GREAT IRISH VOICES

Over 400 years of Irish Oratory

Edited by

Gerard Reid

IRISH ACADEMIC PRESS
DUBLIN · PORTLAND, OR

First published in 1999 by
IRISH ACADEMIC PRESS
44, Northumberland Road, Dublin 4, Ireland
and in the United States of America by
IRISH ACADEMIC PRESS
c/o ISBS, 5804 NE Hassalo Street,
Portland, OR 97213 3644

Website: http://www.iap.ie

British Library Cataloguing in Publication Data
Great Irish Voices: over 400 years of Irish oratory
  1. Speeches, addresses, etc., English – Ireland
  I. Reid, Gerard
  808.8'5'009415
  ISBN 0–7165–2744–8

Library of Congress Cataloguing-in-Publication Data
Great Irish Voices: over 400 years of Irish oratory / [edited by]
  Gerard Reid.
      p.   cm.
  Includes bibliographical references (p.   ) and index.
  ISBN 0–7165–2674–3 (hb)
    1. Speeches, addresses, etc., Irish. 2. Ireland—History—
  —Sources. I. Reid, Gerard, 1969–
  DA905.G72   1998
  941.5—dc21   98–43173
                                                    CIP

Typeset in 11.5 on 13.5 pt Caslon
by Carrigboy Typesetting Services, Co. Cork
Printed by
Creative Print and Design (Wales), Ebbw Vale

Contents

THE GREAT ADVOCATES

THE ULSTER QUESTION

THE RIGHTS OF A MAN

Preface

A MONGST the multitude of speeches, sermons and addresses annually delivered by Irish men and women, only a few are permanently preserved. The remainder are forgotten until eventually the door of oblivion is shut on them. But when words are spoken by men and women who express the thoughts of the times, who speak in clear, simple, direct and captivating language and – even rarer – command the intellect and hearts of those around them, only then do we have words which merit preservation.

The main objective in this present compilation is to bring together a selection of speeches, sermons and addresses from some of Ireland's greatest statesmen and women over the last 1,000 years. The selections are arranged into ten categories, within which the speeches are arranged in chronological order. Introductions, giving background information, are given to each selection. Brief biographical notes are also given on each speaker at the back of the book.

The orations chosen are interesting in themselves and many of them demonstrate enlightening views of historical events. For example, Ireland's stance, both North and South, during World War Two can be seen by reading Éamon de Valera's, Lord Craigavon's and James Dillon's speeches at the time.

These speeches, provide an insight into historical events, even more so than the often differing, and necessarily opinionated accounts of historians. As one will find with many history books, if not all of them, it is rare that they provide us with the speeches of the leading men in Irish history. If and when they do, we are usually given no more than a few lines from any given speech. This is one of the factors that motivated me to compile this anthology of speeches. A speech can give life to one's knowledge of a particular event in time and it can give the reader an insight into the motives and prejudices of the speaker. In many situations these speeches have helped to mould the course of Irish history. The Treaty debates are a notable example.

The great speakers of the Irish past are well represented with Grattan, Burke, O'Connell and Parnell each given considerable attention. The many speeches from the dock are not just of interest because the speakers die for Ireland; they are also interesting for their intrinsic value. In particular, Roger Casement's speech may be taken as a work of great literary importance.

The great Irish lawyers are well represented with John Philpot Curran's speech at Archibald Hamilton Rowan's trial being the most notable. However, no compilation of Irish speeches would be complete without church sermons and, surely Jonathan Swift's is the highlight amongst them.

Unfortunately the anthology features very few women. The main reason for this is that it is only recently that women have become a presence on the political and national stage. For example, on the political stage no woman served as a Government Minister in Ireland between 1922 and 1979. But now, as equality has found its way into society, we see an increasing number of women not only out working, but also in the political arena. Indeed, President Mary Robinson is a prime example.

We also feature very few of today's leading politicians. The reason is quite simple; most of them are not good enough. Most political speeches are "formula" speeches, written with little direct input from the speakers and spoken with little passion or meaning. This decline in the quality of oratory has been apparent for many years as insincerity replaces sincerity, as the ability to articulate declines and, in particular, as the knowledge of the rhythm within a sentence is lost. Listen to the rhythm of the last sentence of Padraig Pearse's oration at the O'Donovan Rossa grave, 'The fools, the fools, the fools! They have left us our Fenian dead, and while Ireland holds these graves, Ireland unfree shall never be at peace.' How many modern orators produce lines like this that stay with us like a good poem does.

Unfortunately, we have only the written words of many of these speeches; the moment of magic at the point of delivery can never be recaptured. All one can do is imagine.

Imagine you are at the Hill of Tara, the site of the fort of the ancient High King of Ireland, on the 15th August, 1843. You have spent two days travelling from the west coast of Ireland to be there. You have had to wait over five hours for the man himself to speak. Finally, when he begins to speak, you become annoyed as not alone can you barely see him, with the large crowd massed in front of you, but you can not even hear him. A steady buzz fills the air. You are not sure what it is. The noise seems to be getting nearer. Then it's upon you, Daniel O'Connell's words being repeated by all the men and women around you. Then you are doing the same and so, slowly, the words of the great Liberator pass through the lines until one million people hear his oration.

The aim has been to bring together all these great speeches and to compile them so that they are easily accessible in one book. They should be read with the pleasure that comes from reading a good book or an exquisite poem and the benefit that comes from understanding the historical figures who called themselves Irish and made us what we are.

GERARD REID
May 1997

For my Nana, Anna Clifford,
A lady of uncommon devotion and love,
A woman who took so little and gave so much,
Loving her was easy,
But telling her so wasn't.
May she always rest in union with the Almighty. Amen.

Speeches from the Dock

Oliver Plunkett
15 June 1681

IN 1672, James, the Duke of York, and the heir apparent to the English crown, converted to Catholicism. Immediately a powerful opposition group came into being within England against James, but the King, Charles II, made a very determined stand to ensure that the succession, on his death, should indeed go to James.

In the midst of this disagreement a Protestant clergyman, Titus Oates, produced a forty-three article document, later expanded to eighty-one, to the effect that the king was to be assassinated at the Pope's orders; that the Pope had plans to take England under his rule and had given a commission to the General of the Jesuits to nominate men to key government and military positions; that the French King had arranged with leading Irishmen the landing of the French army in Ireland, and that all Protestants were to be murdered. Belief in this falsely concocted 'popish plot' quickly spread and soon anti-Catholic frenzy was spreading throughout England.

The Irish administration's overzealous reaction was to arrest many of the leading Irish Catholic clergy including the Primate, Oliver Plunkett, who was brought to Westminster Hall in London and charged with 'high treason, for endeavouring and compassing the King's death, and to levy war in Ireland, and to alter the true religion there, and to induce a foreign power.'

On Wednesday, 15 June, 1681, Oliver Plunkett was brought to the bar to receive his judgement. The clerk of the court asked: 'Oliver Plunkett, hold up thy hand; thou hast been indicted of high treason, thou hast been thereupon arraigned, thou hast thereunto pleaded Not Guilty, and for thy trial hast put thyself upon God and the country, which country hath found thee Guilty; what hast thou to say for thyself, why judgment of death should not pass upon thee, and execution be thereupon awarded according to the law?'

My lord, may it please your lordship, I have something to say, which if
your lordship will consider seriously, may occasion the Court's com-
miseration and mercy. I have, my lord, for this fact been arraigned in
Ireland, and brought to my trial there. At the day of my trial all the
witnesses voluntarily absented themselves, seeing I had records and
witnesses to convince them evidently, and shew what men they were,
and the prepensed malice that they did bear to me, and so finding that
I could clear myself evidently; they absented themselves, on the day of
my trial no Christian appeared, but hither over they came, and procured
that I should be brought hither, where I could not have a jury that knew
the qualities of my adversaries, or who knew me, or the circumstance of
the places, times, and persons, the juries here, as I say, were altogether
strangers to these affairs, and so, my lord, they could not know many
things that conduce to a fair trial, and it was morally impossible they
should know it. I have been accused principally and chiefly for surveying the ports, for fixing upon Carlingford for the landing of the
French, for the having of 70,000 men ready to join with the French, for
collecting money for the agents to this matter, for assisting of the
French and this great Utopian army.

A jury in Ireland consisting of men that lived in that country, or any
man in the world that hath seen Ireland in a map, would easily see
there was no probability that that should be a place fit for the French to
land in, though he never was in Ireland, yet by the map, he would see
they must come between the narrow seas, all along to Ulster, and the
rocks, and such places would make it very dangerous; and by their own
confession it was a poor town, and of no strength, a very small garrison,
which had not been so, if it had been a place of any consideration. And
where I had influence only upon one province, as is well known, though
I had the title of Primate of all Ireland, as the Archbishop of
Canterbury hath of all England; yet the Archbishop of York did not
permit him to meddle with his province; and it is well known by the
gentry there, and those that are accustomed to the place, that in all the
province of Ulster, take men, women, and children of the Roman
Catholics, they could not make up 70,000. This, a jury there, my lord,
had known very well, and therefore the laws of England, which are very
favourable to the prisoner, have provided that there should be a jury of
the place where the fact was committed, as Sir Thomas Gascoigne, as I
have heard, had a Yorkshire jury, though he was tried at London.

And then, after my coming here, I was kept close prisoner for six months, not any Christian was permitted to come to me, nor did I know anything how things stood in the world. I was brought here the third of May to be arraigned, and I did petition your lordship to have some time for my trial, and I would have it put off till Michaelmas, but your lordships did not think fit to grant so long, but only till the eighth of this month, when my witnesses who were ready at the seaside, would not come over without passes, and I could not get over the records without an order from hence; which records would have shewn that some of the witnesses were indicted and found guilty of high crimes, some were imprisoned for robberies, and some of the witnesses were infamous people; so I petitioned on the 8th of this month, that I might have time but for twelve days more: but your lordship thought, when the motion was made, that it was only to put off my trial, and now my witnesses are come to Coventry yesterday morning and they will be here in a few days, and so for want of time to defend myself in, I was exposed to my adversaries, who were some of my own clergy, whom for their debauched lives I have corrected, as is well known there.

I will not deny myself, but that as long as there was any toleration and connivance, I did execute the function of a bishop, and that by the 2nd of Elizabeth is only a praemunire *[a writ charging a person of asserting the papal jurisdiction]*, and no treason. So that, my lord, I was exposed defenceless to my enemies, whereas now my witnesses are come on, that could make all appear. I did beg for twelve days' time, whereby you might have seen as plain as the sun, what those witnesses are, that began the story, and say these things against me. And, my lord, for those depositions of the 70,000 men, and the monies that are collected of the clergy in Ireland, they cannot be true; for they are a poor clergy that have no revenue nor had; they live as the Presbyterians do here, there is not a priest in all Ireland, that hath certainly or un-certainly above threescore pounds a year, and that I should collect of them 40s a piece, for the raising of an army, or for the landing of the French at Carlingford; if it had been brought before a jury in Ireland, it would have been thought a mere romance.

If they had accused me of a praemunire for the exercise of my episcopal function, perhaps they had said something that might have been believed; but my lord, as I am a dying man, and hope for salvation by my Lord and Saviour, I am not guilty of one point of treason they have swore against me, no more than the child that was born but yesterday. I have an attestation under my lord of Essex's hand concerning my good behaviour in Ireland, and not only from him, but from my lord Berkeley, who was also governor there, which the king's attorney saw; but here I was brought, here I was tried, and not having time to bring my witnesses, I could not prove my innocency, as otherwise I might. So that if there be any case in the world that deserves compassion, surely my case does; and it is such a rare case, as I believe you will not find two of them in print, that one arraigned in Ireland, should be tried here afterwards for the same fact. My lord, if there be anything in the world that deserves pity, this does; for I can say, as I hope for mercy, I was never guilty of any one point they have sworn against me, and if my petition for time had been granted, I could have shewn how all was prepensed malice against me, and have produced all circumstances that could make out the innocency of a person. But not having had time enough, and being tried, I am at your mercy.

The Lord Chief Justice then began to give judgement. As he was nearing the end of the judgement, Plunkett interrupted him:

May it please your lordship to give me leave to speak one word. If I were a man that had no care of my conscience in this matter, and did not think of God Almighty, or conscience, or heaven, or hell, I might have saved my life; for I was offered it by divers people here, so I would but confess my own guilt, and accuse others. But, my lord, I had rather die ten thousand deaths, than wrongfully accuse anybody. And the time will come when your lordship will see what these witnesses are, that have come in against me. I do assure your lordship, if I were a man that had not good principles I might easily have saved my life; but I had rather die ten thousand deaths, than wrongfully to take away one farthing of any man's goods, one day of his liberty, or one minute of his life.

The Lord Chief Justice again spoke:

'I am sorry to see you persist in the principles of that religion.'

They are those principles, that even God Almighty cannot dispense withal.

Finally, the sentence was given by the Lord Justice:

'You must go hence to the place from where you came, that is, to Newgate, and from thence you shall be drawn through the city of London to Tyburn; there you shall be hanged by the neck, but cut down before you are dead, your bowels shall be taken out and burnt before your face, your head shall be cut off, and your body divided into four quarters, to be disposed of as his Majesty pleases. And I pray God to have mercy on your soul.'

Plunkett was executed in Tilburn, London on 1 July, 1681, for a crime he did not commit. He was beatified in 1920 and canonized a saint in 1975.

John Sheares
13 June 1798

WITH THE exception of a few names – the most notable of which is Wolfe Tone – most of the leaders of the 1798 rebellion are largely forgotten today in Ireland. One of them, a few nights before his execution, wrote in a letter to his family, 'justice will yet be done to my memory and my fate be mentioned with pride rather than shame . . . if I did not expect the arrival of this justice to my memory, I should be indeed afflicted at the nominal ignominy of my death.'

There is a small street named after him in Cork, but otherwise, the name John Sheares, means little to most. And yet he was one of the leaders of the United Irishmen; one of the men who had masterminded the 1798 rebellion; one of the men who had planned to capture the British Army barracks at Loughlinstown and then to lead an assault on Dublin. But before this plan could be put into action, Sheares was betrayed by a young Irish captain in the Loughlinstown barracks, whom he mistakenly assumed to be loyal to the rebels' plans.

John Sheares and his brother, Henry, were arrested two days before the Rebellion began, on 21 May, 1798. The two young barrister brothers were held in jail until their trial on 12 June when both were sentenced to death by hanging for the crime of high treason.

On the re-assembly of the court to pass sentence, John Sheares spoke:

My Lords, I wish to offer a few words before sentence is pronounced, because there is a weight pressing on my heart much greater than that of the sentence which is to come from the court. There has been, my Lords, a weight pressing on my mind from the first moment I heard the indictment read upon which I was tried; but that weight has been more particularly pressing upon my heart when I found the accusation in the indictment enforced and supported upon the trial. That weight would be left insupportable if it were not for this opportunity of discharging it; I shall feel it to be insupportable since a verdict of my country has stamped that evidence as well founded. Do not think, my Lords, that I am about to make a declaration against the verdict of the jury or the persons connected with the trial; I am only about to call to your recollection a part of the charge at which my soul shudders, and if I had no opportunity of renouncing it before your Lordships and this auditory, no courage would be sufficient to support me. The accusation of which I speak, while I linger here yet a minute, is that of holding out to the people of Ireland a direction to give no quarter to the troops fighting for its defence! My Lords, let me say thus, that if there be any acquaintances in this crowded court – I do not say my intimate friends, but acquaintances – who do not know what I say is truth, I shall be reputed the wretch which I am not; I say if any acquaintance of mine can believe that I could utter a recommendation of giving no quarter to a yielding and unoffending foe, it is not the death which I am about to suffer I deserve – no punishment could be adequate to such a crime. My Lords, I can not only acquit my soul of such an intention, but I declare, in the presence of that God before whom I must shortly appear, that the favourite doctrine of my heart was that no human being should suffer death but when absolute necessity required it. My Lords, I feel a consolation in making this declaration, which nothing else could afford me, because it is not only a justification of myself, but where I am sealing my life with that breath which cannot be suspected of falsehood, what I say may make some impression upon the minds of men not holding the same doctrine. I declare to God I know of no crime but assassination which can eclipse or equal that of which I am accused. I discern no shade of guilt between that and taking away the life of a foe by putting a bayonet to his heart when he is yielding and surrendering. I do request the bench to believe that of me – I do request my country to believe that of me – I am sure God will think that of me. Now, my Lords, I have no favour to ask of the court; my country has decided I am guilty and the law says I shall suffer – it sees that I am ready to suffer. But, my Lords, I have a favour to request of the court that does not relate to myself. My Lords, I have a brother whom I have even loved dearer than myself, but it is not from any affection for him alone that I am induced to make the request. He is a man, and therefore I would hope, prepared to die, if he stood as I do though I do not stand unconnected; but he stands more dearly connected. In short, my Lords, to spare your feelings and I my own, I do not pray that I should not die, but that the husband, the father, the son – all comprised in one person – holding these relations dearer in life to him than any man I know for such a man I do not pray a pardon, for that is not in the power of the court, but I pray a respite for such time as the court in its humanity and discretion shall think proper. You have heard, my Lords, that his private affairs require arrangement. When I address myself to your Lordships, it is with the knowledge you will have of all the sons of our aged mother being gone. Two have perished in the service of the King – one very recently. I only request that disposing of me, with what swiftness either the public mind or justice requires, a respite may be given to my brother, that the family may acquire strength to bear it all. That is all I wish; I shall remember it to my last breath, and I shall offer up my prayers for you to that Being who has endowed us all with the sensibility to feel. That is all I ask. I have nothing more to say.

The two brothers were duly executed and in accordance with the custom of the time John Sheares' head was severed from his body. It is said, however, that Henry Sheares' body was spared that barbarous act.

Wolfe Tone

10 November 1798

THEOBALD WOLFE Tone's place in modern Irish history is assured by the role he played in the lead up to and during the 1798 rebellion. In his memoirs he described his aims as being, 'to subvert the tyranny of our execrable government, to break the connection with England, the never failing source of all our political evils, and to assert the independence of my country.' His means he described as being, 'to unite the whole people of Ireland, to abolish the memory of all past dissensions, and to substitute the common name of Irishmen, in the place of the denominations of Protestant, Catholic, and Dissenter.'

In pursuance of these aims, the Dublin-born Protestant, Wolfe Tone, persuaded the new French government to send a military force to Ireland to help liberate the country from Britain. This force of fourteen thousand men arrived off the south-west coast of Ireland in December, 1796, but due to a combination of bad weather, ill luck and indecision, the troops did not set foot on Irish soil and the venture failed miserably.

A second expedition, in 1798, comprised two small French invasion forces, one of about a thousand men and the other of about three thousand. The former landed at Killala, in County Mayo, and had a limited success. The latter, of which Wolfe Tone was part, was defeated, before ever reaching land, in a naval battle against a British force off the coast of Donegal. Tone himself was captured and charged with treason on 10 November, 1798 in the Royal Barracks, Dublin. After some reservations, the court allowed him to make the following statement:

I mean not to give you the trouble of bringing judicial proof to convict me legally of having acted in hostility to the government of his Britannic Majesty in Ireland. I admit the fact. From my earliest youth I have regarded the connection between Great Britain and Ireland as the curse of the Irish nation, and felt convinced that, whilst it lasted, this country could never be free nor happy. My mind has been confirmed in this opinion by the experience of every succeeding year, and the conclusions which I have drawn from every fact before my eyes. In consequence, I was determined to employ all the powers which my individual efforts could move, in order to separate the two countries. That Ireland was not able of herself to throw off the yoke, I knew; I therefore sought for aid wherever it was to be found. In honourable poverty I rejected offers which, to a man in my circumstances, might be considered highly advantageous. I remained faithful to what I thought the cause of my country, and sought in the French Republic an ally to rescue three millions of my countrymen.

After having being told by the president of the court to confine himself to the charges at hand he continued:

I shall then, confine myself to some points relative to my connection with the French army; Attached to no party in the French Republic – without interest, without money, without intrigue – the openness and integrity of my views raised me to a high and confidential rank in its armies. I obtained the confidence of the Executive Directory, the approbation of my generals, and I will venture to add, the esteem and affection of my brave comrades. When I review these circumstances, I feel a secret and internal consolation which no reverse of fortune, no sentence in the power of this court to inflict, can deprive me of, or weaken in any degree. Under the flag of the French Republic I originally engaged with a view to save and liberate my own country. For that purpose I have encountered the chances of war amongst strangers; for that purpose I repeatedly braved the terrors of the ocean covered, as I knew it to be, with the triumphant fleets of that power which it was my glory and my duty to oppose. I have sacrificed all my views in life; I have courted poverty; I have left a beloved wife unprotected, and children whom I adored, fatherless. After such a sacrifice, in a cause which I have always considered – conscientiously considered – as the cause of justice and freedom, it is no great effort at this day, to add the sacrifice of my life. But I hear it said that this unfortunate country has been a prey to all sorts of horrors. I sincerely lament it. I beg, however, it may be remembered that I have been absent four years from Ireland. To me these sufferings can never be attributed. I designed by fair and open war to procure the separation of the two countries. For open war I was prepared, but instead of that a system of private assassination has taken place. I repeat, whilst I deplore it, that it is not chargeable on me. Atrocities, it seems have been committed on both sides. I do not less deplore them. I detest them from my heart; and to those who know my character and sentiments I may safely appeal for the truth of this assertion; with them I need no justification. In a case like this, success is everything. Success, in the eyes of the vulgar, fixes its merits. Washington succeeded, and Kosciusko *[A Polish rebel]* failed. After a combat nobly sustained – a combat which would have excited the respect and sympathy of a generous enemy – my fate has been to become a prisoner to the eternal disgrace of those who gave the orders. I was brought here in irons like a felon. I mention this for the sake of others; for me, I am indifferent to it. I am aware of the fate which awaits me, and scorn equally the tone of complaint and that of supplication. As to the connection between this country and Great Britain, I repeat it – all that has been imputed to me (words, writings, and actions), I here deliberately avow. I have spoken and acted with reflection and on principle, and am ready to meet the consequences. Whatever be the sentence of the court I am prepared for it. Its members will surely discharge their duty – I shall take care not to be wanting in mine.

Wolfe Tone was sentenced to death by hanging but committed suicide, or – as has been alleged – was murdered, before the sentence could be carried out.

Robert Emmet
19 September 1803

AFTER BEING expelled from Trinity College, Dublin, in 1798 for holding radical political views, the young Protestant, Robert Emmet became the guiding light behind the new United Irishman Executive in Dublin.

After an attempt to capture him failed, Emmet escaped to the Continent where he sought the help of Napoleon Bonaparte in aiding Ireland 'take her place among the nations of the world.' However his attempts failed and after returning to Ireland in October, 1802, he immediately set about laying plans for a rebellion in Dublin on the evening of Saturday, 23 July, 1803.

A trail of disasters led up to the event and when the supposed rebellion started, what Emmet had was not a well-disciplined rebel force, but a mob of thugs and drunkards. One unfortunate victim that night was the humanitarian Lord Kilwarden, the Lord Chief Justice, who found himself quite by accident caught up in the midst of the riot. His coach was surrounded by the rampaging mob and he was dragged to the ground and savagely piked to death. Emmet, who did not know of this action until later deplored it earnestly. As to the riot itself, he conceded, it did not even have the respectability of an insurrection. In all, thirty people lost their lives that night.

Emmet himself escaped but was caught a month later. He was tried at Green Street court-house where he was sentenced to death by hanging. Before sentencing he was asked if he had anything to say. He replied with the following defiant speech:

I am asked what I have to say why sentence of death should not be pronounced on me, according to law. I have nothing to say that can alter your pre-determination, nor that it will become me to say, with any view to the mitigation of that sentence which you are to pronounce and I must abide by. But I have that to say which interests me more than life and which you have laboured to destroy. I have much to say why my reputation should be rescued from the load of false accusation and calumny which has been cast upon it. I do not imagine that, seated where you are, your minds can be so free from prejudice as to receive the least impression from what I am going to utter. I have no hope that I can anchor my character in the breast of a court constituted and trammeled as this is.

I only wish, and that is the utmost that I can expect, that your lordships may suffer it to float down your memories untainted by the foul breath of prejudice, until it finds some more hospitable harbour to shelter it from the storms by which it is buffeted. Were I only to suffer death, after being adjudged guilty by your tribunal, I should bow in silence, and meet the fate that awaits me without a murmur; but the sentence of the law which delivers my body to the executioner will, through the ministry of the law, labour in its own vindication, to consign my character to obloquy; for there must be guilt somewhere, whether in the sentence of the court or in the catastrophe – time must determine. A man in my situation has not only to encounter the difficulties of fortune, and the force of power over minds which it has corrupted or subjugated, but the difficulties of established prejudice. The man dies, but his memory lives. That mine may not perish, that it may live in the respect of my countrymen, I seize upon this opportunity to vindicate myself from some of the charges alleged against me. When my spirit shall be wafted to a more friendly port, when my shade shall have joined the bands of those martyred heroes who have shed their blood on the scaffold and in the field in defense of their country and of virtue, this is my hope: I wish that my memory and my name may animate those who survive me, while I look down with complacency on the destruction of that perfidious government which upholds its domination by blasphemy of the Most High; which displays its power over man as over the beasts of the forest; which sets man upon his brother, and lifts his hand in the Name of God, against the throat of his fellow who believes or doubts a little more or a little less than the government standard, a government which is steeled to barbarity by the cries of the orphans and the tears of the widows it has made.

Here Lord Norbury interrupted Emmet, saying that 'the mean and wicked enthusiasts who felt as he did, were not equal to the accomplishment of their wild designs.'

I appeal to the immaculate God, I swear by the Throne of Heaven, before which I must shortly appear, by the blood of the murdered patriots who have gone before me, that my conduct has been, through all this peril, and through all my purposes, governed only by the conviction which I have uttered, and by no other view than that of the emancipation of my country from the super-inhuman oppression under which she has so long and too patiently travailed; and I confidently hope that, wild and chimerical as it may appear, there is still union and strength in Ireland to accomplish this noblest of enterprises. Of this I speak with confidence, with intimate knowledge, and with the consolation that appertains to that confidence. Think not, my lords, I say this for the petty gratification of giving you a transitory uneasiness. A man who never yet raised his voice to assert a lie will not hazard his character with posterity by asserting a falsehood on a subject so important to his country, and on an occasion like this. Yes, my lords, a man who does not wish to have his epitaph written until his country is liberated, will not leave a weapon in the power of envy, or a pretense to impeach the probity which he means to preserve, even in the grave to which tyranny consigns him.

Here he was again interrupted by Norbury.

Again I say that what I have spoken was not intended for your lordship, whose situation I commiserate rather than envy – my expressions were for my countrymen. If there is a true Irishman present, let my last words cheer him in the hour of his affliction.

Here he was again interrupted. Lord Norbury said he did not sit there to hear treason.

I have always understood it to be the duty of a judge, when a prisoner has been convicted, to pronounce the sentence of the law. I have also understood that judges sometimes think it their duty to hear with patience, and to speak with humanity; to exhort the victim of the laws, and to offer, with tender benignity, their opinions of the motives by which he was actuated in the crime of which he was adjudged guilty. That a judge has thought it his duty so to have done, I have no doubt; but where is the boasted freedom of your institutions, where is the vaunted impartiality, clemency and mildness of your courts of justice if an unfortunate prisoner, whom your policy and not justice is about to deliver into the hands of the executioner, is not suffered to explain his motives sincerely and truly, and to vindicate the principles by which he was actuated? My lord, it may be a part of the system of angry justice to bow a man's mind by humiliation to the purposed ignominy of the scaffold; but worse to me than the purposed shame or the scaffold's terrors would be the shame of such foul and unfounded imputations as have been laid against me in this court. You, my lord, are a judge; I am the supposed culprit. I am a man; you are a man also. By a revolution of power we might exchange places? Though we never could change characters. If I stand at the bar of this court and dare not vindicate my character, what a farce is your justice! If I stand at this bar and dare not vindicate my character, how dare you calumniate it? Does the sentence of death, which your unhallowed policy inflicts on my body, condemn my tongue to silence and my reputation to reproach? Your executioner may abridge the period of my existence; but while I exist I shall not forebear to vindicate my character and motives from your aspersion; and as a man to whom fame is dearer than life, I will make the last use of that life in doing justice to that reputation which is to live after me, and which is the only legacy I can leave to those I honour and love and for whom I am proud to perish. As men, my lords, we must appear on the great day at one common tribunal; and it will then remain for the Searcher of all hearts to show a collective universe, who was engaged in the most virtuous actions or swayed by the purest motives my country oppressor, or –

Here he was interrupted and told to listen to the sentence of the court.

My lords, will a dying man be denied the legal privilege of exculpating himself in the eyes of the community from an undeserved reproach, thrown upon him during his trial, by charging him with ambition and attempting to cast away for paltry consideration the liberties of his country? Why did your lordships insult me? Or rather, why insult justice, in demanding of me why sentence of death should not be pronounced against me? I know my lords, that form prescribes that you should ask the question, the form also presents the right of answering. This, no doubt, may be dispensed with, and so might the whole ceremony of the trial, since sentence was already pronounced at the Castle before the jury was impaneled. Your lordships are but the priests of the oracle, and I insist on the whole of the forms.

I am charged with being an emissary of France. An emissary of France! And for what end? It is alleged that I wished to sell the independence of my country. And for what end? Was this the object of my ambition? And is this the mode by which a tribunal of justice reconciles contradiction? No, I am no emissary; and my ambition was to hold a place among the deliverers of my country, not in power nor in profit, but in the glory of the achievement. Sell my country's independence to France! And for what? Was it a change of masters? No, but for my ambition. O, my country, was it a personal ambition that could influence me? Had it been the soul of my actions, could I not by my education and fortune, by the rank and consideration of my family, have placed myself amongst the proudest of your oppressors. My country was my idol. To it I sacrificed every selfish, every endearing sentiment, and for it I now offer up myself, O God! No, my lords; I acted as an Irishman, determined on delivering my country from the yoke of a foreign and unrelenting tyranny and the more galling yoke of a domestic faction, which is its joint partner and perpetrator in the patricide, from the ignominy existing with an exterior of splendour and a conscious depravity. It was the wish of my heart to extricate my country from this doubly riveted despotism; I wished to place her independence beyond the reach of any power on earth. I wished to exalt her to that proud station in the world. Connection with France was, indeed, intended, but only as far as mutual interest would sanction or require. Were the French to assume any authority inconsistent with the purest independence, it would be the signal for their destruction. We sought their aid and we sought it as we had assurance we should obtain it as auxiliaries in war and allies in peace. Were the French to come as invaders or enemies uninvited by the wishes of the people, I should oppose them to the utmost of my strength. Yes, my countrymen, I should advise you to meet them upon the beach with a sword in one hand and a torch in the other. I would meet them with all the destructive fury of war. I would animate my countrymen to immolate them in their boats, before they had contaminated the soil of my country. If they succeeded in landing, and if forced to retire before superior discipline, I would dispute every inch of the ground, burn every blade of grass, and the last entrenchment of liberty should be my grave. What I could not do myself, if I should fall, I should leave as a last charge to my countrymen to accomplish; because I should feel conscious that life, any more than death, is unprofitable when a foreign nation holds my country in subjection. But it was not as an enemy that the soldiers of France were to land. I looked, indeed, for the assistance of France; but I wished to prove to France and to the world that Irish men deserved to be assisted; that they were indignant at slavery, and ready to assert the independence and liberty of their country. I wished to procure for my country the guarantee which Washington procured for America; to procure an aid which, by its example would be as important as its valour disciplined, gallant, pregnant with science and experience, that of a people who would perceive the good and polish the rough points of our character. They would come to us as strangers and leave us as friends, after sharing in our perils and elevating our destiny. These were my objects; not to receive new task-masters, but to expel old tyrants. It was for these ends I sought aid from France; because France, even as an enemy, could not be more implacable than the enemy already in the bosom of my country.

Here he was interrupted by the court.

I have been charged with that importance in the emancipation of my country as to be considered the keystone of the combination of Irishmen; or, as your lordships expressed it, 'the life and blood of the conspiracy.' You do me honour over much; you have given to the subaltern all the credit of a superior. There are men engaged in this conspiracy who are not only superior to me, but even to your own conceptions of yourself, my lord; men before the splendour of whose genius and virtues I should bow with respectful deference and who would think themselves disgraced by shaking your blood-stained hand.

Here he was interrupted.

What! my lord, shall you tell me on the passage to the scaffold, which that tyranny (of which you are only the intermediary executioner) has erected for my murder, that I am accountable for all the blood that has been shed and will be shed in this struggle of the oppressed against the oppressor; shall thou tell me this, and must I be so very a slave as not to repel it? I do not fear to approach the Omnipotent Judge to answer for the conduct of my whole life; and am I to be appalled and falsified by a mere remnant of mortality here? By you, too, although if it were possible to collect all the innocent blood that you have shed in your unhallowed ministry in one great reservoir, your lordship might swim in it.

Here the judge interrupted.

Let no man dare, when I am dead, to charge me with dishonour; let no man taint my memory by believing that I could have engaged in any cause but that of my country's liberty and independence; or that I could have become the pliant minion of power in the oppression of my country. The Proclamation of the Provisional Government speaks for our views; no inference can be tortured from it to countenance barbarity or debasement at home, or subjection, humiliation or treachery from abroad. I would not have submitted to a foreign oppressor, for the same reason that I would resist the foreign and domestic oppressor. In the dignity of freedom I would have fought upon the threshold of my country, and its enemy would enter only by passing over my lifeless corpse. And am I who lived but for my country, and have subjected myself to the dangers of the jealous and watchful oppressor, and the bondage of the grave, only to give my countrymen their rights and my country her independence, am I to be loaded with calumny and not suffered to resent it? No; God forbid!

Here Norbury told the prisoner that his sentiments and language disgraced his family and education, but more particularly his father, Dr. Robert Emmet, who was a man that would, if alive, discountenance such opinions. To which Emmet replied:

If the spirit of the illustrious dead participate in the concerns and cares of those who were dear to them in this transitory life, O, ever dear and venerated shade of my departed father, look down with scrutiny upon the conduct of your suffering son and see if I have even for a moment, deviated from those principles of morality and patriotism which it was your care to instill into my youthful mind, and for which I am now about to offer up my life! My lords, you are impatient for the sacrifice. The blood which you seek is not congealed by the artificial terrors which surround your victim; it circulates warm and unruffled through the channels which God created for noble purpose, but which you are now bent to destroy for purposes so grievous that they cry to heaven. Be yet patient! I have but a few more words to say. I am going to go to my cold and silent grave. My lamp of life is nearly extinguished. My race is run. The grave opens to receive me and I sink into its bosom. I have but one request to ask at my departure from this world. It is the charity of its silence. Let no man write my epitaph; for as no man who knows my motives dare now vindicate them, let not prejudice or ignorance asperse them. Let them and me rest in obscurity and peace; and my tomb remain uninscribed and my memory in oblivion until other times and other men can do justice to my character. When my country takes her place among the nations of the earth, then, and not till then let my epitaph be written. I have done.

The Manchester Martyrs
1 November 1867

O N 18 SEPTEMBER, 1867, a prison van, taking six prisoners from the police office to the jail, was ambushed by Fenians under a railway arch on Hyde Road in Manchester. The purpose of the ambush was to rescue two Fenian leaders, Colonel Thomas Kelly and Captain Timothy Deasy, who were amongst the prisoners in the van. The rescue proved successful in that both Fenian leaders escaped and were never recaptured. However during the raid a Sergeant Brett, the policeman in the van with the prisoners was killed. How exactly this happened became an extremely controversial issue.

Some accounts of the incident relate that a Fenian called upon Sergeant Brett through the ventilator in the locked door, urging him to surrender, and that the sergeant refused to do so, declaring, 'No, I will do my duty to the last.' Thereupon, a shot from a revolver was fired mortally wounding Sergeant Brett in the head. Other accounts claim that a bullet was fired through the lock of the door with the intent to break it and that the sergeant had his eye to it and was shot accidentally.

Regardless of how the event occurred, the fact remained that a sergeant had been killed, and in the aftermath numerous Irishmen in the Manchester area were rounded up. Amongst those arrested were William Philip Allen, Michael Larkin and Michael O'Brien, all of whom had taken part in the raid. They were tried and found guilty of murder on 1 November, 1867.

The following speeches were made by each of the three from the dock just before they were sentenced to death. The idealistic nature of their speeches raised the level of the entire event far beyond a common crime and clearly made an emotional appeal to the Irish people.

William Philip Allen

No man in this court regrets the death of Sergeant Brett more than I do, and I positively say, in the presence of the Almighty and ever-living God, that I am innocent; aye, as innocent as any man in this court. I don't say this for the sake of mercy, I want no mercy – I'll have no mercy. I'll die, as many thousands have died, for the sake of their beloved land, and in defence of it. I will die proudly and triumphantly in defence of republican principles and the liberty of an oppressed and enslaved people. Is it possible we are asked why sentence should not be passed upon us, on the evidence of prostitutes off the streets of Manchester, fellows out of work, convicted felons-aye, an Irishman sentenced to be hanged when an English dog would have got off. I say positively and defiantly, justice has not been done me since I was arrested. If justice had been done me, I would not have been handcuffed at the pre-investigation in Bridge Street; and in this court justice has not been done me in any shape or form. I was brought up here and all the prisoners by my side were allowed to wear overcoats, and I was told to take mine off. What is the principle of that? There was something in that principle, and I say positively that justice has not been done me. As for the other prisoners, they can speak for themselves with regard to that matter. And now, with regard to the way I have been identified. I have to say that my clothes were kept for four hours by the policemen in Fairfield station and shown to parties to identify me as being one of the perpetrators of this outrage on Hyde Road. Also in Albert station there was a handkerchief kept on my head the whole night, so that I could be identified the next morning in the corridor by the witnesses. I was ordered to leave on the handkerchief for the purpose that the witnesses could more plainly see I was one of the parties who committed the outrage. As for myself, I feel the righteousness of my every act with regard to what I have done in defence of my country. I fear not. I am fearless, fearless of the punishment that can be inflicted on me; and with that, my lords, I have done.

(After a pause.) I beg to be excused one remark more. I return Mr. Seymour and Mr. Jones my sincere heartfelt thanks for their able eloquence and advocacy on my part in this affray. I wish also to return to Mr. Roberts the very same. My name, sir, might be wished to be known. It is not William O'Meara Allen. My name is William Philip Allen. I was born and reared in Bandon, in the county of Cork, and

from that place I take my name; and I am proud of my country, proud of my parentage. My lords, I have done.

Michael Larkin

I have only got a word or two to say concerning Sergeant Brett. As my friend here said, no one could regret the man's death as much as I do. With regard to the charge of pistols and revolvers, and my using them, I call my God as witness that I neither used pistols, revolvers, nor any instrument on that day that would deprive the life of a child, let alone a man. Nor did I go there on purpose to take life away. Certainly, my lords, I do not want to deny that I did go to give aid and assistance to those two noble heroes that were confined in that van – Kelly and Deasy. I did go to do as much as lay in my power to extricate them out of their bondage; but I did not go to take life, nor, my lord, did anyone else. It is a misfortunate there was life taken; but if it was taken it was not done intentionally, and the man who has taken life we have not got him. I was at the scene of action, when there were over, I dare say, 150 people standing by there when I was. I am very sorry I have to say, my lord, but I thought I had some respectable people to come up as witnesses against me; but I am sorry to say as my friend said – I will make no more remarks concerning that. All I have to say, my lords and gentlemen, is that so far as my trial went, and the way it was conducted, I believe I have got a fair trial . . .

So I look to the mercy of God. May God forgive all who have sworn my life away. As I am a dying man, I forgive them from the bottom of my heart. God forgive them.

Michael O'Brien

I shall commence by saying that every witness who has sworn anything against me has sworn falsely. I have not had a stone in my possession since I was a boy. I had no pistol in my possession on the day when it is alleged this outrage was committed. You call it an outrage, I don't. I say further my name is Michael O'Brien. I was born in the county of Cork and have the honour to be a fellow-parishioner of Peter O'Neal Crowley, who was fighting against the British troops at Mitchelstown last March, and who fell fighting against British tyranny in Ireland. I am a citizen of the United States of America, and if Charles Francis Adams had done his duty towards me, as he ought to do in this country, I should not be in this dock answering your questions now. Mr. Adams did not come, though I wrote to him. He did not come to see if I could not find evidence to disprove the charge, which I positively could, if he had taken the trouble of sending or coming to see what I could do. I hope the American people will notice this part of the business.

O'Brien then began reading from a paper he had in his hand.

The right of man is freedom. The great God has endowed him with affections that he may use, not smother them, and a world that may be enjoyed. Once a man is satisfied he is doing right, and attempts to do anything with that conviction, he must be willing to face all the consequences. Ireland, with its beautiful scenery, its delightful climate, its rich and productive lands, is capable of supporting more than treble its population in ease and comfort. Yet no man, except a paid official of the British Government, can say there is a shadow of liberty, that there is a spark of glad life amongst its plundered and persecuted inhabitants. It is to be hoped that its imbecile and tyrannical rulers will be forever driven from her soil amidst the execration of the world. How beautifully the aristocrats of England moralise on the despotism of the rulers of Italy and Dahomey – in the case of Naples with what indignation did they speak of the ruin of families by the detention of its head or some loved member in a prison. Who have not heard their condemnations of the tyranny that would compel honourable and good men to spend their useful lives in hopeless banishment?

At this point the judge interrupted him and advised him to stop his speech. Unperturbed O'Brien continued:

They cannot find words to express their horror of the cruelties of the King of Dahomey because he sacrificed 2,000 human beings yearly, but why don't those persons who pretend such virtuous indignation at the misgovernment of other countries look at home, and see if greater crimes than those they charge against other governments are not committed by themselves or by their sanction? Let them look at London, and see the thousands that want bread there, while those aristocrats are rioting in luxuries and crimes. Look to Ireland; see the hundreds of thousands of its people in misery and want; see the virtuous, beautiful and industrious women who only a few years ago – aye, and yet – are obliged to look at their children dying for want of food. Look at what is called the majesty of the law on one side, and the long deep misery of a noble people on the other. Which are the young men of Ireland to respect – the law that murders or banishes their people or the means to resist relentless tyranny, and ending their miseries for ever under a home government? I need not answer that question here. I trust the Irish people will answer it to their satisfaction soon. I am not astonished at my conviction.

The Government of this country have the power of convicting any person. They appoint the judge; they choose the jury; and by means of what they call patronage (which is the means of corruption) they have the power of making the laws to suit their purposes. I am confident that my blood will rise a hundredfold against the tyrants who think proper to commit such an outrage. In the first place, I say I was identified improperly by having chains on my hands and feet at the time of identification, and thus the witnesses who have sworn to my throwing stones and firing a pistol have sworn to what is false, for I was, as those ladies said, at the jail gates. I thank my counsel for their able defence, and also Mr. Roberts, for his attention to my case.

On 24 November 1867, Allen, Larkin and O'Brien were executed at the new Bailey, Salford, for the murder of Sergeant Brett, a crime of which they were innocent. The cold truth: a man by the name of Peter Rice had fired the fatal shot and had escaped to America along with Kelly and Deasy. Allen, Larkin and O'Brien thereafter became martyrs in the eyes of the Irish, their story being retold in many an Irish ballad.

Roger Casement
30 June 1916

A T THE outbreak of the First World War Roger Casement went to Germany to try and secure military aid for an insurrection against the British, and to form an Irish Brigade from the British prisoners of war which would take part in the fight for Irish freedom. Though unsuccessful in organising an Irish Brigade, he did eventually persuade the Germans to send arms to the Irish.

On the eve of the 1916 Easter Rising in Dublin Casement travelled to Ireland on board a German submarine which was due to rendezvous with the German freighter, the 'Aud.' The freighter which was carrying arms and ammunitions for the forthcoming rebellion went to the wrong meeting-point and was intercepted by the British navy, but was scuttled by its captain before the British could remove the weapons. Meanwhile, Casement had been put ashore near Tralee in County Kerry, but was soon arrested by the local police and sent to London where he was tried for high treason.

Casement's articulate, defiant and powerful speech from the dock is long remembered by all Irishmen.

My Lord Chief Justice, as I wish my words to reach a much wider audience than I see before me here, I intend to read all that I propose to say. What I shall read now is something I wrote more than twenty days ago. I may say, my lord, at once, that I protest against the jurisdiction of this court in my case on this charge, and the argument, that I am now going to read, is addressed not to this court, but to my own countrymen.

There is an objection, possibly not good in law, but surely good on moral grounds, against the application to me here of this old English statute, 565 years old, that seeks to deprive an Irishman today of life and honour, not for 'adhering to the King's enemies', but for adhering to his own people.

When this statute was passed, in 1351, what was the state of mens' minds on the question of a far higher allegiance – that of a man to God and His kingdom? The law of that day did not permit a man to forsake his Church, or deny his God, save with his life. The 'heretic' then, had the same doom as the 'traitor'.

Today a man may forswear God and His heavenly kingdom, without fear or penalty – all earlier statutes having gone the way of Nero's edicts against the Christians, but that constitutional phantom 'the King' can still dig up from the dungeons and torture-chambers of the Dark Ages a law that takes a man's life and limb for an exercise of conscience.

If true religion rests on love, it is equally true that loyalty rests on love. The law that I am charged under has no parentage in love, and claims the allegiance of today on the ignorance and blindness of the past.

I am being tried, in truth, not by my peers of the live present, but by the fears of the dead past; not by the civilization of the twentieth century, but by the brutality of the fourteenth; not even by a statute framed in the language of the land that tries me, but emitted in the language of an enemy land – so antiquated is the law that must be sought today to slay an Irishman, whose offence is that he puts Ireland first.

Loyalty is a sentiment not a law. It rests on love, not on restraint. The government of Ireland by England rests on restraint, and not on law; and since it demands no love, it can evoke no loyalty . . .

Judicial assassination today is reserved only for one race of the King's subjects – for Irishmen, for those who cannot forget their allegiance to the realm of Ireland. The Kings of England as such, had no rights in Ireland up to the time of Henry VIII, save such as rested on compact and mutual obligation entered into between them and certain princes, chiefs, and lords of Ireland. This form of legal right, such as it was, gave no King of England lawful power to impeach an Irishman for high treason under this statute of King Edward III of England until an Irish Act, known as Poyning's Law, the tenth of Henry VII, was passed in 1494 at Drogheda, by the Parliament of the Pale in Ireland, and enacted as law in that part of Ireland. But, if by Poyning's Law an Irishman of the Pale could be indicted for high treason under this Act, he could be indicted in only one way, and before one tribunal – by the laws of the Realm of Ireland and in Ireland. The very law of Poyning, which I believe, applies this statute of Edward III to Ireland, enacts also for the Irishman's defence 'all these laws by which England claims her liberty.'

And what is the fundamental charter of an Englishman's Liberty? That he shall be tried by his peers. With all respect, I assert this court is to me, an Irishman, charged with this offence, a foreign court – this jury is for me, an Irishman, not a jury of my peers to try me on this vital issue, for it is patent to every man of conscience that I have a right, an indefeasible right, if tried at all, under this statute of high treason, to be tried in Ireland, before an Irish court and by an Irish jury. This court, this jury, the public opinion of this country, England, cannot but be prejudiced in varying degrees against me, most of all in time of war. I did not land in England. I landed in Ireland. It was to Ireland I came; to Ireland I wanted to come; and the last place I desired to land was in England.

But for the Attorney-General of England there is only 'England'; there is no Ireland; there is only the law of England, no right of Ireland; the liberty of Ireland and of an Irishman is to be judged by the power of England. Yet for me, the Irish outlaw, there is a land of Ireland, a right of Ireland, and a charter for all Irishmen to appeal to, in the last resort, a charter, that even the very statutes of England itself cannot deprive us of – nay more, a charter that Englishmen themselves assert as the fundamental bond of law that connects the two kingdoms. This charge of high treason involves a moral responsibility, as the very terms of the indictment against myself recite, inasmuch as I committed the acts I am charged with to the 'evil example of others in like case'. What was the evil example I set to others in the like case, and who were these others? The 'evil example' charged is that I asserted the right of my country and the 'others' I appealed to, to aid my endeavour, were my own countrymen. The example was given, not to Englishmen, but to Irishmen, and the 'like case' can never arise in England but only in Ireland. To Englishmen I set no evil example, for I made no appeal to them. I asked no Englishman to help me. I asked Irishmen to fight for their rights. The 'evil example' was only to other Irishmen, who might come after me, and in 'like case' seek to do as I did. How then, since neither my example, nor my appeal was addressed to Englishmen, can I be rightfully tried by them?

If I did wrong in making that appeal to Irishmen to join with me in an effort to fight for Ireland, it is by Irishmen, and by them alone, that I can be rightfully judged. From this court and its jurisdiction I appeal to those I am alleged to have wronged, and to those I am alleged to have injured by my 'evil example' and claim that they alone are competent to decide my guilt or innocence. If they find me guilty, the statute may affix the penalty, but the statute does not override or annul my right to seek judgement at their hands.

This is so fundamental a right, so natural a right, so obvious a right, that it is clear that the Crown were aware of it when they brought me by force and by stealth from Ireland to this country. It was not I who landed in England, but the Crown who dragged me here, away from my own country to which I had returned with a price upon my head, away from my own countrymen whose loyalty is not in doubt, and safe from the judgement of my peers whose judgement I do not shrink from. I admit no other judgement but theirs. I accept no verdict save at their hands.

I assert from this dock that I am being tried here, not because it is just, but because it is unjust. Place me before a jury of my own countrymen, be it Protestant or Catholic, Unionist or Nationalist, Sinn Féineach or Orangemen, and I shall accept the verdict, and bow to the statute and all its penalties. But I shall accept no meaner finding against me, than that of those, whose loyalty I have endangered by my example, and to whom alone I made appeal. If they adjudge me guilty, then guilty I am. It is not I who am afraid of their verdict – it is the Crown. If this is not so, why fear the test? I fear it not. I demand it as my right.

This is the condemnation of English rule, of English-made law, of English government in Ireland, that it dare not rest on the will of the Irish people, but exists in defiance of their will: that it is a rule, derived not from right, but from conquest. But conquest, my lord, gives no title; and, if it exists over the body, it fails over the mind. It can exert no empire over men's reason and judgement and affections; and it is from this law of conquest that I appeal. I would add that the generous expressions of sympathy extended to me from many quarters, particularly from America, have touched me very much. In that country, as in my own, I am sure my motives are understood, and not misjudged – for the achievement of their liberty has been an abiding inspiration to Irishmen, and to all men elsewhere, rightly struggling to be free . . .

I can answer for my own acts and speeches. While one English party was responsible for preaching a doctrine of hatred, designed to bring about civil war in Ireland, the other, and that the party in power, took no active steps to restrain a propaganda that found its advocates in the Army, Navy, and Privy Council – in the House of Parliament, and in the State Church – a propaganda the methods of whose expression were so grossly illegal and utterly unconstitutional that even the Lord Chancellor of England could find only words and no repressive action to apply to them. Since lawlessness sat in high places in England, and laughed at the law as at the custodians of the law, what wonder was it that Irishmen should refuse to accept the verbal protestations of an English Lord Chancellor as a sufficient safeguard for their lives and liberties? I know not how all my colleagues on the Volunteer Committee in Dublin reviewed the growing menace, but those with whom I was in closest cooperation redoubled, in face of these threats from without, our efforts to unite all Irishmen from within. Our appeals were made to Protestant and Unionist as much almost as to Catholic and Nationalist Irishmen.

We hoped that, by the exhibition of affection and goodwill on our part toward our political opponents in Ireland, we should yet succeed in winning them from the side of an English party whose sole interest in our country lay in its oppression in the past, and in the present in its degradation to the mean and narrow needs of their political animosities.

It is true that they based their actions, so they averred, on 'ears for the empire', and on a very diffuse loyalty that took in all the peoples of the empire, save only the Irish. That blessed word empire that bears so paradoxical a resemblance to charity! For if charity begins at home, empire begins in other men's homes, and both may cover a multitude of sins. I, for one, was determined that Ireland was much more to me than empire and, if charity begins at home, so must loyalty. Since arms were so necessary to make our organization a reality, and to give to the minds of Irishmen, menaced with the most outrageous threats, a sense of security, it was our bounden duty to get arms before all else. I decided, with this end in view, to go to America, with surely a better right to appeal to Irishmen there for help in an hour of great national trial, than those envoys could assert for their weekend descents on Ireland, or their appeals to Germany.

If, as the Right Honourable gentleman, the present Attorney-General, asserted in a speech at Manchester, Nationalists would neither fight for Home Rule nor pay for it, it was our duty to show him that we knew how to do both. Within a few weeks of my arrival in the United States, the fund that had been opened to secure arms for the Volunteers of Ireland amounted to many thousands of pounds. In every case the money subscribed, whether it came from the purse of the wealthy man, or from the still readier pocket of the poor man, was Irish gold . . .

We have been told, we have been asked to hope that after this war Ireland will get Home Rule as a reward for the lifeblood shed in a cause which, whomever else its success may benefit, can surely not benefit Ireland. And what will Home Rule be in return for what its vague promise has taken, and still hopes to take away from Ireland? It is not necessary to climb the painful stairs of Irish history – that treadmill of a nation, whose labours are as vain for her own uplifting as the convict's exertions are for his redemption, to review the long list of British promises made only to be broken – of Irish hopes raised, only to be dashed to the ground. Home Rule, when it comes, if come it does, will find an Ireland drained of all that is vital to its very existence unless it be that unquenchable hope we build on the graves of the dead. We are told that if Irishmen go by the thousand to die, not for Ireland, but for Flanders, for Belgium, for a patch of sand in the deserts of Mesopotamia, or a rocky trench on the heights of Gallipoli, they are winning self-government for Ireland. But if they dare to lay down their lives on their native soil, if they dare to dream even that freedom can be won only at home by men resolved to fight for it there, then they are traitors to their country, and their dreams and their deaths are phases of a dishonourable phantasy.

But history is not so recorded in other lands. In Ireland alone, in this twentieth century, is loyalty held to be a crime. If loyalty be something less than love and more than law, then we have had enough of such loyalty for Ireland and Irishmen. If we are to be indicted as criminals, to be shot as murderers, to be imprisoned as convicts, because our offence is that we love Ireland more than we value our lives, then I do not know what virtue resides in any offer of self-government held out to brave men on such terms. Self-government is our right, a thing born in us at birth, a thing no more to be doled out to us, or withheld from us, by another people than the right to life itself – than the right to feel the sun, or smell the flowers, or to love our kind. It is only from the convict these things are withheld, for crime committed and proven and Ireland, that has wronged no man, has injured no land, that has sought no dominion over others – Ireland is being treated today among the nations of the world as if she were a convicted criminal. If it be treason to fight against such an unnatural fate as this, then I am proud to be a rebel, and shall cling to my 'rebellion' with the last drop of my blood. If there be no right of rebellion against the state of things that no savage tribe would endure without resistance, then I am sure that it is better for men to fight and die without right than to live in such a state of right as this. Where all your rights have become only an accumulated wrong, where men must beg with bated breath for leave to subsist in their own land, to think their own thoughts, to sing their own songs, to gather the fruits of their own labours, and even while they beg, to see things inexorably withdrawn from them – then, surely it is a braver, a saner and truer thing to be a rebel, in act and in deed, against such circumstances as these, than to tamely accept it, as the natural lot of men.

My lord I have done . . .

Casement was found guilty of high treason and sentenced to death. An international campaign attempted to have his sentence commuted but it lost momentum when the British government circulated a number of diaries, supposedly containing details of Casement's homosexuality. He was hanged in Pentonville prison on 3 August, 1916.

The Birth of a Nation

Countess Markievicz
1909

COUNTESS MARKIEVICZ made her objectives perfectly clear when she wrote in Bean na hÉireann – a women's journal – in 1909, 'The first step on the road to freedom is to realise ourselves as Irishwomen – not as Irish or merely as women, but as Irishwomen doubly enslaved and with a double battle to fight.'

During the same year she gave a lecture to the young women of the National Literary Society in Dublin. It was published as a pamphlet by Inghinidhe na hÉireann in 1909 and reissued by Cumann na mBán – both women's organisation – in 1918.

She began:

Lecture to National Literary Society

I take it as a great compliment that so many of you, the rising young women of Ireland, who are distinguishing yourselves every day and coming more and more to the front, should give me this opportunity. We older people look to you with great hopes and a great confidence that in your gradual emancipation you are bringing fresh ideas, fresh energies and above all a great genius for sacrifice into the life of the nation.

Now, I am not going to discuss the subtle psychological question of why it was that so few women in Ireland have been prominent in the national struggle, or try to discover how they lost in the dark ages of persecution the magnificent legacy of Maeve, Fheas, Macha and their other great fighting ancestors. True, several women distinguished themselves on the battle fields of 1798, and we have the women of the *Nation* newspaper, of the Ladies' Land League, also in our own day the few women who have worked their hardest in the Sinn Féin movement and in the Gaelic League and we have the women who won a battle for Ireland, by preventing a wobbly Corporation from presenting King

Edward of England with a loyal address. But for the most part our women, though sincere, steadfast Nationalists at heart, have been content to remain quietly at home, and leave all the fighting and the striving to the men.

Lately things seem to be changing . . . so now again a strong tide of liberty seems to be coming towards us, swelling and growing and carrying before it all the outposts that hold women enslaved and bearing them triumphantly into the life of the nation to which they belong.

We are in a very difficult position here, as so many Unionist women would fain have us work together with them for the emancipation of their sex and votes – obviously to send a member to Westminster. But I would ask every nationalist woman to pause before she joined a Suffrage Society or Franchise League that did not include in their programme the Freedom of their Nation. A Free Ireland with No Sex Disabilities in her Constitution should be the motto of all Nationalist Women. And a grand motto it is.

Women, from having till very recently stood so far removed from all politics, should be able to formulate a much clearer and more incisive view of the political situation than men. For a man from the time he is a mere lad is more or less in touch with politics, and has usually the label of some party attached to him, long before he properly understands what it really means . . .

Now, here is a chance for our women. Let them remind their men, that their first duty is to examine any legislation proposed not from a party point of view, not from the point of view of a sex, a trade or a class, but simply and only from the standpoint of their nation. Let them learn to be statesmen and not merely politicians. Let them consider how their action with regard to it may help or hinder their national struggle for independence and nothing else, and then let them act accordingly. Fix your mind on the ideal of Ireland free, with her women enjoying the full rights of citizenship in their own nation, and no one will be able to side-track you, and so make use of you to use up the energies of the nation in obtaining all sorts of concessions – concessions too, that for the most part were coming in the natural course of evolution, and were perhaps just hastened a few years by the fierce agitations to obtain them.

If the women of Ireland would organize the movement for buying Irish goods more, they might do a great deal to help their country. If they would make it the fashion to dress in Irish clothes, feed on Irish food – in fact, in this as in everything, live really Irish lives, they would be doing something great, and don't let our clever Irish colleens test content with doing this individually, but let them go out and speak publicly about it, form leagues, of which 'No English goods' is the war-cry . . .

I daresay you will think this all very obvious and very dull, but Patriotism and Nationalism and all great things are made up of much that is obvious and dull, and much that in the beginning is small, but that will be found to lead out into fields that are broader and full of interest. You will go out into the world and get elected onto as many public bodies as possible, and by degrees through your exertions no public institution – whether hospital, workhouse, asylum, or any other, and no private house – but will be supporting the industries of your country . . .

To sum up in a few words what I want the Young Ireland women to remember from me. Regard yourselves as Irish, believe in yourselves as Irish, as units of a nation distinct from England, your Conqueror, and as determined to maintain your distinctiveness and gain your deliverance. Arm yourselves with weapons to fight your nation's cause. Arm your souls with noble and free ideas. Arm your minds with the histories and memories of your country and her martyrs, her language and a knowledge of her arts, and her industries. And if in your day the call should come for your body to arm, do not shirk that either.

May this aspiration towards life and freedom among the women of Ireland bring forth a Joan of Arc to free our nation!

John E. Redmond

3 August 1914

AFTER WEEKS of negotiations between the Irish Home Rule Party under John Redmond, The Northern Unionists under Edward Carson and the British government under Prime Minister Asquith, the implementation of the Third Home Rule Bill was suspended for six months, or until the end of the expected war with Germany. The question of what was to become of Ulster, the so called 'Ulster Question,' was further left unanswered. Its solution to be agreed before the bill would come into force. Yet even with the problems of Ulster left unsolved it seemed to be a great landmark and triumph for the Irish nationalists.

When Sir Edward Grey, the British Foreign Secretary, spoke about the impending war in the House of Commons on the 3 August, 1914, he was able to say that 'the one bright spot in the very dreadful situation is Ireland. The position in Ireland – and this I should like to be clearly said abroad – is not a consideration among the things we have to take into account now.'

Redmond's immediate reaction to Grey and the looming war with Germany was made clear in the following speech later that day:

Offer of Irish Volunteers to Britain

I hope the house will not consider it improper on my part, in the grave circumstances in which we are assembled, if I intervene for a very few moments. I was moved a great deal by that sentence in the speech of the Secretary of State for Foreign Affairs in which he said that the one bright spot in the situation was the changed feeling in Ireland. In past times, when this Empire had been engaged in these terrible enterprises, it is true it would be the utmost affectation and folly on my part to deny it – the sympathy of the Nationalists of Ireland, for reasons to be found deep down in the centuries of history, has been estranged from this country.

Allow me to say, Sir, that what has occurred in recent years has altered the situation completely. I must not touch, and I may be trusted not to touch, on any controversial topic; but this I may be allowed to say, that a wider knowledge of the real facts of Irish history has, I think, altered the views of the democracy of this country towards the Irish question, and today I honestly believe that the democracy of Ireland will turn with the utmost anxiety and sympathy to this country in every trial and every danger that may overtake it. There is a possibility, at any rate, of history repeating itself. The House will remember that in 1778, at the end of the disastrous American War, when it might, I think, truly be said that the military power of this country was almost at its lowest ebb, and when the shores of Ireland were threatened with foreign invasion, a body of 100,000 Irish Volunteers sprang into existence for the purpose of defending her shores. At first, no Catholic – ah! how sad the reading of the history of those days is! – was allowed to be enrolled in that body of Volunteers, and yet, from the very first day, the Catholics of the South and West subscribed money and sent it towards the arming of their Protestant fellow-countrymen. Ideas widened as time went on, and finally the Catholics in the South were armed and enrolled with their fellow-countrymen of a different creed in the North. May history repeat itself to-day. There are in Ireland two large bodies of Volunteers. One of them sprang into existence in the South. I say to the Government that they may tomorrow withdraw every one of their troops from Ireland. I say that the coast of Ireland will be defended from foreign invasion by her armed sons, and for this purpose armed Nationalist Catholics in the South will be only too glad to join arms with the armed Protestant Ulsterman in the North. Is it too much to hope that out of this situation there may spring a result which will be good, not merely for the Empire, but good for the future welfare and integrity of the Irish nation?

I ought to apologise for having intervened, but while Irishmen generally are in favour of peace, and would desire to save the democracy of this country from all the horrors of war; while we would make every possible sacrifice for that purpose, still, if the dire necessity is forced upon this country, we offer to the Government of the day that they may take their troops away, and that if it is allowed to us, in comradeship with our brethren in the North, we would ourselves defend the coasts of our country.

In all, nearly 200,000 Irishmen fought in the British Army during World War One.

Patrick Pearse
1 August 1915

B Y 1912, Patrick H Pearse had become a convinced militant revolutionary, claiming on one occasion that: 'Bloodshed is a cleansing and a sanctifying thing, and the nation which regards it as the final horror has lost its manhood. There are many things more horrible than bloodshed, and slavery is one of them.'

This aspect of Pearse's character was to dominate the remaining years of his life, and undoubtedly influenced the decision to admit him to full membership of the Irish Republican Brotherhood at the end of 1913.

In 1915, Jeremiah O'Donovan Rossa, the veteran leader of the Fenian Rising of 1867, died in New York. His body was brought back to Dublin and buried in Glasnevin Cemetery on 1 August, 1915. The funeral was arranged as a large propaganda exercise by the Irish Republican Brotherhood and a large crowd gathered at the grave side. After a military salute, Patrick Pearse gave the following short, defiant speech.

Speech at the Grave of O'Donovan Rossa

It has seemed right, before we turn away from this place in which we have laid the mortal remains of O'Donovan Rossa, that one among us should, in the name of all, speak the praise of that valiant man, and endeavour to formulate the thoughts and the hopes that are in us as we stand around his grave. And if there is anything that makes it fitting that I, rather than some other, I rather than one of the grey-haired men who were young with him and shared in his labour and in his suffering should speak here, it is perhaps that I may be taken as speaking on behalf of a new generation that has been rebaptised in the Fenian faith, and that has accepted the responsibility of carrying out the Fenian programme. I propose to you then that, here by the grave of this unrepentant Fenian, we renew our baptismal vows; that, here by the grave of this unconquered and unconquerable man, we ask of God, each one for himself, such unshakeable purpose, such high and gallant courage, such unbreakable strength of soul as belonged to O'Donovan Rossa.

Deliberately here we avow ourselves, as he avowed himself in the dock, Irishmen of one allegiance only. We of the Irish Volunteers, and you others who are associated with us in today's task and duty, are bound together and must stand together henceforth in brotherly union for the achievement of the freedom of Ireland. And we know only one definition of freedom: it is Tone's definition, it is Mitchel's definition, it is Rossa's definition. Let no man blaspheme the cause that the dead generations of Ireland served by giving it any other name and definition than their name and their definition.

We stand at Rossa's grave not in sadness but rather in exaltation of spirit that it has been given to us to come thus into so close a communion with that brave splendid Gael. Splendid and holy causes are served by men who are themselves splendid and holy. O'Donovan Rossa was splendid in the proud manhood of him, splendid in the heroic grace of him, splendid in the Gaelic strength and clarity and truth of him. And all that splendor and pride and strength was compatible with a humility and a simplicity of devotion to Ireland, to all that was olden and beautiful and Gaelic in Ireland, the holiness and simplicity of patriotism of a Michael O'Clery or of an Eoghan O'Growney. The clear true eyes of this man almost alone in his day visioned Ireland as we of today would surely have her: not free merely, but Gaelic as well; not Gaelic merely, but free as well.

In a closer spiritual communion with him now than ever before or perhaps ever again, in a spiritual communion with those of his day, living and dead, who suffered with him in English prisons, in communion of spirit too with our own dear comrades who suffer in English prisons today, and speaking on their behalf as well as our own, we pledge to Ireland our love, and we pledge to English rule in Ireland our hate. This is a place of peace, sacred to the dead, where men should speak with all charity and with all restraint; but I hold it a Christian thing, as O'Donovan Rossa held it, to hate evil, to hate untruth, to hate oppression, and, hating them, to strive to overthrow them. Our foes are strong and wise and wary; but, strong and wise and wary as they are, they cannot undo the miracles of God who ripens in the hearts of young men the seeds sown by the young men of a former generation. And the seeds sown by the young men of 1865 and 1867 are coming to their miraculous ripening today. Rulers and defenders of the realms had need to be wary if they would guard against such processes. Life springs from death; and from the graves of patriot men and women spring nations. The Defenders of this realm have worked well in secret and in the open. They think that they have pacified Ireland. They think that they have purchased half of us and intimidated the other half. They think that they have foreseen everything, think that they have provided against everything; but the fools, the fools, the fools! – they have left us our Fenian dead, and while Ireland holds these graves, Ireland unfree shall never be at peace.

Patrick Pearse
24 April 1916

A T AROUND twelve noon on Easter Monday, 24 April, 1916, a party of one hundred or so Irish Volunteers and Citizen Army members who were marching through the streets of Dublin, as had been their wont for a some months, stopped opposite the General Post Office, and ran into the building from which they proceeded to eject both customers and employees. Soon two flags were flying from the building; the traditional green flag, with a gold harp and a new flag a tricolour made up of green, white and orange.

The 1916 rebellion against the British had started.

A while later, puzzled passers-by, still unsure of what was happening, observed Patrick H. Pearse, who was later to be acclaimed a national hero, read the following proclamation of an Irish Republic from the steps of the General Post Office:

Proclamation of an Irish Republic

Irishmen and Irishwomen: In the name of God and of the dead generations from which she receives her old tradition of nationhood, Ireland, through us, summons her children to her flag and strikes for her freedom.

Having organized and trained her manhood through her secret revolutionary organization, the Irish Republican Brotherhood, and through her open military organizations, the Irish Volunteers, and the Irish Citizen Army, having patiently perfected her discipline, having resolutely waited for the right moment to reveal itself, she now seizes that moment and, supported by her exiled children in America and by gallant allies in Europe, but relying in the first on her own strength, she strikes in full confidence of victory.

We declare the right of the people of Ireland to the ownership of Ireland, and to the unfettered control of Irish destinies, to be sovereign and indefeasible. The long usurpation of that right by a foreign people and government has not extinguished the right, nor can it ever be extinguished except by the destruction of the Irish people. In every generation the Irish people have asserted their right to national freedom and sovereignty; six times during the past three hundred years they have asserted it in arms. Standing on that fundamental right and again asserting it in arms in the face of the world, we hereby proclaim the Irish republic as a sovereign of independent state, and we pledge our lives and the lives of our comrades-in-arms to the cause of its freedom, of its welfare, and of its exaltation among the nations.

The Irish republic is entitled to, and hereby claims, the allegiance of every Irishman and Irishwoman. The republic guarantees religious and civil liberty, equal rights and equal opportunities to all its citizens, and declares its resolve to pursue the happiness and prosperity of the whole nation and of all its parts, cherishing all the children of the nation equally, and oblivious of the differences carefully fostered by an alien government, which have divided a minority from the majority in the past.

Until our arms have brought the opportune moment for the establishment of a permanent national government, representative of the whole people of Ireland, and elected by the suffrages of all her men and women, the Provisional Government, hereby constituted, will administer the civil and military affairs of the republic in trust for the people.

We place the cause of the Irish republic under the protection of the Most High God, whose blessing we invoke upon our arms, and we pray that no one who serves that cause will dishonour it by cowardice, inhumanity, or rapine. In this supreme hour the Irish nation must, by its valour and discipline, and by the readiness of its children to sacrifice themselves for the common good, prove itself worthy of the august destiny to which it is called.

Signed on Behalf of the Provisional Government,

Thomas J. Clarke, Sean MacDiarmada, Thomas MacDonagh, P.H. Pearse, Eamonn Ceannt, James Connolly, Joseph Plunkett

The rebellion, involving 1,600 people, lasted for one week. In that time 450 people had been killed, 2,500 wounded and the centre of Dublin destroyed. W.B.Yeats was later to write of the events in his poem, 'Easter 1916,' 'All changed, changed utterly: A terrible beauty is born.'

John Dillon
11 May 1916

O N THE afternoon of Sunday, 30 of April 1916, as the last group of organised rebels in Jacobs' biscuit factory, under Thomas MacDonagh, were about to surrender, John Dillon, one of the leaders of the Irish Parliamentary Party, wrote to the party leader, John Redmond, who was in London at the time.

'You should urge strongly,' he wrote 'on the Government the extreme unwisdom of any wholesale shooting of prisoners' . . . 'If there were shootings of prisoners on any large scale the effect on public opinion would be disastrous in the extreme. So far the feeling of the population in Dublin is against the Sinn Féiners. But a reaction might very easily be created.'

Three days later, on 3 May, the leaders of the rebellion, Pearse, MacDonagh and Clarke, were executed by firing squad at Kilmainham Gaol in Dublin. If the executions had stopped there, the course of Irish history might have been very different but it did not, and by the time Dillon had reached the House of Commons in London on 11 May, to air his views on the executions, another nine Irishmen had been executed.

His passionate speech that night shocked many of his fellow parliamentarians; it demonstrates how deeply the rising had affected him, as it was to affect the people of Ireland.

Speech in House of Parliament on the Rising

. . . I go on to say a word as to the condition of Dublin itself, and of Ireland, from the point of view of military law. But before I do so I just want to say that the primary object of my Motion is to put an absolute and final stop to these executions. You are letting loose a river of blood, and, make no mistake about it, between two races who, after three hundred years of hatred and of strife, we had nearly succeeded in bringing together . . .

It is the first rebellion that ever took place in Ireland where you had a majority on your side. It is the fruit of our life work. We have risked our lives a hundred times to bring about this result. We are held up to odium as traitors by those men who made this rebellion, and our lives have been in danger a hundred times during the last thirty years because we have endeavoured to reconcile the two things, and now you are washing out our whole life work in a sea of blood. In my opinion, at present the government of Ireland is largely in the hands of the Dublin clubs. The Prime Minister, when I asked him a question yesterday about the government of Ireland, told me that it was in the hands of the military officers, subject to the authority of British Cabinet. In my opinion, and I think I really am speaking on a matter that I know, the British Cabinet has much less power in Ireland today than the Kildare Street Club and certain other institutions. It is they who are influencing the policy of the military authorities. What is the use of telling me, as the Prime Minister told me yesterday that the military authorities acted in close consultation with the civil executive officers of the Irish Government? That was the answer I got to my question. Who are the civil executive officers of the Irish Government? There is no Government in Ireland except Sir John Maxwell and the Dublin clubs, and I defy the Prime Minister to tell us who are the civil officers of the Irish Government with whom the military authorities are acting in consultation. Are we to be informed that Sir Robert Chalmers is the civil officer with whom the military generals are taking careful counsel, and is he so versed in Irish affairs that he can untie the tangle that has defied every British statesman for a hundred years? Everybody in Dublin knows that before the civil officers took to flight out of Dublin the military authorities treated them with undisguised contempt, and from the day martial law was proclaimed civil government came to an absolute end . . .

The worst of the situation is that there are many men in Dublin, I know of my own knowledge, who are going about the streets today openly glorying in the revolt – I mean of the old ascendancy party. What is the talk in the clubs and certain districts in Dublin? It is that this is the best thing that has ever happened in Ireland, because they say it has brought us martial law, and real government into the country, and it will put an end for ever to this rotten Nationalist party . . .

This may horrify you, but I declare most solemnly, and I am not ashamed to say it in the House of Commons, that I am proud of these men. They were foolish; they were misled . . . I say I am proud of their courage, and, if you were not so dense and so stupid, as some of you English people are, you could have had these men fighting for you, and they are men worth having. *[Hon. Members: 'You stopped them.']* That is an infamous falsehood. I and the men who sit around me have been doing our best to bring these men into the ranks of the Army. I say that we have been doing our best to bring these men into the ranks of the Army, and it is the blundering manner in which our country has been ruled which has deprived you of their services. These men require no Compulsory Service Bill to make them fight. Ours is a fighting race, and as I told you when I was speaking before on the Military Service Bill, 'It is not a Military Service Bill that you want in Ireland.' If you had passed a Military Service Bill for Ireland, it would have taken 150,000 men and three months' hard fighting to have dealt with it. It is not a Military Service Bill that you want in Ireland: it is to find a way to the hearts of the Irish people, and when you do that you will find that you have got a supply of the best troops in the whole world. How can we, in the face of these facts, accept the statement of the Prime Minister that according to the best of his knowledge no men are being secretly shot in Ireland? The fact of the matter is that what is poisoning the mind of Ireland, and rapidly poisoning it, is the secrecy of these trials and the continuance of these executions.

Compare the conduct of the Government in dealing with this rebellion with the conduct of General Botha. I say deliberately that in the whole of modern history, taking all the circumstances into account, there has been no rebellion or insurrection put down with so much blood and so much savagery as the recent insurrection in Ireland . . .

As I say, there were some very bad actions, but as regards the main body of the insurgents, their conduct was beyond reproach as fighting men. I admit they were wrong; I know they were wrong; but they fought a clean fight, and they fought with superb bravery and skill, and no act of savagery or act against the usual customs of war that I know of has been brought home to any leader or any organised body of insurgents. I have not heard of a single act, I may be wrong, but that is my impression . . .

What is happening is that thousands of people in Dublin, who ten days ago were bitterly opposed to the whole of the Sinn Féin movement and to the rebellion, are now becoming infuriated against the Government on account of these executions, and, as I am informed by letters received this morning, that feeling is spreading throughout the country in a most dangerous degree . . .

We, I think, have a right, we who speak for the vast majority of the Irish people, and we do; we who have risked a great deal to win the people to your side in this great crisis of your Empire's history: we who have endeavoured, and successfully endeavoured, to secure that the Irish in America shall not go into alliance with the Germans in that country – we, I think, were entitled to be consulted before this bloody course of executions were entered upon in Ireland. God knows the result of flouting our advice, as it has been flouted in the conduct of Irish affairs ever since the Coalition Government was formed, has not been a brilliant one. I think that in this matter we were entitled to be consulted . . .

But it is not murderers who are being executed. It is insurgents who have fought a clean fight, however misguided, and it would he a damned good thing for you if your soldiers were able to put up as good a fight as did these men in Dublin – three thousand men against twenty thousand with machine guns and artillery.

An Honourable Member interrupted him, saying 'evidently you wish they had succeeded.'

That is an infamous falsehood. Who is it said that? It is an abominable falsehood. I say that these men, misguided as they were, have been our bitterest enemies. They have held us up to public odium as traitors to our country because we have supported you at this moment and stood by you in this Great War, and the least we are entitled to is this, that in this great effort which we have made at considerable risk – an effort such as the Honourable Members who interrupted me could never have attempted – to bring the masses of the Irish people into harmony with you, in this great effort at reconciliation – I say, we were entitled to every assistance from the Members of this House and from the Government.

Terence MacSwiney
30 March 1920

ON 20 MARCH, 1920, a party of men armed with rifles – probably Royal Irish Constabulary officers – burst into the home of Tómas MacCurtain, the Lord Mayor of Cork and shot him, killing him instantly.

MacCurtain's death immediately thrust new responsibilities on his deputy, Terence MacSwiney. The two men had been friends for nearly twenty years; together they had been the central figures in the setting up of the Cork branch of the Irish Volunteers in 1913; they had together made the decision not to allow the Cork Volunteers to take part in the 1916 Rising; they had acted as the leaders of the Cork No. 1 Brigade of the IRA and they had served together as mayor and deputy mayor of Cork.

Terence MacSwiney was elected unanimously Lord Mayor of Cork on 30 March, 1920. As he rose from his seat to accept his chain of office, the councillors burst into a sustained round of applause. He began his inaugural speech in Irish, then continued:

Inaugural Speech as Lord Mayor of Cork

I shall be brief as possible. This is not an occasion for many words; least not all, a conventional exchange of compliments and thanks. The circumstances of the vacancy in the office of Lord Mayor governed inevitably the filling of it. And I come here more as a soldier stepping into the breach, than as an administrator to fill the first post in the municipality. At a normal time it would be your duty to find for this post the Councillor most practised and experienced in public affairs. But the time is not normal. We see in the manner in which our late Lord Mayor was murdered an attempt to terrify us all. Our first duty is to answer that threat in the only fitting manner by showing ourselves unterrified, cool and inflexible for the fulfilment of our chief purpose –

the establishment of the independence and integrity of our country – the peace and happiness of our country. To that end I am here.

I was more closely associated than any other here with our murdered friend and colleague both before and since the events of Easter Week, in prison and out of it, in a common work of love for Ireland, down to the hour of his death. For that reason, I take his place. It is, I think, though I say it, the fitting answer to those who struck him down. Following from that, there is a further matter of importance only less great – it touches the efficient continuance of our civic administration. If this recent unbearable aggravation of our persecution by our enemies should cause us to suspend voluntarily the normal discharge of our duties, it would help them very materially in their campaign to overthrow our cause. I feel the future conduct of our affairs is in all our minds. And I think I am voicing the general view when I say that the normal functions of our corporate body must proceed, as far as in our power lies, uninterrupted, with that efficiency and integrity of which our late civic head gave such brilliant promise.

I don't wish to sound a personal note, but this much may be permitted under such circumstances. I made myself active in the selection of our late colleague for the office of Lord Mayor. He did not seek the honour, and would not accept it as such; but, when put to him as a duty, he stepped to his place like a soldier. Before his election, we discussed together in the intimate way we discussed everything touching our common work since Easter Week, we debated together what ought to be done, and what could be done, keeping in mind, as in duty bound, not only the idea line of action, but the practicable line of action at the moment as well. That line he followed with an ability and a success all his own. Gentlemen, you have paid tribute to him on all sides. It will be my duty and steady purpose to follow that line as faithfully as may be in my power, though no man in this company could hope to discharge its functions with his ability and his perfect grasp of public business in all its details as one harmonious whole.

I have thought it necessary to touch on this normal duty of ours, though – and it may seem strange to say it – I feel even at the moment it is a digression. For the menace of our enemies hangs over us, and the essential immediate purpose is to show the spirit that animates us, and how we face the future. Our spirit is but a more lively manifestation of the spirit in which we began the year – to work for the city with a new zeal, inspired by our initial act when we dedicated it and formally attested our allegiance, and by working for our city's advancement with constancy in all honourable ways in her new dignity as one of the first cities of Ireland, to work for and, if need be, to die for.

I would recall some words of mine in the day our first meeting after the election of the Lord Mayor. I realised that most of you in the minority here would be loyal to us, if doing so did not threaten your lives; but that you lacked the spirit and the hope to join with us to complete the work of liberation so well begun. I allude to it here again, because I wish to point out again the secret of our strength and the assurance of our final victory. This contest of ours is not, on our side, a rivalry of vengeance, but one of endurance – it is not they who can inflict most, but they who can suffer most, will conquer – though we do not abrogate our function to demand and see that evil-doers and murderers are punished for their crimes. But it is conceivable that they could interrupt our course for a time; then it becomes a question simply of trust in God and endurance. Those whose faith is strong will endure to the end, and triumph. The shining hope of our time is that the great majority of our people are now strong in that faith.

To you, gentlemen of the minority here, I would address a word. To me it seems – and I don't say it to hurt you – that you have a lively faith in the power of the devil, and but little faith in God. But God is over us. Anyone surveying the events in Ireland for the past five years must see that it is approaching a miracle how our country has been preserved. God has permitted this to be to try our spirits, to prove us worthy of a noble line, to prepare us for a great and noble destiny. You among us who have yet no vision of the future have been led astray by false prophets. The liberty for which we today strive is a sacred thing – inseparably entwined, as body with soul, with that spiritual liberty for which the Saviour of men died, and which is the inspiration and foundation of all just government. Because it is sacred, and death for it is akin to the Sacrifice on Calvary, following far off but akin to that Divine example, in every generation, our best and bravest have died.

Sometimes in our grief we cry out foolish and unthinking words: 'The sacrifice is too great.' But, it is because they were our best and bravest, they had to die. No lesser would save us. Because of it our struggle is holy – our battle is sanctified by their blood, and our victory is assured by their martyrdom. We, taking up the work they left incomplete, confident in God, offer in turn sacrifice from ourselves. It is not we who take innocent blood; we but offer it, sustained by the example of our immortal dead and that divine example which inspires us all – for the redemption of our country. Facing our enemies, we must declare our attitude simply. We ask for no mercy, and we will make no compromise. But to the Divine Author of mercy we appeal for strength to sustain us, whatever the persecution, that we may bring our people victory at the end. The civilised world dare not continue to look on indifferent. But if the rulers of earth fail us, we have yet sure succour in the Ruler of Heaven; and though to some impatient hearts His judgements seem slow, they never fail, and when they fall they are overwhelming and final.

Five months later, on 12 August, 1920, MacSwiney was arrested with ten others at Cork City Hall. He immediately went on hunger strike in protest. On 17 August, MacSwiney was court-martialled at Victoria Barracks, Cork for possession of a police cipher and sentenced to two years imprisonment in England's Brixton Prison. His hunger strike continued unabated and he died 73 days after starting on 24 October, 1920.

Arthur Griffith
19 December 1921

O N THEIR return to Ireland after signing the Treaty with Britain, the five delegates, Griffith, Collins, Barton, Duggan and Duffy, attended a Cabinet meeting to debate and ratify the Treaty. The Cabinet split on whether or not it should be accepted and the Irish President, Éamon De Valera, issued a public statement in which he condemned some of the Treaty terms, in particular the Oath of Allegiance to the King, and stated that he could not recommend the Treaty's ratification. The Dáil was then summoned to debate and vote on the issue.

The chief negotiator of the Treaty was Arthur Griffith, founder of Sinn Féin, and acting Minister for foreign Affairs of the Provisional Government. Although he did not like the compromises of the Treaty, he felt it was the best that could be achieved and so on the 19 December, 1921, the third day of the Treaty debates, he moved the motion that, 'Dáil Éireann approves of the Treaty between Britain and Ireland signed in London, on December 6, 1921.'

Speech at Treaty Debate

Nearly three months ago Dáil Éireann appointed plenipotentiaries to go to London to treat with the British Government and to make a bargain with them. We have made a bargain. We have brought it back. We were to go there to reconcile our aspirations with the association of the community of nations known as the British Empire. That task which was given to us was as hard as was ever placed on the shoulders of men. We faced that task; we knew that whatever happened we would have our critics, and we made up our minds to do whatever was right and disregard whatever criticism might occur. We could have shirked the responsibility. We did not seek to act as the plenipotentiaries; other men were asked and other men refused. We went. The responsibility is on our shoulders; we took the responsibility in London and we take the responsibility in Dublin. I signed that Treaty not as the ideal thing, but fully believing, as I believe now, it is a treaty honourable to Ireland, and safeguards the vital interests of Ireland.

And now by that Treaty I am going to stand, and every man with a scrap of honour who signed it is going to stand. It is for the Irish people – who are our masters *[hear, hear]*, not our servants as some think-it is for the Irish people to say whether it is good enough. I hold that it is, and I hold that the Irish people – that 95 per cent of them believe it to be good enough. We are here, not as the dictators of the Irish people, but as the representatives of the Irish people, and if we misrepresent the Irish people, then the moral authority of Dáil Éireann, the strength behind it, and the fact that Dáil Éireann spoke the voice of the Irish people, is gone, and gone for ever. Now, the President – and I am in a difficult position – does not wish a certain document referred to read. But I must refer to the substance of it. An effort has been made outside to represent that a certain number of men stood uncompromisingly on the rock of the Republic – the Republic, and nothing but the Republic.

It has been stated also here that the man who made this position, the man who won the war – Michael Collins – compromised Ireland's rights. In the letters that preceded the negotiations not once was a demand made for recognition of the Irish Republic. If it had been made we knew it would have been refused. We went there to see how to reconcile the two positions and I hold we have done it. The President does not wish this document to be read. What am I to do? What am I to say? Am I to keep my mouth shut and let the Irish people think about this uncompromising rock?

President de Valera interrupted him briefly, saying 'I will make my position in my speech quite clear.'

What we have to say is this, that the difference in this Cabinet and in this House is between half recognising the British King and the British Empire, and between marching in, as one of the speakers said, with our heads up. The gentlemen on the other side are prepared to recognise the King of England as head of the British Commonwealth. They are prepared to go half in the Empire and half out. They are prepared to go into the Empire for war and peace and treaties, and to keep out for other matters, and that is what the Irish people have got to know is the difference. Does all this quibble of words – because it is merely a quibble of words – mean that Ireland is asked to throw away this Treaty and go back to war? So far as my power or voice extends, not one young Irishman's life shall be lost on that quibble. We owe responsibility to the Irish people. I feel my responsibility to the Irish people, and the Irish people must know, and know in every detail, the difference that exists between us, and the Irish people must be our judges. When the plenipotentiaries came back they were sought to be put in the dock. Well, if I am going to be tried, I am going to be tried by the people of Ireland Now this Treaty has been attacked. It has been examined with a microscope to find its defects, and this little thing and that little thing has been pointed out, and the people are told – one of the gentlemen said it here – that it was less even than the proposals of July. It is the first Treaty between the representatives of the Irish Government and the representatives of the English Government since 1172, signed on equal footing. It is the first Treaty that admits the equality, and because of that I am standing by it. We have come back from London with the Treaty – Saorstát na hÉireann recognised – the Free State of Ireland. We have brought back the flag; we have brought back the evacuation of Ireland after 700 years by British troops and the formation of an Irish army. We have brought back to Ireland her full rights and powers of fiscal control. We have brought back to Ireland equality with England, equality with all nations which form that Commonwealth, and an equal voice in the direction of foreign affairs in peace and war. Well, we are told that that Treaty is a derogation from our status; that it is a Treaty not to be accepted, that it is a poor thing, and that the Irish people ought to go back and fight for something more, and that something more is what I describe as a quibble of words. Now, I shall have an opportunity later on of replying to the very formidably arranged criticism that is going to be levelled at the Treaty to show its defects. At all events, the Irish people are a people of great common sense. They know that a Treaty that gives them their flag and their Free State and their Army is not a sham Treaty, and the sophists and the men of words will not mislead them, I tell you. In connection with the Treaty men said this and said that, and I was requested to get from Mr. Lloyd George a definite statement covering points in the Treaty which some gentlemen misunderstood. This is Mr. Lloyd George's letter:

'Sir, – As doubts may be expressed regarding certain points not specifically mentioned in the Treaty terms, I think is important that their meaning should be clearly understood.

The first question relates to the method of appointment of the Representatives of the Crown in Ireland. Article III of the Agreement lays down that he is to be appointed in like manner as the Governor-General of Canada and in accordance with the practice observed in the making of such appointment. This means that – the Government of the Irish Free State will be consulted so as to ensure a selection acceptable to the Irish Government before any recommendation is made to his Majesty.

The second question is as to the scope of the Arbitration contemplated in Article V regarding Ireland's liability for a share of War Pensions and the Public Debt. The procedure contemplated by the Conference was that the British Government should submit its claim, and that the Government of the Irish Free State should submit any counter-claim to which it thought Ireland entitled.

Upon the case so submitted the Arbitrators would decide after making such further inquiries as they might think necessary; their decision would then be final and binding on both parties. It is, of course, understood that the arbitrator or arbitrators to whom the case is referred shall be men as to whose impartiality both the British Government and the Government of the Irish Free State are satisfied.

The third question relates to the status of the Irish Free State. The special arrangements agreed between us in Articles VI, VII, VIII and IX, which are not in the Canadian constitution, in no way affect status. They are necessitated by the proximity and interdependence of the two islands – by conditions, that is, which do not exist in the case of Canada.

They in no way affect the position of the Irish Free State in the Commonwealth or its title to representation, like Canada, in the Assembly of the League of Nations. They were agreed between us for our mutual benefit, and have no bearing of any kind upon the question of status. It is our desire that Ireland shall rank as co-equal with the other nations of the Commonwealth, and we are ready to support her claim to a similar place in the League of Nations as soon as her new Constitution comes into effect.

The framing of that Constitution will be in the hands of the Irish Government, subject, of course, to the terms of Agreement, and to the pledges given in respect of the minority by the head of the Irish

Delegation. The establishment and composition of the Second Chamber is, therefore, in the discretion of the Irish people. There is nothing in the Articles of Agreement to suggest that Ireland is in this respect bound to the Canadian model.

I may add that we propose to begin withdrawing the Military and Auxiliary Forces of the Crown in Southern Ireland when the Articles of Agreement are ratified.

I am, Sir,

Your obedient Servant,
D. LLOYD GEORGE.

Arthur Griffith continues:

Various different methods of attack on this Treaty have been made. One of them was they did not mean to keep it. Well, they have ratified it, and it can come into operation inside a fortnight. We think they do mean to keep it if we keep it. They are pledged now before the world, pledged by their signature, and if they depart from it they will be disgraced and we will be stronger in the world's eyes than we are to-day. During the last few years a war was waged on the Irish people, and the Irish people defended themselves, and for a portion of that time, when President de Valera was in America, I had at least the responsibility on my shoulders of standing for all that was done in that defence, and I stood for it, I would stand for it again under similar conditions. Ireland was fighting then against an enemy that was striking at her life, and was denying her liberty, but in any contest that would follow the rejection of this offer Ireland would be fighting with the sympathy of the world against her, and with all the Dominions – all the nations that comprise the British Commonwealth – against her.

The position would be such that I believe no conscientious Irishman could take the responsibility for a single Irishman's life in that futile war. Now, many criticisms, I know, will be levelled against this Treaty; one in particular, one that is in many instances quite honest, it is the question of the oath. I ask the members to see what the oath is, to read it, not to misunderstand or misrepresent it. It is an oath of allegiance to the Constitution of the Free State of Ireland and of faithfulness to King George V in his capacity as head and in virtue of the Common citizenship of Ireland with Great Britain and the other nations comprising the British Commonwealth. That is an oath, I say, that any Irishman could take with honour. He pledges his allegiance to his country and to be faithful to this Treaty, and faithfulness after to the head of the British Commonwealth of Nations. If his country were unjustly used by any of the nations of that Commonwealth, or its head, then his allegiance is to his own country and his allegiance bids him to resist *[hear, hear]*.

We took an oath to the Irish Republic, but, as President de Valera himself said, he understood that oath to bind him to do the best he could for Ireland. So do we. We have done the best we could for Ireland. If the Irish people say, 'We have got everything else but the name Republic, and we will fight for it,' I would say to them that they are fools, but I will follow in the ranks. I will take no responsibility. But the Irish people will not do that. Now it has become rather a custom for men to speak of what they did, and did not do, in the past. I am not going to speak of that aspect, except one thing. It is this. The prophet I followed throughout my life, the man whose words and teachings I tried to translate into practice in politics, the man whom I revered above all Irish patriots was Thomas Davis. In the hard way of fitting practical affairs into idealism I have made Thomas Davis my guide. I have never departed in my life one inch from the principles of Thomas Davis, and in signing this Treaty and bringing it here and asking Ireland to ratify it I am following Thomas Davis still.

Later on, when coming to reply to criticism, I will deal with the other matters. Thomas Davis said, 'Peace with England, alliance with England to some extent, and, under certain circumstances, confederation with England; but an Irish ambition, Irish hopes, strength, virtue, and rewards for the Irish.'

That is what we have brought back, peace with England, alliance with England, confederation with England, an Ireland developing her own life, carving out her own way of existence, and rebuilding the Gaelic civilisation broken down at the battle of Kinsale. I say we have brought you that. I say we have translated Thomas Davis into the practical politics of the day. I ask then this Dáil to pass this resolution, and I ask the people of Ireland, and the Irish people everywhere, to ratify this Treaty, to end this bitter conflict of centuries, to end it for ever, to take away that poison that has been rankling in the two countries and ruining the relationship of good neighbours. Let us stand as free partners, equal with England, and make after 700 years the greatest revolution that has ever been made in the history of the world – a revolution of seeing the two countries standing not apart as enemies, but standing together as equals and as friends. I ask you, therefore, to pass this resolution.

After a protracted and sometimes bitter debate the Treaty was ratified on 7 January, 1922, by 64 votes to 57.

Michael Collins
19 December 1921

IMMEDIATELY after signing the Treaty Michael Collins, the IRA commander and reluctant Treaty negotiator, wrote to a friend: 'Think – what have I got for Ireland? Something she has wanted these past seven hundred years. Will anyone be satisfied at the bargain? Will anyone? I tell you this – early this morning I signed my death warrant. I thought at the time how odd, how ridiculous – a bullet may just as well have done the job five years ago. These signatures are the first real step for Ireland. If people will only remember that – the first real step."

At the Treaty debates, Collins was one of the first deputies to support Griffith's motion that 'Dáil Éireann approves of the treaty between Britain and Ireland, signed in London on 6 December, 1921.' His speech, which Ernest Childers, later in the debate described as 'a most able and eloquent speech,' is given below:

Speeach at Treaty Debate

A Chinn Chomhairle, *[Speaker of the House]* much has been said in Private Session about the action of the plenipotentiaries in signing at all or in signing without first putting their document before Cabinet. I want to state as clearly as I can, and as briefly as I can – I promise you to be very brief – what the exact position was. It has been fully explained how the Delegation returned from London that momentous Saturday to meet the Cabinet at home. We came back with a document from the British Delegation which we presented to the Cabinet. Certain things happened at that Cabinet Meeting, and the Delegation, on returning put before the British Delegation as well as they could, their impressions of the decisions. I want to be fair to everybody. I can only say they were decisions in this way, that we went away with certain impressions in our minds and that we did our best faithfully to transmit their impressions to paper in the memorandum we handed into the British Delegation. It was well understood at that meeting that Sir James Craig was receiving a reply from the British Premier on Tuesday morning. Some conclusions between the British Delegation and ourselves had, therefore, to be come to and handed in to the British Delegation on the Monday night. Now, we went with a document which none of us would sign. It must have been obvious, that being so, that in the meantime a document arose which we thought we could sign. There was no opportunity of referring it to our people at home. Actually on the Monday night we did arrive at conclusions which we thought we could agree to and we had to say 'Yes' across the table, and I may that we said 'Yes.' It was later on that same day that the document was signed. But I do not now, and not then, regard my word as being anything more important, or a bit less important, than my signature on a document. Now, I also want to make clear that the answer which I gave and that signature which I put on that document would be the same in Dublin or in Berlin, or in New York or in Paris. If we had been in Dublin the difference in distance would have made this difference, that we would have been able to consult not only the members of the Cabinet but many members of the Dáil and many good friends. There has been talk about 'the atmosphere of London' and there has been talk about 'slippery slopes.' Such talk is beside the point. I knew the atmosphere of London of old and I knew many other things about it of old. If the members knew so much about 'slippery slopes' before we went there why did they not speak then? The slopes were surely slippery, but it is easy to be wise afterwards. I submit that such observations are entirely beside the point. And if my signature has been given in error, I stand by it whether it has or not, and I am not going to take refuge behind any kind of subterfuge. I stand up over that signature and I give the same decision at this moment in this assembly *[applause]*.

It has also been suggested that the Delegation broke down before the first bit of English bluff. I would remind the Deputy who used that expression that England put up quite a good bluff for the last five years here and I did not break down before that bluff *[applause, and a voice, 'That is the stuff']*. And does anybody think that the respect I compelled from them in a few years was in any way lowered during two months of negotiations? That also is beside the point. The results of our labour are before the Dáil. Reject or accept. The President has suggested that a greater result could have been obtained by more skillful handling.

Perhaps so. But there again the fault is not the delegation's; it rests with the Dáil. It is not afterwards the Dáil should have found out our limitations. Surely the Dáil knew it when they selected us, and our abilities could not have been expected to increase because we were chosen as plenipotentiaries by the Dáil. The delegates have been blamed for various things. It is scarcely too much to say that a they have been blamed for not returning with recognition of the Irish Republic. They are blamed, at any rate, for not having done much better. A Deputy when speaking the other day with reference to Canada suggested that what may apply with safety to Canada would not at all apply to Ireland because of the difference in distance from Great Britain. It seemed to me that he did not regard the delegation as being wholly without responsibility for the geographical propinquity of Ireland to Great Britain. It is further suggested that by the result of their labours the delegation made a resumption of hostilities certain. That again rests with the Dáil; they should have chosen a better delegation, and it was before we went to London that should have been done, not when we returned . . .

This Treaty was not signed under personal intimidation. If personal intimidation had been attempted no member of the delegation would have signed it.

At a fateful moment I was called upon to make a decision, and if I were called upon at the present moment for a decision on the same question my decision would be the same. Let there be no mistake and no misunderstanding about that.

I have used the word 'intimidation.' The whole attitude of Britain towards Ireland in the past was an attitude of intimidation, and we, as negotiators, were not in the position of conquerors dictating terms of peace to a vanquished foe. We had not beaten the enemy out of our country by force of arms.

To return to the Treaty, hardly anyone, even those who support it, really understands it, and it is necessary to explain it, and the immense powers and liberties it secures. This is my justification for having signed it, and for recommending it to the nation. Should the Dáil reject it, I am, as I said, no longer responsible. But I am responsible for making the nation fully understand what it gains by accepting it, and what is involved in its rejection. So long as I have made that clear I am perfectly happy and satisfied. Now we must look facts in the face. For our continued national and spiritual existence two things are necessary – security and freedom. If the Treaty gives us these or helps us to get at these, then I maintain that it satisfies our national aspirations. The history of this nation has not been, as is so often said, the history of a military struggle of 750 years; it has been much more a history of peaceful penetration of 750 years. It has not been a struggle for the ideal of freedom for 750 years symbolised in the name Republic. It has been a story of slow, steady, economic encroach by England. It has been a struggle on our part to prevent that, a struggle against exploitation, a struggle against the cancer that was eating up our lives, and it was only after discovering that, that it was economic penetration, that we discovered that political freedom was necessary in order that that should be stopped. Our aspirations, by whatever term they may be symbolised, had one thing in front all the time, that was to rid the country of the enemy strength. Now it was not by any form of communication except through their military strength that the English held this country. That is simply a plain fact which, I think, nobody will deny. It wasn't by any forms of government, it wasn't by their judiciary or anything of that kind. These people could not operate except for the military strength that was always there. Now, starting from that, I maintain that the disappearance of that military strength gives us the chief proof that our national liberties are established. And as to what has been said about guarantees of the withdrawal of that military strength, no guarantees, I say, can alter the fact of their withdrawal, because we are a weaker nation, and we shall be a weaker nation for a long time to come. But certain things do give us a certain guarantee. We are defined as having the constitutional status of Canada, Australia, New Zealand, South Africa. If the English do not withdraw the military strength, our association with those places does give us, to some extent, a guarantee that they must withdraw them. I know that it would be finer to stand alone, but if it is necessary to our security, if it is necessary to the development of our own life, and if we find we cannot stand alone, what can we do but enter into some association? Now I have prepared part of this which I am going to read very carefully. I have said that I am not a constitutional lawyer. I am going to give a constitutional opinion in what I am going to read, and I will back that constitutional opinion against the opinion of any Deputy, lawyer or otherwise, in this Dáil.

Collins then began to read: The status as defined is the same constitutional status in the 'community of nations known as the British Empire,' as Canada, Australia, New Zealand, South Africa. And here let me say that in my judgment it is not a definition of any status that would secure us that status, it is the power to hold and to make secure and to increase what we have gained.

The fact of Canadian and South African independence is something real and solid, and will grow in reality and force as time goes on. Judged by that touchstone, the relations between Ireland and Britain will have a certainty of freedom and equality which cannot be interfered with. England dare not interfere with Canada. Any attempt to interfere with us would be even more difficult in consequence of the reference to the 'constitutional status' of Canada and South Africa.

They are, in effect, introduced as guarantors of our freedom, which makes us stronger than if we stood alone.

In obtaining the 'constitutional status' of Canada, our association with England is based not on the present technical legal position of Canada. It is an old Act, the Canadian Act, and the advances in freedom from it have been considerable. That is the reply to one Deputy who spoke to-day of the real position, the complete freedom equality with Canada has given us. I refer now not to the legal technical status, but to the status they have come to, the status which enables Canada to send an Ambassador to Washington, the status which enables Canada to sign the Treaty of Versailles equally with Great Britain, the status which prevents Great Britain from entering into any foreign alliance without the consent of Canada, the status that gives Canada the right to be consulted before she may go into any war. It is not the definition of that status that will give it to us; it is our power to take it and to keep it, and that is where I differ from the others. I believe in our power to take it and to keep it. I believe in our future civilisation. As I have said already, as a plain Irishman, I believe in my own interpretation against the interpretation of any Englishman. Lloyd George and Churchill have been quoted here against us. I say the quotation of those people is what marks the slave mind. There are people in this assembly who will take their words before they will take my words. That is the slave mind.

The only departure from the Canadian status is the retaining by England of the defences of four harbours, and the holding of some other facilities to be used possibly in time of war. But if England wished to re-invade us she could do so with or without these facilities. And with the 'constitutional status' of Canada we are assured that these facilities could never be used by England for our re-invasion.

If there was no association, if we stood alone, the occupation of the ports might probably be a danger to us. Associated in a free partnership with these other nations it is not a danger, for their association is a guarantee that it won't be used as a jumping-off ground against us. And that same person tells me that we haven't Dominion status because of the occupation of these ports, but that South Africa had even when Simonstown was occupied. I cannot accept that argument. I am not an apologist for this Treaty. We have got rid of the word 'Empire.' For the first time in an official document the former Empire is styled 'The Community of Nations known as the British Empire.' Common citizenship has been mentioned. Common citizenship is the substitution for the subjection of Ireland. It is an admission by them that they no longer can dominate Ireland. As I have said, the English penetration has not merely been a military penetration. At the present moment the economic penetration goes on. I need only give you a few instances. Every day our banks become incorporated or allied to British interests, every day our steamship companies go into English hands, every day some other business concern in this city is taken over by an English concern and becomes a little oasis of English customs and manners. Nobody notices, but that is the thing that has destroyed our Gaelic civilisation. That is a thing that we are able to stop, not perhaps if we lose the opportunity of stopping it now. That is one of the things that I consider is important, and to the nation's life perhaps more important than the military penetration. And this gives us the opportunity of stopping it. Indeed when we think of the thing from that economic point of view it would be easy to go on with the physical struggle in comparison with it.

Do we think at all of what it means to look forward to the directing of the organisation of the nation? Is it one of the things we a prepared to undertake? If we came back with the recognition of the Irish Republic we would need to start somewhere. Are we simply going to go on keeping ourselves in slavery and subjection, forever keeping on an impossible fight? Are we never going to stand on our own feet? Now I had an argument based on a comparison of the Treaty with the second document *[de Valera's alternative Treaty wording]*, and part of the argument was to read the clauses of the second document. In deference to what the President has said I shall not at this stage make use of that argument. I don't want to take anything that would look like an unfair advantage. I am not standing for this thing to get advantage over anybody, and whatever else the President will say about me, I think he will admit that.

At this point President de Valera interrupted him by saying, 'I never said anything but the highest.'

Now I have explained something as to what the Treaty is. I also want to explain to you as one of the signatories what I consider rejection of it means. It has been said that the alternative document does not mean war. Perhaps it does, perhaps does not. That is not the first part of the argument. I say that rejection of the Treaty is a declaration of war until you have beaten the British Empire, apart from any alternative document. Rejection of the Treaty means your national policy is war. If you do this, if you go on that as a national policy, I for one am satisfied. But I want you to go on it as a national policy and understand what it means. I, as an individual, do not now, no more than ever, shirk war. The Treaty was signed by me, not because they held up the alternative of immediate war. I signed it because I would not be one of those to commit the Irish people to war without the Irish people committing themselves to war. If my constituents send me to represent them in war, I do my best to represent them in war. Now I was not going to refer to anything that had been said by the speakers of the Coalition side to-day. I do want to say this in regard to the President's remark about Pitt, a remark, it will be admitted, which was not very flattering to us. Well, now, what happened at the time of the Union? Grattan's Parliament was thrown away without reference to the people and against their wishes. Is the Parliament which this Treaty offers us to be similarly treated? Is it to be thrown away without reference to the people and against their wishes?

Here again he was interrupted. This time by de Valera with the words, 'What Parliament.' Then a member cried, 'the Free State.' And Miss MacSwiney added, 'Which Parliament.'

I would like you to keep on interrupting, because I was looking at a point here. I am disappointed that I was not interrupted more. In our Private Sessions we have been treated to harangues about principle. Not one Deputy has stated a clear, steadfast, abiding principle on which we can stand. Deputies have talked of principle. At different times I have known different Deputies to hold different principles. How can I say, how can anyone say, that these Deputies may not change their principles again? How can anyone say that anybody – a Deputy or a supporter – who has fought against the Irish Nation on principle may not fight against it again on principle? I am not impeaching anybody, but I do want to talk straight. I am the representative of an Irish stock; I am the representative equally with any other member of the same stock of people who have suffered through the terror in the past. Our grand-fathers have suffered from war, and our fathers or some of our ancestors have died of famine. I don't want a lecture from anybody as to what my principles are to be now. I am just a representative of plain Irish stock whose principles have been burned into them, and we don't want any assurance to the people of this country that we are going to betray them. We are one of themselves. I can state for you a principle which everybody will understand, the Principle of 'government by the consent of the governed.' These words have been used by nearly every Deputy at some time or another. Are the Deputies going to be afraid of these words now, supposing the formula happens to go against them?

De Valera again interrupted him with cries of, 'No, no.'

I have heard Deputies remark that their constituents are in favour of this Treaty. The Deputies have got their powers from their constituents and they are responsible to their constituents. I have stated the principle which is the only firm principle in the whole thing.

Now I have gone into more or less a general survey of the Treaty, apart from one section of it, the section dealing with North-East Ulster. Again I am as anxious to face facts in that case as I am in any other case. We have stated that we will not coerce the North-East. We have stated it officially in our correspondence. I stated it publicly in Armagh and nobody has found fault with it. What did we mean? Did we mean we were going to coerce them or we were not going to coerce them? What was the use of talking big phrases about not agreeing to the partition of our country. Surely we recognise that the North-East corner does exist, and surely our intention was that we should take such steps as would sooner or later lead to greater understanding. The Treaty has made an effort to deal with it, and has made an effort, in my opinion, on lines that will lead very rapidly to goodwill, and the entry of the North-East under the Irish Parliament. I do not say it is an ideal arrangement, but if our policy is, as has been stated, a policy of non-coercion, then let somebody else get a better way out of it.

I say that this Treaty gives us, not recognition of the Irish Republic, but it gives us more recognition on the part of Great Britain and the associated States than we have got from any other nation. Again I want to speak plainly. America did not recognise the Irish Republic. As things in London were coming to a close I received cablegrams from America. I understand that my name is pretty well known in America, and what I am going to say now will make me unpopular there for the rest of my life, but I am not going to say anything or hide anything for the sake of American popularity. I received a cablegram from San Francisco, saying, 'Stand fast, we will send you a million dollars a month.' Well, my reply to that is, 'Send us half-a million and send us a thousand men fully equipped.' I received another cablegram from a branch of the American Association for the Recognition of the Irish Republic and they said to me, 'Don't weaken now, stand with de Valera.' Well, let that branch come over and stand with us both. The question before me was were we going to go on with this fight, without referring it to the Irish people, for the sake of propaganda in America? I was not going to take that responsibility. And as this may be the last opportunity I shall ever have of speaking publicly to the Dáil, I want to say that there was never an Irish man placed in such a position as I was by reason of these negotiations. I had got a certain name, whether I deserved it or not, and I knew when I was going over there that I was being placed in a position that I could not reconcile, and that could not in the public mind be reconciled with what they thought I stood for, no matter what we brought back, – and if we brought back the recognition of the Republic – but I knew that the English would make a greater effort if I were there than they would if I were not there, and I didn't care if my popularity was sacrificed or not. I should have been unfair to my own country if I did not go there. Members of the Dáil well remember that I protested against being selected. I want to say another thing. It will be remembered that a certain incident occurred in the South of Ireland, an incident which led to the excommunication of the whole population of that district. At the time I took responsibility for that in our private councils. I take responsibility for it now publicly. I only want to say that I stand for every action as an individual member of the Cabinet, which I suppose I shall be no longer; I stand for every action, no matter how it looked publicly, and I shall always like the men to remember me like that. In coming to the decision I did I tried to weigh what my own responsibility was. Deputies have spoken about whether dead men would approve of it, and they have spoken as to whether children yet unborn will approve of it, but few of them have spoken as to whether the living approve of it. In my own small way I tried to have before my mind what the whole lot of them would think of it. And the proper way for us to look at it is in that way. There is no man here who has more regard for the dead men than I have. I don't think it is fair to be quoting them against us. I think the decision ought to be a clear decision on the documents as they are before us – on the Treaty as it is before us. On that we shall be judged, as to whether we have done the right thing in our own conscience or not. Don't let us put the responsibility, the individual responsibility, upon anybody else. Let us take the responsibility ourselves and let us in God's name abide by the decision.

Éamon de Valera
19 December 1921

F OR THE President of the First Dáil, Éamon de Valera, the Treaty was 'in violent conflict with the wishes of the majority of this nation as expressed freely in elections during the past three years.' He felt that the Treaty negotiators had not got as a good a deal as they should have. He told a private session of Dáil Éireann on the 14 December, 1921: 'I was captaining a team and I felt the team should have played with me to the last and that I should have got the last chance which would have put us over and we might have crossed the bar in my opinion at high tide.'

After Arthur Griffith's motion in the Dáil, on the 19 December, which called for the acceptance of the Treaty by the House, had been seconded by Sean MacKeown, Éamon de Valera stood up to oppose the motion. His speech began:

Speech at Treaty Debate

I think it would scarcely be in accordance with Standing Orders of the Dáil if I were to move directly the rejection of this Treaty. I daresay, however, it will be sufficient that I should appeal to this House not to approve the Treaty. We were elected by the Irish people, and did the Irish people think we were liars when we said that we meant to uphold the Republic, which was ratified by the vote of the people three years ago, and was further ratified – expressly ratified – by the vote of the people at the elections last May? When the proposal for negotiation came from the British Government asking that we should try by negotiation to reconcile Irish national aspirations with the association of nations forming the British Empire, there was no one here as strong as I was to make sure that every human attempt should be made to find whether such reconciliation was possible. I am against this Treaty because it does not reconcile Irish national aspirations with association with the British Government. I am against this Treaty, not because I am a man of war, but a man of peace. I am against this Treaty because it will not end the centuries of conflict between the two nations of Great Britain and Ireland.

We went out to effect such a reconciliation and we have brought back a thing which will not even reconcile our own people much less reconcile Britain and Ireland.

If there was to be reconciliation, it is obvious that the party in Ireland which typifies national aspirations for centuries should be satisfied, and the test of every agreement would be the test of whether the people were satisfied or not. A war-weary people will take things which are not in accordance with their aspirations. You may have a snatch election now, and you may get a vote of the people, but I will tell you, that Treaty will renew the contest that is going to begin the same history the Union began, and Lloyd George is going to have the same fruit for his labours as Pitt had. When in Downing Street proposals to which we could unanimously assent in the Cabinet were practically turned down at the point of the pistol an immediate war was threatened upon our people. It was only then that this document was signed, and the document has been signed by plenipotentiaries, not perhaps individually under duress, but it has been signed, and would only affect this nation as a document signed under duress, and this nation would not respect it.

I wanted, and the Cabinet wanted, to get a document we could stand by, a document that could enable Irishmen to meet Englishmen and shake hands with them as fellow-citizens of the world. That document makes British authority our masters in Ireland. It was said that they had only an oath to the British King in virtue of common citizenship, but you have an oath to the Irish Constitution, and the Constitution will be a Constitution which will have the King of Great Britain as head of Ireland. You will swear allegiance to that Constitution and to the King; and if the representatives of the Republic should ask the people of Ireland to do that which is inconsistent with the Republic, I say they are subverting the Republic. It would be a surrender which was never heard of in Ireland since the days of Henry II; and are we in this generation, which has made Irishmen famous throughout the world, to sign our names to the most ignoble document that could be signed.

When I was in prison in solitary confinement our warders told us that we could go from our cells into the hall, which was about fifty feet by forty. We did go out from our cells to the hall, but we did not give our word to the British jailer that he had the right to detain us in prison because we got that privilege. Again on another occasion we were told that we could get out to a garden party, where we could see the flowers and the hills, but we did not for the privilege of going out to garden parties sign a document handing over our souls and bodies to the jailers. Rather than sign a document which would give British authority in Ireland they should be ready to go into slavery until the Almighty had blotted out their tyrants. If the British Government passed a Home Rule Act or something of that kind I would not have said to the Irish people, 'Do not take it.' I would have said, 'Very well; this is a case of the jailer leading you from the cell to the hall,' but by getting that we did not sign away our right to whatever form of govern-ment we pleased. It was said that an uncompromising stand for a Republic was not made. The stand made by some of them was to try and reconcile a Republic with an association. There was a document presented to this House to try to get unanimity, to see whether the views which I hold could be reconciled to that party which typified the national aspirations of Ireland for centuries. The document was put there for that purpose, and I defy anybody in the House to say other-wise than that I was trying to bring forward before this assembly a document which would bring real peace between Britain and Ireland – a sort of document which we would have tried to get and would not have agreed if we did not get. It would be a document that would give real peace to the people of Great Britain and Ireland and not the officials. I know it would not be a politicians' peace. I know the politician in England who would not take it would risk his political future, but it would be a peace between people, and would be consistent with the Irish people being full masters of everything within their own shores. Criticism of this Treaty is scarcely necessary from this point of view, that it could not be ratified because it would not be legal for this assembly to ratify it, because it would be inconsistent with our position. We were elected here to be the guardians of an independent Irish State – a State that had declared its independence – and this House could no more than the ignominious House that voted away the Colonial Parliament that was in Ireland in 1800 unless we wished to follow the example of that House and vote away the independence of our people. We could not ratify that instrument if it were brought before us for ratification. It is, therefore, to be brought before us not for ratification, because it would be inconsistent, and the very fact that it is inconsistent shows that it could not be reconciled with Irish aspirations, because the aspirations of the Irish people have been crystallised into the form of Government they have at the present time. As far as I was concerned, I am probably the freest man here to express my opinion. Before I was elected President at the Private Session, I said, 'Remember I do not take, as far as I am concerned, oaths as regards forms of Government. I regard myself here to maintain the independence of Ireland and to do the best for the Irish people,' and it is to do the best for the Irish people that I ask you not to approve but to reject this Treaty.

You will be asked in the best interests of Ireland, if you pretend to the world that this will lay the foundation of a lasting peace, and you know perfectly well that even if Mr. Griffith and Mr. Collins set up a Provisional Government in Dublin Castle, until the Irish people would have voted upon it the Government would be looked upon as a usurpation equally with Dublin Castle in the past. We know perfectly well there is nobody here who has expressed more strongly dissent from any attacks of any kind upon the delegates that went to London than I did.

There is no one who knew better than I did how difficult is the task they had to perform. I appealed to the Dáil, telling them the delegates had to do something a mighty army or a mighty navy would not be able to do. I hold that, and I hold that it was in their excessive love for Ireland they have done what they have. I am as anxious as anyone for the material prosperity of Ireland and the Irish people, but I cannot do anything that would make the Irish people hang their heads. I would rather see the same thing over again than that Irishmen should have to hang their heads in shame for having signed and put their hands to a document handing over their authority to a foreign country. The Irish people would not want me to save them materially at the expense of their national honour. I say it is quite within the competence of the Irish people if they wished to enter into an association with other peoples, to enter into the British Empire; it is within their competence if they want to choose the British monarch as their King, but does this assembly think the Irish people have changed so much within the past year or two that they now want to get into the British Empire after seven centuries of fighting? Have they so changed that they now want to choose the person of the British monarch, whose forces they have been fighting against, and who have been associated with all the barbarities of the past couple of years; have they changed so much that they want to choose the King as their monarch? It is not King George as a monarch they choose: it is Lloyd George, because it is not the personal monarch they are choosing, it is British power and authority as sovereign authority in this country. The sad part of it, as I was saying, is that a grand peace could at this moment be made, and to see the difference. I say for instance, if approved by the Irish people, and if Mr. Griffith, or whoever might be in his place, thought it wise to ask King George over to open Parliament he would see black flags in the streets of Dublin. Do you think that that would make for harmony between the two peoples? What would the people of Great Britain say when they saw the King accepted by the Irish people greeted in Dublin with black flags? If a Treaty was entered into, if it was a right Treaty, he could have been brought here [cries of 'no, no']. Yes he could [again cries of 'no, no']. Why not? I say if a proper peace had been made you could bring, for instance, the President of France, the King of Spain, or the President of America here, or the head of any other friendly nation here in the name of the Irish State, and the Irish people would extend to them in a very different way a welcome as the head of a friendly nation coming on a friendly visit to their country, and not as a monarch who came to call Ireland his legitimate possession. In one case the Irish people would regard him as a usurper, in the other case it would be the same as a distinguished visitor to their country. Therefore, I am against the Treaty, because it does not do the fundamental thing and bring us peace. The Treaty leaves us a country going through a period of internal strife just as the Act of Union did.

One of the great misfortunes in Ireland for past centuries has been the fact that our internal problems and our internal domestic questions could not be gone into because of the relationship between Ireland and Great Britain, just as in America during the last Presidential election, it was not the internal affairs of the country were uppermost; it was other matters. It was the big international question. That was the misfortune for America at the time, and it was the great misfortune for Ireland for 120 years, and if the present Pact is agreed on that will continue. I am against it because it is inconsistent with our position, because if we are to say the Irish people don't mean it, then they should have told us that they didn't mean it.

Had the Chairman of the delegation said he did not stand for the things they had said they stood for, he would not have been elected. The Irish people can change their minds if they wish to. The Irish people are our masters, and they can do as they like, but only the Irish people can do that, and we should give the people the credit that they meant what they said just as we mean what we say.

I do not think I should continue any further on this matter. I have spoken generally, and if you wish we can take these documents up, article by article, but they have been discussed in Private Session, and I do not think there is any necessity for doing so.

Therefore, I am once more asking you to reject the Treaty for two main reasons, that, as every Teachta *(Member of Irish Parliament)* knows, it is absolutely inconsistent with our position; it gives away Irish independence; it brings us into the British Empire; it acknowledges the head of the British Empire, not merely as the head of an association, but as the direct monarch of Ireland, as the source of executive authority in Ireland.

The Ministers of Ireland will be His Majesty's Ministers, the Army that Commandant MacKeon spoke of will be His Majesty's Army. You may sneer at words, but I say words mean, and I say in a Treaty words do mean something, else why should they be put down? They have meanings and they have facts, great realities that you cannot close your eyes to. This Treaty means that the Ministers of the Irish Free State will be His Majesty's Ministers and the Irish Forces will be His Majesty's Forces. Well, time will tell, and I hope it won't have a chance, because you will throw this out. If you accept it, time will tell; it cannot be one way in this assembly and another way in the British House of Commons. The Treaty is an agreed document, and there ought to be pretty fairly common interpretation of it. If there are differences of interpretation we know who will get the best of them.

I hold, and I don't mind my words being on record, that the chief executive authority in Ireland is the British Monarch – the British authority. It is in virtue of that authority the Irish Ministers will function. It is to the Commander-in-Chief of the Irish Army, who will be the English Monarch, they will swear allegiance, these soldiers of Ireland. It is on these grounds as being inconsistent with our position, and with the whole national tradition for 750 years, that it cannot bring peace. Do you think that because you sign documents like this you can change the current of tradition? You cannot. Some of you are relying on that 'cannot' to sign this Treaty. But don't put a barrier in the way of future generations.

Parnell was asked to do something like this – to say it was a final settlement. But he said, 'No man has a right to set.' No man 'can' is a different thing. 'No man has a right' – take the context and you know the meaning. Parnell said practically, 'You have no right to ask me, because I have no right to say that any man can set boundaries to the march of a nation.' As far as you can, if you take this you are presuming to set bounds to the onward march of a nation *(applause)*.

John A. Costello
24 November 1948

O N THE 5 September, 1948, a dramatic headline in the Sunday
Independent declared, 'External Relations Act to go.' The controversial External Relations Act of 1936, left Ireland a republic in all
but name. However it still retained, to the dismay of large number of
people, the British Crown as the symbolic head of state.

The recently appointed Taoiseach, John A. Costello, who was in
Canada as a guest of the Canadian Bar Association, reacted to the
article by calling a press conference in Ottawa on 7 September. He
announced to waiting journalists that 'there was no reason why Éire
should not continue in association with Britain but not as a formal
member of the British Commonwealth.' He went on to say that, 'the
External Relations Act was full of inaccuracies and infirmities and the
only thing to do was scrap it.'

Ten weeks later, the Inter-Party Government under Costello introduced the Republic of Ireland Bill to the Dáil.

On 24 November, 1948, during the second stage of the Bill's procedure through the Dáil, Costello told the members why he thought
Ireland should move to republic status:

Introductory Speech on the Republic of Ireland Act

In moving this motion, Sir, it would be the merest hypocrisy on my part
if I did not give expression in public to the feelings of pride which
animate me in being privileged to sponsor this Bill and recommend it
to the Dáil for acceptance. Equally, however, it would be quite unworthy
if I did not express my feelings of deep humility as I approach the
discharge of the duty which I have to fulfil. Those sentiments of humility are genuinely and sincerely felt, and arise from the certain realisation
and knowledge that there are on every side of this House people far

more worthy, who have merited far more than I have, to fulfil the privilege accorded to me by the turn of events.

This Bill which I am introducing and recommending for acceptance to the House is not a Bill merely to repeal a particular statute which has caused much discussion and considerable controversy. It is a Bill which, when enacted, will have consequences which will mark it as a measure ending an epoch and beginning what I hope will be a new and brighter epoch for the people of this country. This Bill will end, and end forever, in a simple, clear and unequivocal way this country's long and tragic association with the institution of the British Crown and will make it manifest beyond equivocation or subtlety that the national and international status of this country is that of an independent republic. It is necessary for me to state what I believe to be the effect of this Bill as clearly and as emphatically as possible so that there can be no arguments in the future, no misunderstandings, no suggestions that lurking around the political structure of this State there is some remnant or residue of that old institution and that politicians might be able to seize upon that for their own purposes, for the purposes of vote-catching or for the purposes of evoking again the anti-British feeling which has been such fruitful ground on which politicians have played for many years past. While it is necessary for me to make as clear as words can make it what we intend and believe to be the purpose and effect of this Bill, it is equally necessary for me to emphasize with equal clarity and force that this measure is not designed nor was it conceived in any spirit of hostility to the British people or to the institution of the British Crown. Least of all is there any notion of hostility to the person who now occupies the throne in England, who has carried out his duties with efficiency and dignity, whose illness we regret and whose recovery we hope will be speedy.

Again, I want to emphasise that this Bill was not conceived nor is it brought into this House in a mood of flamboyant patriotism or aggressive nationalism, nor in a spirit of irresponsible isolationism nor with any desire or intention in any way to dislocate or interrupt the delicate mechanism of that community of nations known as the Commonwealth of Nations with which, in one shape or another, we have had some association over the last quarter of a century. This Bill, as I want to state – and to restate, if necessary – is a constructive proposal, and not one intended to be destructive or to have any centrifugal effect upon another nation or nations, and particularly those nations that form the

Commonwealth of Nations. It is recommended to this Dáil for what it is and what it is intended to be and what I believe it to be; it is recommended as an instrument of domestic peace, of national unity and of international concord and goodwill. We have – and it is hardly necessary for me to say it – had rather too much in the last twenty five years of constitutional law and constitutional lawyers. For twenty five years, we have had arid, futile and unending discussions as to the nature and character of our constitutional position and our constitutional and international relations with Great Britain, with the other members of the Commonwealth of Nations and with other foreign nations of the comity of nations. It is hoped that this Bill will put an end to these arid and futile discussions, and make our international and constitutional position clear beyond all ambiguity and beyond all argument.

It will be necessary for me in the course of the remarks that I have to make in dealing with this Bill to refer critically to the effect of certain measures that have been passed in the years gone by and to suggest the possible effects and repercussions that they may have had upon our constitutional position. I do not intend in the course of my discussions or observations on this measure to enter upon those discussions or observations in a spirit of argument or to press that this or that view is the correct one. What I hope to do is to show that by reason of the legislation of the past 25 years, we have now reached a position which justifies the enactment of this Bill now before the Dáil. I do sincerely desire that the discussion on this measure will neither lead to nor be led into a competition of claims between this Party or that Party, this person or that person as to the part one or other played or did not play in the national events and policies of the past quarter of a century. While I am desirous that that above all should be avoided, I am equally desirous that my object shall be achieved; and I want to say here at the outset that it is my ambition that that object will be achieved. Anything I have to say cannot be regarded as and is not intended to be a justification or apologia or indictment of any Party and, least of all, a personal justification of my own policies or my own past.

I would like in the course of this discussion if acknowledgement were made and recognition given to all Parties and to all persons who each, in whatever measure, contributed a quota or even a mite towards the common cause in the national advancement. We have had, as I indicated, too many constitutional discussions and too many occasions for these arid constitutional arguments. We have as a consequence been too long occupied, divided and frustrated by fruitless and useless controversy and, therefore, I do not want to make this occasion an occasion of further bickering and further controversy, particularly when this Bill was conceived with the primary purpose, as I shall explain later on, and the compelling motives in my mind and in the minds of my colleagues, of bringing unity here in this country and particularly in this part of our country amongst those sections of our people that have hitherto been divided and of putting an end to the bitterness and personalities which have poisoned the stream of our national life blood during the past 25 years.

In that spirit I approach the task that I have to fulfill, and I do earnestly ask Deputies to follow that headline, which I have set for myself and which I hope and trust I shall follow. I earnestly ask Deputies, in the course of the observations I have to make – which, I am afraid, will have to be rather lengthy – to give me the indulgence of their charity if I should, either by word or phrase, stray beyond the bounds of those limits that I have set myself.

This Bill burns no bridges leading either to national unity or to closer friendship with the people of our neighbouring country, Great Britain. It places no obstacle in the way of the progress which we hope to make towards both those goals. I have said, and I want to repeat it again, because I am addressing here today not merely the audience that is immediately listening to me but to a wider audience, that not merely is this measure intended to be a Bill to promote domestic peace and harmony, but it is a measure designed to achieve and one which we believe will achieve a greater measure of friendship and goodwill than has ever existed in the long and tragic association between Great Britain and Ireland. We want to increase that friendship and that goodwill. This Bill is not a mere expression of nationalistic egoism or isolationism. We are a small nation and we require friends. It is only, as we believe, by goodwill and friendship and fellowship and the recognition of our mutual rights and the appreciation of our reciprocal interest that that measure of goodwill and friendship which we wish to achieve shall be achieved.

Doubtless, there have been in the past few weeks some efforts made to bedevil the situation which we are considering here today. The dying embers of reaction and imperialism sent forth a few flickering flames in an effort to light the fires of turmoil and class hatred and hatred between the two peoples and between sections of our peoples here in

Ireland. I am glad to say here today that those efforts have failed; I am glad to say that the fears and apprehensions that were aroused by that poisonous and malicious propaganda can be allayed and be calmed.

It will, I am convinced, when this measure has passed this House, still more when it becomes law, be apparent to the people of this country and to the people in every country that is watching us here now and that has watched us for the last few weeks that as a result of this, this country will be able to take its place, without equivocation, without argument, without subtlety, without having to apologise, explain or discuss as one of the independent nations of the earth, able to do its part and to contribute its quota to the maintenance of peace and the solution of the international problems that face each nation in the world today.

Let me say a few more words about our relations with Great Britain. I believe that as a result of this measure, our relationship with that country will be far closer and far better and will be put upon a better and firmer foundation than it ever has been before. Deputies and those interested will only have to look in retrospect upon the history of this country during the past 25 or 26 years to see that every step made in advance towards the development and the recognition of our national and international sovereignty brought with it, between Great Britain and this country, an additional measure of good feeling and goodwill.

It is a sobering thought that many people who are now in the flower of their manhood and womanhood were not born on the 6th December, 1921, when the Treaty was signed. Many of those do not know anything about the history of the previous years, and the conflicts that took place between this country and Great Britain, but whatever people may think of that Treaty of the 6th December 1921, at least it can be now said in retrospect that it did play its part in bringing about closer relationship and an end of the centuries-old feud between the peoples of these two neighbouring islands.

For ten long years those people who undertook the duty and the task of honouring the signatures to the Treaty walked the via dolorosa of those bitter years, the details of which I do not intend to recall, but at the end of those ten years, when the efforts of the representatives of this country at imperial conferences and international gatherings had borne their fruit, those developments had brought us to the point where we had achieved for this country international recognition as one of the sovereign countries of the world, and we had swept away all the old dead wood of British constitutional theory that lay or appeared to lie in the path of constitutional progress. All those contacts and those controversies that took place both at the imperial conferences and at the international gatherings at which this country was represented, where the efforts of the representatives of this country were directed towards getting complete international recognition for the country and achieving complete freedom for the institutions that were set up under the Treaty, gave their contribution to the goodwill that grew up in spite of all the difficulties and trials of those times between the peoples of these two islands.

After 1932, when the first Government of this State was succeeded by another Government with a different policy, a Government that carried out different Acts, carried out a different policy, as the years went on they too expressed their desire and, be it said, achieved their purpose to some considerable extent of bringing together still more closely the relationship between Great Britain and Ireland and the peoples of these two neighbouring islands. With the Removal of the Oath Act, with the enactment of the Constitution of 1937, with the handing back of the ports, with the recognition of our neutrality during the war, all these things contributed their quota in bringing about the end of those old feuds and bitternesses that divided the peoples of these two islands for centuries.

This measure, in my view, and I recommend it to the Dáil as such, is not merely the logical outcome but the inevitable result of a peaceful political evolution that has gone on here in this country over the past 25 years. During those years we have had close association, some bond of one kind or another, between each of the States and nations forming what is now known as the Commonwealth of Nations. There has been a recognition that this country of ours is a mother country, a country with a spiritual empire beyond the seas and there has grown up, I believe, from my own experience, and particularly from the experiences which I had in Canada during my visit within the last few months, between those nations and this old nation of ours an abundant goodwill and fellow feeling and an intense desire that we should prosper and go the road that our own people wish to walk.

For reasons which I think are cogent it would be unthinkable for us, by the action which this Bill proposes to take, to go further away from those nations with which we have had such long and, I think, such fruitful association in the past twenty five or twenty six years. Great Britain, of course, is the dominant partner in that association. Nothing that can be done by this measure will in any way be a retrograde step in our relations with that country. Our people pass freely from here to England. We have trade and commerce of mutual benefit to each other. We have somewhat the same pattern of life, somewhat the same respect for democratic principles and institutions. The English language in our Constitution is recognised as the second official language of this nation. But we have still stronger ties than even those. Our missionary priests, nuns and brothers have gone to England and have brought the faith there, and are giving no inadequate contribution to the spiritual uplift which is so necessary in the atheistic atmosphere of the world today. We have our teachers there, lay and religious; we have our doctors and professional men there; we have our working men and our craftsmen and our girls who have gone over to earn a living there. All these things would, in normal circumstances, bring about and create and necessitate a feeling of fellowship and goodwill between our two countries. There is no reason why that should not continue. There is no reason why we should not get rid of all these causes of friction which have kept us apart for so many years. This Bill gets rid of one cause of friction and leaves only one to be removed, Partition . . .

. . . Why are we doing this? Why are we doing this now? Why are we leaving the Commonwealth of Nations? Why are we breaking the last tenuous link with the Crown? To these people to whom I address myself here today, people of goodwill, people who are entitled to an answer, I have already addressed the words with which I opened my remarks − that so far from having any feelings of hostility towards Great Britain, the British Crown, or the British people, we want to clear away from our past, the past of this country, all obstacles which are a hindrance to the greater and freer development of good relations between our two countries. Many of those people who are asking these questions and bona fide looking for information upon them, do not know anything at all, or practically anything, about the history of this country or its relationship with Great Britain in the years gone by. They know none of the details of the tragic story of British and Irish relationships. I suppose it is true to say that the vast majority of the British people who are looking now at us and wondering why we are doing this, have not the remotest idea or the smallest conception of the wrongs that were inflicted by their own nation upon this country and the people of this country in the centuries gone by. It is because they are asking for information, wanting to be convinced and genuinely anxious to understand our point of view, that I must take a little time in endeavouring to answer the questions to which I have referred.

In answering these questions, it will be necessary for me to say some hard things about the British Crown and the British people, but those who wish to hear or to read my remarks will take them in the context in which they are uttered and the spirit in which I am making them, as I have to recall those past events or to pass in review some of the tragic circumstances or considerations, in order that those people may know and understand why it has been impossible for this country permanently to accept the institution of the Crown as one of our Irish institutions. Again I want to ask those people, the people of goodwill to whom I am addressing myself, not to be misled by the ignorant, ill-formed, malicious and poisonous propaganda that has been spread by some sections of the Press in the last few weeks, nor to let those sections of the Press twist my remarks, turn them into anything in the nature of an endeavour, on my part or on the part of my colleagues or those who support us, to create anti-British feeling or to give another twist to the lion's tail. I want those people to be informed and, being informed, to appreciate and understand and sympathise with our ideals and our aspirations and accept as genuine our efforts towards the promotion of an ever increasing goodwill between our two countries.

This Bill, as I have said at the outset, will close the long and tragic story of the relations between our two countries based upon an acceptance of the institution of the Crown in such a way as to make it certain that there can be no misconception or ambiguity. We hope that, after this Bill is passed, it will open a new era in our relationships and while one tragic chapter is closed a newer and brighter one will be opened in our international record, in the record between Great Britain and this country. During the whole course of that long sustained struggle for political, civil and religious liberty the Irish people never lost the consciousness that they are not and never were a British people, that they were a race, an Irish race with the distinctive nationality, a distinctive language, an ancient culture all their own. It is impossible for a people who for centuries had fought for and been denied those four essential freedoms of which President Roosevelt spoke and of which it is now so popular to speak – Freedom of Speech, Freedom of Worship, Freedom from Fear and Freedom from Want – to associate those ideas, those four freedoms, with the constitutional forms and ideals of the British common law, with the forms and ideas of the British conquerors. Those conquerors persistently refused those freedoms to the Irish people.

As a learned professor has said quite recently, Professor Wheare, Professor of Constitutional Law – I quote him from the *Sunday Times* of October 24, 1948: 'it is difficult for those who regarded the Crown as the badge of servitude to accept it as the badge of freedom.'

That phrase summarises our whole attitude. We could never accept, no matter what our views may have been or may be, as Irishmen, the Crown as a badge of freedom. To the minds of a lot of people, of most Irish people – I would almost say, all Irish people, because of our instincts and our tradition and our history, the institution of the Crown has been regarded as a badge of servitude and those instincts can never be eradicated from the tradition and the blood of any Irishman.

I mentioned some of the considerations which bore in upon our people and made it impossible for us to regard the Crown as a badge of freedom. In the course of the remarks that I will make later on, I will have to refer to the symbol of the Crown as it was stated to be in the Statute of Westminster and the symbol of free association, but may I here in this context say this, that those of us who worked in the Imperial Conferences of 1926, 1929 and 1930 to clear away all those real or apparent obstacles to freedom for our Legislature or for this country in its international relations, endeavoured to create the situation where that old instinctive feeling of the Crown being the symbol of servitude would be accepted by our people as the symbol of free association, and that they regarded it as nothing else but a symbol.

Having achieved our purpose of getting it stated in the most solemn way that it was a symbol of freedom, a symbol of association, then our effort was to make the position clear in that way to our own people and so to try to reconcile them, at least for a time, to the institution of the British Crown. But no people can be expected willingly and permanently to accept as part of their political institutions the symbol of the British Crown, when fidelity to the Catholic faith, the faith of the vast majority of our Irish people, was throughout the years regarded as disaffection and disloyalty to the British Crown, when love of country became treason to the British Crown, when every attempt to secure personal rights and national liberty was deemed rebellion against the Crown, when entry into the humble homes of Irishmen, to arrest them as a prelude to their gibbering or shooting as demanded in the name of the King. Crown rent, quite rent and rack rents were demanded in the

King's name. The evictions carried out during the land war were carried out to enforce the King's writ. The prosecutions against our patriots, against those who fought in the land war, were carried out by His Majesty's attorneys and sentences were passed by His Majesty's judges. Many of us remember during the days of our childhood, not being taught, but having it almost instinctively in our minds and in our blood, that the harp beneath the crown was the symbol of servitude and that the harp without the crown was the symbol of freedom . . .

Ireland during the Emergency

James Craig
2 September 1939

W ITH THE passage of the Government of Ireland Act through
the British Parliament on 23 December, 1920, Ireland was partitioned into a Northern six county state and a Southern twenty-six county
state.

From that day on, successive Southern governments made great efforts
to sever the imperial connection with Britain. This culminated in the
declaration of neutrality by Dáil Éireann on 2 September, 1939, the day
after Britain had declared war on Germany.

In stark contrast Northern Ireland, after partition, had continued to
maintain and strengthen its constitutional and economic links with
Britain.

On the same day that the Southern Free State government declared
its neutrality, James Craig (or Lord Craigavon), the Northern Ireland
Prime Minister, further reaffirmed Northern Ireland's loyalty to Britain
by offering Northern Ireland's support to the war effort in the following
speech from the Northern Ireland parliament in Stormont:

Speech in Support of the British War Effort

I rise today in a difficult state of affairs so far as we here are concerned.
I would have called the House together earlier, with your permission,
had I thought that any good service would be rendered either to Members
or to the community; but, as will be realised, the situation up to a few
days ago did not, in my opinion, justify calling the House together,
because I felt that it would not be long before some decision was taken
one way or the other which would clear the air so far as being able to
address Honourable Members is concerned.

We are met now after most exhausting endeavours on the part of Mr.
Chamberlain to secure peace throughout the world. He admits it

himself, I am sure with a very sad heart, that all he did on behalf of the country failed and, therefore, we here today are in a state of war, and so are prepared with the rest of the United Kingdom and Empire to face all the responsibilities that are imposed upon Ulster people.

There is no slackening in our loyalty. There is no falling off in our determination to place the whole of our resources at the command of the Government in Britain. They have established now a War Cabinet, and I have already communicated with those of them whom I know best to say privately and, I am sure publicly now as well, that anything we can do here, to facilitate them in the terrible times that lie ahead they have only got to let us know and we will do it. In that I feel I have the backing of the whole House.

We are met also with no mean record behind us of what has been done by the Ulster people. During the past month the response to the call for volunteers has amounted to 45,000, while the actual enrolments in the ordinary forces of the Crown have more than doubled, although hitherto Ulster has stood at the very top so far as enlistment for the army is concerned. That again is a matter of great satisfaction, but much more requires to be done. I am sure the crisis during the next few days will have nerved many of our youth to rally to the colours where they know that not only are they defending their own homes, but the Empire, and where they must know that their own people and womenfolk must be guarded so far as possible from dread bombing or any other machinery of war.

Then I must touch upon another matter. The Government have for some time past been visualising trouble not only from the common enemy, Germany, and her allies but have also been most carefully thinking out plans with regard to the specific dangers in our own area. Orders have been given for the 'B' Special Constabulary to be immediately placed upon the basis they were on before they returned to the drill category, that is to say, patrol category. I would like to explain to the 'B' Special Constabulary three of the reasons which moved the Government to withdraw them temporarily from the category of patrol men. We discovered that a certain amount of exaggerating was being made out of the fact that our 'B' Specials so well patrolled the roads that visitors here on their annual holiday were getting the impression that they were in an armed camp all the time with these men out; that Ulster could not exist without having an armed force going along the roads and lanes of Ulster. We wished, first of all, to give visitors a free run in Ulster without exhibiting the strength which we always have in the background. That is one reason. Another reason was that the harvest was about to come in, and we wanted to release as many men as possible to assist with what will be an important factor in this war – the production of food at home for the people. Then, thirdly, we desired that the men should get more drill, in case, as has happened, we have to turn them out once more to patrol the countryside, especially the Border. Since then there have been some most regrettable incidents, and I have to inform the House that as an additional precaution against sedition and attacks in our midst we took into our care last night forty-five of the IRA and added them to those already in confinement under grave suspicion. There they will remain until the end of the war unless something justifies us in letting them out.

I would like to make a statement with regard to our proposals. We must ensure that we are in complete control, that we are masters of our own house, and not here at the permission of anybody else. We are not here for the citizens to have their lives and property endangered by a lot of cowardly assassins, men who never hesitate to do what they can to destroy the State. Especially at this moment, when the Empire is at war and when every assistance is wanted, nothing should be done to put sand in the wheels of our defence here at home.

There is then the point, who are these men? I can describe them in a sentence. They are the King's enemies. That is the way to describe men who carry on as they did some few hours ago when they dragged the uniform off one of our volunteers going to the front. Are such men not the King's enemies? Can any punishment be too great for them?

I say not, and the Government are determined that whatever precautions are necessary will be taken, and that whatever severity can be dealt out to men of that class this Government is quite powerful enough, thank God, to mete out. It is determined to see that there will be nothing of that kind to disturb the public peace.

I do not often speak like this. This is, as far as I am concerned, my third experience of a great war. I have seen both concerned sides of the picture. I have seen the fighting side, and I have also seen the home side. It is difficult for people at home to realise what war means abroad. Knowing, as I do, how the men abroad day and night look to the home people to keep steadfast and not to allow anything to be given away during their absence, not only do I feel strongly in issuing the solemn warning to the wrongdoers who may crop up in Ulster, but I feel it is necessary to assure those who are boldly going out under the flag of Britain that they will not be neglected or disgraced in their absence.

Éamon de Valera
7 November 1940

IN ACCORDANCE with the Anglo-Irish agreement of 25 April, 1938, the defence facilities at certain Irish harbours, retained by the British Government under the Treaty of 1921, were transferred to the Government of Ireland during the summer of 1938. This part of the agreement had been strongly opposed by Winston Churchill, and from the beginning of the Second World War he made it a major object of policy to secure the recovery of the ports for the defensive purposes of Britain. In the House of Commons on the 5 November, 1940, Churchill stated that the inability to use the south and west coasts of Ireland was 'a most heavy and grievous burden.' This was followed by unfavourable press comment, both in Britain and in the US. Comments in the Economist magazine at the time were typical: 'If the ports become a matter of life and death ... there can only be one way out: we must take them. That would of course revive all the old bitterness. But if bitterness there must be, let us have the bitterness and the bases not the bitterness alone – which is all mere retaliation would provoke.'

De Valera was forced into reply and did so in the Dáil, on 7 November. His official biographers, the Earl of Longford and T.P. O'Neill, later described the following as the 'finest speech of his life.'

Speech Reasserting Ireland's Neutrality

I do not think I would have great difficulty in making what I propose to say relevant to the debate which has just been interrupted, but, in deference to the views expressed this afternoon and to prevent any possibility of misunderstanding, I think it is perhaps better that I should deal with the matter as a completely separate and unconnected affair. I think that every deputy, when he read the statement of the British Prime Minister with reference to our ports, must have wondered somewhat. I do not know whether everybody was prepared to take that statement in the way that I was prepared to take it, as a simple, perhaps natural, expression of regret, or whether it portended something more. I would have refrained from making any comment upon it were it not that it has been followed by an extensive press campaign in Britain itself, and re-echoed in the United States of America, the purport of the campaign being that we should surrender or lease our ports to Britain for the conduct of the war.

Now, the aim of our Government, uniformly, has been to try to bring about good relations between the people of this island and the people of the adjoining island. It has been the prime, the fundamental, motive of most of the things which we did. We realised that these good relations could only be based on the recognition by Britain of our fundamental rights by removing causes which, over the centuries, have made the history of the relations of our two countries such tragic reading. In pursuit of that object we strove with the British Government to get a complete agreement with regard to all the outstanding issues between us. We succeeded to the extent that, with the exception of one outstanding matter, fundamental no doubt, we had settled those outstanding differences in such a way that, if that could only be settled, we could say that the quarrel of the centuries had been ended.

Unfortunately that outstanding matter, the matter of partition, which affects so deeply every man and every woman of Irish blood throughout the world, was left unsettled, and it remained unsettled at the outset of this war. But we had settled the points of difference so far as the immediate territory under the jurisdiction of this Government was concerned, and we had hoped that these matters were settled for ever and that never again was there going to be any question of the right of the people of this part of Ireland to exercise complete sovereignty over this territory and to be able to choose the policy which would best seem to serve the interests of the community that lived in the territory.

No doubt, giving us back what was our own may appear to many to have put a burden upon those who gave it back. To restore that which has been taken does, I suppose, always imply a sacrifice for those who restore it. But, if justice is to be done, that sacrifice has to be faced, and we fully expected that, not merely on the part of the British Government but on the part of the British people, that was completely and fully understood. I want to say before I say much more that, up to the present certainly, it has been understood and that there has not been

since the beginning of this war a single suggestion that this community
of ours was not entitled to act as we have acted and to remain out of
this war.

It is because I am anxious that that should continue that I am choosing this opportunity to address the House and to speak to our people
and to the people of the adjoining island. We have chosen the policy of
neutrality in this war because we believed that it was the right policy for
our people. It is the policy which has been accepted not merely by this
House but by our people as a whole. Anyone who realises what modern
war means, and what it means particularly for those who have not
sufficient air defences, will not have the slightest doubt that that policy
was the right one, apart altogether from any questions of sympathy on
one side or the other.

Now, as I have said, we want friendly relations with the people of
Britain, as we want friendly relations with all other peoples, but we
naturally want them with Britain because Britain is the nearest country
to us on the globe. We have many relations of various kinds which make
it desirable that the two peoples should live in friendship. It was partly
for that reason, and partly because I knew perfectly that it was a condition
of neutrality, that, years before we came into office and several times
since we came into office, I announced that it would be our policy to
use our strength to the utmost to see that this island was not going to
be used as a basis of attack upon Britain. We have never swerved in the
slightest from that declaration. Everything that we could do has been
done to make sure that that policy would be made as effective as it was
within our power to make it.

Before the war, in order to increase our strength and so put us in a
better position to make sure that, in the event of a war and in the event
of our declaring our neutrality, as I expected we would, we should be in
a position to see that that neutrality would be respected by all belligerents, we tried to get arms. We sought them in America; we sought
them in Britain; we sought them on the continent even; and it is no
fault of the Government if our armaments are not even several times
stronger than they are. We did not ask to be given a present of these
arms – we were prepared to buy them; and to the extent to which they
were on offer, either here or in the United States of America, we have
purchased them.

There has been no want of faith, good faith, as far as we are concerned. We have abided by our public as well as by our private promises. It

is a lie to say that German submarines or any other submarines are being supplied with fuel or provisions on our coasts. A most extensive system of coast observation has been established here since the war. I say it is a lie, and I say further that it is known to be a falsehood by the British Government itself.

Having said all that, I now come to the question of our ports. There can be no question of the handing over of these ports so long as this State remains neutral. There can be no question of leasing these ports. They are ours. They are within our sovereignty; and there can be no question, as long as we remain neutral, of handing them over on any condition whatsoever. Any attempt to bring pressure to bear on us by any side – by any of the belligerents – by Britain – could only lead to bloodshed.

Certainly, as long as this Government remains in office, we shall defend our rights in regard to these ports against whoever shall attack them, as we shall defend our rights in regard to every other part of our territory. It would be a strange thing, indeed, if the reason for an attack upon our ports should be that they would be useful. If that is a good reason, then I suppose it is universally a good reason, and it is not necessary for me to point the moral by saying where or for whom.

I want to say to our people that we may be – I hope not – facing a grave crisis. If we are to face it, then we shall do it anyhow, knowing that our cause is right and just and that, if we have to die for it, we shall be dying in that good cause.

James Dillon
17 July 1941

IN MAY, 1939 the Taoiseach, Éamon de Valera, made clear the government's position in the impending war, when he told the Dáil: 'The Government has set the aim of its policy, in the present circumstances, to preserve a position of neutrality. We believe that no other position would be accepted by the vast majority of our people as long as the present position exists.'

On 1 September, 1939 Germany invaded Poland and Europe was cast into war. The following day de Valera summoned the Dáil in order to introduce Emergency legislation which, together with a declaration of neutrality was unanimously passed. An all-party consensus was agreed on neutrality.

During the War years, the only Irish politician to break the all-party consensus on neutrality was James Dillon, the vice-president of Fine Gael. In an interview in 1979, Dillon described why he felt he had to take a stand against neutrality: 'I could never forget that the west coast of Ireland was littered with the bodies of dead English seamen who had been bringing supplies to us. In 1941, the Germans were flying the Cherbourg-Stravanger route up our coasts and dropping magnetic mines into the Atlantic. Britain was at a hairs breath of being cut off from America. The British had no tanks, no oil, no means of bringing US troops to Europe. I felt that the time had come to take a moral stand. I spoke out against Hitler in the Dáil.'

Dillon's speech to the Dáil on 17 July, caused much consternation among Dáil members, as it was at great variance with their thinking, and with that of the vast majority of the Irish population.

Speech Against Neutrality

Recently, a well known Irish political thinker and philosopher wrote the following words: 'Many democrats share the errors of the totalitarians who see in the voice of the State or the leader the very essence of truth and goodness, for on their side they claim that the will of the people is what makes a course of conduct correct, an opinion true – that their decision can be questioned.'

I adopt those words, and though the Government's present policy of indifferent neutrality is the policy of the majority of our people, is the policy of the legitimate, elected Government of this country and, as I believe, the policy supported by the majority of members of the Party to which I belong, I say that it is not the correct course of conduct. I say that it is not in the true interest, moral or material, of the Irish people. I, perhaps, am at fault in not having said this much before but I confess that I forbore from saying it in the hope that the Government of the country and the majority of my fellow countrymen would come of their own volition to share my view. I think, over and above the references which I made to the activities of the Minister for the Co-ordination of Defence in the United States of America, it is right to say that, in addition to his diplomatic activities, indefinite news of ambiguous speeches made by him in various centres of the United States of America lead me to believe that he set out, as the unanimous views of the Irish people, views to which I do not subscribe and to which I believe a considerable number of our people do not subscribe.

I think it is reasonable and right that on this occasion of the Foreign Affairs debate in this House I should at least state my view and in stating it I do not want to avoid any particle of the truth. I do not think that it would be any service to this country or any service to the friends of this country to leave them under any illusion as to what the true situation is. I believe the majority of our people are in favour of the Government's policy of neutrality. That is a plain, patent fact, to which all responsible men must have regard. My view, however, is this: recognising that no responsible man could conceivably wish to see his country at war, nevertheless, when the choice lies between dishonour and material ruin on the one hand and the risk of war upon the other, terrible as that risk may be, frightful as the consequences may be of facing it, I think a nation with our traditions should face that risk of war and refuse to submit to a blackmail of terror designed to make it sell its honour and stake its whole material future on the vain hope that it may be spared the passing pain of effort now.

I now reassert the sovereign right of the Irish people alone to determine what the foreign policy of this State shall be now and for all time.

I reaffirm my conviction that it is the duty of our people and the Government of this country to resist aggression against the sovereignty of this State whence ever it may come, with all the resources at our disposal. But I say that, in the exercise of the sovereign right of the Irish people to determine the foreign policy of the State, we, the Parliament of Ireland, should ascertain precisely what co-operation Great Britain and the United States of America may require to ensure success against the Nazi attempt at world conquest and, as expeditiously as possible, to afford to the United States of America and Great Britain that co-operation to the limit of our resources. I use that word, 'limit', deliberately, and I say that the limit of our resources must be deemed by all reasonable men within this country and outside it to preclude the possibility of sending Irish troops abroad. We have neither the means nor the material with which, to equip such forces. But I do say that our resources extend to ascertaining what accommodation the United States of America and Great Britain may require within our territory to resist the Nazi aggression against the world and, having ascertained it, I do say that we, the Irish people, should afford that accommodation here and now. I would say to my friends in this House and outside it to be on their guard lest the Soviet intervention in this war should confuse their minds and lest it should give rise to any false sense of security.

There may be those who would say that the threat to Western Europe is now past and is oriented. Let them beware, lest what seems a formidable antagonist to the Nazis now might collapse and we would discover the full fury of an unchequered Nazi aggression turned westward to envelop us and all those around us in the course of their campaign. Let those who feel with me that there is only one thing more loathsome than Communism in the world not suffer their minds to be confused by the fact that Soviet Russia is fighting Germany now. Let them ask themselves: if they were being stalked by a man-eating tiger, would they shoot the jaguar that attacked that tiger, or would they not rejoice to see it cripple the aggressor, and give them time and opportunity to prepare their defence? And even though they looked on with equanimity at that jaguar striking down the tiger that sought to destroy them, it would be unnecessary for them to resolve to make a domestic pet of that jaguar when the conflict was over. The fact that Soviet Russia has become locked in deadly conflict with its prototype, Nazi Germany, is a stroke of luck for which Christian civilisation may devoutly thank Providence, but let it create no false sense of security in our minds. The utmost endeavour of all Christian men is requisite if the Nazi threat to Christianity is to be repelled with any casual co-operation that may come our way. I say, Sir, that aid for Great Britain and the United States from this country is called for on spiritual and material grounds. We are fortunate in Ireland that honour and interest coincide, unlike the unhappy countries of Europe, such as Yugoslavia, Holland, Norway, Belgium and Denmark who, finding honour and interest at variance, chose honour and lost all the worldly possessions that they had. That is not our choice . . .

These countries had to make the choice between honour and interest, and they chose honour and they lost all their material goods. This country mercifully finds that its interests and its honour coincide. I say that the honour of this country is involved, because the justification for our existence as a nation is that for 700 years we fought against injustice. We fought and demonstrated our loyalty to the principle of justice before the nations of the world in our resistance to the British imperial claim to make our country a slave country or to thrust upon our people a religion which our people knew to be false. In that fight we sacrificed men, money and material, generation after generation, until we won. That fight was the sheet anchor of resistance in every suffering country in the world, and the beacon of hope to every oppressed people struggling for their liberties from one end of the world to another.

I say today that the German Nazi Axis seeks to enforce on every small nation in Europe the same beastly tyranny that we successfully fought 700 years to prevent the British Empire imposing on this country. I say – and I say it on the authority of Our Holy Father the Pope – that Germany in every small country which she has conquered has sought, not only to establish political domination, but to impose on the conquered peoples an atheist church which derides Christianity and which forbids the people of those States to serve God according to their consciences. I say – and here again I claim the authority of the Holy Father for the statement – that the Nazi domination, in every small State in Europe where it has been established, imposes upon the Christian peoples of those countries the obligation to choose between the Reich and Christ, and that statement is quoted further from the Pastoral Letter from the German Bishops to their own people . . .

Naval and air bases are required in this country by the United States of America and Great Britain at the present time to prevent the Nazi attempt to cut the lifeline between the United States and Britain now.

At present we act the part of Pontius Pilate in asking as between the Axis and the Allies, 'What is truth?' and washing our hands and calling the world to witness that this is no affair of ours. I say we know, as between these parties, what the truth is – that on the side of the Anglo-American Alliance is right and justice and on the side of the Axis is evil and injustice.

And I say it is our affair, inasmuch as resistance to evil and injustice is the affair of every Christian State and every Christian man in this world. At the present time the issue involved is whether Christianity will pass through the catacombs or survive. I am convinced that, if Nazis prevail in the world today Christianity will pass through the catacombs and only those with martyrs' fortitude will retain the Faith. It would be well all of us to ask ourselves the question whether we are sure – each one of us – of martyrs' fortitude; and, if we are not whether we are prepared to put our faith in jeopardy – because we might lose it if we were called on to suffer the torture and persecution that Catholics in Nazi-dominated countries have been called on to suffer in the last four years. I say that it is not doubt as to the right and wrong of the moral issues in this struggle that deters us from making the right decision now. It is fear of the German blitz that deters us.

No prudent man will minimise that danger: no just man will deride that fear. It is a terrible danger: it is a thing of which every honest public representative must feel deeply apprehensive, when he thinks of bringing that danger upon the people for whom he stands trustee. It is only when he is certain that failure to face that danger now, failure to urge his people to face that danger now, is a lesser evil than the consequences of sinking our heads in the sand and turning our backs upon the evil, that he would be justified in the eyes of God in asking them to face it. Were Germany to win this war, the future of Ireland is as certain as the knowledge we have that we are here today. The Germans, if they win this war, will face our country as the conquerors of the world and, in order to maintain that conquest and dominion over the Continent of Europe and the ocean highways of the world, the first thing they will do is to demand and seize naval and air bases on our south-west coast and western seaboard.

Having seized these bases and established their advanced guards in them for the control of the Atlantic highway, the German general staff must say to the German Government: 'We have our bases on the west coast of Ireland, but the hinterland of those bases must be made safe for us; and there are only two ways of making it safe. You have either to exterminate the Irish people in that hinterland or you have to Nazify the whole population of Ireland.' They cannot exterminate our people, and when they attempt to Nazify them, our people will be required to make the choice between the crooked cross of Nazism and the Cross of Christ – and I know the choice our people will make. Let us open our eyes to what that will mean. Our people, in defence of their religion, will be called upon to face a persecution besides which the worst that Oliver Cromwell did in this country will pale into insignificance.

That has been the experience of every Christian country into which the Nazis have found their way. Those who lose their Faith and those who die in defence of their Faith in the course of that persecution will constitute the monument to the leaders amongst us who fail to face the real issue now, and who prefer the illusory hope of safety to the grim duty of facing facts and doing what is right – facing the danger of war while we still have friends to fight beside us, resolved that the day will never dawn when our people will be called upon to face the malignity and might of a Germany, conqueror of the world, face to face with an island standing alone, without friends or hope of help from anywhere.

If Great Britain cannot be guaranteed supplies of food and warlike material from the United States of America she will be defeated by Germany, and the day she falls we fall too. I say that the Atlantic lifeline joining these two champions of democracy and Christian civilisation at the present time is no stronger than its weakest link. British sailors and British ships are bringing England's supplies – and our supplies – through German minefields, German air attack and German submarine attack at the present time. A gap is opening in that lifeline. Extending hands between old friends and new friends, we can close that gap. I know that the closing of it, and acting as the bond between the United States of America and the Commonwealth of Nations at the present time, may bring down upon our heads the fury of the Nazi terror. If what I say is right, then let us face that terror, let us say to them: 'Do what you can to our bodies and our goods, but you cannot destroy our souls: no one ever has, and Nazi Germany never will.' If this course is right, I say that the people of this country are equal to the weight of whatever burden is put upon them in the cause of Right.

If we see our duty and fail to do it now, we seal forever this nation's claim to be free and independent. If we prove unequal to our duty in this time, we shall stand forth amongst the nations of the world as a nation claiming all the privileges of independence but unequal to its burdens. Citizen and soldier must bear together today the perils of war-like times. There was a time in the history of the world when it was, perhaps, one of the most disagreeable tasks a civilian could discharge to suggest that his country was facing war, because it seemed like asking others to go out and bear the heat and burden of the day while he stayed safely at home. That day is past. The dangers of every individual citizen of this State are as great as, or greater than, those of any soldier serving in the field. Ireland has citizens and soldiers who would do her no discredit if tribulation were to come upon her now. The question I ask myself is: has she leaders equal to the great decisions and the terrible responsibilities of the times in which we find ourselves?

I say most deliberately, I say before God, that I believe the fate of Christianity in the whole world is hanging in the balance. I say that what has borne itself in upon my mind, above all other things, is the profound conviction that, if this terrible doctrine should prevail in on the world, Christianity will go to the catacombs. It is the profound con-viction that none amongst us but he who has a martyr's fortitude will keep the faith, if that should happen, that persuades me that it is Ireland's des-tiny and duty to protect her children from that danger. I am convinced that Ireland's action in this time may prove vital. It is a queer fate for Providence to reserve for us, that we, a small, comparatively weak country, should be fated to fill so critical a part in so unprecedented a time. Why that should be is something which is known only to divine Providence which placed us where we are. I believe that we have an opportunity of fulfilling our high destiny and proving our loyalty and devotion to things higher than material property and political considerations. I profoundly believe that the Irish people are equal to that destiny, if properly led. I share with the Taoiseach the desire to see our people a united people in these times. I should like to see our people, all together, forgetting past differences, recognising the magnitude of the issues now involved and recognising the ability of this country in matters of this kind to play not only one man's part but to be a host in action. I should like to see this small weak country of Ireland demonstrate, as it has never been demon-strated in the history of the world before, that it is not by bread alone that man must live and that, whatever may have been the material squabbles that precipitated war in the world, to us the only issue of significance is whether Christianity shall survive and whether mankind all over the world will be left the right to render to God the things that are God's and to render to Caesar the things that are Caesar's. I am convinced that that right is in desperate jeopardy. I am convinced that it is given to us to prove its champion. I am convinced that, were we to accept that charge and face that duty, posterity would have it to tell that in the darkest hours of crisis, when dangers seemed heaviest and perils greatest, Ireland, recognising her destiny, faced it without counting the material cost and that, whatever her material losses were, the undying glory of having stood as a nation for great principles and in defence of the higher freedom had secured for her and her people immortality in human history.

If all the struggle that our fathers made and our grandfathers made meant anything, it must have meant that. They could not have made the sacrifices they made for no other purpose than to give us the right to pass trivial legislation in a Parliament of our own. They meant to give this country a soul, in the deep conviction that their children would keep it a living soul and a burning spirit before the nations of the world. Ours is that glorious opportunity; ours is that terrible responsibility. As it presents itself to me, it is a glorious opportunity. I recognise the appalling nature of the responsibility. I have never said anything in my public life which I feel more sincerely or more deeply and I believe our people are equal to their glorious destiny, equal to bear that burden and the awful responsibility, and I pray God they may yet find leaders who will be worthy of them in this time of crisis.

Following another anti-neutrality speech, this time at the Fine Gael party conference in February 1942, he was forced to resign from the party. He rejoined the party in 1953 and became its leader six years later.

Éamon de Valera
16 May 1945

THE decision of the Irish Government to adopt a strict policy of neutrality during World War II was, and still is, extremely controversial. De Valera, who had been Taoiseach since 1932, argued vehemently, both at the beginning and at the end of the war, that the stance of neutrality was the greatest assertion of Ireland's absolute sovereignty. He also contended that nothing could have given greater moral substance to the newly acquired status of Irish independence than Ireland choosing (and indeed having the capacity to choose) a course independent of Britain.

After the war, Churchill's victory speech, on 13 May, 1945, contained ungracious references to Ireland's neutrality: 'The sense of envelopment which might at any moment turn to strangulation, lay heavy upon us. We had only the north-western approach between Ulster and Scotland through which to bring in the means of life and to send out the forces of war. Owing to the action of Mr. de Valera, so much at variance with the temper and instinct of thousands of southern Irishmen, who hastened to the battle-front to prove their ancient valour, the approaches which the southern Irish ports and airfields could so easily have guarded were closed by the hostile aircraft and U-boats. This was indeed a deadly moment in our life, and if it had not been for the loyalty and friendship of Northern Ireland, we should have been forced to come to close quarters with Mr. de Valera, or perish forever from the earth. However, with a restraint and a poise to which, I venture to say, history will find few parallels, His Majesty's Government never laid a violent hand upon them, though at times it would have been quite easy and quite natural, and we left the de Valera Government to frolic with the German and later with the Japanese representatives to their heart's content.'

Churchill's speech had provided de Valera with an opportunity to show the world how magnanimous a statesman he really was. In what the *Irish Press* referred to as the 'most eagerly awaited public pronouncement for many years,' De Valera responded to Churchill in the following radio broadcast on 16 May 1945:

Reply to Churchill

Certain newspapers have been very persistent in looking for my answer to Mr. Churchill's recent broadcast. I know the kind of answer I am expected to make. I know the answer that first springs to the lips of every man of Irish blood who heard or read that speech, no matter in what circumstances or in what part of the world he found himself. I know the reply I would have given a quarter of a century ago. But I have deliberately decided that that is not the reply I shall make to-night. I shall strive not to be guilty of adding any fuel to the flames of hatred and passion which, if continued to be fed, promise to burn up whatever is left by the war of decent human feeling in Europe.

Allowances can be made to Mr. Churchill's statement, however unworthy, in the first flush of his victory. No such excuse could be found for me in this quieter atmosphere. There are, however, some things which it is my duty to say, some things which it is essential to say. I shall try to say them as dispassionately as I can. Mr. Churchill makes it clear that, in certain circumstances, he would have violated our neutrality and that he would justify his action by Britain's necessity. It seems strange to me that Mr. Churchill does not see that this, if accepted, would mean that Britain's necessity would become a moral code and that when this necessity became sufficiently great, other people's rights were not to count. It is quite true that other great powers believe in this same code – in their own regard – and have behaved in accordance with it. That is precisely why we have the disastrous succession of wars – World War no. 1 and World War no. 2 – and shall it be a World War no. 3?

Surely Mr. Churchill must see that if his contention be admitted in our regard, a like justification can be framed for similar acts of aggression elsewhere and no small nation adjoining a great Power could ever hope to be permitted to go its own way in peace.

It is indeed, fortunate that Britain's necessity did not reach the point when Mr. Churchill would have acted. All credit to him that he successfully resisted the temptation which, I have no doubt, many times assailed him in his difficulties and to which I freely admit many leaders might have easily succumbed. It is, indeed, hard work but acting justly always has its rewards.

By resisting his temptation in this instance, Mr. Churchill, instead of adding another horrid chapter to the already bloodstained record of the relations between England and this country, has advanced the cause of international morality, an important step – one of the most important indeed, that can be taken on the road to the establishment of any sure basis for peace.

As far as the peoples of these two islands are concerned, it may perhaps, mark a fresh beginning towards the realisation of that mutual comprehension to which Mr. Churchill has referred and for which, I hope, he will not merely pray but work also, as did his predecessor who will yet, I believe, find the honoured place in British history which is due to him, as certainly he will find it in any fair record of the relations between Britain and ourselves. That Mr. Churchill should be irritated when our neutrality stood in the way of what he thought he vitally needed, I understand, but that he or any thinking person in Britain or elsewhere should fail to see the reason for our neutrality I find it hard to conceive.

I would like to put a hypothetical question – it is a question I have put to many Englishmen since the last war. Suppose Germany had won the war, had invaded and occupied England, and that after a long lapse of time and many bitter struggles she was finally brought to acquiesce in admitting England's right to freedom, and let England go, all but, let us say, the six southern counties.

These six southern counties, those, let us suppose, commanding the entrance to the narrow seas, Germany had singled out and insisted on holding herself with a view to weakening England as a whole, and maintaining the securing of her own communications through the Straits of Dover. Let us suppose further that after all this had happened, Germany was engaged in a great war in which she could show that she was on the side of the freedom of a number of small nations, would Mr. Churchill as an Englishman who believed that his own nation had as good a right to freedom as any other, not freedom for a part merely, but freedom for the whole – would he, whilst Germany still maintained the partition of his country and occupied six counties of it, would he lead this partitioned England to join with Germany in a crusade? I do not think Mr. Churchill would. Would he think the people of partitioned England an object of shame if they stood neutral in such circumstances? I do not think Mr. Churchill would. Mr. Churchill is proud of Britain's stand alone, after France had fallen and before America entered the war.

Could he not find in his heart the generosity to acknowledge that there is a small nation that stood alone for one year or two, but for several hundred years against aggression; that endured spoilations, famines, massacres in endless succession; that was clubbed many times into insensibility, but that each time on returning consciousness, took up the fight anew; a small nation that could be never got to accept defeat and has never surrendered her soul?

Mr. Churchill is justly proud of his nation's perseverance for freedom against heavy odds. But we in this island are still prouder of our people's perseverance for freedom through all the centuries. We of our time have played our part in that perseverance, and we have pledged ourselves to the dead generations who have preserved intact for us this glorious heritage, that we too will strive to be faithful to the end, and pass on this tradition unblemished.

Many a time in the past there appeared little hope except that hope to which Mr. Churchill referred, that by standing fast a time would come when, to quote his own words, 'the tyrant would make some ghastly mistake which would alter the whole balance of the struggle.'

I sincerely trust, however, that it is not thus our ultimate unity and freedom will be achieved though as a younger man I confess I prayed even for that, and indeed at times saw no other. In latter years, I have had a vision of a nobler and better ending, better for both our people and for the future of mankind. For that I have now been long working. I regret that it is not to this nobler purpose that Mr. Churchill is lending his hand rather than, by the abuse of a people who have done him no wrong, trying to find in a crisis like the present excuse for continuing the injustice of the mutilation of our country.

I sincerely hope that Mr. Churchill has not deliberately chosen the latter course but, if he has, however regretfully we may say it, we can only say, be it so. Meanwhile, even as a partitioned small nation, we shall go on and strive to play our part in the world, continuing unswervingly to work for the cause of true freedom and for peace and understanding between all nations. As a community which has been mercifully spared from the blinding hates and rancours engendered by the present war, we shall endeavour to render thanks to God by playing a Christian part in helping, so far as a small nation can, to bind up some of the gaping wounds of suffering humanity.

Eulogies

Edmund Burke
1 December 1783

O NE OF the first moves of the Fox-North Coalition Government in Britain was to introduce an India Reform Bill. The main aim of the Bill was to introduce legislation to lessen the power of the East India Trading Company, but without allowing it to fall under the control of the British Crown. To cope with this difficulty, Fox and the party's India spokesman, Edmund Burke, proposed the novel, yet radical solution of nominating seven commissioners to oversee the running of the Company. Much criticism was aimed at the Bill but it passed comfortably through the Commons.

Burke delivered his major speech on the Bill during its latter stages in the Commons. Towards its end came what he later described as a 'studied panegyric' of Charles Fox. An extract from that speech is given below:

On Charles Fox

The natives scarcely know what it is to see the grey head of an Englishman. Young men – boys almost – govern there, without society, and without sympathy with the natives. They have no more social habits with the people than if they still resided in England; nor, indeed, any species of intercourse but that which is necessary to making a sudden fortune, with a view to a remote settlement. Animated with all the avarice of age and all the impetuosity of youth, they roll in one after another, wave after wave and there is nothing before the eyes of the natives but an endless, hopeless prospect of new flights of birds of prey and passage, with appetites continually renewing for a food that is continually wasting . . .

And now, having done my duty to the Bill, let me say a word to the author. I should leave him to his own noble sentiments if the unworthy and illiberal language with which he has been treated, beyond all example of parliamentary liberty, did not make a few words necessary; not so much in justice to him as to my own feelings. I must say, then, that it will be a distinction honorable to the age that the rescue of the greatest number of the human race that ever were, so grievously oppressed, from the greatest tyranny that was ever exercised, has fallen to the lot of abilities and dispositions equal to the task; that it has fallen to one who has the enlargement to comprehend, the spirit to undertake, and the eloquence to support, so great a measure of hazardous benevolence. His spirit is not owing to his ignorance of the state of men and things; he well knows what snares are spread about his path, from personal animosity, from court intrigues and possibly from popular delusion. But he has put to hazard his ease, his security, his interest, his power, even his darling popularity, for the benefit of a people whom he has never seen. This is the road that all heroes have trod before him. He is traduced and abused for his supposed motives. He will remember that obloquy is a necessary ingredient in that composition of all true glory. He will remember that it was not only in the Roman customs, but it is in the nature and constitution of things, that calumny and abuse are essential parts for triumph. These thoughts will support a mind, which only exists for honour, under the burden of temporary reproach. He is doing indeed a great good; such as rarely falls to the lot, and almost as rarely coincides with the desires, of any man. Let him use his time. Let him give the whole length of the reins to his benevolence. He is now on a great eminence, where the eyes of mankind are turned to him. He may live long, he may do much. But here is the summit. He never can exceed what he does this day . . .

I have spoken what I think, and what I feel, of the mover of this Bill. An honourable friend of mine, speaking of his merits, was charged with having made a studied panegyric; I don't know what his was. Mine, I am sure, is a studied panegyric; the fruit of much meditation; the result of observation of near twenty years. For my own part, I am happy that I have lived to see this day. I feel myself overpaid for the labours of eighteen years when, at this late period, I am able to take my share, by one humble vote, in destroying a tyranny that exists to the disgrace of this nation, and the destruction of so large a part of the human species.

Owing to pressure from King George III, the Bill was not passed by the House of Lords and, on 18 December, both Fox and North resigned. Burke would never hold office again.

George Bernard Shaw
28 October 1930

ON 28 OCTOBER, 1930, a fund-raising dinner was held in the Savoy Hotel in London, by the Joint British Committee of Ort and Oze for promoting the economic and physical welfare of East European Jews. George Bernard Shaw, then 74 years of age, was asked to speak at the dinner. His speech, which was recorded by the BBC and broadcast in America, honoured the German born, Jewish scientist, Albert Einstein, a man whom Shaw had in 1925, described as having 'lit a fire among the gods of the physicists.'

On Albert Einstein

Napoleon and other great men were makers of empires, but these eight men whom I am about to mention were makers of universes, and their hands were not stained with the blood of their fellow men. I go back twenty-five hundred years, and how many can I count in that period? I can count them on the fingers of my two hands.

Pythagoras, Ptolemy, Kepler, Copernicus, Aristotle, Galileo, Newton, and Einstein – and I still have two fingers left vacant.

Even among those eight men I must make a distinction. I have called them makers of the universe, but some of them were only repairers. Newton made a universe which lasted for three hundred years. Einstein has made a universe, which I suppose you want me to say never stops, but I don't know how long it will last.

These great men, they have been the makers of one side of humanity, which has two sides. We call the one side religion, and we call the other science. Religion is always right. Religion protects us against that great problem which we all must face. Science is always wrong; it is the very artifice of men. Science can never solve one problem without raising ten more problems.

What have all of those great men been doing? Each in turn claimed the other was wrong, and now you are expecting me to say that Einstein proved that Newton was wrong. But you forget that when science reached Newton, science came up against that extraordinary Englishman. That had never happened to it before.

Newton lent a power so extraordinary that if I was speaking fifteen years ago, as I am old enough to have done, I would have said that he had the greatest mind that ever a man was endowed with. Combine the light of that wonderful mind with credulity, with superstition. He knew his people; he knew his language; he knew his own folk; he knew a lot of things; he knew that an honest bargain was a square deal and an honest man was one who gave a square deal.

He knew his universe; he knew that it consisted of heavenly bodies that were in motion, and he also knew the one thing you cannot do to anything whatsoever is to make it move in a straight line. In other words, motion will not go in a straight line.

Mere fact will never stop an Englishman. Newton invented a straight line, and that was the law of gravitation, and when he had invented this, he had created a universe which was wonderful in itself. When applying his wonderful genius, when he had completed a book of that universe, what sort of book was it? It was a book which told you the station of all the heavenly bodies. It showed the rate at which they were travelling; it showed the exact hour at which they would arrive at such and such, a point to make an eclipse. It was not a magical, marvellous thing; it was a matter-of-fact thing.

For three hundred years we believed in that Newtonian universe as I suppose no system has been believed in before. I know I was educated in it and was brought up to believe in it firmly. Then a young professor came along. He said a lot of things, and we called him a blasphemer. He claimed Newton's theory of the apple was wrong.

He said, 'Newton did not know what happened to the apple, and I can prove this when the next eclipse comes.' We said, 'The next thing you will be doing is questioning the law of gravitation.' The young professor said, 'No, I mean no harm to the law of gravitation, but for my part, I can go without it.' 'What do you mean, go without it?' He said, 'I can tell you about that afterward.'

The world is not a rectilinear world, it is a curvilinear world. The heavenly bodies go in curves because that is the natural way for them to go, and so the whole Newtonian universe crumpled up and was succeeded by the Einstein universe. Here in England, he is a wonderful man.

This man is not challenging the fact of science; he is challenging the action of science. Not only is he challenging the action of science, but the action of science has surrendered to his challenge.

Now, ladies and gentlemen, are you ready for the toast? I drink to the greatest of our contemporaries, Einstein.

Speeches of Vision

George Berkeley
1712

GEORGE BERKELEY propounded his ethical theories, in the form of a disquisition on the ethics of civil government, in three talks, delivered in the chapel of Trinity College, Dublin. In 1712, in order to dispel 'false accounts' of the three talks, they appeared together in printed form, under the title, 'Discourse on Passive Obedience.'

The first discourse, from which is taken the crux of his main philosophical standpoint, is given below. The second discourse dealt with anarchy and rebellion as an alternative to passive obedience, whilst the third considered 'the objections drawn from the pretended consequences of non-resistance to the supreme power.'

As a direct result of the three discourses Berkeley's name became associated with Jacobitism. This seriously impeded his career advancement and he was forced eventually to leave Ireland.

Sermon on Passive Obedience

It is not my design to inquire into the particular nature of the government and constitution of these kingdoms; much less to determine concerning the merits of the different parties now reigning in the state. These topics I profess to lie out of my sphere, and they will probably be thought by most men improper to be treated of in an audience almost wholly made up of young persons, set apart from the business and noise of the world, for their more convenient instruction in learning and piety. But surely it is in no respect unsuitable to the circumstances of this place to inculcate and explain every branch of the Law of Nature; or those virtues and duties which are equally binding in every kingdom or society of men under heaven. And of this kind I take to be that Christian Duty of not resisting the supreme Power, implied in my text – 'Whosoever resisteth the Power, resisteth the ordinance of God.'

In treating on which words I shall observe the following method:

First, I shall endeavour to prove that there is an absolute unlimited non-resistance, or passive obedience, due to the supreme civil powers wherever placed in any nation.

Secondly, I shall inquire into the grounds and reasons of the contrary opinion.

Thirdly, I shall consider the objectives drawn from the pretended consequences of non-resistance to the supreme power.

In handling these points I intend not to build on the authority of Holy Scripture, but altogether on the Principles of Reason common to all mankind; and that, because there are some very rational and learned men, who, being verily persuaded an absolute passive subjection to any earthly power is repugnant to right reason, can never bring themselves to admit such an interpretation of Holy Scripture (however natural and obvious from the words) as shall make that a part of Christian religion which seems to them in itself manifestly absurd, and destructive of the original inherent rights of human nature.

I do not mean to treat of that submission which men are, either in duty or prudence, obliged to pay inferior or executive powers; neither shall I consider where or in what persons the supreme or legislative power is lodged in this or that government. Only thus much I shall take for granted: that there is in every civil community, somewhere or other, placed a Supreme Power of making laws, and enforcing the observation of them. The fulfilling of those laws, either by a punctual performance of what is enjoined in them, or, if that be inconsistent with reason or conscience, by a patient submission to whatever penalties the supreme power hath annexed to the neglect or transgression of them, is termed loyalty; as, on the other hand, the making use of force and open violence, either to withstand the execution of the laws, or ward off the penalties appointed by the supreme power, is properly named rebellion.

Now, to make it evident that every degree of rebellion is criminal in the subject I shall, in the first place, endeavour to prove that loyalty is a natural or moral duty; and disloyalty, or rebellion, in the most strict and proper sense, a vice or breach of the law of nature. And, secondly, I propose to show that the prohibitions of vice, or negative precepts of the law of nature, as, 'Thou shalt not commit adultery, Thou shalt not forswear thyself, Thou shalt not resist the supreme power,' and the like, ought to be taken in a most absolute, necessary, and immutable sense: in so much that the attainment of the greatest good, or deliverance from the greatest evil, that can befall any man or number of men in this life, may not justify the least violation of them.

First then, I am to show that Loyalty is a moral duty, and Disloyalty or Rebellion, in the most strict and proper sense, a vice, or breach of the Law of Nature.

Though it be a point agreed amongst all wise men, that there are certain moral rules or laws of nature, which carry with them an eternal and indispensable obligation; yet, concerning the proper methods for discovering those laws, and distinguishing them from others dependent on the humour and discretion of men, there are various opinions. Some direct us to look for them in the Divine Ideas; others in the natural inscriptions on the mind: some derive them from the authority of learned men, and the universal agreement and consent of nations: lastly, others hold that they are only to be discovered by the deductions of reason. The three first methods must be acknowledged to labour under great difficulties; and the last has not that I know, been anywhere distinctly explained, or treated of so fully as the importance of the subject doth deserve.

I hope therefore it will be pardoned, if, in a discourse of passive obedience, in order to lay the foundation of that duty deeper, we make some inquiry into the origin, nature, and obligation of moral duties in general, and the criterions whereby they are to be known.

Self-love being a principle of all others the most universal, and the most deeply engraven in our hearts, it is natural for us to regard things as they are fitted to augment or impair our own happiness and accordingly we denominate them good or evil. Our judgment is ever employed in distinguishing between these two; and it is the whole business of our lives to endeavour, by a proper application of our faculties, to procure the one and avoid the other. At our first coming into the world, we are entirely guided by the impressions of sense; sensible pleasure being the infallible characteristic of present good, as pain is of evil. But, by degrees, as we grow up in our acquaintance with the nature of things, experience informs us that present good is afterwards often attended with a greater evil; and, on the other side, that present evil is not less frequently the occasion of procuring to us a greater future good. Besides, as the nobler faculties of the human soul begin to display themselves, they discover to us goods far more excellent than those which affect the senses . Hence an alteration is wrought in our judgments; we no longer comply with the first solicitations of sense, but stay to consider the remote consequences of an action: what good may be hoped, or what evil feared from it, according to the wonted course of things. This obliges us frequently to overlook present momentary enjoyments, when they come in competition with greater and more lasting goods; though too far off, or of too refined a nature as to affect our senses.

But, as the whole Earth and the entire duration of those perishing things contained in it is altogether inconsiderable, or, in the prophet's expressive style, 'less than nothing' in respect of Eternity, who sees not that every reasonable man ought so to frame his actions as that they may most effectually contribute to promote his eternal interest? And, since it is a truth, evident by the light of nature, that there is a sovereign omniscient Spirit, who alone can make us for ever happy, or for ever miserable; it plainly follows that a conformity to His will, and not any prospect of temporal advantage, is the sole rule whereby every man who acts up to the principles of reason must govern and square his actions. The same conclusion doth likewise evidently result from the relation which God bears to His creatures. God alone is maker and preserver of all things. He is, therefore, with the most undoubted right, the great legislator of the world; and mankind are, by all the ties of duty, no less than interest, bound to obey His laws.

Hence we should – above all things endeavour to trace out the Divine will, or the general design of Providence with regard to mankind, and the methods most directly tending to the accomplishment of that design. And this seems the genuine and proper way for discovering the laws of nature. For, laws being rules directive of our actions to the end intended the legislator, in order to attain the knowledge of God's laws, we ought first to inquire what that end is which He designs should be carried on by human actions. Now, as God is a being of infinite goodness, it is plain the end He proposes is good. But, God enjoying in Himself all possible perfection, it follows that it is not His own good, but that of His creatures. Again, the moral actions of men are entirely terminated within themselves, so as to have no influence on the other orders of intelligences or reasonable creatures; the end therefore to be procured by them can be no other than the good of men. But, as nothing in a natural state can entitle one man more than another to the favour of God, except only moral goodness; which, consisting in a conformity to the laws of God, doth presuppose the being of such laws, and law ever supposing an end, to which it guides our actions – it follows that, antecedent to the end proposed by God, no distinction can be conceived between men: that end therefore itself, or general design of Providence, is not determined or limited by any respect of persons. It is not therefore the private good of this or that man, nation, or age, but the general well-being of all men, of all nations, of all ages of the world, which God designs should be procured by the concurring actions of each individual.

Having thus discovered the great end to which all moral obligations are subordinate, it remains that we inquire what methods are necessary for the obtaining of that end.

The well-being of mankind must necessarily be carried on in one of these two ways. Either, first, without the injunction of any certain universal rules of morality; only by obliging every one, upon each particular occasion, to consult the public good, and always to do that which to him shall seem, in the present time and circumstances, most to conduce to it: or, secondly, by enjoining the observation of some determinate, established laws, which, if universally practised, have, from the nature of things, an essential fitness to procure the well-being of mankind; though, in their particular application, they are sometimes, through untoward accidents, and the perverse irregularity of human wills, the occasions of great sufferings and misfortunes, it may be, to very many good men.

Against the former of these methods there lie several strong objections. For brevity I shall mention only two:

First, it will thence follow that the best men, for want of judgment, and the wisest, for want of knowing all the hidden circumstances and consequences of an action, may very often be at a loss how to behave themselves; which they would not be, in case they judged of each action by comparing it with some particular precept, rather than by examining the good or evil which in that single instance it tends to procure: it being far more easy to judge with certainty, whether such or such an action be a transgression of this or that precept, than whether it will be attended with more good or ill consequences. In short, to calculate the events of each particular action is impossible; and, though it were not, would yet take up too much time to be of use in the affairs of life.

Secondly, if that method be observed, it will follow that we can have no sure standard to which, comparing the actions of another, we may pronounce them good or bad, virtues or vices. For, since the measure and rule of every good man's actions is supposed to be nothing else but his own private disinterested opinion of what makes most for the public good at that juncture; and, since this opinion must unavoidably in different men, from their particular views and circumstances, be very

different: it is impossible to know, whether any one instance of par-
ricide or perjury, for example, be criminal. The man may have had his
reasons for it; and that which in me would have been a heinous sin may
be in him a duty. Every man's particular rule is barred in his own breast,
invisible to all but himself, who therefore can only tell whether he
observes it or no. And, since that rule is fitted to particular occasions, it
must ever change as they do: hence it is not only various in different
men, but in one and the same man at different times.

From all which it follows, there can be no harmony or agreement
between the actions of good men: no apparent steadiness or consistency
of one man with himself; no adhering to principles: the best actions
may be condemned, and the most villainous meet with applause. In a
word, there ensues the most horrible confusion of vice and virtue, sin
and duty, that can possibly be imagined. It follows, therefore, that the
great end to which God requires the concurrence of human actions
must of necessity be carried on by the second method proposed, namely,
the observation of certain, universal, determinate rules or moral precepts,
which, in their own nature, have a necessary tendency to promote the
well-being of the sum of mankind, taking in all nations and ages, from
the beginning to the end of the world.

Hence, upon an equal comprehensive survey of the general nature,
the passions, interests, and mutual respects of mankind; whatsoever
practical proposition doth to right reason evidently appear to have a
necessary connexion with the Universal well-being included in it, is to
be looked upon as enjoined by the will of God. For, he that willeth the
end doth will the necessary means conducive to that end; but it hath
been shewn that God willeth the universal well-being of mankind
should be promoted by the concurrence of each particular person;
therefore, every such practical proposition necessarily tending thereto is
to be esteemed a decree of God, and is consequently a law to man.

These propositions are called laws of nature, because they are universal,
and do not derive their obligation from any civil sanction, but immediately from the Author of nature himself. They are said to be stamped
on the mind, to be engraven on the tables of the heart, because they are
well known to mankind, and suggested and inculcated by conscience.
Lastly, they are termed eternal rules of reason, because they necessarily
result from the nature of things, and may be demonstrated by the
infallible deductions of reason.

And, notwithstanding that these rules are too often, either by the
unhappy concurrence of events, or more especially by the wickedness of

perverse men who will not conform to them, made accidental causes of misery to those good men who do, yet this doth not vacate their obligation: they are ever to be esteemed the fixed unalterable standards of moral good and evil; no private interest, no love of friends, no regard to the public good, should make us depart from them. Hence, when any doubt arises concerning the morality of an action, it is plain this cannot be determined by computing the public good which in that particular case it is attended with, but only by comparing it with the Eternal Law of Reason. He who squares his actions by this rule can never do amiss, though thereby he should bring himself to poverty, death, or disgrace: no, not though he should involve his family, his friends, his country, in all those evils which are accounted the greatest and most insupportable to human nature. Tenderness and benevolence of temper are often motives to the best and latest actions; but we must not make them the sole rule of our actions: they are passions rooted in our nature, and, like all other passions, must be restrained and kept under, otherwise they may possibly betray us into as great enormities as any other unbridled lust. Nay, they are more dangerous than other passions, in so much as they are more plausible, and apt to dazzle and corrupt the mind with the appearance of goodness and generosity.

For the illustration of what has been said, it will not be amiss, if from the moral we turn our eyes on the natural world. And, surely, it is not possible for free intellectual agents to propose a nobler pattern for their imitation than Nature; which is nothing else but a series of free actions, produced by the best and wisest Agent. But, it is evident that those actions are not adapted to particular views, but all conformed to certain general rules, which being collected from observation, are by philosophers termed laws of nature. And these indeed are excellently suited to promote the general well-being of the creation: but, what from casual combinations of events, and what from the voluntary motions of animals, it often falls out, that the natural good not only of private men but of entire cities and nations would be better promoted by a particular suspension, or contradiction, than an exact observation of those laws. Yet, for all that, nature still takes its course; nay, it is plain that plagues, famines, inundations, earthquakes, with an infinite variety of pains and sorrows – in a word, all kinds of calamities public and private, do arise from a uniform steady observation of those General Laws which are once established by the Author of Nature, and which He will not change or deviate from upon any of those accounts, how wise or benevolent so ever it may be thought by foolish men to do so. As for the miracles recorded in Scripture, they were always wrought for confirmation of some doctrine or mission from God, and not for the sake of the particular natural goods, as health or life, which some men might have reaped from them. From all which it seems sufficiently plain that we cannot be at a loss which way to determine, in case we think God's own methods the properest to obtain His ends, and that it is our duty to copy after them, so far as the frailty of our nature will permit.

Thus far in general, of the nature and necessity of Moral Rules, and the criterion or mark whereby they may be known. As for the particulars, from the foregoing discourse, the principal of them may without much difficulty be deduced.

It hath been shewn that the Law of Nature is a system of such rules or precepts as that, if they be all of them, at all times, in all places, and by all men observed, they will necessarily promote the well-being of mankind, so far as it is attainable by human actions. Now, let any one who hath the use of reason take but an impartial survey of the general frame and circumstances of human nature, and it will appear plainly to him that the constant observation of truth, for instance, or of justice, and chastity hath a necessary connexion with their universal well-being; that, therefore they are to be esteemed virtues or duties; and that 'Thou shalt not forswear thyself,' 'Thou shalt not commit adultery,' 'Thou shalt not steal,' are so many unalterable moral rules, which to violate in the least degree is vice or sin. I say, the agreement of these particular practical propositions with the definition or criterion premised doth so clearly result from the nature of things, that it were a needless digression, in this place, to enlarge upon it.

And, from the same principle, by the very same reasoning, it follows that loyalty is a moral virtue, and 'Thou shalt not resist the supreme Power' a rule or law of nature, the least breach whereof hath the inherent stain of moral turpitude.

The miseries inseparable from a state of anarchy are easily imagined. So insufficient is the wit or strength of any single man, either to avert the evils, or procure the blessings of life, and so apt are the wills of different persons to contradict and thwart each other, that it is absolutely necessary several independent powers be combined together, under the direction (if I may so speak) of one and the same will – I mean the Law of the Society. Without this there is no politeness, no order, no peace, among men, but the world is one great heap of misery and confusion; the strong as well as the weak, the wise as well as the foolish, standing on all sides exposed to all those calamities which man can be liable to, in a state where he has no other security than the not being possessed of any thing which may raise envy or desire in another. A state by so much more ineligible than that of brutes as a reasonable creature hath a greater reflexion and foresight of miseries than they. From all which it plainly follows, that Loyalty, or submission to the supreme authority, hath, if universally practised in conjunction with all other virtues, a necessary connexion with the well-being of the whole sum of mankind; and, by consequence, if the criterion we have laid down be true, it is, strictly speaking, a moral duty, or branch of natural religion. And, therefore, the least degree of rebellion is, with the utmost strictness and propriety, a sin; not only in Christians, but also in those who have the light of reason alone for their guide. Nay, upon a thorough and impartial view, this submission will, I think, appear one of the very first and fundamental laws of nature; inasmuch as it is civil government which ordains and marks out the various relations between men, and regulates property; thereby giving scope and laying a foundation for the exercise of all other duties. And, in truth, whoever considers the condition of man will scarce conceive it possible that the practice of any one moral virtue should obtain, in the naked, forlorn state of nature. . . .

I shall therefore endeavour to make it yet more plain, that 'Thou shalt not resist the Supreme Power' is an undoubted precept of morality; as will appear from the following considerations:

First, then, submission to government is a point important enough to be established by a moral rule. Things of insignificant and trifling concern are, for that very reason, exempted from the rules of morality. But government, on which so much depend the peace, order, and well-being, of mankind, cannot surely be thought of too small importance to be secured and guarded by a moral rule. Government, I say, which is itself the principal source under heaven of those particular advantages for the procurement and conservation whereof several unquestionable Moral rules were Prescribed to men.

Secondly, obedience to government is a case universal enough to fall under the direction of a law of nature. Numberless rules there may be for regulating affairs of great concernment, at certain junctures, and to some particular persons or societies, which, not withstanding, are not to be esteemed moral or natural laws, but may be either totally abrogated or dispensed with; because the private ends they were intended to promote respect only some particular persons, as engaged in relations not founded in the general nature of men; who, on various occasions, and in different postures of things, may prosecute their own designs by different measures, as in human prudence shall seem convenient. But what relation is there more extensive and universal than that of subject and law? This is confined to no particular age or climate, but universally obtains, at all times, and in all places, wherever men live in a state exalted above that of brutes. It is, therefore, evident that the rule forbidding resistance to the Law or Supreme Power is not, upon pretence of any defect in point of universality, to be excluded from the number of the laws of nature.

Thirdly, there is another consideration which confirms the necessity of admitting this rule for a moral or natural law, namely because the case it regards is of too nice and difficult a nature to be left to the judgment of and determination of each private person. Some cases there are so plain and obvious to judge of that they may safely be trusted to the prudence of every reasonable man. But in all instances to determine, whether a civil law is fitted to promote the public interest; or whether submission or resistance will prove most advantageous in the consequence; or when it is that the general good of a nation may require an alteration of government, either in its form, or in the hands which administer it; these are points too arduous and intricate, and which require too great a degree of parts, leisure, and liberal education, as well as disinterestedness and thorough knowledge in the particular state of a kingdom, for every subject to take upon him the determination of them. From which it follows that, upon this account also, Non-resistance, which in the main, nobody can deny to be a most profitable and wholesome duty, ought not to be limited by the judgment of private persons to particular occasions, but esteemed a most sacred law of nature.

The foregoing arguments do, I think, make it manifest, that the precept against rebellion is on a level with other moral rules. Which will yet further appear from this fourth and last consideration. It cannot be denied that right reason doth require some common stated rule or measure, whereby subjects ought to shape their submission to the Supreme Power; since any clashing or disagreement in this point must unavoidably tend to weaken and dissolve the society. And it is unavoidable that there should be great clashing, where it is left to the breast of each individual to suit his fancy with a different measure of obedience. But this common stated measure must be either the general precept forbidding resistance, or else the public good of the whole nation; which last, though it is allowed to be in itself something certain and determinate, yet, for as much as men can regulate their conduct only by what appears to them, whether in truth it be what it appears or no; and, since the prospects men form to themselves of a country's public good are commonly as various as its landscapes, which meet the eye in several situations: it clearly follows, that to make the public good the rule of obedience is, in effect, not to establish any determinate, agreed, common measure of loyalty, but to leave every subject to the guidance of his own particular mutable fancy.

From all which arguments and considerations it is a most evident consideration that the law prohibiting rebellion is in strict truth a law of nature, universal reason, and morality. But to this it will perhaps be objected by some that, whatever may be concluded with regard to resistance from the tedious deductions of reason, yet there is I know not what turpitude and deformity in some actions, which at first blush shows them to be vicious; but they, not finding themselves struck with such a sensible and immediate horror at the thought of rebellion, cannot think it on a level with other crimes against nature. To which I answer: that it is true, there are certain natural antipathies implanted in the soul, which are ever the most lasting and insurmountable; but, as custom is a second nature, whatever aversions are from our early childhood continually infused into the mind give it so deep a stain as is scarce to be distinguished from natural complexion. And, as it doth hence follow, that to make all the inward horrors of soul pass for infallible marks of sin were the way to establish error and superstition in the world, so, on the other hand, to suppose all actions lawful which are unattended with those starts of nature would prove of the last dangerous consequence to virtue and morality. For, these pertaining to us as men, we must not be directed in respect of them by any emotions in our blood and spirits, but by the dictates of sober and impartial reason. And if there be any who find they have a less abhorrence of rebellion than of other villanies, all that can be inferred from it is, that this part of their duty was not so much reflected oil, or so early and frequently inculcated into their hearts, as it ought to have been. Since without question there are other men who have as thorough an aversion for that as for any other crime.

Again, it will probably be objected that submission to government differs from moral duties in that it is founded in a contract, which, upon the violation of its conditions, doth of course become void, and in such case rebellion is lawful: it hath not therefore the nature of a sin or crime which is in itself absolutely unlawful, and must be committed on no pretext whatsoever. Now, passing over all inquiry and dispute concerning the first obscure rise of government, I observe its being founded on a contract may be understood in a two fold sense: either, first, that several independent persons, finding the insufferable inconvenience of a state of anarchy, where every one was governed by his own will, consented and agreed together to pay an absolute submission to the decrees of some certain legislative; which, though sometimes they may bear hard on the subject, yet must surely prove easier to be governed by than the violent humours and unsteady opposite wills of a multitude of savages. And, in case we admit such a compact to have been the original foundation of civil government, it must even on that supposition be held sacred and inviolable.

Or, secondly, it is meant that subjects have contracted with their respective sovereigns or legislators to pay, not an absolute, but conditional and limited, submission to their laws; that is, upon condition, and so far forth, as the observation of them shall contribute to the public good: reserving still to themselves a right of superintending the laws, and judging whether they are fitted to promote the public good or not and (in case they or any of them think it needful) of resisting the higher powers, and changing the whole frame of government by force: which is a right that all mankind, whether single persons or societies, have over those that are deputed by them. But, in this sense, a contract cannot be admitted for the ground and measure of civil obedience, except one of these two things be clearly shown: either first that such a contract is an express known part of the fundamental constitution of a nation, equally allowed and unquestioned by all as the common law of the land or, secondly, if it be not express, that it is at least necessarily implied in the very nature or notion of civil polity, which supposes it is a thing manifestly absurd, that a number of men should be obliged to live under an unlimited subjection to civil law, rather than continue wild and independent of each other. But to me it seems most evident that neither of those points will ever be proved.

And till they are proved beyond all contradiction, the doctrine built upon them ought to be rejected with detestation. Since, to represent the higher powers as deputies of the people manifestly tends to diminish that awe and reverence which all good men should have for the laws and government of their country. And to speak of a condition, limited loyalty, and I know not what vague and undetermined contracts, is a most effectual means to loosen the bands of civil society; than which nothing can be of more mischievous consequence to mankind. But, after all, if there be any man who either cannot or will not see the absurdity and perniciousness of those notions, he would, I doubt not, be convinced with a witness, in case they should once become current, and every private man take it in his head to believe them true, and put them in practice.

But there still remains an objection which hath the appearance of some strength against what has been said. Namely, that, whereas civil polity is a thing entirely of human institution, it seems contrary to reason to make submission to it part of the law of nature and not rather of the civil law. For, how can it be imagined that nature should dictate or prescribe a natural law about a thing which depends on the arbitrary humour of men, not only as to its kind or form, which is very various and mutable, but even as to its existence; there being no where to be found a civil government set up by nature. In answer to this, I observe, first, that most moral precepts do presuppose some voluntary actions, or pacts of men, and are nevertheless esteemed laws of nature. Property is assigned, the signification of words ascertained, and matrimony contracted, by the agreement and consent of mankind; and, for all that, it is not doubted whether theft, falsehood, and adultery be prohibited by the law of nature. Loyalty, therefore, though it should suppose and be the result of human institutions, may, for all that, be of natural obligation. – I say, secondly, that, notwithstanding particular societies are formed by men, and are not in all places alike, as things esteemed natural are wont to be, yet there is implanted in mankind a natural tendency or disposition to a social life. I call it natural, because it is universal, and because it necessarily results from the differences which distinguish man from beast; the peculiar wants, appetites, faculties, and capacities of man being exactly calculated and framed for such a state, in so much that without it, it is impossible he should live in a condition in any degree suitable to his nature. And, since the bond and cement of society is a submission to its laws, it plainly follows that this duty hath an equal right with any other to be thought a law of nature. And surely that precept which enjoins obedience to civil laws cannot itself, with any propriety, be accounted a civil law; it must therefore either have no obligation at all on the conscience, or, if it hath, it must be derived form the universal voice of nature and reason.

Edmund Burke
3 November 1774

A S THE general election neared in the autumn of 1774, the Irish-born Edmund Burke realised that his seat as a Member of Parliament for Wendover was insecure and chose to stand instead as a candidate for Bristol.

After the poll closed on 3 November, Burke delivered a speech in Bristol's Guildhall, contesting the words of the previous speaker who stated that, 'it has ever been my opionion that the electors have the right to instruct their member.' This speech has long since been accepted as the definitive statement of the duties of a Parliamentarian, but it did not please many of the Bristol electors who saw his role as simply fighting 'Bristol's corner.'

Duties of a Politician

I owe myself, in all things, to all the freemen of this city. My particular friends have a demand on me that I should not deceive their expectations. Never was cause or man supported with more constancy, more activity, more spirit. I have been supported with a zeal indeed and heartiness in my friends, which (if their object had been at all proportioned to their endeavours) could never be sufficiently commended. They supported me upon the most liberal principles. They wished that the members for Bristol should be chosen for the city, and for their country at large, and not for themselves.

So far they are not disappointed. If I possess nothing else, I am sure I possess the temper that is fit for your service. I know nothing of Bristol but by the favours I have received and the virtues I have seen exerted in it.

I shall ever retain, what I now feel, the most perfect and grateful attachment to my friends – and I have no enmities, no resentment. I never can consider fidelity to engagements and constancy in friendships but with the highest approbation, even when those noble qualities are employed against my own pretensions. The gentleman who is not fortunate as I have been in this contest, enjoys in this respect a consolation full of honour both to himself and to his friends. They have certainly left nothing undone for his service.

As for the trifling petulance which the rage of party stirs up in little minds, though it should show itself even in this court, it has not made the slightest impression on me. The highest flight of such clamorous birds is winged in an interior region of the air. We hear them, and we look upon them just as you, gentlemen, when you enjoy the serene air on your lofty rocks, look down upon the gulls that skim the mud of your river when it is exhausted of its tide.

I am sorry I cannot conclude without saying a word on a topic touched upon by my worthy colleague. I wish that topic had been passed by at a time when I have so little leisure to discuss it. But since he has thought proper to throw it out, I owe you a clear explanation of my poor sentiments on that subject.

He tells you that 'the topic of instructions has occasioned much altercation and uneasiness in this city;' and he expresses himself – if I understand him rightly – in favour of the coercive authority of such instructions.

Certainly, gentlemen, it ought to be the happiness and glory of a representative to live in the strictest union, the closest correspondence, and the most unreserved communication with his constituents. Their wishes ought to have great weight with him; their opinion high respect; their business unremitted attention. It is his duty to sacrifice his repose, his pleasure, his satisfactions, to theirs; and, above all, ever, and in all cases, to prefer their interest to his own.

To deliver an opinion is the right of all men; that of constituents is a weighty and respectable opinion, which representative ought always to rejoice to hear, and which he ought always most seriously to consider. But authoritative instructions, mandates issued which the member is bound blindly and implicitly to obey, to vote and to argue for, though contrary to the clearest conviction of his judgement and conscience: these are things utterly unknown to the laws of this land, and which arise from a fundamental mistake of the whole order and tenor of our constitution.

Parliament is not a congress of ambassadors from different and hostile interests, which interests each must maintain, as – agent and advocate, against other agents and advocates; but Parliament is a deliberative assembly of one nation with one interest – that of the whole: where, not the local purposes, not local prejudices ought to guide, but the general good, resulting from the general reason of the whole. You choose a member, indeed; but when you have chosen him, he is not a member of Bristol, but he is a member of Parliament. If the local constituent should have an interest or should form an hasty opinion, evidently opposite to the real good of the rest of the community, the member for that place ought to be as far, as any other, from any endeavour to give it effect. I beg pardon for saying so much on this subject. I have been unwillingly drawn into it, but I shall ever use a respectful frankness of communication with you. Your faithful friend, your devoted servant, I shall be to the end of my life; a flatterer you do not wish for.

But his unbiased opinion, his mature judgement, his enlightened conscience, he ought not to sacrifice to you – to any man, or to any set of men living. These he does not derive from your pleasure; no, nor from the law and the constitution. They are a trust from Providence, for the abuse of which he is deeply answerable. Your representative owes you, not his industry only, but his judgement; and he betrays, instead of serving you if he sacrifices it to your opinion.

My worthy colleague says his will ought to be subservient to yours. If that be all, the thing is innocent. If government were a matter of will upon any side, yours, without question, ought to be superior. But government and legislation are matters of reason and judgement, and not of inclination; and what sort of reason is that in which the determination precedes the discussion? In which one set of men deliberate, and another decide? And where those who form the conclusion are perhaps three hundred miles distant from those who hear the arguments?

Edmund Burke
9 September 1780

AS THE general election of autumn 1780 approached, the Member of Parliament for Bristol, Edmund Burke, knew that he would have to face much hostility from his constituents. They had four main criticisms: firstly, the excessive sympathy he had shown towards America and the detrimental consequences such sympathy had on Bristol's trade with the colonies; secondly, his favouring of Ireland rather than Bristol in the argument over the liberalisation of trade; thirdly, his support for the act which sought to mitigate the 'savgery,' as Burke called it, of the existing law which could impose a sentence of life imprisonment on those in debt; and fourthly, his support for the repeal of the anti-Catholic legislation which he said had the effect of making an Irish Catholic 'a foreigner in his own land.

On 6 September, 1780 Burke came before his constituents to answer these charges. At the close of the meeting he was encouraged to go on with the canvass. But declined to put his name forward for election, feeling that the opposition against him was too great. Three days later he delivered the following speech:

Speech Declining Election

Gentlemen, – I decline the election. It has ever been my rule through life to observe a proportion between my efforts and my objects. I have never been remarkable for a bold, active, and sanguine pursuit of advantages that are personal to myself.

I have not canvassed the whole of this city in form; but I have taken such a view of it as satisfies my own mind that your choice will not ultimately fall upon me. Your city, gentlemen, is in a state of miserable distraction; and I am resolved to withdraw whatever share my pretensions may have had in its unhappy divisions. I have not been in haste. I have tried all prudent means. I have waited for the effect of all contingencies. If I were fond of a contest, by the partiality of my numerous friends, whom you known to be among the most weighty and respectable people of the city. I have the means of a sharp one in my hands; but I thought it far better, with my strength unspent, and my reputation unimpaired, to do early and from foresight that which I might be obliged to do from necessity at last.

I am not in the least surprised, nor in the least angry at this view of things. I have read the book of life for a long time, and I have read other books a little. Nothing has happened to me but what has happened to men much better than me, and in times and in nations full as good as the age and country that we live in. To say that I am no way concerned would be neither decent nor true. The representation of Bristol was an object on many accounts dear to me, and I certainly should very far prefer it to any other in the kingdom. My habits are made to it; and it is in general more unpleasant to be rejected after a long trial than not to be chosen at all.

But, gentlemen, I will see nothing except your former kindness, and I will give way to no other sentiments than those of gratitude. From the bottom of my heart I thank you for what you have done for me. You have given me a long term, which is now expired. I have performed the conditions, and enjoyed all the profits to the full; and I now surrender your estate into your hands without being in a single tile or a single stone impaired or wasted by my use. I have served the public for fifteen years. I have served you, in particular, for six. What is past is well stored. It is safe and out of the power of fortune. What is to come is in wiser hands than ours, and He in whose hands it is, best knows whether it is best for you and me that I should be in Parliament, or even in the world.

Gentlemen, the melancholy event of yesterday reads to us an awful lesson against being too much troubled about any of the objects of ordinary ambition. The worthy gentleman who has been snatched from us at the moment of the election, and in the middle of the contest, while his desires were as warm and his hopes as eager as ours, has feelingly told us what shadows we are, and what shadows we pursue *[Mr. Coombe, one of his competitors in the election, died suddenly the night before]*.

It has been usual for a candidate who declines, to take his leave by a letter to the sheriffs; but I received your trust in the face of day, and in the face of day I accept your dismission. I am not − I am not at all ashamed to look upon you, nor can my presence discompose the order of business here. I humbly and respectfully take my leave of the sheriffs, the candidates, and the electors, wishing heartily that the choice may be for the best at a time which calls, if ever time did call, for service that is not nominal. It is no plaything you are about. I tremble when I consider the trust I have presumed to ask. I confided perhaps too much in my intentions. They were really fair and upright; and I am bold to say that I ask no ill thing for you when, on parting from this place, I pray that whomever you choose to succeed me, he may resemble me exactly in all things except in my abilities to serve and my fortune to please you.

Burke was appointed a candidate in the constituency of Malton, and was elected Member of Parliament by them in the 1780 election.

Douglas Hyde
25 November 1892

WILLIAM BUTLER Yeats made an accurate analysis of something that began happening in Ireland during the late 1880s when he wrote, 'A true literary consciousness – national to the centre – seems gradually to be forming.' This movement has come to be best described as the Irish literary revival.

Yeats and Douglas Hyde were to the forefront of this movement. In 1892, they founded the Irish National Literary Society, with the prime aim 'to encourage and stimulate a new school of literature which would be thoroughly and distinctly Irish, though in the English language.'

At one of its meetings on 25 November, 1893, Douglas Hyde delivered the following lecture entitled, 'The Necessity for De-anglicizing Ireland.'

Lecture on the Importance of De-Anglicizing Ireland

If we take a bird's-eye view of our island today, and compare it with what it used to be, we must be struck by the extraordinary fact that the nation which was once, as every one admits, one of the most classically learned and cultured nations in Europe, is now one of the least so; how one of the most reading and literary peoples has become one of the least studious and most un-literary, and how the present art products of one of the quickest, most sensitive, and most artistic races on earth are now only distinguished for their hideousness.

I shall endeavour to show that this failure of the Irish people in recent times has been largely brought about by the race diverging during this century from the right path, and ceasing to be Irish without becoming English. I shall attempt to show that with the bulk of the people this change took place quite recently, much more recently than most people imagine, and is, in fact, still going on. I should also like to call attention to the illogical position of men who drop their own language to speak

English, of men who translate their euphonious Irish names into English monosyllables, of men who read English books, and know nothing about Gaelic literature, nevertheless protesting as a matter of sentiment that they hate the country which at every hand's turn they rush to imitate.

I wish to show you that in anglicizing ourselves wholesale we have thrown away with a light heart the best claim which we have upon the world's recognition of us as a separate nationality. What did Mazzini say? What is Goldwin Smith never tired of declaiming? What do the *Spectator and Saturday Review* harp on? That we ought to be content as an integral part of the United Kingdom because we have lost the notes of nationality, our language and customs.

It has always been very curious to me how Irish sentiment sticks in this half-way house; how it continues to apparently hate the English, and at the same time continues to imitate them; how it continues to clamour for recognition as a distinct nationality, and at the same time throws away with both hands what would make it so. If Irishmen only went a little further they would become good Englishmen in sentiment also. But – illogical as it appears – there seems not the slightest sign or probability of their taking that step.

It is the curious certainty that, come what may, Irishmen will continue to resist English rule, even though it should be for their good, which prevents many of our nation from becoming unionists upon the spot. It is a fact, and we must face it as a fact, that although they adopt English habits and copy England in every way, the great bulk of Irishmen and Irishwomen over the whole world are known to be filled with a dull, ever-abiding animosity against her, and – right or wrong – to grieve when she prospers, and joy when she is hurt. Such movements as Young Irelandism, Fenianism, Land Leagueism, and parliamentary obstruction seem always to gain their sympathy and support. It is just because there appears no earthly chance of their becoming good members of the empire that I urge that they should not remain in the anomalous position they are in, but since they absolutely refuse to become the one thing, that they become the other; cultivate what they have rejected, and build up an Irish nation on Irish lines.

But you ask, why should we wish to make Ireland more Celtic than it is – why should we de-anglicize it at all? I answer because the Irish race is at present in a most anomalous position, imitating England and yet apparently hating it. How can it produce anything good in literature, art, or institutions as long as it is actuated by motives so contradictory?

Besides, I believe it is our Gaelic past which, though the Irish race does not recognize it just at present, is really at the bottom of the Irish heart, and prevents us becoming citizens of the empire as, I think, can be easily proved . . .

Let us suppose for a moment – which is impossible – that there were to arise a series of Cromwells in England for the space of one hundred years, able administrators of the empire, careful rulers of Ireland, developing to the utmost our national resources, whilst they unremittingly stamped out every spark of national feeling, making Ireland a land of wealth and factories, whilst they extinguished every thought and every idea that was Irish, and left us, at last after a hundred years of good government, fat, wealthy, and populous, but with all our characteristics gone, with every external that at present differentiates us from the English lost or dropped; all our Irish names of places and people turned into English names; the Irish language completely extinct; the O's and the Macs dropped; our Irish intonation changed, as far as possible by English schoolmasters into something English; our history no longer remembered or taught; the names of our rebels and martyrs blotted out; our battlefields and traditions forgotten; the fact that we are not of Saxon origin dropped out of sight and memory, and let me now put the question – how many Irishmen are there who would purchase material prosperity at such a price? It is exactly such a question as this and the answer to it that shows the difference between the English and Irish race. Nine Englishmen out of ten would jump to make the exchange, and I as firmly believe that nine Irishmen out of ten would indignantly refuse it.

And yet this awful idea of complete anglicization, which I have put here before you in all its crudity is, and has been, making silent inroads upon us for nearly a century. Its inroads have been silent because, had the Gaelic race perceived what was being done, or had they been once warned of what was taking place in their own midst, they would I think, never have allowed it. When the picture of complete anglicization is drawn for them in all its nakedness Irish sentimentality becomes suddenly a power and refuses to surrender its birthright.

What lies at the back of the sentiments of nationality with which the Irish millions seem so strongly leavened; what can prompt them to applaud such sentiments as

'They say the British empire owes much to Irish hands,
That Irish valour fixed her flag o'er many conquered lands

And ask if Erin takes no pride in these her gallant sons,
Her Wolseleys and her Lawrences, her Wolfes and Wellingtons.
Ah ! these were of the empire – we yield them to her fame,
And ne'er in Erin's orisons are heard their alien name
But those for whom her heart beats high and benedictions swell,
They died upon the scaffold and they pined within the cell.'

Of course it is a very composite feeling which prompts them; but I believe that what is largely behind it is the half unconscious feeling that the race which at one time held possession of more than half Europe, which established itself in Greece, and burned infant Rome, is now almost extirpated and absorbed elsewhere making its last stand for independence in this island of Ireland; and do what they may the race of today cannot wholly divest itself from the mantle of its own past. Through early Irish literature, for instance, we can best form some conception of what that race really was, which, after overthrowing and trampling on the primitive peoples of half Europe, was itself forced in turn to yield its speech, manners, and independence to the victorious eagles of Rome. We alone of the nations of Western Europe escaped the claws of those birds of prey; we alone developed ourselves naturally upon our own lines outside of and free from all Roman influence; we alone were thus able to produce an early art and literature, our antiquities can best throw light upon the pre-Romanized inhabitants of half Europe, and we are our father's sons. . . .

What we must endeavour to never forget is this, that the Ireland of today is the descendant of the Ireland of the seventh century; then the school of Europe and the torch of learning. It is true that Northmen made some minor settlements in it in the ninth and tenth centuries, it is true that the Normans made extensive settlements during the succeeding centuries, but none of these broke the continuity of the social life of the island. Dane and Norman drawn to the kindly Irish breast issued forth in a generation or two fully Irishized, and more Hibernian than the Hibernians themselves, and even after the Cromwellian plantation the children of numbers of the English soldiers who settled in the south and midlands, were after forty years' residence, and after marrying Irish wives, turned into good Irishmen, and unable to speak a word of English, while several Gaelic poets of the last century have, like Father English, the most unmistakably English names. In two points only was the continuity of the Irishism of Ireland damaged. First, in the northeast of Ulster, where the Gaelic race was expelled and the land planted with aliens, whom our dear mother Erin, assimilative as she is, has hitherto found it difficult to absorb, and in the ownership of the land, eight-ninths of which belongs to people many of whom have always lived, or live, abroad, and not half of whom Ireland can be said to have assimilated.

During all this time the continuation of Erin's national life centred, according to our way of looking at it, not so much in the Cromwellian or Williamite landholders who sat in College Green, and governed the country, as in the mass of the people whom Dean Swift considered might be entirely neglected, and looked upon as mere hewers of wood and drawers of water; the men who, nevertheless, constituted the real working population, and who were living on in the hopes of better days; the men who have since made America, and have within the last ten years proved what an important factor they may be in wrecking or in building the British empire. These are the men of whom our merchants, artisans, and farmers mostly consist, and in whose hands is today the making or marring of an Irish nation. But, alas, quantum mutatus ab illo! *[How much changed from that man]*. What the battleaxe of the Dane, the sword of the Norman, the wile of the Saxon were unable to perform, we have accomplished ourselves. We have at last broken the continuity of Irish life, and just at the moment when the Celtic race is presumably about to largely recover possession of its own country, it finds itself deprived and stripped of its Celtic characteristics, cut off from the past, yet scarcely in touch with the present. It has lost since the beginning of this century almost all that connected it with the era of Cuchullain and of Ossian, that connected it with the christianizers of Europe, that connected it with Brian Boru and the heroes of Clontarf, with the O'Neills and O'Donnells, with Rory O'More, with the wild geese, and even to some extent with the men of 1798. It has lost all that they had – language, traditions, music, genius and ideas. Just when we should be starting to build up anew the Irish race and the Gaelic nation as within our own recollection Greece has been built up anew – we find ourselves despoiled of the bricks of nationality. The old bricks that lasted eighteen hundred years are destroyed; we must now set to, to bake new ones, if we can, on other ground and of other clay. Imagine for a moment the restoration of a German-speaking Greece.

In 1893, Hyde broke away from the Irish National Literary Society and with Eoin O'Neill and Father Eugene O'Growney, founded the Gaelic League, with the declared objective of saving the Irish language.

Éamon de Valera
17 March 1943

1943 MARKED the fiftieth anniversary of the founding of the Gaelic League, an organisation set up to preserve and encourage the study of Irish. With an election looming the Taoiseach and Fianna Fáil leader, Éamon de Valera, used this as his major theme when he broadcast over the radio, on 17 March, 1943.

The historian, Prof. J.J. Lee, recently described it as 'an election speech masquerading in the guise of a festival homily,' a typical comment on what has become de Valera's most ridiculed, misquoted and mocked speech.

After an introduction in Irish, de Valera continued:

Dream Speech

Before the present war began I was accustomed on St. Patrick's Day to speak to our kinsfolk in foreign lands, particularly in the United States, and to tell them year by year on the progress being made towards building up the Ireland of their dreams and ours – the Ireland that we believe is destined to play, by its example and its inspiration, a great part as a nation among nations.

Acutely conscious though we all are of the misery and desolation in which the greater part of the world is plunged, let us turn aside for a moment to that ideal Ireland that we would have. That Ireland which we dreamed of would be the home of a people who valued material wealth only as the basis of right living, of a people who were satisfied with frugal comfort and devoted their leisure to the things of the spirit – a land whose countryside would be bright with cosy homesteads, whose fields and villages would be joyous with the sounds of industry, with the romping of sturdy children, the contests of athletic youths and the laughter of comely maidens, whose firesides would be forums for the wisdom of serene old age. It would, in a word, be the home of a people living the life that God desires that man should live.

With the tidings that make such an Ireland possible, St. Patrick came to our ancestors 1,500 years ago, promising happiness here as well as happiness hereafter. It was the pursuit of such an Ireland that later made our country worthy to be called the Island of Saints and Scholars. It was the idea of such an Ireland, happy, vigorous, spiritual, that fired the imagination of our poets, that made successive generations of patriotic men give their lives to win religious and political liberty, and that will urge men in our own future generations to die, if need be, so that these liberties may be preserved.

One hundred years ago the Young Irelanders, by holding up the vision of such an Ireland before the people, inspired our nation and moved it spiritually as it had hardly been moved since the golden age of Irish civilisation. Fifty years after the Young Irelanders, the founders of the Gaelic League similarly inspired and moved the people of their day, as did later the leaders of the Volunteers. We of this time, if we have the will and the active enthusiasm, have the opportunity to inspire and move our generation in like manner. We can do so by keeping this thought of a noble future for our country constantly before our minds, ever seeking in action to bring that future into being, and ever remembering that it is to our nation as a whole that future must apply.

Thomas Davis, laying down the national programme for his generation, spoke first of the development of our material resources as he saw them, of the wealth that lay in our harbours, our rivers, our bogs and our mines. Characteristically, however, he passed on to emphasise the still more important development of the resources of the spirit:

'Our young artisans must be familiar with the arts of design and the natural sciences connected with their trade; and so of our farmers; and both should, beside, have that general information which refines and expands the mind, that knowledge of Irish history and statistics that makes it national and those accomplishments and sports which make leisure profitable and home joyous. Our cities must be stately with sculpture, pictures and buildings, and our fields glorious with peaceful abundance.'

'But this is an utopia!' he exclaimed, but when questioned, 'Is it?' he answered: 'No: but the practicable (that is, the attainable) object of those who know our resources. To seek it is the solemn, unavoidable duty of every Irishman.'

Davis's answer should be our answer also. We are aware that Davis was mistaken in the extent of some of the material resources which he catalogued, but we know, none the less, that our material resources are sufficient for a population much larger than we have at present, if we consider their use with a due appreciation of their value in a right philosophy of life. And we know also that the spiritual resources which Davis asked the nation to cultivate are inexhaustible.

For many the pursuit of the material is a necessity. Man, to express himself fully and to make the best use of the talents God has given him, needs a certain minimum of comfort and leisure. A section of our people have not yet this minimum. They rightly strive to secure it, and it must be our aim and the aim of all who are just and wise to assist in the effort. But many have got more than is required and are free, if they choose, to devote themselves more completely to cultivating the things of the mind, and in particular those which mark us out as a distinct nation.

The first of these latter is the national language. It is for us what no other language can be. It is our very own. It is more than a symbol; it is an essential part of our nationhood. It has been moulded by the thought of a hundred generations of our forebearers. In it is stored the accumulated experience of a people, our people, who even before Christianity was brought to them were already cultured and living in a well-ordered society. The Irish language spoken in Ireland today is the direct descendant, without break, of the language our ancestors spoke in those far-off days.

As a vehicle of three thousand years of our history, the language is for us precious beyond measure. As the bearer to us of a philosophy, of an outlook on life deeply Christian and rich in practical wisdom, the language today is worth far too much to dream of letting it go. To part with it would be to abandon a great part of ourselves, to lose the key of our past, to cut away the roots from the tree. With the language gone we could never aspire again to being more than half a nation.

For my part, I believe that this outstanding mark of our nationhood can be preserved and made forever safe by this generation. I am indeed certain of it, but I know that it cannot be saved without understanding and co-operation and effort and sacrifice. It would be wrong to minimise the difficulties. They are not slight. The task of restoring the language as the everyday speech of our people is a task as great as any nation ever undertook. But it is a noble task. Other nations have succeeded in it, though in their case, when the effort was begun, their national language was probably more widely spoken among their people than is ours with us. As long as the language lives, however, on the lips of the people as their natural speech in any substantial part of this land we are assured of success if – if we are in earnest.

It is a task in which the attitude of the individual is what counts most. It is upon the individual citizen, upon you who are listening to me, that the restoration of the language finally depends. The State and public institutions can do much to assist, but if the individual has not the inclination or the will-power to make the serious efforts initially required or to persevere till reasonable fluency is attained, outside aids will be of little use. The individual citizen must desire actively to restore the language and be prepared to take the pains to learn it and to use it, else real progress cannot be made.

Today there is no dearth of books and reading matter and other facilities for those who wish to begin their study or to improve their knowledge. Twenty years of work in the schools has brought some knowledge of the language to hundreds of thousands of our young people. If these make it a practice to read and to speak it to one another, even a little at the beginning, particularly in the case of those living in the same house, they will add to their store continually through conversation until all sense of effort has disappeared and the words and phrases come naturally and correctly as they are needed. Each additional person who speaks the language makes the task of all the others easier. Each one who opposes the language and each one who knowing it fails to use it makes the task of those striving to restore it more difficult. For those who can speak it, to neglect doing so, whenever and wherever it can be under-stood, is a betrayal of those who gave their lives so that not merely a free but an Irish-speaking nation might be possible. Were all those who now have a knowledge of the language to speak it consistently on all occasions when it could reasonably be spoken, our task would be easy.

Let us all then, do our part this year. The restoration of the unity of the national territory and the restoration of the language are the greatest of our uncompleted national tasks. Let us devote this year especially to the restoration of the language; let the year be one in which the need for this restoration will be constantly in our thoughts and the language itself as much as possible on our lips.

The physical dangers that threaten, and the need for unceasing vigilance in the matters of defence as well as unremitting attention to the serious day-to-day problems that the war has brought upon us, should not cause us to neglect our duty to the language. Time is running against us in this matter of the language.

We cannot afford to postpone our effort. We should remember also that the more we preserve and develop our individuality and our characteristics as a distinct nation, the more secure will be our freedom and the more valuable our contribution to humanity when this war is over.

Bail ó Dhia oraibh agus bail go gcuire sé ar an obair atá romhainn. Go gcúmhdai Dia sinn agus gur fiú sinn choiche, mar náisiún, na tiolacaí a thug Pádraig chugainn. Go dtuga an tuilechumhachtadh. A thug slán sinn go dtí seo ón anacháin is ón mí-ádh atá ar oiread sin náisiún eile de bharr an chogaidh seo, scath agus didean dúinn go dtí an deireadh, agus go ndeonaí sé agus fiú sinn cion uasal a dhéanamh sa saol nua atá romhainn.

Mary Robinson
3 December 1990

O N 5 JANUARY, 1990, Dick Spring, the leader of the Labour Party, revealed in the course of a radio interview his intent to ensure an election for the next President of Ireland. So determined was he, in fact, that he told the astonished interviewer that he was prepared to run himself if a suitable candidate was not forthcoming. Following the formulation of a 'job description' for the President, and with no sign of any obvious candidate, the name of Mary Robinson, a barrister and academic of some note, and an ex-member of the Labour Party, was mentioned. It was quickly agreed that she would make a suitable candidate and the surprised Robinson became the Labour Party's nominee for President.

Her opponents in the election were Austin Currie (Fine Gael nominee) and Brian Lenihan (Fianna Fáil nominee). Austin Currie was an ex-member of the SDLP and a TD of only one year duration. He was not well known in Southern Ireland and he put up no real opposition to Robinson. Brian Lenihan, the Tánaiste and Minister for Defence, did. But his campaign was effectively ruined, however, after he denied phoning President Hillery to try to persuade him not to dissolve the Dáil following the budget crisis of 1982, an allegation later found to be true. To further damage his campaign the Taoiseach, Charles Haughey, fired Lenihan, following political pressure from Fianna Fáil's coalition partners, the Progessive Democrats.

Large amounts of money were spent in attempting to tarnish Mary Robinson's campaign. A series of press advertisements were taken out, with captions like 'is the left right for the park?' and urging the electorate to vote for Lenihan if 'you want to stop radical socialists taking over the Presidency.' In spite of this Mary Robinson won the Presidential election by an impressive majority of over 86,000.

On 3 December, 1990, Mary Robinson was inaugurated President of Ireland, the first woman to hold that position. She began her inauguration speech as follows:

Inaugural Speech as President

Citizens of Ireland, mná na hÉireann agus fir na hÉireann, you have chosen me to represent you and I am humbled by and grateful for your trust.

The Ireland I will be representing is a new Ireland, open, tolerant, inclusive. Many of you who voted for me did so without sharing all my views. This, I believe, is a significant signal of change, a sign, however modest, that we have already passed the threshold to a new, pluralist Ireland.

The recent revival of an old concept of the fifth province expresses this emerging Ireland of tolerance and empathy. The old Irish term for province is 'coicead,' meaning 'fifth' and yet, as everyone knows, there are only four geographical provinces on this island. So where is the fifth? The fifth province is not anywhere here or there, north or south, east or west. It is a place within each of us – that place that is open to the other, that swinging door which allows us to venture out and others to venture in. Ancient legends divide Ireland into four quarters and a 'middle,' although they differed about the location of this middle or fifth province. While Tara was the political centre of Ireland, tradition has it that this fifth province acted as a second centre, a necessary balance. If I am a symbol of anything I would like to be a symbol of this reconciling and healing fifth province.

My primary role as President will be to represent this state. But the state is not the only model of community with which Irish people can and do identify. Beyond our state there is a vast community of Irish emigrants extending not only across our neighbouring island – which has provided a home away from home for several Irish generations – but also throughout the continents of North America, Australia, and of course Europe itself. There are over seventy million people living on this globe who claim Irish descent. I will be proud to represent them. And I would like to see Áras an Uachtaráin, my official residence, serve – on something of an annual basis – as a place where our emigrant communities could send representatives for a get-together of the extended Irish family abroad.

There is another level of community which I will represent. Not just the national, not just the global, but the local community. Within our state there are a growing number of local and regional communities determined to express their own creativity, identity, heritage and initiative in new and exciting ways. In my travels around Ireland I have found local community groups thriving on a new sense of self-confidence and self-empowerment. Whether it was groups concerned with adult education, employment initiative, women's support, local history and heritage, environmental concern or community culture, one of the most enriching discoveries was to witness the extent of this local empowerment at work.

As President I will seek to the best of my abilities to promote this growing sense of local participatory democracy, this emerging movement of self-development and self-expression which is surfacing more and more at grassroots level. This is the face of modern Ireland.

Ba mhaith liom a rá go bhfuair mé taithneamh agus pléisiúr as an taisteal a rinne mé le míosa anuas ar fuaid na hÉireann. Is fíor álainn agus iontact an tar atá againn, agus is álainn an pobal iad muintir na hÉireann.

Fuair mé teachtaireacht ón bpobal seo agus mé a dul timpeall: 'Teastaíonn Uachtarán uainn gur féidir linn bheith bo, bródúil aisti, ach, níos mó ná sin, gur féidir linn bheith bródúil lena chéile – toisc gus Éireannaigh sinn, agus go bhfuil traidisiúin agus cultúr álainn againn.'

Is cuid an-tábhachtach don gcultúr sin an Ghaeilge – an teanga bheo – fé má atá á labhairt sa Ghaeltacht agus ag daoine eile ar fuaid na hÉireann.

Tá aistear eile le déanamh anois agam – aistear cultúrtha, leis an saibhreas iontach atá sa teanga Ghaeilge a bhaint amach díom féin.

Tá súil agam go leanfaidh daoine eile má atá ar mo nós fhéin – beagán as cleachtadh sa Ghaeilge – agus go raghaimíd ar aghaidh le chéile le taithneamh agus pléisiúr a fháil as ár dteanga álainn féin.

The best way we can contribute to a new and integrated Europe of the 1990s is by having a confident sense of our Irishness. Here again we must play to our strengths – take full advantage of our vibrant cultural resources in music, art, drama, literature and film: value the role of our educators, promote and preserve our unique environmental and geographical resources of relatively pollution free lakes, rivers, landscapes and seas; encourage, and publicly support local initiative projects in aquaculture, forestry, fishing, alternative energy and small-scale technology.

Looking outwards from Ireland, I would like on your behalf to contribute to the international protection and promotion of human rights.

One of our greatest natural resources has always been, and still is, our ability to serve as a moral and political conscience in world affairs. We have a long history in providing spiritual, cultural, and social assistance to other countries in need – most notably in Latin America, Africa and other Third World countries. And we can continue to promote these values by taking principal and independent stands on issues of international importance.

As the elected President of this small democratic country I assume office in a vital moment in Europe's history. Ideological boundaries that have separated East from West are withering away at an astounding pace. Eastern countries are seeking to participate as full partners in a restructured and economically buoyant Europe. The stage is set for a new common European home based on respect for human rights, pluralism, tolerance and openness to new ideas. The European Convention on Human Rights – one of the finest achievements of the Council of Europe – is asserting itself as the natural Constitution for the new Europe. These developments have created one of the major challenges for the 1990s.

If it is time, as Joyce's Stephen Dedalus remarked, that the Irish began to forge in the smithy of our souls 'the uncreated conscience of our race' – might we not take on the still 'uncreated conscience' of the wider international community? Is it not time that the small started believing again that it is beautiful, that the periphery can rise up and speak out on equal terms with the centre, that the most outlying island community of the European Community really has something 'strange and precious' to contribute to the sea-change presently sweeping through the entire continent of Europe? As a native of Ballina, one of the most western towns of the most western province of the most western nation in Europe, I want to say – 'The West's awake!'

I turn now to another place close to my heart, Northern Ireland. As the elected choice of the people of this part of our island I want to extend the hand of friendship and of love to both communities in the other part. And I want to do this with no hidden agendas, no strings attached. As the person chosen by you to symbolise this Republic and to project our self-image to others, I will seek to encourage mutual understanding and tolerance between all the different communities sharing this island.

In seeking to do this I shall rely to a large extent on symbols. But symbols are what unite and divide people. Symbols give us our identity, our self-image, our way of explaining ourselves to ourselves and to others. Symbols in turn determine the kinds of stories we tell; and the stories we tell determine the kind of history we make and remake. I want Áras an Uachtaráin to be a place where people can tell diverse stories – in the knowledge that there is someone there to listen.

I want this Presidency to promote the telling of stories – stories of celebration through the arts and stories of conscience and of social justice. As a woman, I want women who have felt themselves outside history to be written back into history, in the words of Eavan Boland, 'finding a voice where they found a vision.'

May God direct me so that my Presidency is one of justice, peace and love. May I have the fortune to preside over an Ireland at a time of exciting transformation when we enter a new Europe where old wounds can be healed, a time when, in the words of Seamus Heaney, 'hope and history rhyme.' May it be a Presidency where I, the President, can sing to you, citizens of Ireland, the joyous refrain of the fourteenth century Irish poet as recalled by W.B. Yeats:

'I am of Ireland . . . come dance with me in Ireland.'
Go raibh míle maith agaibh go léir.

Mary Robinson
2 February 1995

IRELAND HAS had a long and painful history of emigration. During this century waves of people – as much as 50,000 in some years – have left the country. One result of this has been a drop in the Irish population. Even greater has been the impact that emigration has had on the social fabric and confidence of the Irish nation.

In the 1990 Presidential election campaign the future President, Mary Robinson, vowed to provide a direct link with these emigrants when she said 'There are over seventy million people living on the globe who claim Irish descent. I will be proud to represent them.'

Shortly after taking up residence in Áras an Uachtaráin, she made a most celebrated gesture to Irish people throughout the world, by putting a light on in her kitchen window. It burned night and day, and was her way of symbolising an everlasting welcome for the extended Irish family. During her term as President she crisscrossed the world visiting and meeting many of these emigrants.

On the 2 February, 1995 President Robinson addressed a joint sitting of the Houses of the Oireachtas on the subject of the Irish diaspora:

Speech entitled Cherishing the Irish Diaspora

Four years ago I promised to dedicate my abilities to the service and welfare of the people of Ireland. Even then I was acutely aware of how broad that term the people of Ireland is and how it resisted any fixed or narrow definition. One of my purposes here today is to suggest that, far from seeking to categorise or define it, we widen it still further to make it as broad and inclusive as possible.

At my inauguration I spoke of the seventy million people worldwide who can claim Irish descent. I also committed my Presidency to cherishing them – even though at the time I was thinking of doing so in a purely symbolic way. Nevertheless, the simple emblem of a light in the window, for me, and I hope for them, signifies the inextinguishable nature of our love and remembrance on this island for those who leave it behind.

But in the intervening four years something has occurred in my life which I share with many deputies and senators here and with most Irish families. In that time I have put faces and names to many of those individuals.

In places as far apart as Calcutta and Toronto, on a number of visits to Britain and the United States, in cities in Tanzania and Hungary and Australia, I have met young people from throughout the island of Ireland who felt they had no choice but to emigrate. I have also met men and women who may never have seen this island but whose identity with it is part of their own self-definition. Last summer, in the city of Cracow, I was greeted in Irish by a Polish student, a member of the Polish-Irish Society. In Zimbabwe I learned that the Mashonaland Irish association had recently celebrated its centenary. In each country visited I have met Irish communities, often in far-flung places, and listened to stories of men and women whose pride and affection for Ireland has neither deserted them nor deterred them from dedicating their loyalty and energies to other countries and cultures. None are a greater source of pride than the missionaries and aid workers who bring such dedication, humour and practical commonsense to often very demanding work. Through this office, I have been a witness to the stories these people and places have to tell.

The more I know of these stories the more it seems to me an added richness of our heritage that Irishness is not simply territorial. In fact Irishness as a concept seems to me at its strongest when it reaches out to everyone on this island and shows itself capable of honouring and listening to those whose sense of identity, and whose cultural values, may be more British than Irish. It can be strengthened again if we turn with open minds and hearts to the array of people outside Ireland for whom this island is a place of origin. After all, emigration is not just a chronicle of sorrow and regret. It is also a powerful story of contribution and adaptation. In fact, I have become more convinced each year that this great narrative of dispossession and belonging, which so often had its origins in sorrow and leave-taking, has become – with a certain amount of historic irony – one of the treasures of our society. If that is so then our relation with the diaspora beyond our shores is one which can instruct our society in the values of diversity, tolerance and fair-mindedness.

To speak of our society in these terms is itself a reference in shorthand to the vast distances we have travelled as a people. This island has been inhabited for more than five thousand years. It has been shaped by pre-Celtic wanderers, by Celts, Vikings, Normans, Huguenots, Scottish and English settlers. Whatever the rights or wrongs of history, all those people marked this island, down to the small detail of the distinctive ship-building of the Vikings, the linen-making of the Huguenots, the words of Planter balladeers. How could we remove any one of these things from what we call our Irishness? Far from wanting to do so, we need to recover them so as to deepen our understanding.

Nobody knows this more than the local communities throughout the island of Ireland who are retrieving the history of their own areas. Through the rediscovery of that local history, young people are being drawn into their past in ways that help their future. These projects not only generate employment; they also regenerate our sense of who we were. I think of projects like the Céide Fields in Mayo, where the intriguing agricultural structures of settlers from thousands of years ago are being explored through scholarship and field work. Or Castletown House in Kildare where the grace of our Anglo-Irish architectural heritage is being restored with scrupulous respect for detail. The important excavations at Navan Fort in Armagh are providing us with vital information about early settlers whose proved existence illuminates both legend and history. In Ballance House in Antrim the Ulster-New Zealand Society have restored the birthplace of John Ballance, who became Prime Minister of New Zealand and led that country to be the first in the world to give the vote to women.

Varied as these projects may seem to be, the reports they bring us are consistently challenging in that they may not suit any one version of ourselves. I for one welcome that challenge. Indeed, when we consider the Irish migrations of the seventeenth, eighteenth, nineteenth and twentieth centuries our preconceptions are challenged again. There is a growing literature which details the fortunes of the Irish in Europe and later in Canada, America, Australia, Argentina. These important studies of migration have the power to surprise us. They also demand from us honesty and self-awareness in return. If we expect that the mirror held up to us by Irish communities abroad will show us a single familiar identity, or a pure strain of Irishness, we will be disappointed. We will overlook the fascinating diversity of culture and choice which looks back at us. Above all we will miss the chance to have that dialogue with our own diversity which this reflection offers us.

This year we begin to commemorate the Irish famine which started one hundred and fifty years ago. All parts of this island – north and south, east and west – will see their losses noted and remembered, both locally and internationally. This year we will see those local and global connections made obvious in the most poignant ways. But they have always been there.

Last year, for example, I went to Grosse Ile, an island on the St. Lawrence river near Quebec city. I arrived in heavy rain and as I looked at the mounds which, together with white crosses, are all that mark the mass graves of the five thousand or more Irish people who died there, I was struck by the sheer power of commemoration. I was also aware that, even across time and distance, tragedy must be seen as human and not historic, and that to think of it in national terms alone can obscure that fact. And as I stood looking at Irish graves, I was also listening to the story of the French-Canadian families who braved fever and shared their food, who took the Irish into their homes and into their heritage.

Agus is ón dul i dtír ar Grosse Ile ar a dtugtar freisin Oileán na nGael a shíolraigh an bhean a d'inis an scéal sin dom. Labhair sí liom as Fraincis agus is le bród ar leith a labhair sí Gaeilge liom a bhí tógtha aici ona muitir roimpi. Dá mhéad taistil a rinne mé sea is mó a chuaigh sé i bhfedhm orm gur tháining an Ghaeilge slán ó aimsir an ghorta agus go bhfuil sí le cloisteáil i gcanúintí New York agus Toronto agus Sydney, gan trácht ar Camden Town. Tá scéal ann féin sa Ghaeilge den teacht slán agus den chur in oiriúint.

Ach ar ndóigh bhí seasamh aici i bhfad roimhe seo mar theanga léinn san Eoraip. Tá stair na hEorpa ar bharr a teanga ag an Ghaeilge. Tá cuntas tugtha ina cuid litríochta nach bhfuil in aon áit eile ar chultúr na hEorpa roimh theacht na Rómhánach. Ní inoadh ar bith mar sin go bhfuil staidéar á dhéanamh uirthi in ollscoileanna ó Ghlascú go Moscó agus ó Seattle go Indiana. Agus cén fáth go deimhin go mbeadh inoadh ar bith orm gur as Gaeilge a chuir an macléinn ón bPolainn fáilte romham go Cracow.

Is le pléisiúr agus le bród a éistim le Gaeilge á labhairt i dtíortha eile agus tugann sé pléisiúr dom freisin nuair a chloisin rithimí ár n-amhrán agus ár bhfilíochta á nglacadh chucu féin ag teangacha agus traidisiúin eile. Cruthaíonn sé seo rud atá ar eolas cheana ag mílte Éireannach thar lear, gur féidir grá agus ómós d'Éirinn agus don Ghaeilge agus do chultúr na d'Éireann a chur in iúl ina lán bealaí agus ina lán teangacha.

Indeed, the woman who told me that story had her own origins in the arrival at Grosse Ile. She spoke to me in her native French and, with considerable pride, in her inherited Irish. The more I have travelled the more I have seen that the Irish language since the famine has endured in the accents of New York and Toronto and Sydney, not to mention Camden Town. As such it is an interesting record of survival and adaptation. But long before that, it had standing as a scholarly European language. The Irish language has the history of Europe off by heart. It contains a valuable record of European culture from before the Roman conquest there. It is not surprising therefore that it is studied today in universities from Glasgow to Moscow and from Seattle to Indiana. And why indeed should I have been surprised to have been welcomed in Cracow in Irish by a Polish student? I take pleasure and pride in hearing Irish spoken in other countries just as I am moved to hear the rhythms of our songs and our poetry finding a home in other tongues and other traditions. It proves to me what so many Irish abroad already know: that Ireland can be loved in any language.

The weight of the past, the researches of our local interpreters and the start of the remembrance of the famine all, in my view, point us towards a single reality: that commemoration is a moral act, just as our relation in this country to those who have left it is a moral relationship. We have too much at stake in both not to be rigorous.

We cannot have it both ways. We cannot want a complex present and still yearn for a simple past. I was very aware of that when I visited the refugee camps in Somalia and more recently in Tanzania and Zaire. The thousands of men and women and children who came to those camps were, as the Irish of the 1840s were, defenceless in the face of catastrophe. Knowing our own history, I saw the tragedy of their hunger as a human disaster. We, of all people, know it is vital that it be carefully analysed so that their children and their children's children be spared that ordeal. We realise that while a great part of our concern for their situation, as Irish men and women who have a past which includes famine, must be at practical levels of help, another part of it must consist of a humanitarian perspective which springs directly from our self-knowledge as a people. Famine is not only humanly destructive, it is culturally disfiguring. The Irish who died at Grosse Ile were men and women with plans and dreams of future achievements. It takes from their humanity and individuality to consider them merely as victims.

Therefore it seemed to me vital, even as I watched the current tragedy in Africa, that we should uphold the dignity of the men and women who suffer there by insisting there are no inevitable victims. It is important that in our own commemoration of famine, such reflections have a place. As Tom Murphy has eloquently said in an introduction to his play FAMINE: 'a hungry and demoralised people becomes silent.' We cannot undo the silence of our own past, but we can lend our voice to those who now suffer. To do so we must look at our history, in the light of this commemoration, with a clear insight which exchanges the view that we were inevitable victims in it, for an active involvement in the present application of its meaning. We can examine in detail humanitarian relief then and relate it to humanitarian relief now and assess the inadequacies of both. And this is not just a task for historians. I have met children in schools and men and women all over Ireland who make an effortless and sympathetic connection between our past suffering and the present tragedies of hunger in the world. One of the common bonds between us and our diaspora can be to share this imaginative way of re-interpreting the past. I am certain that they, too, will feel that the best possible commemoration of the men and women who died in that famine, who were cast up on other shores because of it, is to take their dispossession into the present with us, to help others who now suffer in a similar way.

Therefore I welcome all initiatives being taken during this period of commemoration, many of which can be linked with those abroad, to contribute to the study and understanding of economic vulnerability. I include in that all the illustrations of the past which help us understand the present. In the Famine Museum in Strokestown there is a vivid and careful retelling of what happened during the Famine. When we stand in front of those images I believe we have a responsibility to understand them in human terms now, not just in Irish terms then. They should inspire us to be a strong voice in the analysis of the cause and the cure of conditions that predispose to world hunger, whether that involves us in the current debate about access to adequate water supplies or the protection of economic migrants. We need to remember that our own diaspora was once vulnerable on both those counts. We should bear in mind that an analysis of sustainable development, had it existed in the past, might well have saved some of our people from the tragedy we are starting to commemorate.

I chose the title of this speech – Cherishing the Irish Diaspora – with care. Diaspora, in its meaning of dispersal or scattering, includes the many ways, not always chosen, that people have left this island.

To cherish is to value and to nurture and support. If we are honest we will acknowledge that those who leave do not always feel cherished. As Eavan Boland reminds us in her poem 'The Emigrant Irish,'

'Like oil lamps we put them out the back,
Of our houses, of our minds.'

To cherish also means that we are ready to accept new dimensions of the diaspora. Many of us over the years – and I as President – have direct experience of the warmth and richness of the Irish-American contribution and tradition, and its context in the hospitality of that country. I am also aware of the creative energies of those born on this island who are now making their lives in the United States and in so many other countries. We need to accept that in their new perspectives may well be a critique of our old ones. But if cherishing the diaspora is to be more than a sentimental regard for those who leave our shores, we should not only listen to their voice and their viewpoint. We have a responsibility to respond warmly to their expressed desire for appropriate dialogue and interaction with us by examining in an open and generous way the possible linkages. We should accept that such a challenge is an education in diversity which can only benefit our society.

Indeed there are a variety of opportunities for co-operation on this island which will allow us new ways to cherish the diaspora. Many of those opportunities can be fruitfully explored by this Oireachtas. Many will be taken further by local communities. Some are already in operation. Let me mention just one example here. One of the most understandable and poignant concerns of any diaspora is to break the silence: to find out the names and places of origin. If we are to cherish them, we have to assist in that utterly understandable human longing. The Irish Genealogical Project, which is supported by both governments, is transferring handwritten records from local registers of births, deaths and marriages, on to computer. It uses modern technology to allow men and women, whose origins are written down in records from Kerry to Antrim, to gain access to them. In the process it provides employment and training for young people in both technology and history. And the recent establishment of a council of genealogical organisations, again involving both parts of this island, shows the potential for voluntary co-operation.

I turn now to those records which are still only being written. No family on this island can be untouched by the fact that so many of our young people leave it. The reality is that we have lost, and continue every day to lose, their presence and their brightness. These young people leave Ireland to make new lives in demanding urban environments. As well as having to search for jobs, they may well find themselves lonely, homesick, unable to speak the language of those around them; and, if things do not work out, unwilling to accept the loss of face of returning home. It hardly matters at that point whether they are graduates or unskilled. What matters is that they should have access to the support and advice they need. It seems to me therefore that one of the best ways to cherish the diaspora is to begin at home. We need to integrate into our educational and social and counselling services an array of skills of adaptation and a depth of support which will prepare them for this first grueling challenge of adulthood.

The urgency of this preparation, and its outcome, allows me an opportunity to pay tribute to the voluntary agencies who respond with such practical compassion and imagination to the Irish recently arrived in other countries. I have welcomed many of their representatives to Áras an Uachtaráin and I have also seen their work in cities such as New York and Melbourne and Manchester, where their response on a day-to-day basis may be vital to someone who has newly arrived. It is hard to overestimate the difference which personal warmth and wise advice, as well as practical support, can make in these situations.

I pay a particular tribute to those agencies in Britain – both British and Irish – whose generous support and services, across a whole range of needs, have been recognised by successive Irish governments through the Dion project. These services extend across employment, housing and welfare and make a practical link between Irish people and the future they are constructing in a new environment. Compassionate assistance is given, not simply to the young and newly arrived, but to the elderly, the sick including those isolated by HIV or AIDS, and those suffering hardship through alcohol or drug dependency or who are in prison. Although I think of myself as trying to keep up with this subject, I must say I was struck by the sheer scale of the effort which has been detailed in recent reports published under the auspices of the Federation of Irish Societies. These show a level of concern and understanding which finds practical expression every day through these agencies and gives true depth to the meaning of the word cherish.

When I was a student, away from home, and homesick for my family and my friends and my country, I walked out one evening and happened to go into a Boston newsagent's shop. There, just at the back of the news stand, almost to my disbelief, was *The Western People*. I will never forget the joy with which I bought it and took it back with me and found, of course, that the river Moy was still there and the Cathedral was still standing. I remember the hunger with which I read the news from home. I know that story has a thousand versions. But I also know it has a single meaning. Part of cherishing must be communication. The journey which an Irish newspaper once made to any point outside Ireland was circumscribed by the limits of human travel. In fact, it replicated the slow human journey through ports and on ships and airplanes. Now that journey can be transformed, through modern on-line communications, into one of almost instantaneous arrival.

We are at the centre of an adventure in human information and communication greater than any other since the invention of the printing press. We will see our lives changed by that. We still have time to influence the process and I am glad to see that we in Ireland are doing this. In some cases this may merely involve drawing attention to what already exists. The entire Radio 1 service of RTE is now transmitted live over most of Europe on the Astra satellite. In North America we have a presence through the Galaxy satellite. There are several internet providers in Ireland and bulletin boards with community databases throughout the island. The magic of e-mail surmounts time and distance and cost. And the splendid and relatively recent technology of the World Wide Web means that local energies and powerful opportunities of access are being made available on the information highway.

The shadow of departure will never be lifted. The grief of seeing a child or other family member leave Ireland will always remain sharp and the absence will never be easy to bear. But we can make their lives easier if we use this new technology to bring the news from home. As a people, we are proud of our story-telling, our literature, our theatre, our ability to improvise with words. And there is a temptation to think that we put that at risk if we espouse these new forms of communication. In fact we can profoundly enrich the method of contact by the means of expression, and we can and should – as a people who have a painful historic experience of silence and absence – welcome and use the noise, the excitement, the speed of contact and the sheer exuberance of these new forms.

This is the second time I have addressed the two Houses of the Oireachtas as provided under the Constitution. I welcome the opportunity it has given me to highlight this important issue at a very relevant moment for us all. The men and women of our diaspora represent not simply a series of departures and losses. They remain, even while absent, a precious reflection of our own growth and change, a precious reminder of the many strands of identity which compose our story. They have come, either now or in the past, from Derry and Dublin and Cork and Belfast. They know the names of our townlands and villages. They remember our landscape or they have heard of it. They look to us anxiously to include them in our sense of ourselves and not to forget their contribution while we make our own. The debate about how best to engage their contribution with our own has many aspects and offers opportunities for new structures and increased contact.

If I have been able to add something to this process of reflection and to encourage a more practical expression of the concerns we share about our sense of ourselves at home and abroad then I am grateful to have had your attention here today. Finally, I know this Oireachtas will agree with me that the truest way of cherishing our diaspora is to offer them, at all times, the reality of this island as a place of peace where the many diverse traditions in which so many of them have their origins, their memories, their hopes are bound together in tolerance and understanding.

Union and the Fight for Home Rule

Henry Grattan
19 April 1780

TOWARDS the end of the 15th century, alarmed by the use of the Irish Parliament by the old English settlers, the English government set out to curb the power of the Irish Parliament. Poynings Law, an act passed by Sir Richard Poyning the Kings Viceroy to Ireland in 1494, made the Irish Parliament's right to legislate subject to approval by the English Government. The system of patronage further ensured that the English government had a majority in the Irish Parliament.

On the 19 April, 1780, the barrister Henry Grattan put forward the motion in the Irish Parliament that 'the Lords and Commons of Ireland are the only powers competent to make laws to bind Ireland.' The gravity of the occasion on which the speech was delivered and the significance of its political content give it an elevated position in the history of the legislative relations between Britain and Ireland.

The following is the text of that speech:

Call for Ireland to have an Independant Legislator

Sir, I have entreated an attendance on this day that you might, in the most public manner, deny the claim of the British Parliament to make law for Ireland, and with one voice, lift up your hands against it.

If I had lived when the ninth of William [*An act made in the 9th Year of the reign of William III*] took away the woollen manufacture, or when the sixth of George the First declared this country to be dependent, and subject to laws to be enacted by the Parliament of England, I should have made a covenant with my own conscience to seize the first moment of rescuing my country from the ignominy of such acts of power; or, if I had a son, I should have administered to him an oath that he would consider himself a person separate and set apart for the discharge of so important a duty; upon the same principle am I now come to move a declaration of right, the first moment occurring, since my time, in which such a declaration could be made with any chance of success, and without aggravation of oppression.

Sir, it must appear to every person, that, notwithstanding the import of sugar, and export of woollens, the people of this country are not satisfied – something remains, the greater work is behind; the public heart is not well at ease. To promulgate our satisfaction; to stop the throats of millions with the votes of Parliament; to preach homilies to the Volunteers; to utter invectives against the people, under pretence of affectionate advice, is an attempt, weak, suspicious, and inflammatory.

You cannot dictate to those whose sense you are entrusted to represent; your ancestors, who sat within these walls, lost to Ireland trade and liberty; you, by the assistance of the people, have recovered trade; you still owe the Kingdom liberty; she calls upon you to restore it.

The ground of public discontent seems to be, 'We have gotten commerce, but not freedom,' the same power which took away the export of woollens and the export of glass, may take them away again; the repeal is partial, and the ground of repeal is upon a principle of expediency.

Sir, expedient is a word of appropriated and tyrannical import; expedient is an ill-omened word, selected to express the reservation of authority, while the exercise is mitigated; expedient is the ill-omened expression of the Repeal of the American Stamp Act. England thought it expedient to repeal that law; happy had it been for mankind, if, when she withdrew the exercise, she had not reserved the right! To that reservation she owes the loss of her American empire at the expense of millions, and America the seeking of liberty through a sea of bloodshed. The repeal of the woollen act, similarly circumstanced, pointed against the principle of our liberty, present relaxation, but tyranny in reserve, may be a subject for illumination to a populace, or a pretence for apostacy to a courtier, but cannot be the subject of settled satisfaction to a freeborn, an intelligent, and an injured community. It is, therefore, they consider, the free trade as a trade de facto, and not de jure, a license to trade under the Parliament of England, not a free trade under the charters of Ireland as a tribute to her strength; to maintain which she must continue in a state of armed preparation, dreading the approach of a general peace, and attributing all she holds dear to the calamitous condition of the British interest in every quarter of the globe. This dissatisfaction, founded upon a consideration of the liberty we have lost, is increased when they consider the opportunity they are losing; for if this nation, after the death-wound given to her freedom, had fallen on her knees in anguish, and besought the Almighty to frame an occasion in which a weak and injured people might recover their rights, prayer could not have asked, nor God have furnished, a moment more opportune for the restoration of liberty, than this, in which I have the honour to address you.

England now smarts under the lesson of the American War; the doctrine of imperial legislature she feels to be pernicious; the revenues and monopolies annexed to it she has found to be untenable; she lost the power to enforce it; her enemies are a host, pouring upon her from all quarters of the earth; her armies are dispersed; the sea is not hers; she has no minister, no ally, no admiral, none in whom she long confides, and no general whom she has not disgraced; the balance of her fate is in the hands of Ireland; you are not only her last connection, you are the only nation in Europe that is not her enemy. Besides, there does, of late, a certain damp and spurious supineness overcast her arms and councils, miraculous as that vigour which has lately inspirited yours – for with you everything is the reverse; never was there a Parliament in Ireland so possessed of the confidence of the people; you are the greatest political assembly now sitting in the world; you are at the head of an immense army; nor do we only possess an unconquerable force, but a certain unquenchable public fire, which has touched all ranks of men like a visitation.

Turn to the growth and spring of your country, and behold and admire it; where do you find a nation who, upon whatever concerns the rights of mankind, expresses herself with more truth or force, perspicuity or justice? Not the set phrase of scholastic men, not the tame unreality of court addresses, not the vulgar raving of a rabble, but the genuine speech of liberty, and the unsophisticated oratory of a free nation.

See her military ardour, expressed, not only in forty thousand men, conducted by instinct as they were raised by inspiration, but manifested in the zeal and promptitude of every young member of the growing community. Let corruption tremble; let the enemy, foreign or domestic, tremble; but let the friends of liberty rejoice at these means of safety and this hour of redemption. Yes; there does exist an enlightened sense of rights, a young appetite for freedom, a solid strength, and a rapid fire, which not only put a declaration of right within your power, but put it out of your power to decline one. Eighteen counties are at your bar; they stand there with the compact of Henry, with the charter of

John, and with all the passions of the people. 'Our lives are at your service, but our liberties – we received them from God; we will not resign them to man.'

The people of that country [*England*] are now waiting to hear the Parliament of Ireland speak on the subject of their liberty; it begins to be made a question in England whether the principal persons wish to be free; it was the delicacy of former parliaments to be silent on the subject of commercial restrictions, lest they should show a knowledge of the fact, and not a sense of the violation; you have spoken out, you have shown a knowledge of the fact, and not a sense of the violation.

On the contrary, you have returned thanks for a partial repeal made on a principle of power; you have returned thanks as for a favour, and your exultation has brought your charters, as well as your spirit, into question, and tends to shake to her foundation your title to liberty; thus you do not leave your rights where you found them. You have done too much not to do more; you have gone too far not to go on; you have brought yourselves into that situation in which you must silently abdicate the rights of your country, or publicly restore them. It is very true you may feed your manufacturers, and landed gentlemen may get their rents, and you may export woollen, and may load a vessel with baize, serges, and kerseys, and you may bring back again directly from the plantations sugar, indigo, speckle-wood, beetle root, and panellas. But liberty, the foundation of trade, the charters of the land, the independency of Parliament, the securing, crowning, and the consummation of everything are yet to come. Without them the work is imperfect, the foundation is wanting, the capital is wanting, trade is not free, Ireland is a colony without the benefit of a charter, and you are a provincial synod without the privileges of a Parliament . . .

There is no policy left for Great Britain but to cherish the remains of her Empire, and do justice to a country who is determined to do justice to herself, certain that she gives nothing equal to what she received from us when we gave her Ireland.

With regard to this country, England must resort to the free principles of government, and must forgo that legislative power which she has exercised to do mischief to herself; she must go back to freedom, which, as it is the foundation of her Constitution, so it is the main pillar of her empire; it is not merely the connection of the Crown, it is a constitutional annexation, an alliance of liberty, which is the true meaning and mystery of the sisterhood, and will make both countries one arm and one soul, replenishing from time to time, in their immortal connection, the vital spirit of law and liberty from the lamp of each others light. Thus combined by the ties of common interest, equal trade, and equal liberty, the constitution of both countries may become immortal, a new and milder empire may arise from the errors of the old, and the British nation assume once more her natural station – the head of mankind.

That there are precedents against us I allow – acts of power I would call them, not precedent; and I answer the English pleading such precedents, as they answered their kings when they urged precedents against the liberty of England: such things are the weakness of the times; the tyranny of one side, the feebleness of the other, the law of neither; we will not be bound by them; or rather, in the words of the Declaration of Right: 'No doing judgement, proceeding, or anywise to the contrary, shall be brought into precedent or example.' Do not then tolerate a power – the power of the British Parliament over this land, which has no foundation in utility or necessity, or empire, or the laws of England, or the laws of Ireland, or the laws of nature, or the laws of God – do not suffer it to have a duration in your mind.

Do not tolerate that power which blasted you for a century, that power which shattered your loom, banished your manufacturers, dishonoured your peerage, and stopped the growth of your people; do not, I say, be bribed by an export of woollen, or an import of sugar, and permit that power which has thus withered the land to remain in your country and have existence in your pusillanimity.

Do not suffer the arrogance of England to imagine a surviving hope in the fears of Ireland; do not send the people to their own resolves for liberty, passing by the tribunals of justice and the high court of Parliament; neither imagine that, by any formation of apology, you can palliate such a commission to your hearts, still less to your children, who will sting you with their curses in your grave for having interposed between them and their Maker, robbing them of an immense occasion, and losing an opportunity which you did not create and can never restore.

Hereafter, when these things shall be history, your age of thraldom and poverty, your sudden resurrection, commercial redress, and miraculous armament, shall the historian stop at liberty, and observe – that here the principal men among us fell into mimic trances of gratitude they were awed by a weak ministry, and bribed by an empty treasury and when liberty was within their grasp, and the temple opened her folding doors, and the arms of the people clanged, and the zeal of the nation urged and encouraged them on, that they fell down, and were prostituted at the threshold?

I might, as a constituent, come to your bar, and demand my liberty. I do call upon you, by the laws of the land and their violation, by the instruction of eighteen counties, by the arms, inspiration, and providence of the present moment, tell us the rule by which we shall go – assert the law of Ireland – declare the liberty of the land.

I will not be answered by a public lie in the shape of an amendment; neither, speaking for the subjects freedom, am I to hear of faction. I wish for nothing but to breathe, in this our island, in common with my fellow subjects, the air of liberty. I have no ambition, unless it be the ambition to break your chain and contemplate your glory. I never will be satisfied so long as the meanest cottager in Ireland has a link of the British chain clanking to his rags; he may be naked, he shall not be in iron; and I do see the time is at hand, the spirit is gone forth, the declaration is planted; and though great men shall apostatize, yet the cause will live; and though the public speaker should die, yet the immortal fire shall outlast the organ which conveyed it, and the breath of liberty, like the word of the holy man, will not die with the prophet, but survive him.

I shall move you, 'That the King's most excellent Majesty, and the Lords and Commons of Ireland, are the only power competent to make laws to bind Ireland.'

The motion was lost.

Henry Grattan
16 April 1782

A T THE beginning of 1782, the Irish Volunteers, which had originally been set up to defend Ireland from a possible French invasion, passed a motion that 'a claim of any body of men, other than the King, Lords and Commons of Ireland, to bind this kingdom is unconstitutional, illegal and a grievance.' This strengthened the hand of Irish parliamentarians like Henry Grattan, who wanted Ireland to have a legislature independent of Britain.

On 16 April, 1782, a mere two years after his first attempt had failed, Grattan's resolutions demanding legislative independence were passed triumphantly by the Irish Parliament.

That night, Grattan addressed the Irish Parliament in a buoyant mood:

Celebratory speech following the Passing of the Resolutions by the Irish Parliament calling for an Independent Legislator

I am now to address a free people: ages have passed away, and this is the first moment in which you could be distinguished by that appellation.

I have spoken on the subject of your liberty so often, that I have nothing to add, and have only to admire by what heaven-directed steps you have proceeded until the whole faculty of the nation is braced up to the act of her own deliverance.

I found Ireland on her knees, I watched over her with a paternal solicitude; I have traced her progress from injuries to arms, and from arms to liberty. Spirit of Swift! Spirit of Molyneux! Your genius has prevailed. Ireland is now a nation. In that new character I hail her, and bowing to her august presence, I say, Esto perpetua! [*Let it be forever*]

She is no longer a wretched colony, returning thanks to her governor for his rapine, and to her king for his oppression; nor is she now a squabbling, fretful secretary, perplexing her little wits, and firing her furious statutes with bigotry, sophistry, disabilities, and death, to transmit to posterity insignificance and war . . .

You, with difficulties innumerable, with dangers not a few, have done what your ancestors wished, but could not accomplish; and what your posterity may preserve, but will never equal: you have moulded the jarring elements of your country into a nation. You had not the advantages which were common to other great countries; no monuments, no trophies, none of those outward and visible signs of greatness, such as inspire mankind and connect the ambition of the age which is coming on with the example of that going off, and form the descent and concatenation of glory; no, you have not had any great act recorded among all your misfortunes, nor have you one public tomb to assemble the crowd, and spread to the living the language of integrity and freedom.

Your historians did not supply the want of monuments; on the contrary, these narrators of your misfortunes, who should have felt for your wrongs, and have punished your oppressors with oppressions, natural scourges, the moral indignation of history, compromised with public villainy and trembled; they excited your violence, they suppressed your provocation, and wrote in the chain which entrammelled their country. I am come to break that chain, and I congratulate my country, who, without any of the advantages I speak of, going forth, as it were, with nothing but a stone and a sling, and what oppression could not take away, the favour of Heaven, accomplished her own redemption, and left you nothing to add and everything to admire.

Within six months the British yielded to Grattan's demands and the Irish Parliament was allowed to legislate for Ireland independent of the London Parliament. For the next twenty years, the Irish Parliament was to create its own laws until it was bribed into passing the Act of Union, in 1800.

Henry Flood
1783

AFTER 1782, the Irish Parliament enjoyed an ostensible independence from Britain in that it originated its own legislation. But the
power of the Privy Council and the King over Irish law still remained,
as did the rather conservative Civil Service.

Henry Flood's recognition of this inconclusiveness prompted him to
call on the British Government to renounce all external controls over
the Irish Parliament. This was eventually agreed to and the Act of
Renunciation, as it was known, declared that the, 'right claimed by the
people of Ireland, to be bound only by laws enacted by His Majesty and
the Parliament of the Kingdom in all cases whatever – shall be, and it is
hereby declared to be, established and ascertained for ever, and shall at
no time hereafter be questioned or questionable.'

The following is Flood's speech on Renunciation in the Irish
Parliament:

Celebratory speech following the passing of the Act of Renunciation

A voice from America shouted to liberty, the echo of it caught your
people as it passed along the Atlantic, and they renewed the voice till it
reverberated here. What followed? All the propositions that had been
separately reprobated were now collectively adopted; the representatives
of the people articulated at length the sense of their constituents. The
case of Ireland originally stated by the great Molyneux, and burned at
the revolution by the Parliament of England, is not now afraid of the
fire; it has risen from that phoenix urn, and with the flames of its cradle
it illuminates our isle! What is the result? It is now in your power, and I
trust it will be in your wisdom to do final justice to the rights and
interests of your country for me, I hope I have not been peculiarly

wanting to them. At an early period of my life, on a question of embargo, in consequence of a proclamation founded on a British Act of Parliament, I brought the criminal gazette within these walls, and at your Bar I arraigned the delinquent. The House was alarmed, and I withdrew my question, on the proclamation being withdrawn. If you ask why I did not pursue it to a formal declaration of right, I answer, for I wish to be answerable to you for every part of my life: I answer that the time was not ripe for it. The first spring of the constitution is the elective power of the people: till that was reinforced by limiting the duration of Parliaments, little could be done. The people wanted constitutional privilege; till the fabric of usurpation, founded on the law of Poynings, had been shaken to its foundation, little could be done; the Parliament wanted conscious dignity till the people were armed; everything could not be done; the nation wanted military power. These were necessary antecedents. The public mind wanted much cultivation. The seed, too, was necessary to be sown, and if I have not been wanting to the preparations of the soil, may I not be permitted to watch over the harvest? To that harvest too, as well as to every other, a prosperous season was necessary, and that season presented itself in the American war. When, therefore, the honourable member [*Grattan*] in the sunshine of that season, and of his own abilities, brought forward a declaration of rights in Lord Buckingham's Government, after that administration had amended his proposition for the purpose of defeating it, I stepped forward, in office as I was, and at the hazard of that office, rescued the principle from the disgrace of a postponement, or from the ruin of rejection. In this session, too, I hope that my humble efforts have not been peculiarly wanting. In ability I will yield to many, in zeal to none; and, if I have not served the public cause more than many men, this at least I may say, I have sacrificed as much to it. Do you repent of that sacrifice? If I am asked, I answer 'No.' Who could repent of a sacrifice to truth and honour, to a country that he loves, and to a country that is grateful? Do you repent of it? No. But I should not rejoice in it, if it were only to be attended with a private deprivation, and not to be accompanied by all its gains to my country. I have a peculiar right, therefore, to be solicitous and ardent about the issue of it, and no man shall stop me in my progress.

Were the voice with which I utter this, the last effort of an expiring nature; were the accent which conveys it to you, the breath that was to waft me to that grave to which we all tend, and to which my footsteps rapidly accelerate, I would go on; I would make my exit by a loud demand of your rights; and I call upon the God of truth and liberty who has often favoured you, and who has of late looked down upon you with such a peculiar grace and glory of protection, to continue to you his inspirings – to crown you with the spirit of his completion, and to assist you against the errors of those that are honest, as well as against the machinations of all that are not so.

I will now move you, that the opinion of all the judges be desired on the following question: 'Does the repeal of the Declaratory Act amount, in legal construction, to a repeal or renunciation of the legal principle on which the Declaratory Act grounded itself?'

Nothing ever was more judicious than the conduct of this occasion. She has so embarrassed Great Britain abroad, and you were so strong at home, that she could not deny the repeal of the Declaratory law. Yet it must ever be her wish to retain the principle of it, because it is the principle of power, which no nation has ever relinquished while it could maintain it.

If there be a pride of England, there is a pride of Ireland too. Now I ask which ought to give way, for one must, and I answer impartially, that which has the worst foundation. Now which is that? The pride of England in this case, is the pride of wrong, and the pride of usurpation. The pride of Ireland is the pride of right, the pride of justice, the pride of constitution. I will not ask you after that, which ought to give way; but it is wrong to put this question principally upon pride.

But time is not necessary, negotiation alone is sufficient to undo you; you were not born to be negotiators; the negotiator is a dark, austere, inexorable character; you are soft, open, and persuadable; you have not the detailed knowledge, the systematical procrastination, the suspicious reserve, or the frigid perseverance of a negotiator. When have you negotiated that you have not lost? You negotiated at the Restoration, you negotiated at the Revolution, you negotiated at the augmentation of your army, you negotiated your free trade, you negotiated the Mutiny Bill. When have you demanded that you have not succeeded, and when have you negotiated that you have not been deceived?

There never was a time which required more consideration than the present; the national exertion began in the last year of Lord Buckingham's administration, it is now drawing to a period, and whether that shall be glorious or otherwise depends on your wisdom. A short view of what we have done will be a guide to what we should do. We had groaned for a century under an increasing usurpation; the American war broke out, and whilst we were called upon to shed our blood for Great Britain, we were insulted with the application of that principle to Ireland which had revolted America; our feelings were exasperated by the application, and our trade was ruined by the war; we saw ourselves beggars in fact, and slaves in assertion. The merchants flew to a non-importation agreement, the people flew to arms. Amidst this perturbation Parliament assembled, and we amended our address by the demand of a free constitution, that is of an exclusive legislature, on which all freedom of trade must depend; and therefore it was, that I did originally differ with some gentlemen, for I asserted that they had not obtained that freedom of trade of which they had boasted, because they had not obtained that freedom of Parliamentary constitution, without which a freedom of trade could not exist. We received from England a dilatory answer. We shortened our money grants to the crown – we shortened them to the subject. And the Irish public, creditors to their immortal honour, embarked so fully with the rights of the nation, as cheerfully to accept of a six months' security. This rapid succession of sober and consistent efforts struck like lightning on the Ministry and Parliament of England; all obstacles gave way; our demand was to be granted in all its plentitude; all the British statutes restrictive of our foreign commerce were to be repealed; and on that constitutional principle on which alone it would be welcome – a principle, which in that early period of this question, I took the first opportunity to lay down in clear, unambiguous, and categorical terms. What was that principle? That, having a Parliament of our own, our foreign trade was necessarily free, and subject to no restrictions as to our ports, but such as our Parliament might impose. This principle, we were told, was admitted by England, as to our foreign trade, and pleaded by her in return, as to her own ports, and those of her own colonies. She admitted the principle which we claimed, and she said she would open to us her colony ports, on equal regulation of trade. The tidings of this emancipation, as it was idly called, landed in Ireland. The Post Office was illuminated by an emissary of the Castle; the College took fire in the next instance by an unhappy contagion, and the city caught the flame in a regular and sympathetic succession. All sober consideration was lost in an ignorant clamour, and the steady pulse of the public yielded to a fever of exultation. What was the consequence? England saw that we were surprised at our success, saw that we had asked more than we expected, concluded that we would accept of infinitely less, and determined that should be as little as she could. First, then, she determined not to repeal all her laws restrictive of our foreign commerce, yet, whilst an atom of such restriction remains, the total impeachment of your Constitution remains; when, therefore, an artful resolution was prepared for this House, on that occasion, expressive of satisfaction in that enlargement of our foreign trade, I exclaimed against that word. If you thank the British Parliament, I said, for the enlargement of our foreign trade, you admit she can restrain it, you admit her legislative authority gain little in commerce, and you lose everything in constitution. I objected to the word foreign, therefore; it belies Ireland and it deceives Great Britain. The independent gentlemen of the day, however, did not feel, did not take up the principle, yet, though they did not take it up that day, they have felt it since; and though the word was universally admitted then, there is not a man in the nation that would not reject it now. Such was the first of this business. Let us see how much worse we made it in the progress of negotiation. The language of England was the language of common sense. Ireland must have equal regulations of trade, she said, but equal taxes on home consumption she did not say; equal regulations of trade may subsist between a poor country and a rich one, but equal taxes on consumption cannot. Now what has your negotiation made of it? You have made your arrangement a tax-law in part, which ought to have been a trade-law in the whole; that is to say, instead of a regulation in trade, you made it a regulation against trade, and a caustic regulation too. What regulation, indeed, can be much more adversary to trade, than a heavy tax on a raw material imported for the purpose of trade, and for the end of manufacture? So pernicious are such taxes, that the ministers in England, whose profusion has brought them to that country, have endeavoured to extenuate their malignity by two regulations; to console the manufacturer, they tell him that they will open to him the foreign market, by giving him a drawback on his manufactures exported, equal to the tax on imported material. And they tell him besides that they will shut up the home market, and give him a monopoly of it. How? By laying a prohibitory duty on the manufacture imported from abroad and what have they done as to manufactured sugars? They have laid a prohibitory duty upon them when imported into England from any other part of the world, Ireland even not excepted. What have we done? We have laid the same prohibitory duty on sugars imported into Ireland from any other part of the world; but we have excepted England whereas she did not except Ireland. Now, there was much more reason for our excepting England than there was for her excepting Ireland, and why? Because Ireland could never, by any possibility, be a rival in sugars to England in the English market, but England is actually a very formidable rival to Ireland in the Irish market. What is the fact? The Irish manufacturer of sugars has but one rival in the world, and that is the English manufacturer of them. And what have we done? We have given him the fullest security against all those that are not his rivals. And we have not given it to him against the only manufacturers that are his rivals; we have given him perfect protection where he is in no danger, and we have not given it to him where he is in all danger. We have done worse by him, we have not only given him as much security against his only rivals, as against those who are not at all his rivals; but we have not left him as much security against his only rivals as he always had before; that is to say, the duty on the imported manufacture now bears a less proportion than ever it did before to the duty on the imported raw materials. By consequence his peril is greater, as his protection is less; and his security being diminished, his danger is enhanced. But this is not all; you have not done for him what England originally pointed out to you in his favour: she proposed equality as the principle of your regulation of trade; we adopted it religiously in that part to which it was not applicable, and, where it was pernicious, I mean in the tax part; and we only deserted it in the trade part, where alone it was applicable, and where alone it was beneficial. Such was the spirit in which we negotiated our free trade. Let us take care how we negotiate our free Constitution but the error of that arrangement does not stop here. Its first principle was erroneous; it set out with this maxim: that you were to pay for this as if it were an enlargement, and that you were to pay for it in tax, as if you had not paid it otherwise before. But what is the truth? The sugars of Spain, Portugal, and France would supply your manufactures, as well as the British West Indian Islands, and generally better; if, whilst you retained those markets, England had opened her colony ports too, this would have been a new market, which is always an advantage to the buyer. But what is the case now? You are suffered to go to the colony market of England, which is the English market in effect, and which is therefore her advantage; but you give up for this all other, and some better markets, which is your advantage. Instead of its being an enlargement, therefore, this is more properly a restriction and instead of England's granting you a boon in this matter, it is you that gave her a monopoly. Now, a monopoly is so much against the giver, and so much in favour of the obtainer of it, that no nation in its senses ever gives it to another. And if a part of an empire gives it to the head, it cannot be on a principle of trade, because a principle of trade is a principle of gain, whereas this is a principle of loss. On what principle alone can it be given? On a principle of empire. That is to say, in other words, it is a tax or a tribute, and that of the heaviest nature; but, if you were to pay for it in taxes, besides paying for it by monopoly, it would be absurd to pay for it more than it was worth. Now take the whole West India commerce, take the utmost proportion of that commerce that could ever fall to your lot, take the utmost proportion of clear profit that can be supposed to accrue from that quantity of trade, and then take the utmost proportion of that clear profit that can be afforded to revenue, and I say it would never amount to that sum which you have agreed to pay on the instant for the contingency of this direct trade, with this additional absurdity, that if you should not be able to establish it, these additional duties will be equally payable upon your old circuitous trade, which before was free from them. Will you trust negotiation again? This arrangement cannot be justified on any commercial principle. Was any constitutional advantage obtained by it? Far from it: the very principle of the arrangement is hostile to the Constitution; it gives to the British Parliament a virtual power of taxing you; for what is the principle of it? That when England taxes a colony produce, you must tax it equally or give up the trade. Thus this arrangement leaves both your trade and your money at the mercy of the Ministry and Parliament of England. Combine this with another law of the same period, the Mutiny Bill, therefore, and see what the result of both is. You complained that the British Parliament should make even a twelve-months law for your army; and what did you do to remedy it? You made an Act, that she should do it for ever. The two greatest powers in the management of human concerns, are the power of the purse, and the power of the sword. You did by these two laws, for so much, delegate away both of these great powers from yourselves to the British Parliament; that is to say, in the very moment that you talked of recovering your own authority, and denying that of the British legislature, you did everything you could to strengthen the power of that Parliament which you meant to overthrow, and to weaken the power of that Parliament which you meant to establish. I do not speak these things in order to say what is disagreeable to any man living, much less to say anything disagreeable to that body, in defence of whose privileges I have lived these two and twenty years, and in defence of whose privileges I will die. I speak them from a deep conviction of their necessity. You see how you have been negotiated out of everything, and how dangerous it is to negotiate again. You see how dangerous it is to exult too soon, or to imagine that anything of this kind is done, while anything remains undone. You see what a miserable end was made of Lord Buckingham's last session of Parliament, though it began with so much splendour; and as a part of this session has trod the steps of its glory, would warn the conclusion of it against the steps of its decline. To put a stop, therefore, to the danger of negotiation, and to accelerate the safety of an immediate repeal, and of a final Renunciation, I move the resolution I have before stated to you.

William Conyngham Plunket

23 January 1799

ON 22 JANUARY, 1799 Lord Cornwallis, the Lord Lieutenant in Ireland, opened the first session of the Irish Parliament with a rousing call for Union with Britain. 'The more I have reflected on the situation and circumstances of this kingdom,' he said, 'considering on the one hand the strength and stability of Great Britain, and on the other hand, these divisions which have shaken Ireland to its foundations, the more anxious I am for some permanent adjustment which may extend the advantages enjoyed by our sister kingdom to every part of this island.'

A most animated and protracted debate followed, the first of many such on the proposed Union with Britain. It continued unabated for twenty-two hours. Shortly before daybreak on the morning of the 23rd, the young Enniskillen-born barrister, William Conyngham Plunket – later Lord Plunket – rose to address the audience. What followed was according to Sir Jonah Barrington 'the ablest speech ever heard in that Parliament . . . perfect in eloquence, and unanswerable in reasoning.'

Anti-Act of Union Speech

Sir, I shall make no apology for troubling you at this late hour, exhausted though I am, in mind and body, and suffering, though you must be under a similar pressure. This is a subject which must arouse the slumbering, and might almost reanimate the dead. It is a question whether Ireland shall cease to be free. It is a question involving our dearest interests forever.

Sir, I congratulate the house on the manly temper with which this measure has been discussed. I congratulate them on the victory, which I already see they have obtained; a victory which I anticipate from the bold and generous sentiments which have been expressed on this side of the house, and which I see confirmed in the doleful and discomfited visages of the miserable group whom I see before me. Sir, I congratulate you on the candid avowal of the noble lord who has just sat down. He has exposed this project in its naked hideousness and deformity. He has told us that the necessity of sacrificing our independence flows from the nature of our connexion. It is now avowed that this measure does not flow from any temporary cause; that it is not produced in consequence of any late rebellion, or accidental disturbance in the country; that its necessity does not arise from the danger of modern political innovations, or from recent attempts of wicked men to separate this country from Great Britain. No, we are now informed by the noble lord, that the condition of our slavery is engrafted on the principle of our connexion, and that by the decrees of fate, Ireland has been doomed a dependant colony from her cradle.

I trust that after this barefaced avowal there can be little difference of opinion. I trust that every honest man who regards the freedom of Ireland, or who regards the connexion with England, will, by his vote on this night, refute this unfounded and seditious doctrine. Good God, sir, have I borne arms to crash the wretches who propagated the false and wicked creed, 'that British connexion was hostile to Irish freedom,' and am I now bound to combat it, coming from the lips of the noble lord who is at the head of our administration.

But Sir, in answer to the assertion of the noble lord. I will quote the authority of the Duke of Portland, in his speech from the throne, at the end of the session, 1782, 'that the two kingdoms are now one, indissoluble, connected by unity of constitution and unity of interest, that the danger and security, the prosperity and calamity of the one must mutually affect the other; that they stand and fall together.' I will quote the authority of the king, lords, and commons of Ireland, who asserted and established the constitution of our independent parliament founded on that connexion; and the authority of the king, lords, and commons of Great Britain, who adopted and confirmed it. With as little prospect of persuasion has the noble lord cited to us the example of Scotland; and as little am I tempted to purchase, at the expense of two bloody rebellions, a state of poverty and vassalage, at which Ireland, at her worst state, before she attained a free trade or a free constitution, would have spurned.

But Sir, the noble lord does not seem to repose very implicit confidence in his own arguments, and he amuses you by saying, that in adopting this address you do not pledge yourselves to a support of the measure in any future stage. Beware of this delusion. If you adopt this address you sacrifice your constitution. You concede the principle, and any future inquiries can only be as to the terms. For them you need entertain no solicitude, on the terms you can never disagree. Give up your independence, and Great Britain will grant you whatever terms you desire. Give her the key, and she will confide everything to its protection. There are no advantages you can ask which will grant, exactly for the same reason that the unprincipled spendthrift will subscribe, without reading it, the bond which he has no intention of ever discharging. I say, therefore, that if you ever mean to make a stand for the liberties of Ireland, now, and now only, is the moment for doing it.

But, Sir, the freedom of discussion which has taken place on this side of the house has, it seems, given great offence to gentlemen on the treasury bench. They are men of nice and punctilious honour, and they will not endure that anything should be said which implies a reflection on their untainted and virgin integrity. They threatened to take down the words of an honourable gentleman who spoke before me, because they conveyed an insinuation; and I promised them on that occasion, that if the fancy for taking down words continued, I would indulge them in it to the top of their bent. Sir, I am determined to keep my word with them, and I now will not insinuate, but I will directly assert, that base and wicked as is the object proposed, the means used to effect it have been more flagitious and abominable.

Do you choose to take down my words? Do you dare me to the proof?

Sir, I had been induced to think that we had at the head of the executive government of this country a plain, honest soldier, unaccustomed to, and disdaining the intrigues of politics, and who, as an additional evidence of the directness and purity of his views, had chosen for his secretary a simple and modest youth, *puer ingenui vultus ingenuique pudoris* [*boy of noble countenance and natural modesty*], whose inexperience was the voucher of his innocence; and yet I will be bold to say, that during this royalty of this unspotted veteran, and during the administration this unassuming stripling – within these last six weeks, a system of black corruption has been carried on within the walls of the castle which would disgrace the annals of the worst period of the history of either country.

Do you choose to take down my words?

I need call no witness to your bar to prove them. I see two Right Honourable gentlemen sitting within your walls, who had long and faithfully served the crown, and who have been dismissed, because they dared to express a sentiment in favour of their country. I see another gentlemen, who has been forced to resign his place as commissioner of the revenue because he refused to co-operate in this dirty job of a dirty administration.

Do you dare to deny this?

I say that at this moment the threat of dismissal from office is suspended over the heads of the members who now sit around me, in order to influence their votes on the question of this night, involving everything that can be sacred or dear to man.

Do you desire to take down my words? Utter the desire, and I will prove the truth of them at your bar.

Sir, I would warn you against the consequences of carrying this measure by such means as this, but that I see the necessary defeat of it in the honest and universal indignation which the adoption of such means excites. I see the protection against the wickedness of the plan in the imbecility of its execution; and I congratulate my country, that when a design was formed against her liberties, the prosecution of it was entrusted to such hands as it is now placed in.

The example of the Prime Minister of England, imitable in its vices, may deceive the noble lord. The minister of England has his faults. He abandoned in his latter years the principle of reform, by professing which he had attained the early confidence of the people of England, and in the whole of his political conduct he has shown himself haughty and intractable; but it must be admitted that he is endowed by nature with a towering and transcendent intellect, and that the vastness of his resources keeps pace with the magnificence and unboundedness of his projects. I thank God, that it is much more easy for him to transfer his apostacy and his insolence than his comprehension and his sagacity; and I feel the safety of my country in the wretched feebleness of her enemy. I cannot fear that the constitution which has been founded by the wisdom of sages, and cemented by the blood of patriots and of heroes, is to be smitten to its centre by such a green and sapless twig as this.

Sir, the noble lord has shown much surprise that he should hear a doubt expressed concerning the competence of Parliament to do this act. I am sorry that I also must contribute to increase the surprise of the noble lord. If I mistake not, his surprise will be much augmented before this question shall be disposed of; he shall see and hear what he has never before seen or heard, and be made acquainted with sentiments to which, probably, his heart has been a stranger.

Sir, I, in the most express terms, deny the competency of Parliament to do this act. I warn you, do not dare to lay your hands on the Constitution. I tell you, that if, circumstanced as you are, you pass this Act, it will be a nullity, and that no man in Ireland will be bound to obey it. I make the assertion deliberately, I repeat it, and I call on any man who hears me to take down my words. You have not been elected for this purpose. You are appointed to make laws, and not legislatures. You are appointed to act under the Constitution, not to alter it. You are appointed to exercise the functions of legislators, and not to transfer them. And if you do so, your act is a dissolution of the Government. You resolve society into its original elements, and no man in the land is bound to obey you.

Sir, I state doctrines which are not merely founded on the immutable laws of justice and of truth. I state not merely the opinions of the ablest men who have written on the science of government, but I state the practice of our Constitution as settled at the era of the revolution, and I state the doctrines under which the House of Hanover derives its title to the throne. Has the King a right to transfer his Crown? Is he competent to annex it to the Crown of Spain or any other country? No, but he may abdicate it, and every man who knows the constitution knows the consequence – the right reverts to the next in succession, if they all abdicate, it reverts to the people. The man who questions this doctrine, in the same breath must arraign the Sovereign on the throne as an usurper. Are you competent to transfer your legislative rights to the French Council of five hundred? Are you competent to transfer them to the British Parliament? I answer, No. When you transfer you abdicate, and the great original trust reverts to the people from whom it issued. Yourselves you may extinguish, but Parliament you cannot extinguish. It is enthroned in the hearts of the people.

It is enshrined in the sanctuary of the Constitution. It is immortal as the island which it protects. As well might the frantic suicide hope that the act which destroys his miserable body should extinguish his eternal soul. Again, I therefore warn you, do not dare to lay your hands on the Constitution; it is above your power.

Sir, I do not say that Parliament and the people, by mutual consent and co-operation, may not change the form of the Constitution. Whenever such a case arises it must be decided on its own merits – but that is not this case. If the Government considers this a season peculiarly fitted for experiments on the Constitution, they may call on the people. I ask you are you ready to do so? Are you ready to abide the event of such an appeal? What is it you must, in that event, submit to the people? Not this particular project; for if you dissolve the present form of government, they become free to choose any other – you fling them to the fury of the tempest – you must call on them to unhouse themselves of the established Constitution, and to fashion to themselves another. I again ask, is this the time for an experiment of this nature? Thank God, the people have manifested no such wish; so far as they have spoken, their voice is decidedly against this daring innovation. You know that no voice has been uttered in its favour, and you cannot be infatuated enough to take confidence from the silence which prevails in some parts of the Kingdom. If you know how to appreciate that silence, it is more formidable than the most clamorous opposition – you may be rived and shivered by the lightning before you hear the peal of the thunder.

But, Sir, we are told that we should discuss this question with calmness and composure. I am called on to surrender my birthright and my honour, and I am told I should be calm and should be composed. National pride! Independence of our country! These, we are told by the Minister, are only vulgar topics fitted for the meridian of the mob, but unworthy to be mentioned to such an enlightened assembly as this; they are trinkets and gewgaws fit to catch the fancy of childish and unthinking people like you, Sir, or like your predecessor in that chair, but utterly unworthy the consideration of this house, or of the matured understanding of the noble lord who condescends to instruct it. Gracious God! We see a Pery re-ascending from the tomb, and raising his awful voice to warn us against the surrender of our freedom, and we see that the proud and virtuous feelings which warmed the breast of that aged and venerable man are only calculated to excite the contempt of this young philosopher, who has been transplanted from the nursery to the Cabinet to outrage the feelings and understanding of the country . . .

Let me ask again, how was the rebellion put down? By the zeal and loyalty of the gentlemen of Ireland rallying round – what? – a reed shaken by the winds; a wretched apology for a minister, who neither knew how to give nor where to seek protection? No! but round the laws and Constitution and independence of the country. What were the affections and motives that called us into action? To protect our families, our properties, and our liberties. What were the antipathies by which we were excited? Our abhorrence of French principles and French ambition.

What was it to us that France was a republic? I rather rejoiced when I saw the ancient despotism of France put down. What was it to us that she dethroned her monarch? I admired the virtues and wept for the suffering of the man; but as a nation it affected us not. The reason I took up arms, and am ready still to bear them against France, is because she intruded herself upon our domestic concerns – because with the rights of man and the love of freedom on her tongue, I see that she has the lust of dominion in her heart – because wherever she has placed her foot, she has erected her throne; and to be her friend or her ally is to be her tributary or her slave.

Let me ask, is the present conduct of the British minister calculated to augment or to transfer that antipathy? No, Sir, I will be bold to say, that licentious and impious France, in all the unrestrained excesses which anarchy and atheism have given birth to, has not committed a more insidious act against her enemy than is now attempted by the professed champion of civilized Europe against a friend and an ally in the hour of her calamity and distress – at a moment when our country is filled with British troops – when the loyal men of Ireland are fatigued with their exertions to put down rebellion; efforts in which they had succeeded before these troops arrived – whilst our Habeas Corpus Act is suspended – whilst trials by court martial are carrying on in many parts of the kingdom – whilst the people are taught to think that they have no right to meet or to deliberate, and whilst the great body of them are so palsied by their fears, and worn down by their exertions, that even this vital question is scarcely able to rouse them from their lethargy – at the moment when we are distracted by domestic dissensions – dissensions artfully kept alive as the pretext for our present subjugation and the instrument of our future thraldom!

Yes, Sir, I thank administration for this measure. They are, without intending it, putting an end to our dissensions – through this black cloud which they have collected over us, I see the light breaking in upon this unfortunate country. They have composed our dissensions – not by formenting the embers of a lingering and subdued rebellion – not by hallooing the Protestant against the Catholic and the Catholic against Protestant – not by committing the north against the south – not by inconsistent appeals to local or to party prejudices; no, but by the removal of this atrocious conspiracy against the liberties of Ireland, they have subdued every petty and subordinate distinction. They have united every rank and description of men by the pressure of this grand and momentous subject; and I tell them that they will see every honest and independent man in Ireland rally round her Constitution, and merge every other consideration in his opposition to this ungenerous and odious measure. For my own part, I will resist it to the last gasp of my existence and with the last drop of my blood, and when I feel the hour of my dissolution approaching, I will, like the father of Hannibal, take my children to the altar and swear them to eternal hostility against the invaders of their country's freedom.

Sir, I shall not detain you by pursuing this question through the topics which it so abundantly offers. I shall be proud to think my name be handed down to posterity in the same roll with these disinterested patriots who have successfully resisted the enemies of their country. Successfully I trust it will be. In all events, I have my exceeding great reward; I shall bear in my heart the consciousness of having done my duty, and in the hour of death I shall not be haunted by the reflection of having basely sold or meanly abandoned the liberties of my native land. Can every man who gives his vote on the other side this night lay his hand upon his heart and make the same declaration? I hope so. It will be well for his own peace. The indignation and abhorrence of his countrymen will not accompany him through life, and the curses of his children will not follow him to his grave.

In 1800, the Act of Union was passed by the Irish and British Parliaments. The Irish Parliament was disbanded and one hundred Irish Parliamentarians became members of the new British and Irish Parliament in London.

Henry Grattan
26 May 1800

THE ACT OF UNION, in 1800 brought about the Parliamentary Union between Great Britain and Ireland, and the abolition of the Irish Parliament.

The British Prime Minister, William Pitt the Younger, described the Union in the House of Commons as, 'the voluntary association of two great countries, which seek their common benefit in one Empire, in which each will retain its proportionate weight and importance, under the security of equal laws, reciprocal affection, and inseparable interests, and in which each will acquire a strength that will render it invincible.'

Grattan's last speech, in the Irish Parliament was made on 26 May, 1800, before the vote on the Act of Union, with the knowledge that many of the Irish Lords had already been bribed and intimidated by the British Government into voting for the Union.

Anti-Act of Union Speech

The Constitution may for a time be so lost; the character of the country cannot be so lost. The ministers of the Crown will, or may, perhaps, at length find that it is not so easy to put down for ever an ancient and respectable nation, by abilities, however great, and by power and by corruption, however irresistible. Liberty may repair her golden beams, and with redoubled heat animate the country: the cry of loyalty will not long continue against the principles of liberty; loyalty is a noble, a judicious and a capacious principle, but in these countries loyalty, distinct from liberty, is corruption, not loyalty.

The cry of the connection will not, in the end, avail against the principles of liberty. Connection is a wise and a profound policy; but connection without an Irish Parliament is connection without its own principle, without analogy of condition, without the pride of honour that should attend it; is innovation, is peril, is subjugation – not connection. The cry of disaffection will not, in the end, avail against the principles of liberty.

Identification is a solid and imperial maxim, necessary for the preservation of freedom, necessary for that of empire; but, without union of hearts – with a separate government – and without a separate Parliament, identification is extinction, is dishonour, is conquest – not identification.

Yet I do not give up the country. I see her in a swoon, but she is not dead. Though in her tomb she lies helpless and motionless, still there is on her lips a spirit of life, and on her cheek a glow of beauty

> 'Thou art not conquered; beauty's ensign yet
> Is crimson in thy lips, and in thy cheeks,
> And death's pale flag is not advanced there.'

While a plank of the vessel sticks together, I will not leave her. Let the courtier present his flimsy sail, and carry the light bark of his faith, with every new breath of wind. I will remain anchored here, with fidelity to the fortune of my country, faithful to her freedom, faithful to her fall.

Daniel O'Connell
15 August 1843

THE REPEAL Association was founded in 1840, under the careful control of Daniel O'Connell. Its primary objective was the repeal of the Act of Union.

In the course of 1843, O'Connell spoke at a series of vast, public demonstrations throughout Ireland. At these meetings he asserted that only a native Irish Parliament under the Crown of Britain and Ireland could bring about the measures needed to improve the conditions of everyday life in Ireland.

Though a man in his sixties, he spoke at over thirty such meetings in 1843 and to such effect that the British Government, under Robert Peel, felt 'the empire shaken to its foundations.'

The largest of all these 'monster meetings' was held at Tara, County Meath, the seat of the ancient High Kings of Ireland. The 'Times' reported that one million people came to see and hear O'Connell. After his carriage had spent many hours moving through the crowds to get to the hill, he finally addressed the meeting from the summit. When the cheering subsided, he began:

Speech at Tara

It would be the extreme of affectation in me to suggest that I have not some claims to be the leader of this majestic meeting. It would be worse than affectation – it would be drivelling folly, if I were not to feel the awful responsibility of the part I have taken in this majestic movement imposed upon me (*hear, hear.*) I feel responsibility to my country, responsibility to my Creator. Yes, I feel the tremulous nature of that responsibility – Ireland is aroused, is aroused from one end to another. Her multitudinous population have but one expression and one wish, and that is the extinction of the Union, the restoration of her nationality.

Suddenly, someone cried, 'there will be no compromise.'

Who is it that talks of compromise? I am not here for the purpose of making anything like a schoolboy's attempt at declamatory eloquence; I am not here to revive in your recollection any of those poetic imaginings respecting the spot on which we stand, and which have really become as familiar as household words; I am not here to exaggerate the historical importance of the spot on which we are congregated – but it is impossible to deny that Tara has historical recollections that give to it an importance, relatively, to other portions of the land, and deserves to be so considered by every person who comes to it for political purposes, and gives it an elevation and point of impression in the public mind that no other part of Ireland can possibly have. History may be tarnished by exaggeration, but the fact is undoubted that we are at Tara of the Kings. We are on the spot where the monarchs of Ireland were elected, and where the chieftains of Ireland bound themselves by the sacred pledge of honour and the tie of religion to stand by their native land against the Danes or any other stranger [*cheers*]. This is emphatically the spot from which emanated the social power – the legal authority – the right to dominion over the furthest extremes of the island, and the power of concentrating the force of the entire nation for the purpose of national defence. On this important spot I have an important duty to perform. I here protest in the face of my country, in the face of my Creator – in the face of Ireland and her God, I protest against the continuance of the unfounded and unjust Union. My proposition to Ireland is that the Union is not binding upon us; it is not binding, I mean, upon conscience it is void in principle. It is void as matter of right and it is void unconstitutional law. I protest everything that is sacred, without being profane, to the truth of my assertion there is really no union between the two countries.

My proposition is that there was no authority vested in any person to pass the Act of Union. I deny the authority of the Act, I deny the competency of the two legislatures to pass that Act. The English legislature had no such competency – that must be admitted by every person. The Irish legislature had no such competency; and I arraign the Union, therefore, on the ground of the incompetency of the bodies that passed it. No authority could render it binding but the authority of the Irish people, consulted individually through the counties, cities, towns, and villages; and if the people of Ireland called for the Union, then it was binding on them, but there was no other authority that could make it binding. The Irish Parliament had no such authority; they were elected to make laws and not legislatures, and it had no right to the authority which alone belonged to the people of Ireland. The trustee might as well usurp the right of the person who trusts him; the servant might as well usurp the power of the master; the Irish Parliament were elected as our trustees, we were their masters – they were but our servant and they had no right to transfer us to any other power on the face of the earth. This doctrine is manifest, and would be admitted by every person; if it were applied to England, would any person venture to assert that the Parliament of England should have the power to transfer its privileges to make laws from England to the legislative chamber of France. Would any person be so insane as to admit it, and that insanity would not be misstated even if they were allowed to send over their representatives to France? Yes, every person would admit in that case that the Union was void.

I have no higher affection for England than for France. They are both foreign authorities to me. The highest legal authority in England has declared us aliens in blood, aliens in religion, and aliens in language from the English. Let no person groan him – I thank him for the honesty of the expression. I never heard of any other act of honesty on his part, and the fact of his having committed one act of honesty ought to recommend him to your good graces. I can refer you to the principle of constitutional law, and to Locke on government, to show that the Irish Parliament had no power or authority to convey itself away. I will only detain you on that point by citing the words of Lord Chancellor Plunket. He declared in the Irish House of Commons that they had no right to transfer the power of legislation from the country. He called upon them to have his words taken down, and he defied the power of Lord Castlereagh to have him censured for the expression, limiting the authority of Parliament. He said to them that they could not transfer their authority, that the maniacal suicide might as well imagine that the blow by which he destroyed his miserable body could annihilate his immortal soul, as they to imagine they could not annihilate the soul of Ireland, her constitutional right. The illustration is a happy one. I am here the representative of the Irish nation, and in the name of that great, that virtuous, that moral, temperate, brave, and religious nation, I proclaim the Union a nullity, for it is a nullity in point of right. Never was any measure carried by such iniquitous means as the Union was carried. The first thing that taints it in its origin, and makes it, even if it were a compact, utterly void, is the fraud committed in formenting discord in the country, and encouraging the rebellion until it broke out, and in making that rebellion and the necessity for crushing it the means of taking from Ireland her constitution and her liberties. There was this second fraud committed on her, that at the time of the passing of the Act of Union Ireland had no legal protection; the habeas corpus was suspended, martial law was proclaimed, trial by jury was at an end, and the lives and liberties of all the King's subjects in Ireland were at the mercy of the courts martial. Those among you who were old enough at the time remember when the shriek from the triangle was heard from every village and town, and when the troops would march out from Trim and lay desolate the country for nine or ten miles around. The military law was established in all its horrors throughout every district of the country and the people were trampled in the dust under the feet of the yeomanry, army, and fencibles. The next fraudulent device to which England had recourse in order to carry this infamous measure, and to promote her own prosperity on the ruins of Irish nationality, was to take the most effective means in order to prevent the Irish people from meeting to remonstrate against the insult and the injury which was about to be inflicted upon them. The Union was void no less from the utter incompetency of the contracting parties to enter into any such contract than by reason of the fact, that it was carried into operation by measures most iniquitous, atrocious and illegal; the habeas corpus act was suspended, torture, flogging, pitch caps, and imprisonment were the congenial agencies whereby England endeavored to carry her infamous designs, and executions upon the gallows for no other crime than that of being suspected to be suspicious, were of daily occurrence in every part of the kingdom. Thus it was that they endeavored to crush the expression of the people's feelings, whom they resolved to plunder and degrade. The people were not permitted to assemble together for the purpose of remonstrating against the Union. Meetings convened by the officers of justice – by the high sheriffs of counties, were dispersed at the point of the bayonet. The people were not permitted to meet together for remonstrance, but they got up petitions in every direction, to testify their feelings upon the subject, and although no less than seven hundred and seven thousand signatures were signed to petitions against the Union, despite of all the corrupt influence of the Government, more than three thousand wretches could not be found to sign a petition in favour of the measure.

The next impeachment which I bring against the Union is that it was brought about not only by physical force, but by bribery the most unblushing and corruption the most profligate. One million two hundred and seventy-five thousand pounds were expended upon the purchase of rotten boroughs alone, and no less a sum than two millions of money were lavished upon peculation unparalleled, and bribery the most enormous and most palpable that ever yet disgraced the annals of humility. There was not an office, civil, military, or ecclesiastical in the county, which was not flung open to due Unionist as the pence and wages of his political depravity. Six or seven judges bought their seats upon the bench by giving in their adhesion to the Union; and having no claim to wear the ermine other than that which was to be derived from the fact of their being recreants to their country, they continued in right of this during their lives to inflict the effects of their iniquity upon the people whom they betrayed. Twelve bishops obtained their seats by voting for the Union, for the spirit of corruption spared nothing. Men were made prelates, generals, admirals, commissioners for supporting the ministry in this infamous design, and every office in the revenue and customs was placed at the disposal of those who were base enough to sell their country for a mess of porridge. In fact, corruption was never known to have been carried before or since to such excess in any country of the world, and if such a contract, if contract it could be called, was to be binding on the Irish nation, there was no longer any use for honesty or justice in the world. But strong as was the influence of corruption on the human mind, the victory which the English ministry achieved was slow and by no means easy of accomplishment, for the intimidation to the death upon the one hand, and bribery on the other, were impotent to procure a majority for them in the Irish House of Commons in the first session, when the bill was introduced. On the contrary, when the first attempt was made to frustrate our liberties, there was a majority of eleven against the Union Bill. But the despoiler was not easy to be foiled, nor was he apt to be disheartened by a single failure. The work of corruption was set on foot with redoubled energy, and the wretches who were not so utterly abandoned as to suffer themselves to be bribed for the direct and positive purpose of giving their vote for the Union, accepted bribes on the condition of withdrawing from the House altogether, and accordingly they vacated their seats, and in their place stepped in Englishmen and Scotchmen who knew nothing of Ireland, and who were not impeded by any conscientious scruples whatever from giving their unqualified sanction to any plot of the English, how infamous so ever, to oppress and plunder the country. By these accumulated means the Union was carried and the fate of Ireland sealed. But the monster evil of the Union is the financial robbery which by its means was practiced upon Ireland. A scandalous injustice thus inflicted would be in itself sufficient even in the absence of other arguments – even if other arguments were wanting – to render the Union void and of no effect. At the passing of that fatal act – badge of our ruin and disgrace – Ireland owed only twenty millions, England owed four hundred and forty six millions, and the equitable terms on which the contract was based, whereby both countries were to be allied and identified – identified indeed! – were these, that England was generously to undertake the liability of one-half of her national debt, on condition that we would undertake the responsibility of one-half of hers. This is not a befitting time nor season to enter into minute details relative to the particulars of this financial swindle, but I may be permitted to direct your attention to this very obvious fact, that whereas England has only doubled her debt since the passing of the Union, the increase of the national debt of Ireland during the same period cannot with justice be estimated on a different ratio, and that consequently Ireland, at the very highest calculation, cannot in realist and as of her own account, owe a larger sum than forty millions; and I will tell you, my friends, that never will we consent to pay one shilling more of a national debt than that. I say it in the name and on behalf of the Irish nation. But I will tell you this, as a secret, and you may rely upon it as a truth, that in point of fact we do not owe one farthing more than thirty millions; and in proof of the truth of this assertion, I beg leave to refer you to a work published by a very near and dear relative of mine – my third son, the member for Kilkenny – who, by the most accurate statistical calculations, and by a process of argument intelligible to the humblest intellect, has made the fact apparent to the world, that according to the terms of honest and equitable dealing, as between both countries, Ireland's proportion of the national debt cannot be set down at a larger sum than I state, thirty millions. I am proud that there is a son of mine who, after the Repeal shall have been carried, will be able to meet the cleverest English financier of them all, foot to foot and hand to hand, and prove by arguments most incontestable how grievous and intolerable is the injustice which was inflicted upon our country in this respect by the Union. The project of robbing Ireland by joining her legislatively with England was no new scheme which entered the minds of the English for the first time about the year, 1800. It was a project which was a favourite theme of dissertation with all the English essayists for years previous to the period when it was carried into practical effect, and the policy towards Ireland, which their literary men were continually urging upon the English people for their adoption, was similar to that of the avaricious housewife who killed the goose who laid her golden eggs. Yes, such was the course they pursued towards Ireland, and you will deserve the reputation of being the lineal descendants of that goose if you be such ganders as not to declare in a voice of thunder that no longer shall this system of plunder be permitted to continue.

My next impeachment of the Union is founded upon the disastrous effects which have resulted therefrom to our commercial and manufacturing interests, as well as to our general national interests. Previous to the Union, the county Meath was filled with the seats of noblemen at Semen! What a contrast does its present state present! I, on Monday read at the Association a list of the deserted mansions which are now to be found ruined and desolate in your country. Even the spot where the Duke of Wellington – famed the world over for his detestation of his country – drew his first breath, instead of bearing a noble castle, or splendid mansion, presented the aspect of ruin and desolation, and briars and nettles adequately marked the place that produced him. The county of Meath was at one time studded thickly with manufactories in every direction, and an enormous sum was expended yearly in wages, but here, as in every other district of the country, the eye was continually shocked with sights which evidenced with but too great eloquence the lamentable decay which has been entailed upon our country by the Union. The linen trade at one period kept all Ulster in a state of affluence and prosperity. Kilkenny was for ages celebrated for its extensive blanket manufactures and Cork also – and Carrick-on-Suir, and in a thousand other localities, too numerous to mention, thousands were kept in constant and lucrative employment, at various branches of national industry, from year's end to year's end, before the passing of the Union. But this is no longer the case, and one man is not now kept in employment for a thousand who were employed before the Union. The report of the English commissioners themselves has declared this appalling fact to the world that one-third of our population are in a state of actual destitution; and yet, in the face of all this, men may be found who, claiming to themselves the character of political honesty, stand up and declare themselves in favour of the continuance of the Union. It is no bargain; it was a base swindle. Had it, indeed, been a fair bargain, the Irish would have continued faithful to it to the last, regardless of the injuries which it might have entailed upon them for the Irish people have been invariably faithful to their contracts; whereas England never yet made a promise which she did not violate, nor ever entered into a contract which she did not shamelessly and scandalously outrage. Even the Union itself, beneficial as it is to England, is but a living lie to Ireland. Everybody now admits the mischief that the Union has produced to Ireland. The very fact of its not being a compact is alone sufficient to nullify the Union, and on that ground I here proclaim, in the name of the Irish nation, that it is null and void. It is a union of legislators, but not a union of nations. Are you and I one bit more of Englishmen now than we were twenty or forty years ago? If we had a Union would not Ireland have the same parliamentary franchise that is enjoyed by England? But calling it a Union, could anything be more unjust on the part of England than to give her own people a higher and more extensive grade of franchise? And to the Irish people a more limited and an extinguishing and perishing franchise. She has given to her people an extended municipal reform, and to Ireland a wretched and miserable municipal reform. Even within the last week a plan was brought forward by Lord Elliot and the [*sneers*] Attorney-General Smith, that will have the effect of depriving one-third of those who now enjoy the franchise of its possession. No, the Union is void, but it is more peremptorily void on the ground of the ecclesiastical revenues of the counts being left to support a church of a small portion of the people. In England the ecclesiastical revenues of the country are given to the clergy that the majority of the people believe to teach the truth. In Scotland the ecclesiastical revenues are, or at least were up to a late period, paid to the clergy of the majority of the people; but the Irish people are compelled to pay the clergy of a small minority, not amounting to more than the one-tenth of the people of the entire island. The Union was effected against all constitutional principle by the most atrocious fraud – by the most violent and most iniquitous exercise of force, by the most abominable corruption and bribery, by the shifting of Irish members out of their seats, and the putting of Englishmen and Scotchmen into their places; and that was followed by the destruction of our commerce, by the annihilation of our manufactures, by the depreciation of our farmers – and you know I speak the truth when I talk of the depression of the farming interests by financial robbery, on an extensive scale to be sure, but a robbery on that very account, only the more iniquitous, fiendish, and harsh. I contend, therefore, that the Union is a nullity; but do I, on that account, advise you to turn out against it? No such thing. I advise you to act quietly and peaceably and in no other way.

Then a voice cried, 'any way you like.'

Remember that my doctrine is that 'the man who commits a crime gives strength to the enemy,' and you should not act in any manner that would strengthen the enemies of your country. You should act peaceably and quietly, but firmly and determinedly. You may be certain that your cheers here today will be conveyed to England.

The vast assemblage here commenced cheering in the most deafening and enthusiastic manner, and the distant lines of people on the limits of the assembly were seen waving their hats and handkerchiefs in response.

Yes, the overwhelming majestic of your multitude will be taken to England, and will have its effect there. The Duke of Wellington began by threatening us. He talked of civil war, but he does not say a single word of that now. He is now getting eyelet holes made in the old barracks, and only think of an old general doing such a thing, just as if we were going to break our heads against stone walls. I am glad to find that a great quantity of brandy and biscuits has been latterly imported, and I hope the poor soldiers get some of them. But the Duke of Wellington is not now talking of attacking us, and I am glad of it; but I tell him this – I mean no disrespect to the brave, the gallant, and the good conducted soldiers that compose the Queen's army; and all of them that we have in this country are exceedingly well conducted. There is not one of you that has a single complaint to make against any of them. They are the bravest army in the world and therefore I do not mean to disparage them at all, but I feel it to be a fact, that Ireland, roused as she is at the present moment, would, if they made war upon us, furnish women enough to beat the entire of the Queen's forces. At the last fight for Ireland, when she was betrayed by having confided in England's honour, but oh! English honour will never again betray our land, for the man will deserve to be betrayed who would confide again in England. I would as soon think of confiding in the cousin-German of a certain personage having two horns and a hoof. At that last battle, the Irish soldiers, after three days fighting, being attacked by fresh troops, faltered and gave way, and 1,500 of the British army entered the breach. The Irish soldiers were fainting and retiring when the women of Limerick threw themselves between the contending forces, and actually stayed the progress of the advancing enemy. I am stating matter of history to you, and the words I use are not mine, but those of Parson Story, the chaplain of King William, who describes the siege, and who admits that the Limerick women drove back the English soldiers from fifteen to thirty paces. Several of the women were killed, when a shriek of horror resounded from the ranks of the Irish. They cried out, 'Let us rather die to the last man than that our women should be injured,' and then they threw themselves forward, and, made doubly valiant by the bravery of the women, they scattered the Saxon and the Dane before them. Yes, I have women enough in Ireland to beat them if necessary; but, my friends, it is idle to imagine that any statesman ever existed who could resist the cry that Ireland makes for justice . . .

We will break no law. See how we have accumulated the people of Ireland for this Repeal Year. When, on the 2nd of January, I ventured to call it the Repeal Year, every person laughed at me. Are they laughing now? It is our turn to laugh at present. Before twelve months more, the Parliament will be in College Green. I said the Union did not take away from the people of Ireland their legal rights. I told you that the Union did not deprive the people of that right, or take away the authority to have self-legislation. It has not lessened the prerogatives of the Crown, or taken away the rights of the Sovereign, and amongst them is the right to call her Parliament wherever the People are entitled to it, and the people of Ireland are entitled to have it in Ireland. And the Queen has only tomorrow to issue her writs and get the Chancellor to seal them, and if Sir Edward Sugden does not sign them she will soon get an Irishman that will, to revive the Irish Parliament. The towns which sold their birthright have no right to be reckoned amongst the towns sending members to Parliament. King James the First, in one day, created forty boroughs in Ireland, and the Queen has the same right as her predecessor to do so. We have a list of the towns to return members according to their population, and the Queen has only to order writs to issue, and to have honest ministers to advise her to issue those wants, and the Irish Parliament is revived by its own energy, and the force of the Sovereign's prerogative. I will only require the Queen to exercise her perogative, and the Irish people will obtain their nationality again. If, at the present moment, the Irish Parliament was in existence, even as it was in 1800, is there a coward amongst you – is there a wretch amongst you so despicable that would not die rather than allow the Union to pass?

Another voice interrupted him, 'Yes, to the last man.'

Let every man who, if we had an Irish Parliament, would rather die than allow the Union to pass lift up his hands. Yes, the Queen will call that Parliament; you may say it is the act of her ministry, if you please. To be sure it would be the act of her ministry, and the people of Ireland are entitled to have their friends appointed to the ministry. The Irish Parliament will then assemble, and I defy all the generals, old and young, and all the old women in pantaloons. Nay, I defy all the chivalry of the earth to take away that Parliament from us again. Well, my friends, may I ask you to obey me in the course of conduct I point out to you, when I dismiss you to-day; when you have heard the resolutions put, I am sure you will go home with the same tranquillity with which you came here, every man of you; and if I wanted you again, would you not come again to Tara Hill for me? Remember me, I lead you into no peril. If danger existed, it would arise from some person who would attack us, for we will attack nobody; and if that danger exists you will not find me in the rear rank. The Queen will be able to restore our Parliament to us. The absentee drains, which caused the impoverishment of the country, will be at an end – the wholesale ejectment of tenants and turning them out on the highway the murdering of tenants by the landlords shall be at an end. The rights of the landlords will be respected, but their duties shall be enforced – an equitable tenure will take the place of the cruel tyranny of the present code of laws, and the protection of the occupying tenants of Ireland be inscribed on the banner of Repeal. Carry home with you my advice. Let there be peace and quiet, law and order, and let every one of you enroll yourselves Repealers – men, women, and children. Give me three millions of Repealers, and I will soon have them. The next step is being taken, and I announce to you from this spot, that all the magistrates that have been deprived of the communion of the peace shall be appointed by the Association to settle all the disputes and differences in their neighbourhood. Keep out of the petty sessions court, and go to them on next Monday. We will submit a plan to choose persons to be arbitrators to settle the differences of the people without expense, and I call upon every man that wishes to be thought the friend of Ireland, to have his disputes settled by the arbitrators, and not again to go to the petty sessions. We shall shortly have the preservative society to arrange the means of procuring from her Majesty the exercise of her prerogative, and I believe I am able to announce to you that twelve months cannot possibly elapse without having a hurrah for our Parliament in College Green. Remember, I pronounce the Union to be null – to be obeyed, as an injustice must be obeyed, when it is supported by law until we have the royal authority to set the matter right, and substitute our own Parliament. I delight at having this day presided over such an assemblage on Tara Hill. Those shouts that burst from you were enough to recall to life the Kings and Chiefs of Ireland. I almost fancy that the spirits of the mighty dead are hovering over us, that the ancient Kings and Chiefs of Ireland are from yonder clouds listening to us. Oh, what a joyous and cheering sound is conveyed in the chirrup for Old Ireland! It is the most beautiful, the most fertile – the most abundant, the most productive country on the face of the earth. It is a lovely land, indented with noble harbours, intersected with transcendent, translucent streams divided by mighty estuaries. Its harbours are open at every hour for every tide, and are sheltered from every storm that can blow from any quarter of Heaven. Oh, yes, it is a lovely land and where is the coward that would not dare to die for it! Yes, our country exhibits the extreme of civilization, and your majestic movement is already the admiration of the civilised world. No other country could produce such an amount of physical force, coupled with so much decorum and propriety of conduct. Many thousands of persons assembled together, and, though they have force sufficient to carry any battle that ever was fought, they separate with the tranquillity of schoolboys breaking up in the afternoon. I wish you could read my heart, to see how deeply the love of Ireland is engraven upon it, and let the people of Ireland, who stood by me so long, stand by me a little longer, and Ireland shall be a nation again.

Thomas Francis Meagher
28 July 1846

IN 1846, with the famine worsening in Ireland, the Tory government, under Robert Peel, attempted to pass a Coercion Bill to deal with the problem of agrarian violence. In response, the Repeal Association, under the leadership of Daniel O'Connell came to an agreement with the Whig opposition and together they obstructed the passing of the Bill. This caused great anger amongst the younger sections of the Association. These Young Irelanders, as they were known, went so far as to say that it was a betrayal of Repeal.

As tension between O'Connell and the Young Irelanders, grew, a series of fiery debates took place on the issue of the alliance with the Whigs and on the hypothetical subject of the use of physical force.

With the issues still unresolved, a second series of debates took place on 27 and 28 July. This time without the ailing O'Connell. On the last day the divisions in the Repeal Association seemed to be lessening until the Young Irelander, Thomas Francis Meagher rose to address the hostile audience:

Sword Speech

My Lord Mayor, I will commence as Mr. Mitchel concluded, by an allusion to the Whigs. I fully concur with my friend, that the most comprehensive measures which the Whig Minister may propose will fail to lift this country up to that position which she has the right to occupy, and the power to maintain. A Whig Minister, I admit, may improve the province but he will not restore the nation. Franchises, tenant compensation bills, liberal appointments, may ameliorate but they will not exalt. They may meet the necessities – they will not call forth the abilities of the country. The errors of the past may be repaired – the hopes of the future will not be fulfilled. With a vote in one pocket, a lease in the

other, a full 'justice' before him at the petty sessions-in the shape of a
'restored magistrate' – the humblest peasant may be told that he is free;
but, my lord, he will not have the character of a freeman, his spirit to
dare, his energy to act. From the stateliest mansion down to the poorest
cottage in the land, the inactivity, the meanness, the debasement, which
provincialism engenders, will be perceptible . . .

   A good government may, indeed, redress the grievances of an injured
people; but a strong people can alone build up a great nation. To be
strong, a people must be self-reliant, self-ruled, self-sustained. The
dependence of one people upon another, even for the benefits of legislation, is the deepest source of national weakness. By an unnatural law
it exempts a people from their just duties, their just responsibilities.
When you exempt a people from these duties, from these responsibilities,
you generate in them a distrust in their own powers. Thus you enervate,
if you do not utterly destroy, that spirit which a sense of these responsibilities is sure to inspire, and which the fulfillment of these duties
never fails to invigorate. Where this spirit does not actuate, the country
may be tranquil – it will not be prosperous. It may exist; it will not
thrive. It may hold together; it will not advance. Peace it may enjoy –
for peace and serfdom are compatible. But, my lord, it will neither
accumulate wealth, nor win a character. It will neither benefit mankind
by the enterprise of its merchants, nor instruct mankind by the examples
of its statesmen. I make these observations, for it is the custom of some
moderate politicians to say, that when the Whigs have accomplished
the pacification of the country, there will be little or no necessity for
Repeal. My lord, there is something else, there is everything else, to be
done when the work of 'pacification' has been accomplished – and here
it is hardly necessary to observe, that the prosperity of a country is,
perhaps, the sole guarantee for its tranquillity, and that the more universal
the prosperity the more permanent will be the repose. But the Whigs
will enrich as well as pacify! Grant it, my lord. Then do I conceive that
the necessity for Repeal will augment. Great interests demand great
safeguards. The prosperity of a nation requires the protection of a senate.
Hereafter a national senate may require the protection of a national
army. So much for the extraordinary affluence with which we are threatened; and which it is said by gentlemen on the opposite shore of the
Irish sea, will crush this Association, and bury the enthusiasts who
clamour for Irish nationality, in a sepulchre of gold. This prediction,
however, is feebly sustained by the ministerial programme that has lately

appeared. On the evening of the 16th, the Whig Premier, in answer to a question that was put to him by the member for Finsbury, Mr. Duncombe, is reported to have made this consolatory announcement:

'We consider that the social grievances of Ireland are those which are most prominent and to which it is most likely to be in our power to afford, not a complete and immediate remedy, but some remedy, some kind of improvement, so that some kind of hope may be entertained that, some ten or twelve years hence, the country will, by the measures we undertake, be in a far better state with respect to the frightful destitution and misery which now prevail in that country. We have that practical object in view.'

After that most consolatory announcement, my lord, let those who have the patience of Job and the poverty of Lazarus, continue in good faith to wait on Providence and the Whigs continue to entertain some kind of hope that if not a complete and immediate remedy, at least some remedy, some improvement will place this country in a far better state than it is at present, some ten or twelve years hence. After that, let those who prefer the periodic boons of a Whig Government to that which would be the abiding blessing of an Irish Parliament – let those who deny to Ireland what they assert for Poland – let those who would inflict, as Henry Grattan said, an eternal disability upon this country, to which Providence has assigned the largest facilities for power – let those who would ratify the 'base swap,' as Mr. Sheil once stigmatised the Act of Union, and who would stamp perfection upon that deed of perfidy let such men 'Plod on in sluggish misery, Rotting from sire to sire, from age to age, Proud of their trampled nature.'

But we, my lord, who are assembled in this hall, and in whose hearts the Union has not bred the slave's disease – we who have not been imperialised – we are here, with the hope to undo that work, which, forty-six years ago, dishonoured the ancient peerage, and subjugated the people of our country.

My lord, to assist the people of Ireland to undo that work I came to this hall. I came to repeal the Act of Union. I came here for nothing else. Upon every other question, I feel myself at perfect liberty to differ from each and every one of you. Upon questions of finance, questions of a religious character, questions of an educational character, questions of municipal policy, questions that may arise from the proceedings of the legislature – upon all these questions, I feel myself at perfect liberty to differ from each and every one of you. Yet more, my lord, I maintain that it is my right to express my opinion upon each of these questions, if necessary. The right of free discussion I have here upheld. In the exercise of that right I have differed, sometimes, from the leader of this Association, and would do so again. That right I will not abandon – I shall maintain it to the last. In doing so, let me not be told that I seek to undermine the influence of the leader of this Association and am insensible to his services. My lord, I am grateful for his services, and will uphold his just influence. This is the first time I have spoken in these terms of that illustrious man, in this hall . . .

No, my lord, I am not ungrateful to the man who struck the fetters off my arms, whilst I was yet a child, and by whose influence, my father – the first Catholic who did so for two hundred years sat – for the last two years, in the civic chair of an ancient city. But, my lord, the same God who gave to that great man the power to strike down an odious ascendancy in this country, and enabled him to institute in this land the glorious law of religious equality – the same God gave to me a mind that is my own – a mind that has not been mortgaged to the opinions of any man, or any set of men a mind that I was to use and not surrender.

My lord, in the exercise of that right which I have here endeavoured to uphold – a right which this Association should preserve inviolate, if it desires not to become a despotism. In the exercise of that right I have differed from Mr. O'Connell on previous occasions, and differ from him now. I do not agree with him in the opinion he entertains of my friend, Charles Gavan Duffy – that man whom I am proud indeed to call my friend – though he is a 'convicted prisoner,' and suffered for you in Richmond Prison. I do not think he is a 'maligner.' I do not think he has lost, or deserves to lose, the public favour. I have no more connection with the *Nation* than I have with the *Times*. I, therefore, feel no delicacy in appearing here this day in defence of its principles, with which I avow myself identified. My lord, it is to me a source of true delight and honest pride to speak this day in defence of that great journal. I do not fear to assume the position, exalted though it be, it is easy to maintain it. The character of that journal is above reproach. The ability that sustains it has won a European fame. The genius of which it is the offspring, the truth of which it is the oracle, have been recognised, my lord, by friends and foes. I care not how it may be assailed – I care not howsoever great may be the talent, howsoever high may be the position, of those who now consider it their duty to impeach its writings – I do think that it has won too splendid a reputation to lose the influence it has acquired. The people, whose enthusiasm has been kindled by the impetuous fire of its verse, and whose sentiments have been ennobled by the earnest purity of its teaching will not ratify the censure that has been pronounced upon it in this hall. Truth will have its day of triumph, as well as its day of trial; and I foresee that the fearless patriotism which, in those pages, has braved the prejudices of the day, to enunciate grand truths, will triumph in the end. My lord, such do I believe to be the character, such do I anticipate will be the fate of the principles that are now impeached. This brings me to what may be called the question of the day. Before I enter upon that question, however, I will allude to one observation which fell from the honourable member for Kilkenny [*John O'Connell*], and which may be said to refer to those who expressed an opinion that has been construed into a declaration of war.

The honourable gentleman said – in reference, I presume, to those who dissented from the resolutions of Monday – that 'Those who were loudest in their declarations of war, were usually the most backward in acting up to these declarations.'

My lord, I do not find fault with the honourable gentleman for giving expression to a very ordinary saying, but this I will say, that I did not volunteer the opinion he condemns – to the declaration of that opinion I was forced. You left me no alternative – I should compromise my opinion, or avow it. To be honest, I avowed it. I did not do so to brag, as they say. We have had too much of that bragging in Ireland. I would be the last to initiate the custom. Well, I dissented from those 'peace resolutions' – as they are called. Why so? In the first place, my lord, I conceive that there was not the least necessity for them. No member of this Association suggested an appeal to arms. No member of this Association advised it. No member of this Association would be so infatuated as to do so. In the existing circumstances of the country, an excitement to arms would be senseless and wicked, because irrational. To talk nowadays of repealing the Act of Union by force of arms would be to rhapsodize ... There might be a riot in the street – there would be no revolution in the country. The secretary, Mr. Crean, will far more effectually promote the cause of Repeal, by registering votes in Green Street than registering fire-arms in the Head Police Office. Conciliation Hall on Burgh Quay is more impregnable than a rebel camp on Vinegar Hill. The hustings at Dundalk will be more successfully stormed than the Magazine in the Park. The registry club, the reading room, the polling booths, these are the only positions in the country we can occupy. Voters' certificates, books, pamphlets, newspapers, these are the only weapons we can employ. Therefore, my lord, I cast my vote in favour of the peaceful policy of this Association. It is the only policy we can adopt. If that policy be pursued with truth, with courage, with fixed determination of purpose, I firmly believe it will succeed.

But, my lord, I dissented from the resolutions before us, for other reasons. I stated the first – I now come to the second. I dissented from them, for I felt that by assenting to them, I should have pledged myself to the unqualified repudiation of physical force in all countries, at all times, and under every circumstance. This I could not do. For, my lord, I do not abhor the use of arms in the vindication of national rights. There are times when arms will alone suffice, and when political call for a drop of blood, and many thousand drops of blood. Opinion, I admit, will operate against opinion. But as the honourable member for Kilkenny has observed, force must be used against force. The soldier is proof against an argument – but he is not proof against a bullet. The man that will listen to reason – let him be reasoned with, but it is the weaponed arm of the patriot that can alone prevail against battalioned despotism.

Then, my lord, I do not condemn the use of arms as immoral, nor do I conceive it profane to say, that the King of Heaven – the Lord of Hosts – the God of Battles, bestows His benediction upon those who unsheath the sword in the hour of a nation's peril.

From that evening on which, in the valley of Bethulia, He nerved the arm of the Jewish girl to smite the drunken tyrant in his tent, down to this day, in which He has blessed the insurgent chivalry of the Belgian priest, His Almighty hand hath ever been stretched forth from His throne of Light, to consecrate the flag of freedom – to bless the patriot's sword! Be it in the defence, or be it in the assertion of a people's liberty, I hail the sword as a sacred weapon; and if, my lord, it has sometimes taken the shape of the serpent and reddened the shroud of the oppressor with too deep a dye, like the anointed rod of the High Priest, it has at other times, and as often, blossomed into celestial flowers to deck the freeman's brow.

Abhor the sword and stigmatise the sword? No, my lord, for in the passes of the Tyrol it cut to pieces the banner of the Bavarian, and through those cragged passes struck a path to fame for the peasant insurrectionist of Inspruck!

Abhor the sword and stigmatise the sword? No, my lord, for, at its blow, a giant nation started from the waters of the Atlantic, and by its redeeming magic, and in the quivering of its crimson light, the crippled colony sprang into the attitude of a proud republic – prosperous, limitless, and invincible!

Abhor the sword – stigmatise the sword? No, my lord, for it swept the Dutch marauders out of the fine old towns of Belgium – scourged them back to their own phlegmatic swamps – and knocked their flag and sceptre, their laws and bayonets, into the sluggish waters of the Scheldt.

My lord, I learned that it was the right of a nation to govern herself – not in this hall, but upon the ramparts of Antwerp. This, the first article of a nation's creed, I learned upon those ramparts, where freedom was justly estimated, and the possession of the precious gift was purchased by the effusion of generous blood.

My lord, I honour the Belgians, I admire the Belgians, I love the Belgians, for their enthusiasm, their courage, their success, and I for one, will not stigmatise, for I do not abhor the means by which they obtained a Citizen King, a Chamber of Deputies.

At this point Mr. John O'Connell, the son of Daniel O'Connell, interrupted Meagher and declared that as these sentiments were against those of the founder of the Association, either Meagher and anyone supporting him should leave or else the Association should cease to be. There were angry shouts as another Young Irelander, Smith O'Brien, protested, and with the hall ringing to the sounds of enthusiastic shouts of, 'O'Connell! O'Connell!' Smith O'Brien abruptly left the hall, quickly followed by Meagher and the other Young Irelanders.

Isaac Butt
20 March 1874

THE NEWLY formed Home Rule League, under the leadership of Isaac Butt, won 59 out of the 103 Irish seats in the 1874 General Election. Despite their election successes the Home Rulers appeared almost unprepared for the parliamentary session when it opened in March, 1874. Their uncertainty and divided counsel were revealed in a meeting held in Dublin at which they committed themselves to forming a 'separate and distinct party' which would demand unity on only one single issue, Irish Home Rule. On all other issues, even those concerned with important Irish matters, Home Rule M.P. s were permitted to do as they pleased.

On 19 March, 1874, Queen Victoria's opening address to the British Parliament was read out by the Lord Chancellor, due to the Queen's ill health. In the course of the address, the Queen outlined the matters which she felt warranted 'grave consideration' in the coming Parliamentary session. Ireland was not mentioned in the address and so the next day Isaac Butt, the leader of the Home Rulers, proposed that the following amendment be added to the Speech from the throne:

'We also think it right humbly to represent to Your Majesty that dissatisfaction prevails very extensively in Ireland with the existing system of Government in that country, and that complaints are made that under that system the Irish people do not enjoy the full benefit of the Constitution and of the free principles of the law; and we humbly assure Your Majesty that we shall regard it as the duty of Parliament, on the earliest opportunity, to consider the origin of this dissatisfaction with a view to the removal of all just causes of discontent.'

He then went on to explain his amendment and the reason for it:

Home Rule Speech

I think there is one result of this dissatisfaction in Ireland, as exhibited by the recent elections, to which no person can be indifferent, and which no wise statesman can disregard. For the first time since the Act of Union, a majority – I will call it a decisive majority of Irish members – has been returned pledged to seek such a modification of the arrangements of the Union as would give to Irishmen in Ireland the right of managing their own affairs. I refer to this fact as evidence of dissatisfaction with the existing state of things. The Irish members who have been returned as Home Rulers are a decisive majority of the Irish representatives, and these have not been pledged to any mere vague declaration in favour of Home Rule. Those who have thought it right to endeavour to excite the attention of the country to the question of Home Rule have deliberately prepared and put before the country the plan contained in the Resolution, which, I venture to say, is framed in terms as clear and distinct as possible. We ask that Ireland shall have the management of all exclusively Irish affairs. Our plan would relieve the House of business which it has not the time, and, I may say, without disrespect, the capacity, to manage. Our plan would not in the slightest degree affect the perogative of the Crown or the stability of the Empire. We see no reason why an Irish Parliament could not manage exclusively Irish affairs without endangering the stability of the Empire. Has the grant of Parliaments to Canada, Australia, and other Colonies endangered the stability of the Empire? I believe I speak for every member who has been returned for Ireland on the Home Rule principle, when I say that we repudiate, in the strongest terms, the slightest wish to break up the unity of the Empire, or to bring about a collision between England and Ireland. We make no secret that they have all been elected to put forward the claim of Ireland to Home Rule, and, whether rightly or wrongly, we have come to an agreement among ourselves that we will act separately and independently of all existing political combinations in this House.

Whether this course is wise or not, it certainly is a new feature in Irish politics, and one that cannot be overlooked. We take up this position because we cannot acquiesce in anything that appears to us to imply that there is nothing in the state of Ireland that requires a remedy. In taking up this position I feel that we have taken a great responsibility upon ourselves, and I know the difficulty of our position.

I know the prejudice which the statement that we have determined to act independently of political combinations must naturally provoke, but I would ask this House to judge us by our conduct. We would pursue a course very different from anything like faction. I think I may base the first part of this Amendment upon the mere fact that a majority of the Irish members are returned expressly to endeavour to obtain for Ireland self-government. I know not what stronger proof can be given of the dissatisfaction existing in Ireland. This dissatisfaction has been constitutionally expressed. It has not been expressed by any disturbances, such as on former occasions have been noticed in the Queen's Speech. The Irish people have made this great political movement at a time when perfect tranquillity prevails throughout the country, and in all the agitation by which the result has been brought about there has been nothing unconstitutional or illegal. It has been expressed through that political franchise which has been given to them for the purpose of declaring their political opinion. Ireland at present is in a state of perfect tranquillity. The Assizes that have just closed have ended in every place with congratulations from the Judges upon the peaceableness of the different counties. In the last Summer Assizes in the city I have the honour to represent [*Limerick*], white gloves were given to the Judge, there not being a single prisoner to be tried. In the city of Cork, another great city in the south of Ireland, the very same thing occurred. I think the dissatisfaction in Ireland calls upon the House, I will not say to alter or reverse any policy that has been hitherto pursued with reference to Ireland, but certainly to review calmly and deliberately that policy, and ascertain the causes that have given rise to the dissatisfaction as to the management of Irish affairs by this House.

I think I need not go far to justify the second part of this Amendment, which affirms that the Irish people complain that they have not had the full benefits of the Constitution of England. I believe that at this moment Ireland is under a code of law which for severity has not its parallel in any European State. I will not speak for a moment of the law that prevails all over Ireland independently of the will of the Lord Lieutenant. The Lord Lieutenant has power, by proclamation, to make it illegal in any district to carry arms without a licence from a police magistrate; and any man having a gun, a pistol, or dagger is liable, unless he have a magistrate's licence, to imprisonment for two years. Of the thirty-two counties in Ireland, twenty-six have been proclaimed; the greater part of five others has been proclaimed; and there is just one county in Ireland, designated Tyrone, which is free from proclamation. Of the eight counties and cities, Carrickfergus only is free from proclamation. Now, this, I think, is a very startling state of things in Ireland. But more than this – at any time of the night, in any district where this law prevails, any policeman holding a warrant may demand to be admitted into any house in a proclaimed district, and may break open the door if admittance be refused, to search the house for arms; one hundred and nineteen of these general warrants are now in operation. Even this is not all. By proclamation the Lord Lieutenant may make it a crime to be out of doors after dark; while by another proclamation he can empower the police to seize any stranger; and a large portion of Ireland is at present under this law. By another proclamation any magistrate or police officer may demand admittance to any man's house, and ransack his papers for the purpose of comparing the handwriting with the handwriting of a threatening letter. Let it not be insinuated that these powers are never used. They are in daily and constant use. On one occasion a number of young men, one of whom was the son of a respectable merchant, determined to play 'Hamlet.' A police inspector, hearing of this, went to the theatre, arrested the young gentleman, and kept him in prison from Saturday night till Monday morning, when he was brought before a magistrate on a charge of having arms in his possession.

Cases like this are of frequent occurrence in Ireland. Under the pretext of searching for arms the police often seek to procure evidence of robberies and thefts, and these powers may be abused for many other purposes. I care not how these provisions may be defended, for I am sure they are not necessary.

This, I think, amply justified me in saying that Ireland does not enjoy the advantages of the British Constitution, nor the free principles of the English law. These powers are in constant use. With regard to arresting persons after sunset, I will tell the House what occurred on the fifth of the present month, according to an account which appeared in a very respectable newspaper. Early in the morning on that day a band went to attend an election meeting. In going through the town they played some tune which, however, was not a party tune – and the young people of the place were naturally attracted by the music. The crowd cheered, and then a policeman thought fit to think an offence had been committed against the law. Subsequently, the constable followed two young men, whom he knew perfectly well, a distance of two miles, and at six minutes to six o'clock, just after sunset, he told them they were out under suspicious circumstances. Thereupon he carried them to jail, where they were detained until they were brought before a magistrate the next day. Is this a state of things that ought to be endured in a country which is nominally under the British Constitution? The police in Ireland are in truth a military force. A high Conservative authority has said they are ten times as numerous as they need be for the purpose of keeping the peace; and the late Lord Mayo said that, by converting them into a military force, their efficiency as detectors of crime has been destroyed. The existing laws make the police the masters of the daily life of the people. Indeed the police have been termed an 'army of occupation' and when the civil power of a country is confided to such an army, the law is identified with the idea of conquest. But how does Ireland stand with regard to other matters? In the first place, the franchise is not the same as in England. When the late Reform Act was passed for England, household suffrage was introduced into the boroughs; whereas in Ireland no one can vote in a borough unless he have a rating qualification above £4. Moreover, the franchise in Ireland is encumbered by so many vexatious rules about rating that it is difficult for anybody to obtain a vote. In England, with a population of 26,000,000, as many as 1,200,000 enjoy the town franchise; while in Ireland, with a population of 5,000,000 there are just 50,000 town voters, of whom 30,000 are to be found in Belfast, Dublin, Cork and Limerick. In the whole of the rest of Ireland only 20,000 persons are admitted to what ought to be a popular franchise. Perhaps it may be said that the town population of Ireland is not so large as that of England. This is doubtless true, but in England one man out of every eight has the franchise, whereas in Ireland only one man out of every twenty has it. I will ask you whether the Irish people have the full benefit of the Constitution which has been established in England? It is a strange circumstance that the progress of Liberal opinions leads to this divergence between the English and the Irish franchises. Formerly they were the same in both countries, but shortly after the passing of Catholic Emancipation the forty shilling freeholders were abolished, and by the Reform Act the franchise in Ireland was made higher than in England. There is also a difference between the municipal franchise in the two countries. In Ireland – the poorer country, be it remembered – a man cannot take part in a municipal election unless he occupies a house worth £10 a year, but in England every householder has a right to vote. Again, how are fiscal affairs managed in Ireland? A Grand Jury is summoned in every county for the purpose of finding bills and discharging the criminal administration of justice, and the members of this body, who are not elected by the people, are made the guardians of the whole county expenditure, which amounts throughout the whole of Ireland to £1,200,000 a year. In fact, the whole system of Government in Ireland is based on distrust of the people, just as the whole system of Government in England is based upon trust of the people.

This circumstance, I think, justifies the complaint of the people of Ireland that they have not the benefit of the Constitution. In accordance with an old principle of the British Constitution, sheriffs in all towns are elected by the people, and this was the case in Ireland until Liberal legislation reformed the corporations, and took from them this power of electing sheriffs. Do not the facts I have mentioned justify me in asking the House to recede from its policy of coercion and distrust? The conclusion has been reluctantly forced upon me, that conceding to Ireland a Parliament to manage its own affairs is the only way to establish a perfect Constitutional Government in that country. I am persuaded that any candid Englishman who will examine the peculiar condition of Ireland, and the differences which exist between Ireland and England, will arrive, as I have done, at the conclusion that the only way to have a really Constitutional Government in Ireland is to allow the representatives of the people, freely chosen by the people, to administer their own affairs. However, the Amendment I am about to move does not express any opinion on this point. All I now ask the House to say is that Ireland has not the benefit of the Constitution, and to consider a remedy. The Amendment ought to commend itself to the common sense and candour of English gentlemen. A new state of things has arisen in Ireland, and an opportunity is now given to the House of Commons to review its policy with regard to that country. I do not at present ask the House to concede Home Rule to Ireland. That question remains to be discussed, and perhaps to be discussed for many years. But first the advocates of Home Rule must satisfy the English people that they are not happy seeking separation. Ireland has given up the idea of separation, because she has before her the prospect of obtaining another and a far better thing. I do not believe Ireland will ever be content with the existing state of things but if Englishmen approach the subject with unprejudiced minds, there will be no difficulty in framing a measure which will make Ireland contented, while the integrity of the Empire will be perfectly maintained.

We are now entering upon a new phase of Irish politics. It is not my wish to say one word of disrespect towards the Right Honourable gentleman opposite [*Mr. Disraeli*], who by his genius has raised himself to the exalted position he at present occupies. The Right Honourable gentleman is now, for the first time in his life in power, although he has previously been in office. Ireland is a field large enough for the ambition of any man if he can reconcile that country cordially to the British nation, and dispel every trace of disloyalty to the British Crown. I believe it is possible to do this by wise legislation. There may be a veiled policy as well as a veiled rebellion. It will be a mistake, however, if the Right Honourable gentleman conceives that other questions will not have to be dealt with. If a policy of conciliation is pursued towards Ireland, the Right Honourable gentleman will not find himself obstructed by Irish representative; but if he unfortunately pursues a different course, he will find himself disappointed. But however great our wish to relieve the House of Commons from the management of exclusively Irish affairs, for which we believe the House unfit, while these affairs are managed in the House, and we continue members of it, a duty devolved upon us which will be discharged by not offering factious Opposition to any measures for the benefit of Ireland, from whichever side of the House, such measures may emanate.

I think I have shown that a crisis has arisen in the affairs of Ireland, presenting new phases; that those gentlemen who have associated themselves for the purpose of obtaining self-government for Ireland are bound not to acquiesce in an Address which infers that things shall remain as they are; and it is with this view that I now place in the hands of the Speaker the Amendment which I have prepared.

The amendment was rejected.

Charles Stewart Parnell
21 January 1885

IN 1884, the Westminster Parliament passed the Representation of the People Act which established the principle of 'one man, one vote,' and at the same time increased both the number of Parliamentary seats on offer to Ireland, and the number of people who could vote.

Parnell realised that the Irish Parliamentary Party could benefit immensely from the increased number of voters in Ireland. So certain was he that the party could win eighty percent of the seats in Ireland in the upcoming election that he felt he could reject Joseph Chamberlain's local government scheme [offering limited devolution].

This he did in Cork on 21 January 1885 in what has become his most widely quoted speech:

Speech at Cork

I go back from the consideration of these questions to the Land Question, in which the labourers question is also involved and the manufacturers' question. I come back and every Irish politician must be forcibly driven back to the consideration of the great question of National Self – Government for Ireland [*cheers*]. I do not know how this great question will be eventually settled. I do not know whether England will be wise in time and concede to constitutional arguments and methods the restitution of that which was stolen from us towards the close of the last century [*cheer*]. It is given to none of us to forecast the future, and just as it is impossible for us to say in what way or by what means the National question may be settled, in what way full justice may be done to Ireland, so it is impossible for us to say to what extent that justice should be done. We cannot ask for less than restitution of Grattan's Parliament [*renewed cheering*]. But no man has the right to fix the boundary to the march of a nation [*great cheers*]. No man has a right to say to his country: 'Thus far shalt thou go, and no further;' and we have never attempted to fix 'Ne plus ultra' [*no further*] to the progress of Ireland's nationhood, and we never shall [*cheers*].

But gentlemen, while we leave those things to time, circumstances, and the future, we must each one of us resolve in our own hearts that we shall at all times do everything which within us lies to obtain for Ireland the fullest measure of her rights [*applause*]. In this way we shall avoid difficulties and contentions amongst each other. In this way we shall not give up anything which the future may put in favour of our country, and while we struggle today for that which may seem possible for us with our combination, we must struggle for it with the proud consciousness, and that we shall not do anything to hinder or prevent better men who may come after us from gaining better things than those for which we now contend [*prolonged applause*].

The Great Advocates

Bishop of Ossory
1324

RICHARD DE LEDREDE, a Franciscan monk, fresh from the papal court at Avignon, was appointed Bishop of Ossory in 1317. He was the catalyst for the Alice Kyteler witch trial at Kilkenny in 1324.

Kyteler a well connected lady with four husbands, none of whose names she ever adopted, was supported by her brother-in-law, Lord Arnold, one of the most powerful men in Ireland.

In the parliament convened at Dublin in May, 1324, Lord Arnold called for the country to unite against Ledrede whom he accused of slandering the country by stating that, 'the Irish are all heretics.' The Bishop then spoke in reply:

Trial of Allice Kytler

Venerable fathers and lords, many statements have been made by this noble and powerful lord in front of you, but they are not all completely true, for there are very many privileges of the church which could not very well be listed in one little document. There is no doubt but that kings and leaders of this world administer their temporal laws and make laws and statutes. So does our lord the Pope, vicar of Christ, have liberty to administer and regulate spiritual affairs, especially in matters of the faith, its observation and protection wherefore we and all of you, even kings and leaders, must obey him.

As for what was said in the third place, that we defamed you and your country by saying that you are all heretics and excommunicated, with all due respect to such a great and powerful man, that's not true: for when criminals are found among law-abiding citizens, it does not redound to the infamy of law-abiding citizens unless they have aided and abetted the crimes. For among the disciples of Christ, Judas the traitor was discovered, and among many holy men many evil men are found. Likewise in our diocese, in the midst of many law-abiding decent people, we have found one diabolical den, more foul than any that has ever been found in the kingdom or dominion of the lord king of England. When we proceeded to purge this den, as we are bound to do under the duties of our office, we endured no little opposition, unheard of in modern times.

In honour of the power and wealth of our adversaries, we donned episcopal vestments, and carrying the host, accompanied by many priests and clergy, we earnestly sought help from you, Lord Arnold, in your own province, because of your office, to flush out these heretics. But you paid no respect to your creator. With insults and much violence you roughly threw us from your sight and out of the judicial court – yes, you threw us, our own lord, Jesus, the king of all things, and even ourselves, your father the bishop. You flatly refused to help the church in a matter of the faith. You forbore to swear an oath as laid down in the canonical texts, to the damnation of the faith and infinite scandal of the people, and you knew this would bring the sentence of excommunication onto your head.

Nor should you believe that our lord, the most holy vicar of Christ, would have sent you a bishop, nourished in the bosom of the holy Roman church, who in a matter of the faith would fear your power, threats and terrors. Rather, we are ready, with God's help, to endure not only prison if we must, but also death. Therefore, we leave it to your judgement and to the judgement of the prelates and other nobles, whether or not these are the words and deeds of the faithful or of others.

Arnold jumped up and angrily answered the bishop thus: 'You will certainly be obstructed at every turn.'

If you and your henchmen obstruct us, you will find we are ready to meet you with a joyful spirit rejoicing in the faith of Christ.

Whereupon Arnold and his knights left the hall.

Eventually the Bishop succeeded in bringing Alice Kyteler to trial but she escaped before she could be burned. Her lady in waiting and one of her sons were not so lucky.

Edmund Burke
15–19 February 1788

WARREN HASTINGS, was Governor-General of India for eleven years. As such he had been instrumental in extending the rule of Britain over India. His victories, moreover, had added greatly to the national wealth, with the rich spoils of the vanquished being distributed throughout Britain. In 1786, he returned to Britain a national hero.

A few men, of whom Edmund Burke was both the most vocal and the most prominent, were concerned about the precise moral character of the actions performed by Hastings in carrying out his duties, and pushed for his impeachment on charges of 'high crimes and misdemeanours.'

The trial of Warren Hastings was the great political trial of the era. It ran for 145 days over a period of seven years. The trial opened in Westminster Hall, before the House of lords, on the 13 February, 1788. After two days of preliminaries, Burke spoke for four days and delivered a passionate and thunderous indictment of Hastings' activities. Below is an extract from that speech:

Warren Hastings Trial

The crimes, which we charge in these articles, are not lapses, defects, errors, of common human frailty, which, as we know and feel, we can allow for. We charge this offender with no crimes, that have not arisen from passions, which it is criminal to harbour; with no offences, that have not their root in avarice, rapacity, pride, insolence, ferocity, treachery, cruelty, malignity of temper; in short, in nothing, that does not argue a total extinction of all moral principle; that does not manifest an inveterate blackness of heart, dyed in grain with malice, vitiated, corrupted, gangrened to the very core. If we do not plant his crimes in those vices, which the breast of man is made to abhor, and the spirit of all laws, human and divine, to interdict, we desire no longer to be heard upon this occasion. Let everything that can be pleaded on the ground of surprise or error, upon those grounds be pleaded with success: we give up the whole of those predicaments. We urge no crimes, that were not crimes of forethought. We charge him with nothing, that he did not commit upon deliberation; that he did not commit against advice, supplication, and remonstrance; that he did not commit against the direct command of lawful authority; that he did not commit after reproof and reprimand, the reproof and reprimand of those, who are authorized by the laws to reprove and reprimand him. The crimes of Mr. Hastings are crimes not only in themselves, but aggravated by being crimes of contumacy. They were crimes not against forms, but against those eternal laws of justice, which are our rule and our birthright. His offences are not, in formal, technical language, but in reality, in substance, and effect, high crimes and high misdemeanours.

So far as to the crimes. As to the criminal, we have chosen him on the same principle on which we selected the crimes. We have not chosen to bring before you a poor, puny, trembling delinquent, misled, perhaps, by those, who ought to have taught him better, but who have afterwards oppressed him by their power, as they had first corrupted him by their example. Instances there have been many, wherein the punishment of minor offences, in inferior persons, has been made the means of screening crimes of an high order, and in men of high description. Our course is different. We have not brought before you an obscure offender, who, when his insignificance and weakness are weighed against the power of the prosecution, gives even to public justice something of the appearance of oppression. No my lords, we have brought before you the first man of India in rank, authority, and station. We have brought before you the chief of the tribe, the head of the whole body of eastern offenders; a captain-general of iniquity, under whom all the fraud, all the peculation, all the tyranny, in India, are embodied, disciplined, arrayed, and paid. This is the person, my lords, that we bring before you. We have brought before you such a person, that, if you strike at him with the firm and decided arm of justice, you will not have need of a great many more examples. You strike at the whole corps, if you strike at the head . . .

My lords, I do not mean now to go farther than just to remind your lordships of this – that Mr. Hastings' government was one whole system of oppression, of robbery of individuals, of spoliation of the public, and of supersession of the whole system of the English government, in order to vest in the worst of the natives all the power that could possibly exist in any government; in order to defeat the ends which all governments ought, in common, to have in view. In the name of the Commons of England, I charge all this villainy upon Warren Hastings, in this last moment of my application to you.

I, therefore, charge Mr. Hastings with having destroyed, for private purposes, the whole system of government by the six provincial councils, which he had no right to destroy.

I charge him with having delegated to others that power, which the Act of Parliament had directed him to preserve unalienably in himself.

I charge him with having formed a committee to be mere instruments and tools, at the enormous expense of £62,000 per annum.

I charge him with having appointed a person their dewan, to whom these Englishmen were to be subservient tools; whose name to his own knowledge, was by the general voice of India, by the general recorded voice of the company, by recorded official transactions, by everything, that can make a man known, abhorred, and detested, stamped with infamy and with giving him the whole power, which he had thus separated from the council general, and from the provincial councils.

I charge him with taking bribes of Gunga Govin Sing.

I charge him with not having done that bribe service, which fidelity, even in iniquity, requires at the hands of the worst of men.

I charge him with having robbed those people, of whom he took the bribes.

I charge him with having fraudulently alienated the fortunes of widows.

I charge him with having, without right, title, or purchase, taken the lands of orphans, and given them to wicked persons under him.

I charge him with having removed the natural guardians of a minor rajah, and with having given that trust to a stranger, Debi Sing, whose wickedness was known to himself and all the world; and by whom the rajah, his family, and dependants were cruelly oppressed.

I charge him with having committed to the management of Debi Sing three great provinces; and thereby, with having wasted the country, ruined the landed interest, cruelly harassed the peasants, burnt their houses, seized their crops, tortured and degraded their persons, and destroyed the honour of the whole female race of that country.

In the name of the Commons of England, I charge all this villainy upon Warren Hastings, in this last moment of my application to you.

My lords, what is it, that we want here to a great act of national justice? Do we want a cause, my lords? You have the cause of oppressed princes, of undone women of the first rank, of desolated provinces, and of wasted kingdoms.

Do you want a criminal, my lords? When was there so much iniquity ever laid to the charge of any one? No, my lords, you must not look, you must not look to punish any other such delinquent from India. Warren Hastings has not left substance enough in India to nourish such another delinquent.

My lords, is it a prosecutor you want? You have before you the Commons of Great Britain as prosecutors; and, I believe, my lords, that the sun, in his beneficent progress round the world, does not behold a more glorious sight than that of men, separated from a remote people by the material bounds and barriers of nature, united by the bond of a social and moral community; all the Commons of England resenting, as their own, the indignities and cruelties, that are offered to all the people of India.

Do we want a tribunal? My lords, no example of antiquity, nothing in the modern world, nothing in the range of human imagination, can supply us with a tribunal like this. My lords, here we see virtually in the mind's eye that sacred majesty of the Crown, under whose authority you sit, and whose power you exercise. We see in that invisible authority what we all feel in reality and life, the beneficent powers and protecting justice of his majesty. We have here the heir – apparent to the Crown, such as the fond wishes of the people of England wish an heir – apparent of the Crown to be. We have here all the branches of the royal family in a situation between majesty and subjection, between the sovereign and the subject – offering a pledge in that situation for the support of the rights of the Crown, and the liberties of the people, both which extremities they touch. My lords, we have a great hereditary peerage here; those, who have their own honour, the honour of their ancestors, and of their posterity, to guard; and who will justify, as they have always justified, that provision in the Constitution, by which justice is made an hereditary office. My lords, we have here a new nobility who have arisen and exalted themselves by various merits, by great military services, which have extended the fame of this country from the rising to the setting sun; we have those, who by various civil merits and various civil talents have been exalted to a situation, which they well deserve, and in which they will justify the favour of their sovereign, and the good opinion of their fellow subjects, and make them rejoice to see those virtuous characters, that were the other day upon a level with them, now exalted above them in rank, but feeling with them in sympathy what they felt in common with them before. We have persons exalted from the practice of the law, from the place, in which they administered high, though subordinate, justice, to a seat here, to enlighten with their knowledge, and to strengthen with their votes those principles, which have distinguished the courts, in which they have presided.

My lords, you have here also the lights of our religion; you have the bishops of England. My lords, you have that true image of the primitive church in its ancient form, in its ancient ordinances, purified from the superstitions and the vices, which a long succession of ages will bring upon the best institutions. You have the representatives of that religion, which says, that their God is love, that the very vital spirit of their institution is charity; a religion, which so much hates oppression, that, when the God, whom we adore, appeared in human form, he did not appear in a form of greatness and majesty, but in sympathy with the lowest of the people – and thereby made it a firm and ruling principle, that their welfare was the object of all government; since the person, who was the Master of Nature, chose to appear himself in a subordinate situation. These are the considerations, which influence them, which animate them, and will animate them, against all oppression; knowing, that He, who is called first among them, and First among us all, both of the flock that is fed, and of those who feed it, made Himself 'the servant of all.'

My lords, these are the securities which we have in all the constituent parts of the body of this house. We know them, we reckon, we rest upon them, and commit safely the interests of India and of humanity into your hands. Therefore, it is with confidence, that, ordered by the Commons:

I impeach Warren Hastings, Esq., of high crimes and misdemeanours.

I impeach him in the name of the Commons of Great Britain in Parliament assembled, whose parliamentary trust he has betrayed.

I impeach him in the name of all the commons of Great Britain, whose national character he has dishonoured.

I impeach him in the name of the people of India, whose laws, rights, and liberties he has subverted; whose properties he has destroyed, whose country he has laid waste and desolate.

I impeach him in the name, and by virtue of those eternal laws of justice, which he has violated.

I impeach him in the name of human nature itself, which he has cruelly outraged, injured, and oppressed in both sexes, in every age, rank, situation, and condition of life.

My lords, at this awful close, in the name of the Commons and surrounded by them, I attest the retiring, I attest the advancing generations, between which, as a link in the great chain of eternal order, we stand. We call this nation, we call the world to witness, that the Commons have shrunk from no labour; that we have been guilty of no prevarication; that we have made no compromise with crime; that we have not feared any odium whatsoever, in the long warfare which we have carried on with the crimes, with the vices, with the exorbitant wealth, with the enormous and overpowering influence of Eastern corruption.

My lords, it has pleased Providence to place us in such a state that we appear every moment to be upon the verge of some great mutations. There is one thing, and one thing only, which defies all mutation: that which existed before the world, and will survive the fabric of the world itself – I mean justice; that justice which, emanating from the Divinity, has a place in the breast of every one of us, given us for our guide with regard to ourselves and with regard to others, and which will stand, after this globe is burned to ashes, our advocate or our accuser, before the Great Judge, when He comes to call upon us for the tenor of a well-spent life.

My lords, the Commons will share in every fate with your lordships; there is nothing sinister which can happen to you, in which we shall not all be involved; and, if it should so happen that we shall be subjected to some of those frightful changes which we have seen – if it should happen that your lordships, stripped of all the decorous distinctions of human society, should, by hands at once base and cruel, be led to those scaffolds and machines of murder upon which great kings and glorious queens have shed their blood, amidst the prelates, amidst the nobles, amidst the magistrates, who supported their thrones – may you in those moments feel that consolation which I am persuaded they felt in the critical moments of their dreadful agony!

My lords, if you must fall, may you so fall! But, if you stand – and stand I trust you will – together with the fortune of this ancient monarchy, together with the ancient laws and liberties of this great and illustrious kingdom, may you stand as unimpeached in honour as in power; may you stand, not as a substitute for virtue, but as an ornament of virtue, as a security for virtue; may you stand long, and long stand the terror of tyrants; may you stand the refuge of afflicted nations; may you stand a sacred temple, for the perpetual residence of an inviolable justice!

The trial took seven years, at the end of which Hastings was acquitted of all charges.

Richard Brinsley Sheridan
13 June 1788

RICHARD BRINSLEY Sheridan, the Irish born dramatist and author, like Edmund Burke, was an uncompromising and earnest supporter of the impeachment of the ex Governor-General of India, Warren Hastings. Following a brilliant speech against him, in the House of Commons, the public eagerly awaited Sheridan's address at the Hastings trial.

Public curiosity was so aroused that as much as fifty pounds was paid for a seat. On the night of the 2 June many people slept at local coffee-houses so as to be sure of reaching the door of Westminster Hall in time – a precaution which proved warranted, as by six thirty the next morning the entrance area was crowded. When the door opened, there was a rush for seats and those lucky enough to get in had to wait three hours for Sheridan to arrive.

After a nervous beginning, Sheridan spoke for four and a half hours. On the 6 June, he continued, and again on the 10 June, but in the course of his speech that day he was taken ill, and the court was adjourned until the 13 June, when he brought the speech to a triumphant conclusion.

Edmund Burke declared afterwards that 'of all the various species of oratory, of every kind of eloquence that have been heard in ancient or modern times, whatever the acuteness of the Bar, the dignity of the senate, or the morality of the pulpit could furnish, had not been equal to what the House had that day heard in Westminster Hall.'

Below is the conclusion of the speech made by Sheridan on the 13 June:

Warren Hastings Trial

The inquiry which now only remains, my lords, is, whether Mr. Hastings is to be answerable for the crimes committed by his agents. It has been fully proved that Mr. Middleton signed the treaty with the superior begum [*women of high rank in Oude, a province in India*] in October, 1778. He also acknowledged signing some others of a different date, but could not recollect the authority by which he did it! These treaties were recognized by Mr. Hastings, as appears by the evidence of Mr. Purling, in the year 1780. In that of October 1778, the jaghire was secured, which was allotted for the support of the women in the khord mahal. But still the prisoner pleads that he is not accountable for the cruelties which were exercised. His is the plea which tyranny, aided by its prime minister, treachery, is always sure to set up. Mr. Middleton has attempted to strengthen this ground by endeavouring to claim the whole infamy in these transactions, and to monopolize the guilt! He dared even to aver, that he had been condemned by Mr. Hastings for the ignominious part he had acted. He dared to avow this, because Mr. Hastings was on his trial, and he thought he never would be arraigned; but in the face of this court, and before he left the bar, he was com-pelled to confess that it was for the lenience, and not the *seterio* of his proceedings, that he had been reproved by the prisoner.

It will not, I trust, be concluded that because Mr. Hastings has not marked every passing shade of guilt, and because he has only given the bold outline of cruelty, he is therefore to be acquitted. It is laid down by the law of England, that law which is the perfection of reason, that a person ordering an act to be done by his agent is answerable for that act with all its consequences, 'Quod facit per alium, facit per se' [What one does through another person one does oneself]. Middleton was appointed, in 1777, the confidential agent, the second-self of Mr. Hastings. The Governor-General ordered the measure. Even if he never saw, nor heard afterward of its consequences, he was therefore answerable for every pang that was inflicted, and for all the blood that was shed. But he did hear, and that instantly, of the whole. He wrote to accuse Middleton of forbearance and of neglect . . .

After this, my lords, can it be said that the prisoner was ignorant of the acts, or not culpable for their consequences? It is true, he did not direct the guards, the famine, and the bludgeons; he did not weigh the fetters, nor number the lashes to be inflicted on his victims; but yet he is just as guilty as if he had borne an active and personal share in each transaction. It is as if he had commanded that the heart should be torn from the bosom, and enjoined that no blood should follow. He is in the same degree accountable to the law, to his country, and to his conscience, and to his God!

The prisoner has endeavoured also to get rid of a part of his guilt, by observing that he was but one of the supreme council and that all the rest had sanctioned those transactions with their approbation. Even if it were true that others did participate in the guilt, it cannot tend to diminish his criminality . . .

When, my lords, the Board of Directors received the advices which Mr. Hastings thought proper to transmit, though unfurnished with any other materials to form their judgement, they expressed very strongly their doubts, and properly ordered an inquiry into the circumstances of the alleged disaffection of the begums, declaring it, at the same time, to be a debt which was due to the honour and justice of the British nation. This inquiry, however, Mr. Hastings thought it absolutely necessary to elude . . . All this, however, my lords is nothing to the magnificent paragraph which concludes this communication. 'Besides' says he, 'I hope it will not be a departure from official language to say, that the majesty of justice ought not to be approached without solicitation. She ought not to descend to inflame or provoke, but to withhold her judgement until she is called on to determine.'

But, my lords, do you, the judges of this land, and the expounders of its rightful laws – do you approve of this mockery and call it the character of justice, which takes the form of right to excite wrong? No, my lords, justice is not this halt and miserable object; it is not the ineffective bauble of an Indian pagod; it is not the portentous phantom of despair; it is not like any fabled monster, formed in the eclipse of reason, and found in some unhallowed grove of superstitious darkness and political dismay!

No, my lords, in the happy reverse of all this, I turn from the disgusting caricature to the real image! Justice I have now before me august and pure! The abstract idea of all that would be perfect in the spirits and the aspirings of men! – where the mind rises; where the heart expands; where the countenance is ever placid and benign; where her favourite attitude is to stoop to the unfortunate; to hear their cry and to help them; to rescue and relieve, to succour and save; majestic, from its mercy; venerable, from its utility; uplifted, without pride; firm, without obduracy; beneficent in each preference; lovely, though in her frown!

On that justice I rely: deliberate and sure, abstracted from all party purpose and political speculation; not on words, but on facts. You, my lords, who hear me, I conjure, by those rights which it is your best privilege to preserve; by that fame which it is your best pleasure to inherit; by all those feelings which refer to the first term in the series of existence, the original compact of our nature, our controlling rank in the creation. This is the call on all to administer to truth and equity, as they would satisfy the laws and satisfy themselves, with the most exalted bliss possible or conceivable for our nature; the self-approving consciousness of virtue, when the condemnation we look for will be one of the most ample mercies accomplished for mankind since the creation of the world! My lords, I have done.

At the end of the seven-year trial, Hastings was acquitted of all charges.

John Philpot Curran
29 January 1794

IN 1791, THE United Irishmen was founded with the aim of uniting all Irishmen, whatever religion, in an effort to counteract the weight of English influence in Ireland, and securing a reform of government and Parliament. On the publication of a document appealing to the Dublin branch of the Irish Volunteers to follow their cause, the Secretary of the United Irishmen, Archibald Hamilton Rowan, was arrested and charged with sedition.

John Philpot Curran, a leading barrister of the time, defended Rowan.

The following is an extract from Rowan's defence, which the English statesman, Alfred Boughman described as 'the greatest speech of an advocate in ancient and modern times.'

Trial of Archibald Rowan

Gentlemen the representation of our people is the vital principle of their political existence; without it they are dead, or they live only to servitude; without it there are two estates acting upon and against the third, instead of acting in cooperation with it; without it, if the people are oppressed by their judges, where is the tribunal to which the judges can be amenable? Without it, if they are trampled upon and plundered by a minister, where is the tribunal to which the offender shall be amenable? Without it, where is the ear to hear, or the heart to feel, or the hand to redress their sufferings? Shall they be found, let me ask you, in the accursed bands of imps and minions that bask in their disgrace, and fatten upon their spoils, and flourish upon their ruin? But let me not put this to you as a merely speculative question. It is a plain question of fact: rely upon it, physical man is everywhere the same; it is only the various operations of moral causes that gives variety to the social or individual character and condition. How otherwise happens it that modern slavery looks quietly at the despot, on the very spot where Leonidas expired? The answer is Sparta has not changed her climate, but she has lost that government which her liberty could not survive.

I call you, therefore, to a plain question of fact. This paper recommends a reform in Parliament. I put that question to your consciences. Do you think it needs that reform? I put it boldly and fairly to you, do you think the people of Ireland are represented as they ought to be? Do you hesitate for an answer? If you do, let me remind you that, until last year, three million of your countrymen have by the express letter of the law, been excluded from the reality of actual, and even from the phantom of virtual representation. Shall we then be told that this is the affirmation of a wicked and seditious incendiary? If you do not feel the mockery of such a charge, look at your country. In what state do you find it? Is it in a state of tranquillity and general satisfaction? These are traces by which good are ever to be distinguished from bad governments, without any very minute inquiry or speculative relinement. Do you feel that a veneration for the law, a pious and humble attachment to the Constitution, form the political morality of the people? Do you find that comfort and competency among your people which are always to be found where a government is mild and moderate, where taxes are imposed by a body who have an interest in treating the poorer orders with compassion, and preventing the weight of taxation from pressing sore upon them?

Gentlemen, I mean not to impeach the state of your representation; I am not saying that it is defective, or that it ought to be altered or amended; nor is this a place for me to say whether I think that three millions of the inhabitants of a country, whose whole number is but four, ought to be admitted to any efficient situation in the state. It may be said, and truly, that these are not questions for either of us directly to decide; but you cannot refuse them some passing consideration. At least when you remember that on this subject the real question for your decision is, whether the allegation of a defect in your constitution is so utterly unfounded and false, that you can ascribe it only to the malice and perverseness of a wicked mind, and not to the innocent mistake of an ordinary understanding; whether it may not be mistake; whether it can be only sedition?

And here, gentlemen, I own I cannot but regret that one of our countrymen should be criminally pursued for asserting the necessity of a reform, at the very moment when that necessity seems admitted by the Parliament itself; that this unhappy reform shall, at the same moment, be a subject of legislative discussion and criminal prosecution. Far am I from imputing any sinister design to the virtue or wisdom of our Government; but who can avoid feeling the deplorable impression that must be made oil the public mind when the demand for that reform is answered by a criminal information! I am the more forcibly impressed by this consideration, when I consider that when this information was first put on the file, the subject was transiently mentioned in the House of Commons. Some Circumstance retarded the process of the inquiry there, and the progress of the information was equally retarded here. On the first day of the session you all know that subject was again brought forward in the House of Commons, and, as if they had slept together, this prosecution was also revived in the Court of King's Bench, and that before a jury taken from a panel partly composed of those very Members of Parliament who, in the House of Commons, must debate upon this subject as a measure of public advantage, which they are here called upon to consider as a public crime.

This paper, gentlemen, insists upon the necessity of emancipating the Catholics of Ireland, and that is charged as part of the libel. If they had waited another year, if they had kept this prosecution impending for another year, how much would remain for a jury to decide upon, I should be at a loss to discover. It seems as if the progress of public information was eating away the ground of the prosecution. This part of the libel has unluckily received the sanction of the legislature. In that interval our Catholic brethren have obtained that admission, which, it seems, it was a libel to propose; in what way to account for this, I am really at a loss. Have any alarms been occasioned by the emancipation of our Catholic brethren? Has the bigoted malignity of any individual been crushed or has the stability of the government been weakened; or is one million of subjects stronger than four millions? Do you think that the benefit they received should be poisoned by the sting of vengeance? If you think so, you must say to them – 'You have demanded emancipation and you have got it; but we abhor your persons, we are outraged at your success, and we will stigmatize by criminal prosecution the adviser of that relief which you have obtained from the voice of your country.' I ask you, do you think, as honest men, anxious for the public tranquillity, conscious that there are wounds not yet completely cicatrized, that you ought to speak this language at this time, to men who are too much disposed to think that in this very emancipation they have been saved from their own Parliament by the humanity of their sovereign?

Or do you wish to prepare them for the revocation of these improvident concessions? Do you think it wise or humane at this moment to insult them, by sticking up in a pillory the man who dared to stand forth as their advocate? I put it to your oaths; do you think that a blessing of that kind, that a victory obtained by justice over bigotry and oppression, should have a stigma cast upon it by an ignominious sentence upon men bold and honest enough to propose that measure? To propose the redeeming of religion from the abuses of the church, the reclaiming of three millions of men from bondage, and giving liberty to all who had a right to demand it; giving, I say in the so much censured words of this paper, giving 'universal emancipation!' I speak in the spirit of the British law, which makes liberty commensurate with and inseparable from British soil; which proclaims even to the stranger and sojourner, the moment he sets his foot upon British earth, that the ground on which he treads is holy, and consecrated by the genius of universal emancipation. No matter in what language his doom may have been pronounced; no matter what complexion incompatible with freedom an Indian or an African sun may have burnt upon him; no matter in what disastrous battle his liberty may have been cloven down; no matter with what solemnities he may have been devoted upon the altar of slavery; the first moment he touches the sacred soil of Britain, the altar and the god sink together in the dust; his soul walks abroad in her own majesty; his body swells beyond the measure of his chains, that burst from around him; and he stands redeemed, regenerated, and disenthralled, by the irresistible genius of 'universal emancipation.'

Through the defence was most ably conducted by Curran, the jury, some member of which were said to have been bribed, took a mere ten minutes to reach a verdict of guilty. The court sentenced Rowan to 'pay his Majesty a sum of five hundred pounds, and to be imprisoned for two years.' However, soon after being jailed Rowan escaped and spent an unhappy time in revolutionary France. He was, therefore, out of Ireland when the 1798 Rebellion took place and was eventually able to receive a pardon from the Irish Courts.

The Ulster Question

Edward Carson
11 February 1914

IN 1910, the Dublin-born Edward Carson was elected head of the Irish Unionist party. He immediately took a leading role in opposing the passage of the Third Irish Home Rule Bill through the British Parliament. The Bill's passage into law was inevitable following the removal, in 1911, of the House of Lord's power to veto legislation, though two attempts to pass the Bill failed in 1912 and 1913.

At the beginning of 1914, next to the maintenance of peace in Europe, the most important political issue facing the British Government was the Irish question. In his opening address to Parliament on the 10 February, King George V told the members that the Home Rule Bill would again be submitted for consideration. 'My earnest wish,' he said, was 'that that the good will and co-operation of men of all parties and creeds may heal dissension and lay the foundations of a lasting peace.' The British Prime Minister, Henry Asquith, enlarged on the King's opening address to Parliament by expressing his own hopes and desires.

In the debate that followed, Edward Carson, expressed his utter detestation at the Government's plans. His speech, which Asquith would later describe as 'impeccable' is given below.

Anti-Home Rule speech

Ulster is not asking for concessions. Ulster is asking to be let alone. When you talk of concessions, what you really mean is, we want to lay down what is the minimum of wrong we can do to Ulster. Let me tell you that the results of two years delay and the treatment we have received during these two years have made your task and made our task far more difficult. You have driven these men to enter into a covenant for their mutual protection. No doubt you have laughed at their covenant. Have a good laugh at it now. Well, so far as I am concerned, I am not the kind of man who will go over to Ulster one day and say, 'Enter into a covenant,' and go over next day and say, 'Break it.' But there is something more. You have insulted them. I do not say the Prime Minister has done so. I would be wrong if I were to say that he has done so. He has treated them seriously, but the large body of his Colleagues in the rank and file of his party have taken every opportunity of jeering at these men, of branding them as braggarts and bluffers and cowards, and all the rest of it. Well, do not you see that having done that, these men can never go back, and never will go back, and allow these gibes and insults and sneers to prove true.

The Speech from the Throne talks of the fears of these men. Yes, they have, I think, genuine fears for their civil and religious liberty under the Bill, but do not imagine that that is all that these men are fighting for. They are fighting for a great principle, and a great ideal. They are fighting to stay under the Government which they were invited to come under, under which they have flourished, and under which they are content, and to refuse to come under a Government which they loathe and detest. Men do not make sacrifices or take up the attitude these men in Ulster have taken up on a question of detail or paper safeguards. I am not going to argue whether they are right or wrong in resisting. It would be useless to argue it's because they have thoroughly made up their minds, but I say this: If these men are not morally justified when they are attempted to be driven out of one Government with which they are satisfied, and put under another which they loathe, I do not see how resistance ever can be justified in history at all.

There was one point made by the Prime Minister yesterday, and repeated by Lord Morley in another place which I should like to deal with for one moment, although it has been already referred to by my Right Honourable friend last night. The Prime Minister said, it is 'as the price of peace that any suggestion we make will be put forward' and he elaborated that by saying that he did not mean the mere abandonment of resistance, but that he meant that the Bill, if these changes were made, as I understand him, should as the price of the changes be accepted generally by opponents in Ireland, and in the unionist party, so as to give, as he hoped, a good chance and send off to the Bill. If he means that as the condition of the changes in the Bill we are to support the bill or take any responsibility whatever for it, I tell him we never can do it. Ulster looms very largely in this controversy, simply because Ulster has a strong right arm, but there are Unionists in the south and west who loath the bill just as much as we Ulster people loath it, whose difficulties are far greater, and who would willingly fight, as Ulster would fight, if they had the numbers. Nobody knows the difficulties of these men better than I do. Why, it was only the other day some of them ventured to put forward as a business proposition that this Bill would be financial ruin to their businesses, saying no more, and immediately they were boycotted, and resolutions were passed, and they were told that they ought to understand as Protestants that they ought to be thankful and grateful for being allowed to live in peace among the people who are there. Yes, we can never support the Bill which hands these people over to the tender mercies of those who have always been their bitterest enemies. We must go on whatever happens, opposing the bill to the end. That we are entitled to do; that we are bound to do. But I want to speak explicitly about the exclusion of Ulster. I am not at all sure that I entirely understood what the Prime Minister said yesterday in his speech on this subject. In one part of the speech I understood him to say that he did not, in making these changes, which are eventually to be put upon the Table of the House, reject the exclusion of Ulster as a possibility. In another part of his speech he said: 'There is nothing we will do, consistent with the maintenance of the fundamental principles of the Bill, in the solution of this question, to avoid the terrible calamity of civil war or bloodshed.' If I take these two passages together I suppose I am entitled to say that the exclusion of Ulster is not opposed to the fundamental principles of the Bill.

Now that is a very important matter. If the exclusion of Ulster is not shut out, and if at the same time the Prime Minister says he cannot admit anything contrary to the fundamental principles of the Bill, I think it follows that the exclusion of Ulster is not contrary to the fundamental principles of the Bill. If that is so, are you really going on to these grave difficulties in the future that the gracious speech from the throne deals with, and not going to make your offer now, at once, with a view, not to our adopting the Bill, but to putting an end to resistance in Ulster. Why do you hesitate? Surely something that is not fundamental to the principles of the Bill is a thing that you may readily concede, rather than face these grave difficulties which you yourselves admit to exist. I can only say this to the Prime Minister: If the exclusion for that purpose is proposed, it will be my duty to go to Ulster at once and take counsel with the people there; for I certainly do not mean that Ulster should not be any pawn in any political game. I say once more, that no responsible leader, unless he were a lunatic, as the secretary of state says I am.

The Secretary of State for War interrupted him and apologised for implying that he was a lunatic.

No responsible man, whether he was a leader or follower, could possibly go to the people, under any condition, and say, 'We are offered something,' but say to them for political purposes, 'You ought to prepare to fight for it rather than accept it;' and I am not going to do anything of the kind.

On the other hand I say this, that if your suggestions – no matter what paper safeguards you put, or no matter what other methods you may attempt to surround these safeguards with for the purpose of raising what I call 'your reasonable atmosphere' – if your suggestions try to compel these people to come into a Dublin Parliament, I tell you I shall, regardless of personal consequences, go on with these people to the end with their policy of resistance. Believe me, whatever way you settle the Irish question, there are only two ways to deal with Ulster. It is for statesmen to say which is the best and right one. She is not a part of the community which can be bought. She will not allow herself to be sold. You must therefore either coerce her if you go on, or you must, in the long run, by showing that good government can come under the Home Rule Bill, try and win her over to the case of the rest of Ireland. You probably can coerce her – though I doubt it. If you do, what will be the disastrous consequences not only to Ulster, but to this country and the Empire? Will my fellow countryman, the Leader of the Nationalist party, have gained anything? I will agree with him – I do not believe he wants to triumph any more than I do. But will he have gained anything if he takes over these people and then applies for what he used to call – at all events his party used to call – the enemies of the people to come in and coerce them into obedience? No, Sir, one false step taken in relation to Ulster will, in my opinion, render for ever impossible a solution of the Irish question. I say this to my Nationalist fellow countrymen, and, indeed, also to the Government: you have never tried to win over Ulster. You have never tried to understand her position. You have never alleged, and can never allege, that this Bill gives her one atom of advantage. Nay, you cannot deny that it takes away many advantages that she has as a constituent part of the United Kingdom.

You cannot deny that in the past she had produced the most loyal and law-abiding part of the citizens of Ireland. After all that, for these two years, every time we came before you your only answer to us – the majority of you, at all events – was to insult us, and to make little of us. I say to the leader of the Nationalist party, if you want Ulster, go and take her, or go and win her. You have never wanted her affections; you have wanted her taxes. . . .

In September, 1914, the Home Rule Bill became law, with the qualification that its implementation should be suspended until the end of the war, and that Parliament should then make special provisions for Ulster.

This Home Rule Bill allowed for the setting up of an Irish Parliament and Executive to deal with purely domestic affairs, while reserving for the British Parliament all matters affecting the Crown, the defence forces, international affairs and war and peace.

William Butler Yeats
17 October 1924

THE CONSTITUTION adopted by the first Parliament of the Irish Free State provided for the creation of two houses, the Dáil and the Seanad. Members of the former were to be elected by the people whilst members of the latter were to be appointed by the Dáil and by the Executive Council of the President.

W.B. Yeats became a member of the First Irish Senate on the 11 December, 1922. He was appointed to advise the government on matters concerning education, literature and the arts.

During his six years in the Seanad, Yeats spoke mainly on these topics, yet one of his most memorable Seanad speeches concerned the motion before the House on 17 October, 1924, 'that the interests of the country as a whole would be best served by an agreed solution of the outstanding problems affecting the relations between the Irish Free State and Northern Ireland.'

Speech on Northern Ireland in Senate

I do not think the Senator who has just spoken fully understands the resolution. We are not asking the Government to withdraw from the Commission [*a commission set up to decide on the boundaries between the six counties of Northern Ireland and the twenty six of the Southern, Irish Free State*] and we are not asking that the Commission should come to an end. We perfectly understand the Government's promise to those people. The Government promised those people the Treaty and they are bound to give the people of this country the Treaty; they cannot give anything else but the Treaty. What the resolution suggests is that before the Commission has reported, President Cosgrave, without giving anything away whatever, should make another appeal to the North to meet him in counsel. He is surrendering nothing. I think we quite recognise that nothing will probably come out of that appeal of President Cosgrave. To some extent we have to think of the future: we have to think of educating the next generation.

Results of a very evil kind may happen from the report of the Commission no matter what way it reports, and it is exceedingly important that no responsibility for those results should lie with the Government of the Free State. I have no hope of seeing Ireland united in my time, or of seeing Ulster won in my time; but I believe it will be won in the end, and not because we fight it, but because we govern this country well. We can do that, if I may be permitted as an artist and a writer to say so, by creating a system of culture which will represent the whole of this country and which will draw the imagination of the young towards it.

Now, I have spoken very seriously, but I want to turn from serious-ness to a fact that has been burning in my imagination since this meeting began – a discovery I made which has lightened this serious subject for me. I have been looking for a historical precedent for the remarkable fact that certain Englishmen who afterwards became Cabinet Ministers and in other ways rose to the highest positions in the State went over to Ulster about fifteen years ago and armed the people at a time of entire peace and urged them, and are now urging them, to use these arms against us. I have found a historical precedent which establishes that it is an old custom of the British Government. I have found that Edmund Burke in the middle of the 18th century drew attention to a very remarkable item in the Estimates of the year. It was an item of so much money for the purchase of five gross of scalping knives, which scalping knives were intended to be given to the American Indians that they might scalp the French.

After further discussion, the motion was carried.

Cahir Healy
24 April 1934

BY 1932, Northern Ireland was so badly affected by the world depression that unemployment soared to over 76,000, or 28% of the workforce. This coupled with the grim conditions of the unemployed, led to the formation of various Revolutionary Worker's Groups. These groups organised Catholic and Protestant workers, to bind together in a series of marches and strikes across the North throughout 1932 and 1933.

Despite the increasing solidarity of both Catholic and Protestant workers there was still an undercurrent of sectarianism. This was brought to the fore through the actions of the Ulster Protestant League, formed in 1931, which had as one of its main objectives the safeguarding of the employment of Protestants.

Sectarianism retreated during the rail strike of 1932 but raised its murky head again during the following summer, when government ministers openly stirred religious tensions. None were more bigoted than Basil Brooke, the Minister for Agriculture, who suggested the slogan, 'Protestants employ Protestants.'

On 24 April, 1934, Cahir Healy, the political leader of the Northern Ireland Nationalists, in response to the increasing number of sectarian statements by Government Ministers, proposed in the Northern Ireland House of Commons, 'that in the opinion of this House the campaign against the employment of Catholics promulgated by the Minister of Agriculture and expressly sanctioned by the Prime Minister is a grave violation of the rights and liberties of the minority placed under the rule of the Northern Government.'

He continued:

Speech on Minority Rights

We have put down this motion not to elicit what the Government policy on the matter is, because we know that already, but rather to give supporters of the Government in this House and outside an opportunity of saying whether they approve of the declaration of the Minister of Agriculture who has advised audiences on more than one occasion not to employ Catholics. We have been told that these statements, as well as the declaration of the Prime Minister, have shocked many Protestants both inside and outside this House and they have failed to find any justification for the practice either in the New Testament or in present day conditions here. These statements are not merely anti-Catholic, they are anti-Christian. Some supporters of the Government in this House have told us that they employ Catholics and that they will continue to do so notwithstanding the slogan of the Minister of Agriculture, 'No Catholic need apply.' Those Honourable Members live on terms of neighbourly friendship with Catholics and I trust that despite the interference of the Prime Minister they will continue to do so.

The policy is not a new one. The Right Honourable Member for Enniskillen [*Sir Edward Archdale*], who was then Minister for Agriculture, declared on the 31st March, 1925 that out of 109 officials in his Department only four were Roman Catholics, and he apologised for even having four in the service of the Government on the plea that three of them were civil servants turned over to him, 'whom I had to take when we began.' Some of those four have since gone, so I assume he can now breathe in peace.

The Prime Minister was not slow in making clear his own position in this matter. At Drumbanagher on 12th of July, 1932, he said: 'Ours is a Protestant Government, and I am an Orangeman.'

At Belfast on 3rd of September, 1932, he said: 'I do not care a snap of my fingers so long as I have the staunch, loyal, and Protestant majority at my back. I will carry on as I have begun.'

We know how he began. He began by interning 500 Nationalists, many of them from the most peaceful parts of the Six Counties, but not a single man of his own gunmen in Belfast was interned. He began by gerrymandering local government areas, even in places where the Nationalists in relation to the Protestants were as two and a quarter to one. They were left without any control of the local councils. He drove the Nationalists out of every public position where it was possible to do so, and he made, and continues to make, public appointments on sectarian and political grounds, totally ignoring merit. That is how he began, and that is how he continues.

Like attracts like. The present Minister of Agriculture, like his predecessor, was not slow to take the hint. The more intolerant the policy the better apparently it would please the Prime Minister, and so on 12th July last when he saw his present post in sight he went on a public platform at Newtownbutler and set about stirring up sectarian and political bias in a district that to my knowledge was hitherto free from any taint of these things. This is what he said. 'Many in the audience employ Catholics, but I have not one about my place.' One would think he was describing vermin of some kind.

'Catholics are out to destroy Ulster with all their might and power. They want to nullify the Protestant vote, take all they can out of Ulster and then see it to go to hell.' You will note he makes no distinction between Catholics in this declaration. The ex-service man who risked his life in the Great War is put on a level with people like myself, who believe that the best thing for all Irishmen is a united Ireland, and that it would be a better place for all than a divided Ireland can ever be. People whose ancestors were in this country before the first of the planters proceeded to drive out the inhabitants, are to be on the same level and to be treated alike. Notwithstanding the plain precepts of the New Testament this godly Churchman's plan is plainly to extirpate his fellow Christians and to starve them to death, if, indeed, theirs is not going to be a sadder fate.

The Right Honourable Gentleman returned to the congenial task on 12th August last in Enniskillen. This time, however, he made a distinction which, in practice, leaves it exactly as it stood. He said: 'In Northern Ireland the Catholic population is increasing to a great extent . . . 97 per cent of Roman Catholics in Ireland are disloyal and disruptive.' You will notice his statistics. 'If they, in Ulster, allow Roman Catholics to work on their farms they are traitors to Ulster.'

By the way, the cry about people coming across the Border is flatly contradicted by the Honourable Baronet's own organisation which met in Enniskillen on 10th April last. It is reported there that the Unionist majority shows some increase since the previous revision, notwithstanding which, you will be surprised to hear, the association reported a small debit balance, which hardly looks as if the loyalists of Fermanagh were so enthusiastically behind the Right Honourable Gentleman as he makes out. A debit balance remains. That cuts plainly across the declaration and the statements made in this Parliament recently, when the Representation of the People Bill was introduced. I fear that neither fact nor consistency will trouble the people at the back of this anti-Christian crusade.

I confess I did expect that when the Member for Lisnaskea received his portfolio as Minister he would have recognised the obligations of a Minister of the Crown. But in common with others, I did not reckon on the degree of anti-Catholic hate which seems to boil up in him periodically like a spring. At Derry, on 19th March, he confirmed his pre-Ministerial, anti-Christian, and anti-Catholic programme, as follows: 'When I made that declaration' – that is, the declaration of Newtownbutler – 'I did so after careful consideration. What I said was justified. I recommend people not to employ Roman Catholics, who are 99 per cent disloyal.'

You will notice that in Newtownbutler it was 97 per cent. They had increased by 2 per cent so that this extraordinary Minister of Agriculture seems to have had a new census made of the whole of the Catholics in the Six Counties. He proceeded: 'One paper admitted that 100 per cent of the Roman Catholics were Nationalists and, therefore, out for the destruction of the Ulster Constitution. What I said had nothing to do with a man's method of religion. That is no concern of anybody's, but when that religion is so politically minded and is out to destroy us as a body, it does concern us then. I will continue to criticise and to take what action I can. What astonishes me is that these people are rather hurt because of my utterance.'

It is interesting to see that the Honourable Baronet is now prepared to allow Catholics to practise their religion. I am sure we are all obliged to him for that concession. In fact, we are not to be molested if we are found going to Mass. In that respect it resembles Cromwell's boast after Drogheda – that he had left two friars alive out of the thousand people massacred. But in other respects there is no difference in the policy of 'to Hell or Connaught' practised by the leader of the Ironsides and the Lisnaskea Cromwell, whose slogan is – 'Don't employ Catholics – starve them.'

Let me draw the attention of the House to the British Act of 1920, under which it receives its authority. There was some fear at the time that the minorities in the North and South might be subject to penalties indirectly on account of religion. So Section 5 of the Government of Ireland Act, 1920, expressly stipulated that: 'In the exercise of their power to make laws under this Act the Parliament of Northern Ireland shall not make a law so as directly or indirectly to establish or endow any religion or prohibit or restrict the free exercise thereof, or give a

preference, privilege or advantage, or impose any disability or disad-
vantage on account of religious belief or religious or ecclesiastical status.'

This House has already legislated in the matter of education, so as
directly to penalise Catholics. It is true the Prime Minister claims that
if Catholics transfer their schools to the secular Protestant authority
they can secure the terms which are now available to the members of
every other creed. He knows perfectly well that course is impossible.

. Catholics cannot conscientiously transfer the religious teaching of
the young to any secular authority, even if it were done without religious or political bias, which cannot be found in the Six Counties. The
Minister for Agriculture, seeing the prime Minister break the undertaking
he accepted under the 1920 Act, thought he would go one better. Not
only would he penalise Catholics, but he would extirpate them by
denying them the right to work. It is quite clear that the Government
has, therefore decided in practice, to drive a coach and four through the
undertaking which the British Government gave the Irish minorities.

There is no Catholic on the Bench in Northern Ireland, where the
Catholics are in a majority over any other creed. When Catholics holding
public positions die or resign they are being replaced by Protestants. I
have no objection to the appointment of a person of any creed, provided it
is made on merit, but I do protest against this disgraceful discrimination
which the Government has been pursuing for a considerable time.

The Right Honourable Gentleman claims that Catholics are not
loyal. Loyal to what? I will show later that the only type of loyalty
which this Government recognises is that which helps them to remain
upon the Treasury Bench. When they speak of loyalty they mean
loyalty to His Majesty the Prime Minister. The King governs through
his Ministers, and the Administration here does not know the day
when a Socialist Government may replace the National one, so they
stipulate for a conditional loyalty to the Throne, just so long as it suits.
We have not forgotten 1914 and the Provisional Government set up
here. We may live to see the praters about loyalty to the Constitution
take their guns again and go out to attack the King's troops.

The Orange Order, which is the shadow and power behind the
Government, was born to stir up strife amongst neighbours and has,
unwittingly perhaps, carried out that policy at intervals since. Its loyalty
can be judged from the fact that a Commission held that it was responsible for the attempt to oust Queen Victoria from the Throne, and to
set its own nominee – the Duke of Cumberland, in her place. The riots

which disgraced the cities of Derry and Belfast from 1813 to 1886 were traced to that Order by the successive Royal Commissions which sat to take evidence. It had to be suppressed by a British Statute not less than four times in that interval.

When I spoke of the Orange mob recently to describe the rather rowdy elements which mainly made up the processions following the Member for Derry City, he protested. I would point out, however, that it was a Royal Commissioner who first used the term 'mob' to describe the drum-beating brethren, not I. I gladly admit that there are many decent men in the Order, but they are not allowed to think for themselves; they are being saturated with anti-Catholic dope and then used as the vocal tools of better-informed people, who have their own axes to grind.

The Minister of Agriculture objects to our changing the Government by the vote. That is the primary purpose of the Representation of the People Bill recently introduced. Nationalists are described as disloyal because they would change the Government by constitutional means. The Right Honourable Member for Lisnaskea [*Sir Basil Brooke*] has a particular grievance against myself, because he says I would do my best to bring Ulster into a united Ireland by the power of the vote or by peaceful penetration. I have never used the term peaceful penetration, but I see no objection to it. If Nationalists are not permitted to work for a united Ireland by the vote, I ask you what other means are left to them? You are coming to the time when Nationalist exercise of the franchise anywhere will almost seem a wasted effort.

I warn you now that you are moulding a policy that may soon drive Nationalists out of this house altogether. At the moment they see little use in playing politics with people who do not possess even the most elementary notion of justice or fair play. They are indeed beginning to ask themselves if it is worth while keeping representatives here. They might achieve their desire for a united Ireland more readily by encouraging the rise of an independent Unionist party. There are not many constituencies in the North and the Nationalists holding the balance of power might occupy here in a few years the strong position which Parnell occupied in British politics in the eighties. You are preparing for that position now.

Whatever may be their views of the Government or laws, however much they may long for the day when they will see an end to such an intolerant and sectarian administration, and have a united government

for the whole country, Nationalists are at the moment observing the law
as well as any other class in the Six Counties. And therefore they ought
to be treated as good citizens are treated in every country in the world.
Hitler has not prosecuted the Jews nearly so much nor so subtly nor so
long as you have persecuted the Catholics in the Six Counties. The
world's Press proclaim his crime; it is still silent as to yours. But on this
question of loyalty I think you have the slenderest right to speak. Your
past belies your present professions of loyalty. On the Treasury Bench I see
some of the men who in 1914 set up an illegal Provisional Government
in opposition to the King's Government. One of the military chiefs of
the time described the present residence of the Prime Minister as a
veritable arsenal from which armed men marched to the Liverpool boat
to meet Sir Edward Carson. The Speaker of the House asked him at
this point to stop 'travelling very wide of the motion he has put down.'

The whole case made before now and up to this moment is this, that
the Nationalists are not loyal, and surely I am entitled to meet that case
in this way, by showing that the people who make that charge are
themselves not loyal, and have no right to make it. My memory goes
back to the 1914 episode out of which this whole Parliament arose, and
I remember the importation of arms into the ports of Larne and Bangor. I
remember the gun-running. I remember the declarations made by Right
Honourable and Honourable Members of this House as to the degree
of their loyalty, and I want to put those declarations in contrast with the
position of Nationalists, some thousands of whom in the Great War
gave up their lives hoping that it was a war in defence of small nation-
alities. I should like for one minute to quote here some of the declarations that were made at that time. Mr. Gerard, who was the American
Ambassador to Germany, said in My Four Years in Germany:

'The raising of the Ulster Army by Sir Edward Carson ... was reported
by the German spies as a real and serious revolutionary movement, and
of course it was believed by the Germans that Ireland would rise in
rebellion the moment war was declared.'

The Belfast *Evening Telegraph* on 27th August, 1913, stated: 'Sir
Edward Carson had the honour of receiving an invitation to dine with
the Kaiser last week at Hamburg.'

That is an interesting thing in view of the challenge of Nationalist
disloyalty.

Captain Craig, MP is reported in the *Morning Post* of 9th January,
1911 to have said: 'There is a spirit spreading, which I can testify to

from my personal knowledge, that Germany and the German Emperor would be preferred to the rule of John Redmond.'

Then Mr Robert Thompson, M.P., chairman of the Belfast Harbour Board, on 8th April, 1912, said: 'We are promised a large measure of support from Canada . . . Germany has been looking after Ulster developments. She has the drawings completed of every dock we have in the Harbour . . . still more, she has an officer named to carry out the necessary campaign.'

And this is from a report of a speech made by Sir Edward Carson in the Criterion Restaurant, London, on 24th June, 1912: 'It has been said he ought to be sent to jail . . . he intended when he went over to Ulster to break every law that was possible.'

Again at Blenheim, on 23rd July, 1912, Sir Edward Carson said: 'They may tell us if they like that that is treason. It is not for men who have such stakes as we have at issue to trouble about the cost.'

At Derry, on 20th September, 1912, Sir Edward Carson said: 'Let no man make light of signing the Covenant. It was signed by soldiers in uniform, policemen and great lawyers. Any man who having made this pledge goes back on it, or fails at the critical moment, let him beware. He is a betrayer of his brother.'

In an interview with a representative of the *Daily Telegraph* on 20th April, 1914, Sir Edward Carson, said: 'Had the operations started by the Constabulary of seizing the Old Town Hall the Unionist Headquarters proceeded . . . as a high percentage of Belfast's male population carry revolvers . . . long before the police could have arrived the streets would have been running in blood.'

Mr. William Moore, KC, M.P., speaking at Birkenhead on 10th March, 1913 said: 'I have no doubt, if Home Rule is carried, its baptism in Ireland will be a baptism in blood.'

This is from an open letter which appeared in the *Coleraine Constitution* in July, 1913: 'Can King George sign the Home Rule Bill? Let him do so and his Empire shall perish as true as God rules heaven . . . Therefore, let King George sign the Home Rule Bill; he is no longer my King.'

Sir Edward Carson at Belfast on 12th July, 1913, declared: 'The Army are with us.'

The Irish Churchman, 14th November, 1913, stated: 'It may not be known to the rank and file of Unionists that we have the offer of aid from a powerful continental monarch, who, if Home Rule is forced on the Protestants of Ireland, is prepared to send an army sufficient to relieve England of any further trouble in Ireland by attaching it to his dominion . . . The Protestants of Ireland will welcome this continental deliverer as their forefathers, under similar circumstances, did once before.'

Sir William Johnson-Hicks, speaking on 6th December, 1913, said: 'The people of Ulster have behind them the Unionist Party . . . In God's name they said to the Prime Minister; 'Let your armies and batteries fire. Fire if you dare! Fire and be damned.'

My last quotation is from a speech delivered by Sir Edward Carson in Armagh on 4th October, 1913. He said: 'If anything could add to the gratification which I feel at the present moment it is that there should stand beside me here the Lord Primate of Ireland, a very good specimen, if I may say so, of a brother rebel.'

Mr. Speaker, I ask the Prime Minister a question through you. Who was it that first imported arms into this country?

Did not the Irish Republican Army merely march in the footsteps of the gentleman who is now the King's Prime Minister in Northern Ireland? I shall be told that your treason was of the conditional type. You knew and Sir Edward Carson knew you would never be obliged to make good in the flesh your promises to the mob. And you were right in that. For you, the ringleaders in rebellion, there was to be the Government Bench and the profitable post of a law lord. For Casement, Pearse, Connolly and the rest there was to be a bullet at dawn and a grave in quick lime. That is how justice is administered.

The old proverb has it: 'Treason never does prosper.' Why? When treason prospers men do not call it treason. Treason has prospered with you. You have achieved place and power by treason. There can be no better authority upon disloyalty than the Prime Minister and his pale shadows, the Ministers for Home Affairs and Agriculture.

Nationalists, whom you twit with disloyalty, never said they would prefer the Kaiser to the King in the days when war was in sight. No, instead, they sent out their sons to die for an ideal. They have been disillusioned by you. When someone said it was a war to make the world safe for democracy, he was merely telling a lie. They have read the declaration of the Minister for Agriculture. 'I have not a Catholic about my place,' and they know that whatever proof of loyalty they could give would not secure them the humble position of a rate collector in any County of the North. If the sons of some of them turn away from Constitutionalism, can you wonder? They look at you and they see that the only way to succeed is by treason and physical force. You may reply that because we tried to upset the Government in 1921 and 1922 that is your justification for anything and everything. In so far as it went we merely imitated your own policy and methods.

Honourable Members opposite may ask me what about Mr. O'Kelly. The rather loose statement of the Vice-President of the Free State recently has caused quite a sensation up here. The people remember 1914 and since, and know that if he meant his threat which he probably did not he would be merely adopting the means you used to climb to power and partition this country. You have not the least fear of anyone in the Free State deposing you by physical force so long as the British Army is intact. It may suit your policy of stirring up sectarian strife to use such threats with which to frighten every independently minded Protestant up here and cause him to fall in behind the Orange Order, which calls the tune to which you all must dance every time.

The leaders of the Orange Order talk big of 'civil and religious liberty' once or twice a year, but in practice this only means liberty for themselves. The extent of the liberty of thought the Orange Order are prepared to give anyone can be gauged by their outlawing Senator Gyle for being present in the room of the late Mr. Devlin when some friend was making a prayer. I must offer my sympathy to certain members here who find themselves in an Organisation so devoid of Christian charity and lacking in any knowledge of Christianity. I wish they had the courage to step outside its darkened wall into the light or liberty, of real Christianity.

In these circumstances it is now clear that the Prime Minister desires Nationalists to have votes only on condition that he has an assurance that they are always going to remain a minority. Because they aim at changing the Government itself, or the form of the Government, by constitutional means, he gets angry and says their voting power must be reduced to a minimum. If gerrymandering will not do it – where one Unionist vote is equal to two and a quarter Nationalist votes – he will resort to everything calculated to prevent Nationalists getting any votes. He wants to secure that opposition must never be able to get a majority at all.

The Representation of the People Bill is the beginning; it is by no means the end of the chapter of rebellion opened by the Prime Minister in 1914. In pursuance of this policy, should there be such a landslide from the supporters of the Government, as we believe possible in a reasonable time, the Prime Minister will not hesitate to trample upon the British Constitution again, take up the gun, and set up a dictatorship. The man who says that a Catholic must not get work because he is desirous of getting rid of a Government which made rebellion fashionable in 1914, will not hesitate to substitute once more the rule of the gun for the will of the people.

Nationalists now see whither they are drifting. The Prime Minister desires them to clear out of politics altogether. His opponents may regard his opinion in that respect as carrying more wisdom than he suspects. We accept it partially. We will not allow ourselves to become an official Opposition in this House. We will only intervene when we feel that we can expose injustice. But we reserve the right to come in or stay outside, as and when our people may decide. If bad feelings develop in the North, to the loss of trade, the business people will know where the scheme originated.

Nationalists have been anxious, while reserving their right as to the form of Government under which they live, to do their best to promote the welfare of the Six Counties. They have been desirous of forgetting old sectarian animosities and cultivating friendship with all creeds and classes. The Prime Minister is afraid that such a policy – the uniting of Orange and Green – might eventually lead to a new political orientation in the North, so he has called out the dogs of war in the persons of the Honourable and learned Member for Derry [Mr. Murphy] and the Minister of Agriculture, who sees a long period in his profitable office if he can only keep up the old hates, the old sectarian strife. I am glad that I was born poor, so that I can live without such spoils of office. I would rather go out on the roadsides and break stones in all sorts of weather than hold office by such degrading tactics.

We rejoice that the mass of the Northern Protestants are not likely to heed such an unchristian lead. They realise that a policy of that sort would be a great set-back to their own business or trade. Even the Members behind the Government, who employ many Catholics, are not likely to dismiss one merely because the Minister for Agriculture desires it. No political party in Great Britain would exist for a year if it advocated the restriction to its public services of people of a particular Christian church. It would be regarded as a scandal and would bring down any Government which attempted it. We know there is today no place for a Catholic in any public office. They are banned more effectively by the bigotry, secret and open, of the Northern Ministers, than they were in the days before the passing of Catholic Emancipation. But for all that, we are far from despairing. We have assurances from many Protestants that they abhor your policy and have no intention of paying the least heed to it.

We believe the justice of our case will triumph over your intolerance. The mass of the Protestant people, after all, get nothing more from you than we. It is only the select few, the friends and associates of the members of the Government, who share the plums of office. And whatever you may do by legislation we tell you now that we are not to be driven from the Six Counties. Like the Jews, we were born to suffering and persecution, and we love the land and its associations. What Elizabethans failed in doing you cannot accomplish. What Cromwell attempted in vain you will also attempt in vain. God and right are with us and these will prevail over all your machinations. This is not the last generation. Neither will your threats cause us to change our ideals, of a united and free Ireland.

James Craig
24 April 1934

A FTER CAHIR Healy, the political leader of the Northern Ireland Nationalists, proposed the motion in the Northern Ireland Parliament 'that in the opinion of this House the campaign against the employment of Catholics promulgated by the Minister of Agriculture and expressly sanctioned by the Prime Minister is a grave violation of the rights and liberties of the minority placed under the rule of the Northern Government,' the Northern Ireland Prime Minister, James Craig, offered an alternative motion for consideration by the House.

The motion suggested by Craig was 'that in the opinion of this House the employment of disloyalists entering Northern Ireland is prejudicial, not only to the interests of law and order and the safety of the State, but also to the prior claims of loyal Ulster-born citizens seeking employment.'

He then went on to answer the charges brought against himself and some of his Ministers by Healy:

Reply to Healy

I may have some little difficulty in replying to all the charges that have been made against the Government, and, particularly, against myself this afternoon. When I came down here I thought I was to deal more with the implication that lay in the Motion by the Nationalist Party than to be ready to go back along history and to touch upon matters which have now drifted into the years that lie behind. But in case there should be any impression left in the mind of Honourable Members opposite that I desire to shirk the responsibility which I take on my shoulders from time to time, I will say here and now quite frankly, as this happens to be the actual anniversary of the gun running into Ulster that saved the Province to Great Britain and the Empire, that if I had to do it again I would go through it every step if as a result we were able to cling, as we have always done, to those loyal men in other parts of the Empire who wished us well and were only too delighted that our action saved Ulster for the Empire.

Then the Honourable Member [*Mr. Healy*] rails and jeers at the Orange Institution and places some of the blame on that Order. He says we are all mere puppets in the hands of those who are in that ancient and honourable Institution. I suppose I am about as high up in the Orange Institution as anybody else. I am very proud indeed to be Grand Master of the loyal County of Down. I have filled that office many years, and I prize that far more than I do being Prime Minister. I have always said I am an Orange man first and a politician and Member of this Parliament afterwards. Therefore, if Honourable Members think for a moment that by taunts and jeers at the Orange Institution they will make me withdraw in the slightest degree anything I have done in my capacity as a loyal Orangeman, they make a very great mistake.

Then to come down a little bit more definitely to some of the charges of partiality and persecution of the Nationalists in the Ulster area, may I just recall that when the Honourable Members of the Nationalist Party were elected to this House under Proportional Representation, for which they seem to have such affection, they were exactly in the same position as they are in here today when elected for single-Member constituencies? So anxious were my colleagues and myself to be absolutely fair when the redistribution of seats took place that we did not actually call upon the Act of 1920, which permitted us to do away with Proportional Representation after a trial of the Act, for three years.

My colleagues and I were most meticulously anxious that there should be no mistakes made about the redistribution of seats and, therefore, in order to make astutely certain that we were not going beyond what was right and fair towards the Opposition, we allowed, not one, but actually two General Elections to take place under Proportional Representation and on each occasion the number of Nationalist Members returned to this House was, to all intents and purposes exactly the same as the number of seats the Honourable Members now hold. No man can charge us with being unfair in a matter of that kind. Where does the unfairness come in? Do the Nationalist members want twenty seats? How many seats do they want? They have got the same number of seats as under the Act of 1920, after a trial of two General Elections.

At this point Mr. Healy interrupted him saying: 'Is the Prime Minister now speaking of local government?

The Honourable Member in his very bland way pretends to misunderstand. If he had been listening he would have heard me say that it was with regard to Proportional Representation for this House: I am coming to this other matter in a moment. Therefore, I honestly think that these charges are more for the sake of outside consumption than with any thought that they will impress my Honourable Friends behind me with the idea that they have been dealing in any harsh or unfriendly manner.

Now I come to the question of local government. When this Government took office we sent down – I am speaking now entirely from memory – the Deputy Recorder of Belfast, a learned King's Counsel, and a man whom everybody respected in his profession. He was quite free of the Government or of any taint of the Government either before the Act of 1920 or after it. We sent him down throughout the country in order that he should map out what should be the proper local government areas for Ulster. We left the matter entirely to him.

He went round, and he issued an advertisement for every county and every local authority into whose areas he went, saying that on certain days he would sit in order to hear the evidence, not of Orangemen, not of loyalists, but of everyone inside that area, the Nationalists as well as the others. And what happened? What help did Honourable Members opposite give to him? What help did their party give to him? They boycotted his court. They refused to allow anybody to go near him to give evidence. They left the whole business entirely in his own hands, and he did the best he could in fairness to the people in making out a proper schedule for local government for Northern Ireland. What answer has the honourable member of South Fermanagh to give to that? Or the honourable member for West Tyrone?

Mr. Donnelly, the member for West Tyrone, replied by telling the audience that the scheme for Tyrone was prepared months in advance by the Orangemen.

I am delighted that the Orange body showed themselves to be alert and able to come forward and help in a matter of that kind. I may say, from my experience of Tyrone, that it is not often the Nationalists are caught napping in a matter like that. Now, let me go on again to what the Government had to set up in the first instance. We established first of all a Committee of this House, on which all the members were thoroughly represented, in order to see that there was fair play so far as the Royal

Ulster Constabulary were concerned. I think nearly all the members on that committee are still here, and they will be able to correct me if I go beyond accuracy. If I remember aright there were no Members of the Government on this committee. This committee reported to the House that they thought it would be fair to give representation in the Royal Ulster Constabulary on the basis of the proportion of the Nationalists to the loyalists in the area, or, if Honourable Members like me to put it this way, two thirds to the Protestants and one-third to the Roman Catholics.

That was according to the recognised population, and it has been the basis on which a great many of our actions have been carried through since then. What happened? Once again, although about 1,000 places out of 3,000 were kept open for the Roman Catholics to come along and take their part in helping to develop and to police Ulster, there was a boycott. They were not allowed to join. They were told, 'No, nothing must be done to enable the Ulster Government to get well established.' That is a very significant fact. I do not think it is sufficiently realised by honourable Members opposite that the blame, far from resting on this side of the House rests on that side of the House, or, rather, with those whom they represent for having said, 'No, we are not going to allow you to take part in a matter of this kind.'

Then the Honourable Member for South Fermanagh made a strong attack in regard to the judiciary because there was no Roman Catholic sitting on the Northern Bench. Let me remind you that the first Lord Chief Justice of Northern Ireland was a Roman Catholic, and a very distinguished one, a man whom everyone respected. I can only say that if there was another man like him in the ranks of the learned Gentleman's religious denomination there would be nothing to prevent his reaching the same high and distinguished position as was occupied by my old good friend, Sir Denis Henry.

I have never yet known a country prosper where appointments to the judiciary were made on religious grounds. [*Honourable Members: Hear, hear*] I think it would be a fatal mistake if whoever had an opportunity of recommending to His Majesty the names for the high position of judges in this land had to take into consideration a man's religion. As long as I have anything to do with it, I say here quite frankly and openly, that that aspect will never enter into my mind. Only the best man who can be had for the position will be recommended. These matters are all readily answered, I think, to the satisfactin of any fair-minded man.

I will refer next to the speech of the Honourable Members for West Tyrone [*Mr. Donnelly*]. I am very glad he has admitted something along the lines of the Amendment which the Government has seen fit to put down to this Vote of want of confidence, for that is really what it amounts to. When my colleagues have passed the Resolution it will read like this: –

'That in the opinion of this House the employment of disloyalists entering Northern Ireland is prejudicial, not only to the interests of law and order and the safety of the State, but also to the prior claims of loyal Ulster-born citizens seeking employment.'

All through this debate the charges made by honourable Members opposite have been grossly exaggerated. Since we took up office we have tried to be absolutely fair towards all the citizens of Northern Ireland. Actually, on an Orange platform, I, myself, laid down the principle, to which I still adhere, that I was Prime Minister not of one section of the community but of all, and that as far as I possibly could I was going to see that fair play was meted out to all classes and creeds without any favour whatever on my part.

Mr Leeke, cried, 'What about your Protestant Parliament?'

The Honourable Member must remember that in the South they boasted of a Catholic State. They still boast of Southern Ireland being a Catholic State. All I boast of is that we are a Protestant Parliament and a Protestant State. It would be rather interesting for historians of the future to compare a Catholic State launched in the South with a Protestant State launched in the North and to see which gets on the better and prospers the more. It is most interesting for me at the moment to watch how they are progressing. I am doing my best always to top the bill and to be ahead of the South.

As I have said, there is a great deal of exaggeration in the statements made to-day. Are memories so short that Honourable Members opposite have forgotten that those who came into this Northern area at a certain period of our career came for the purpose of preventing the Ulster Government from being established. We will never forget the death of our old colleague, Mr. Twaddell, and there are two honourable Members of this House who bear the marks of bullets because of their loyalty in helping the Government to maintain law and order. Those people, I always believe, came from outside. Is it any wonder that we should take precautions and advise our own people in this area to beware of persons of that type coming into Ulster in order to recreate all the turmoil, murder, bloodshed, and trouble from which we formerly suffered.

May I just for a moment mention what happens in our Dominions in regard to the prohibition of foreigners and other persons coming into those countries. I am reading extracts from the regulations governing the admission of immigrants into certain British Dominions and also into Kenya. Persons likely to endanger the safety of the State, and they are the persons referred to in this Amendment, are not admitted. Take Canada:

(a) Persons who believe in or advocate the overthrow by force or violence of the Government of Canada or of constituted law and authority, or who disbelieve in or are opposed to organised government, or who advocate the assassination of public officials, or who advocate or teach the unlawful destruction of property.

(b) Persons who are members of or affiliated with any Organisation entertaining or teaching disbelief in our opposition to organized government or advocating or teaching the duty, necessity, or propriety of the unlawful assaulting or killing of any officer or officers either of specific individuals or of officers generally, of the Government of Canada or of any other organised government, because of his or their local character, or advocating or teaching, the unlawful destruction of property.

Take New Zealand. The persons not admitted there are: Persons who are disaffected or disloyal, or of such a character that their place would be injurious to the peace, order, and good government of the Dominion.

Take South Africa. Who is refused admission there? Any person who from information received from any government [whether British or Foreign] through official or diplomatic channels, is deemed by the Minister to be an undesirable inhabitant of or visitor to the Union.

Take Kenya. Admission is refused to: Any person deemed by the Immigration Officer, from information received from a reliable source, to be an undesirable immigrant.

These are the types of persons to whom my Right Honourable Friend the Minister of Agriculture [*Basil Brooke*] was referring, and to whom I am referring in the Government's Amendment to this proposed Resolution. We are not afraid at all of the population which we at the present moment have to govern. Not one bit. We are quite prepared to give and, as I say, we do give the fairest play to all. It is all nonsense to say that the party represented by honourable Members opposite are penalised. They always talk about the Education Act. The Education Act does not mention them in any one word. There is no differentiation. The Education Act is alarmed so accurately that all can benefit, and so far as other things are concerned I think I have dealt with them fully.

Now we can deal with our own population perfectly well, but we do say and we do think it right to give warning to the people that they should not employ people coming over the Border who may be drifting into this part to destroy the constitution and to start over again the trouble which we overcame in 1920, 1921, and 1922. Is it any wonder we should do so? I should look upon myself as lacking in my duty to the people of Ulster if I did not take every precaution to see that such happening does not take place.

Let me deal with the second part, which is still one to be borne in mind, but before I pass on to that I would just remind Honourable Members that only today the British Government have introduced a Bill which is called the Incitement to Disaffection Bill. That Bill is going through the British House of Commons at the present moment. It is to deal with any endeavour to seduce any person serving in His Majesty's forces from his duty or allegiance to His Majesty. All that we here desire to see is that allegiance to His Majesty – which, thank God, the great majority of the loyal Ulster people wish always to maintain – shall not be impaired by people who come in here to help to break the last link between Great Britain and Ireland. They are attempting to do that in the South. That is an attempt to which we will be no party here. Therefore we are justified in taking all the steps we have taken in order to safeguard our position to the best of our ability. We have anticipated the British Government because in our Civil Authorities Act we are able to deal with crime and outrage and threats just as strong as the British Government will be able to deal with the sowing disaffection in His Majesty's forces.

I wish now to deal very shortly with the point that we can here quite readily and appropriately absorb our own natural increase in population from year to year. I think that industry, which is on the turn, will be able to pick up the unemployed of whom there are, I agree, far too many, some 63,000 in our midst. But I do not see why the loyal Ulster artisan should pay contributions in order to maintain people who come from the other side and who compete with them in the market here for labour, and until that 63,000 is fully absorbed it is only fair to place every obstacle we can in the way of people coming across the Border from the Free State and after a certain time qualifying for taking the jobs of our people here.

I do claim that over and above law and order and the safety of the Province there are strong arguments why we should protect our own loyal workingmen and if any preference is given they should be given that preference over anyone coming across the Border. We have a long way to go yet. I think we should take every means as early as possible to urge the public to employ only loyalists. I say only loyalists. I do not care what their religion may be. I say as long as they are loyal people we will engage them and we will give them every chance and will help them, but we must be particular to see that none of these men can burrow underneath our constitution, working day and night to destroy Ulster which took us so long to build up.

Before I close I would just like to say that fortunately for us there is no great hardship in the recommendation or advice which my Right Honorable Friend gave.

I would ask the genial and kindly Member for South Fermanagh [*Mr. Healy*] what hardship there will be if he uses his strong political influence to keep people in the Free State and says to them: 'You who are not able to find work stay there. Do not come into Ulster. It is the most bigoted and horribly blackmouth place upon earth. Do not come in here. Stay in that glorious country, that part where it is overflowing with milk and honey, that new Jerusalem. Stay there and for God's sake do not put your noses across the border.'

Surely an appeal of that sort would sink into the minds of the Honorable Member's people. Let them all find their employment in their own area, and then we will have a better chance of picking up the unemployed upon the exchanges that already exist in the Ulster area. Let us be consistent in all these matters, and let us also never forget another matter, and this is of very great importance in the border counties. I do not suppose from the date that Mr. Redmond on the one hand and Lord Carson and myself on the other hand attended the conference at Buckingham Palace – I do not suppose from that day to this that the Counties of Tyrone and Fermanagh have ever been out of my mind. They must get all the support they ask for. They must get all the help they require, and so far as I am concerned and my colleagues in the Government are concerned it will never be refused them. Never. I do not mind going a step further and saying that the Government will be ready to pass even stronger legislation if it is found necessary to prevent anything I have hinted at to-day happening. We will not hesitate for one moment to make safe and sure what we have there and what we intend to hold. [*Honourable Members: Hear, hear*]

Terence O'Neill
9 December 1968

A S THE CIVIL Rights Movement grew in number and determination, the Northern Ireland Prime Minister, Captain Terence
O'Neill, made a series of reforms designed to reduce discrimination
against Catholics. These reforms included the abolition of the
Londonderry Corporation with its unfairly-elected Unionist majority,
the appointment of an Ombudsman to arbitrate grievances, and new
legislation to ensure the fair allocation of state housing.

Nevertheless, the situation remained potentially explosive and with
feelings rising on both sides of the religious and political divide, O'Neill
felt it necessary to appeal directly to the people of Northern Ireland.
On the 9 December, 1968, he appeared on television to say:

O'Neills TV Broadcast on the Worsening
Troubles in Northern Ireland

Ulster stands at the crossroads. I believe you know me well enough by
now to appreciate that I am not a man given to extravagant language.
But I must say to you this evening that our conduct over the coming
days and weeks will decide our future. And as we face this situation, I
would be failing in my duty to you as your Prime Minister if I did not
put the issues, calmly and clearly, before you all. These issues are far
too serious to be determined behind closed doors, or left to noisy
minorities. The time has come for the people as a whole to speak in a
clear voice.

For more than five years now I have tried to heal some of the deep
divisions in our community. I did so because I could not see how an
Ulster divided against itself could hope to stand. I made it clear that a
Northern Ireland based upon the interests of any one section rather
than upon the interests of all could have no long-term future.

Throughout the community many people have responded warmly to my words. But if Ulster is to become the happy and united place it could be there must be the will throughout our Province and particularly in Parliament to translate these words into deeds.

In Londonderry and other places recently, a minority of agitators determined to subvert lawful authority played a part in setting light to highly inflammable material. But the tinder for that fire in the form of grievances real or imaginary, had been piling up for years.

And so I saw it as our duty to do two things. First, to be firm in the maintenance of law and order, and in resisting those elements which seek to profit from any disturbances. Secondly, to ally firmness with fairness, and to look at any underlying causes of dissension which were troubling decent and moderate people. As I saw it, if we were not prepared to face up to our problems, we would have to meet mounting pressure both internally, from those who were seeking change, and externally from British public and parliamentary opinion, which had been deeply disturbed by the events in Londonderry.

That is why it has been my view from the beginning that we should decide – of our own free will and as a responsible Government in command of events – to press on with a continuing programme of change to secure a united and harmonious community. This indeed, has been my aim for over five years.

Moreover, I knew full well that Britain's financial and other support for Ulster, so laboriously built up could no longer be guaranteed if we failed to press on with such a programme.

I am aware, of course, that some foolish people have been saying: 'Why should we bow the knee to a Labour Prime Minister? Let's hold out until a Conservative Government returns to power, and then we need do nothing.' My friends, that is a delusion. This letter is from Mr. Edward Heath, and it tells me – with the full authority of the Shadow Cabinet and the expressed support of my old friend Sir Alec Douglas-Home – that a reversal of the policies which I have tried to pursue would be every bit as unacceptable to the Conservative Party. If we adopt an attitude of stubborn defiance we will not have a friend left at Westminster.

I make no apology for the financial and economic support we have received from Britain. As a part of the United Kingdom, we have always considered this to be our right. But we cannot be a part of the United Kingdom merely when it suits us. And those who talk so glibly about acts of impoverished defiance do not know or care what is at stake.

Your job, if you are a worker at Short's or Harland & Wolff; your subsidies if you are a farmer; your pension, if you are retired – all these set aspects of our life, and many others, depend on support from Britain. Is a freedom to pursue the un-Christian path of communal strife and sectarian bitterness really more important you than all the benefits of the British Welfare State?

But this is not all. Let me read to you some words from the Government of Ireland Act, 1920 – the Act of the British Parliament on which Ulster's Constitution is founded. 'Notwithstanding the establishment of the Parliament of Northern Ireland . . . the supreme authority of the Parliament of the United Kingdom shall remain unaffected and undiminished over all persons, matters and things in [Northern] Ireland and every part thereof.'

Because Westminster has trusted us over the years to use the powers of Stormont for the good of all the people of Ulster, a sound custom has grown up that Westminster does not use its supreme authority in fields where we are normally responsible. But Mr. Wilson made it absolutely clear to us that if we did not face up to our problems the Westminster Parliament may well decide to act over our heads. Where would our Constitution be then?

What shred of self-respect would be left to us? If we allowed others to solve our problems because we had not the guts – let me use a plain word – the guts to face up to them, we would be utterly shamed.

There are, I know, today some so-called loyalists who talk of independence from Britain – who seem to want a kind of Protestant Sinn Fein. These people will not listen when they are told that Ulster's income is £200 million a year but that we can spend £300 million – only because Britain pays the balance.

Rhodesia, in defying Britain from thousands of miles away, at least has an Air Force and an Army of her own. Where are the Ulster armoured divisions or the Ulster jet planes? They do not exist and we could not afford to buy them. These people are not merely extremists. They are lunatics who would set a course along a road which could only lead at the end into an all-Ireland Republic. They are not loyalists but disloyalists: disloyal to Britain, disloyal to the Constitution, disloyal to the Crown, disloyal – if they are in public life – to the solemn oaths they have sworn to Her Majesty The Queen.

But these considerations, important though they are, are not my main concern. What I seek – and I ask for the help and understanding of you all – is a swift end to the growing civil disorder throughout Ulster. For as matters stand today, we are on the brink of chaos, where neighbour could be set against neighbour. It is simple-minded to imagine that problems such as these can be solved by repression. I for one am not willing to expose our police force to indefinite insult and injury. Nor am I prepared to see the shopkeepers and traders of Ulster wrecked and looted for the benefit of the rabble. We must tackle root causes if this agitation is to be contained. We must be able to say to the moderate on both sides: come with us into a new era of co-operation, and leave the extremists to the law. But this I also say to all, Protestant or Roman Catholic, Unionist or Nationalist: disorder must now cease. We are taking the necessary measures to strengthen our police forces. Determined as we are to act with absolute fairness, we will also be resolute in restoring respect for the laws of the land.

Some people have suggested that I should call a general election. It would, in my view, be utterly reprehensible to hold an election against a background of bitterness and strife. I have spoken to you in the past about the grounds – well of moderate opinion. Its presence was seen three years ago when we fought an election on a manifesto which would stand inspection in any Western democracy and we swept the country on a non-sectarian platform. Those who would sow the wind by having a bitter election now would surely reap the whirlwind.

And now I want to say a word directly to those who have been demonstrating for civil rights. The changes which we have announced are genuine and far-reaching changes and the Government as a whole is totally committed to them. I would not continue to preside over an administration which would water them down or make them meaningless. You will see when the members of the Londonderry Commission are appointed that we intend to live up to our words that this will be a body to command confidence and respect. You will see that in housing allocations we mean business. You will see that legislation to appoint an Ombudsman will be swiftly introduced. Perhaps you are not entirely satisfied; but this is democracy, and I ask you now with all sincerity to call you people off the streets and allow an atmosphere favourable to change to develop. You are Ulstermen yourselves. You know we are all of us stubborn people, who will not be pushed too far. I believe that most of you want change, not revolution. Your voice has been heard, and clearly heard. Your duty now, is to play your part in taking the heat out of the situation before blood is shed.

But I have a word too for all those others who see in change a threat to our position in the United Kingdom. I say to them, Unionism armed with justice will be a stronger cause than Unionism armed merely with strength. The bully-boy tactics we saw in Armagh are no answer to these grave problems: but they incur for us the contempt of Britain and the world, and such contempt is the greatest threat to Ulster. Let the Government govern and the police take care of law and order.

What in any case are these changes which we have decided must come? They all amount to this: that in every aspect of our life, justice must not only be done but be seen to be done to all sections of the community. There must be evident fairness as between one man and another.

The adoption of such reforms will not I believe, lose a single seat at Stormont for those who support the Unionist cause and indeed some may be gained. And remember that it is with Stormont that the power of decision rests for maintaining our Constitution.

And now a further word to you all. What kind of Ulster do you want? A happy and respected Province, in good standing with the rest of the United Kingdom? Or a place continually torn apart by riots and demonstrations, and regarded by the rest of Britain as a political outcast? As always in a democracy, the choice is yours. I will accept whatever your verdict may be. If it is your decision that we should live up to the words 'Ulster is British' which is part of our creed, then my services will be at your disposal to do what I can. But if you should want a separate, inward-looking, selfish and divided Ulster then you must seek for others to lead you along that road, for I cannot and will not do it. Please weigh well all that is at stake, and make your voice heard in whatever way you think best so that we may know the views not of the few but of the many. For this is truly a time of decision, and in your silence all that we have built up could be lost. I pray that you will reflect carefully and decide wisely. And I ask all our Christian people, whatever their denomination, to attend their places of worship on Sunday next to pray for the peace and harmony of our country.

The response to O'Neill's appeal was phenomenal. In the weeks that followed nearly 150,000 people signed messages endorsing the sentiments of the television broadcast. Yet within six months he had resigned his position as leader of the Unionist Party and Prime Minister of Northern Ireland as it became increasingly doubtful that the Unionists would support his reform policies.

Jack Lynch
13 August 1969

IN JANUARY, 1967 the Northern Ireland Civil Rights Association was formed to campaign for increased civil rights for Catholics. The first civil rights march was held in Dungannon in August, 1968 and passed off without incident. Future marches, however, often resulted in violence and soon images of baton-yielding police were being beamed all over the world.

In June, 1969 southern Ireland saw Fianna Fáil, under the leadership of Jack Lynch, frustrate its rivals by winning the general election with an increased majority. One of the first issues to confront the Lynch Government was the increased violence on the streets of Northern Ireland and the increasing republican sympathies of the Southern Irish towards the Northern Catholics.

After the overzealous reaction of the Royal Ulster Constabulary [RUC] and the Ulster Special Constabulary [the B-Specials] to rioting in Derry, Jack Lynch, gave the following broadcast on RTE television on the evening of 13 August:

Lynch's TV Broadcast on the Worsening Troubles in Northern Ireland

It is with deep sadness that you, Irish men and women of goodwill, and I, have learned of the tragic events which have been taking place in Derry and elsewhere in the North in recent days. Irishmen in every part of this island have made known their concern at these events. This concern is heightened by the realisation that the spirit of reform and intercommunal co-operation has given way to the forces of sectarianism and prejudice. All people of goodwill must feel saddened and disappointed at this backward turn in events and must be apprehensive for the future.

The Government fully share these feelings and I wish to repeat that we deplore sectarianism and intolerance in all the forms wherever they occur. The Government have been very patient and have acted with great restraint over several months past. While we made our views known to the British Government on a number of occasions, both by direct contact and through our diplomatic representatives in London, we were careful to do nothing that would exacerbate the situation. But it is clear now that the present situation cannot be allowed to continue.

It is evident also, that the Stormont Government is no longer in control of the situation. Indeed the present is the inevitable outcome of the policies pursued by successive Stormont Governments. It is clear also, that the Irish Government can no longer stand by and see innocent injured and perhaps worse.

It is obvious that the RUC is no longer accepted as an impartial police force. Neither would the employment of British troops be acceptable nor would they be likely to restore peaceful conditions, certainly not in the long term. The Government have therefore, requested the British Government to apply immediately to the United Nations for the urgent dispatch of a peace-keeping force to the Six Counties of Northern Ireland and have instructed the Irish Permanent Representative to the United Nations to inform the Secretary-General of this request. We have also asked the British Government to see to it that police attacks on the people of Derry should cease immediately.

Very many people have been injured and some of them seriously. We know that many of these do not wish to be treated in Six-County hospitals. We have therefore, directed the Irish Army authorities to have field hospitals established in County Donegal adjacent to Derry and at other points along the Border where they may be necessary.

Recognising however, that the re-unification of the national territory can provide the only permanent solution for the problem, it is our intention to request the British Government to enter into early negotiations with the Irish Government to review the present constitutional position of the Six Counties of Northern Ireland.

These measures which I have outlined to you seem to the Government to be those most immediately and urgently necessary.

All men and women of goodwill will hope and pray that the present deplorable and distressing situation will not further deteriorate but that it will soon be ended, firstly, by the granting of full equality of citizenship to every man and woman in the Six-County area regardless of class, creed or political persuasion and eventually, by the restoration of the historic unity of our country.

Three days later the British army was ordered onto the streets of Northern Ireland. The B Specials were placed under army control and a committee was set up to decide on how best the RUC could be reorganised.

Brian Faulkner
28 March 1972

IN MARCH 1971, with the political crisis in Northern Ireland worsening, James Chichester Clarke resigned as Prime Minister and his place was taken by Brian Faulkner. Faulkner selected a cabinet with a wide range of ideological view points and made a bid for the support of the main Nationalist party, the Social Democratic and Labour Party, by inviting its members to join various parliamentary committees. But following Faulkner's refusal to set up a public inquiry into the death of two local men killed by the British army whilst rioting in Derry in July, the SDLP withdrew from Stormont and tensions increased between the Nationalist communities and the British army and the Unionists.

Faulkner, introduced internment without trial in August, 1971. Casualties soared, whilst there had been thirty deaths up to the 9 August, there were a further 143 before the year was out. The situation deteriorated further at the start of 1972 when thirteen civil rights protesters were shot dead by the British Army in Derry, in what became known as Bloody Sunday. Relations between the Nationalists and their government reached an all-time low.

In March, 1972 the British Prime Minister, Edward Heath, sought complete British control of Northern Ireland security, justice and law and order. When Faulkner and his cabinet refused, the British government temporarily dismissed the Stormont Government and Parliament and introduced direct rule from London. William Whitelaw was appointed Northern Ireland Secretary.

On 28 March, the Northern Ireland Parliament was adjourned and Brian Faulkner made the following brief statement.

The Ulster Question

282

Final speech as Prime Minister in Northern Ireland Parliament

Mr. Speaker, Sir, I propose on this occasion to make a brief statement. My colleagues and I have made absolutely clear why and how it was that we reached a state of total disagreement with the United Kingdom Government and I do not propose to repeat this today. We have, however arranged that my own statement issued later that day by the Cabinet as a whole, should be placed formally on record as a White Paper, of which copies are now being made available to Hon. Members. As for what has followed upon that disagreement, others than we are responsible for it and must answer for it in another place.

I simply want to say this, as we in the present Government meet this House for the last time. For over 50 years the Government and the Parliament of Northern Ireland, and through them the people of Northern Ireland as a whole, have been given devoted service by servants of the Crown. We think of the men of the Royal Ulster Constabulary, of the Ulster Special Constabulary and of the Royal Ulster Constabulary Reserve – all forces, for which Government have answered to this House – and of the sacrifices they have made. In all these forces there have served some of the most splendid, brave and patriotic men the United Kingdom is ever likely to see.

We pay tribute, too, to the Civil Service, which as always worked with loyalty and dedication and which has risen with such cheerful courage to meet the challenges and the dangers of these recent years. And, of course, we have very much in our minds the loyal servants of this House, in great positions and in small, who have sought with total impartiality to serve, irrespective of party, all those all down the years who have been sent here by the people. They know what is in all our minds today – that there is only one authentic voice in any country and that is its elected democratic voice.

Before we adjourn today, I have no doubt that other Right Hon. and Hon. Members may wish to be heard here. We in the Government, however, will have nothing to add as such. We have explained our position. We have taken our stand. We leave our record over the last few days and as a whole to be judged by the country and by posterity.

I conclude with this final word as the government of Ulster is about to pass, temporarily at least, into other hands. I have always been proud to lead the present team in Government, but never so proud as last week. We stood firm and we stood together. When we faced a hard and unpalatable decision no hint of any other interest than the interest of the whole country was heard at the Cabinet table. We did what we believed to be right, for that is the spirit in which Ulster should always be served.

Could I just express the wish and – since I believe in its power – the prayer that we will seek peace, but that it will be peace with justice in our native land? Please God.

At the end of the one year prorogation, the Stormont government and Parliament was abolished and replaced by a new Northern Ireland Assembly.

Garret Fitzgerald
15 March 1984

FOLLOWING THE 1982 general election the Labour Party, under Dick Spring, decided to form a coalition government with the Fine Gael Party, under Garret Fitzgerald. When the Dáil reconvened on 26 November, Fitzgerald was appointed Taoiseach and Spring Tánaiste.

One of the key policy areas for the incoming government was Northern Ireland. A new initiative was needed as the sectarian and political crisis lay in stalemate. Fitzgerald, together with John Hume, the leader of the Northern Irish party, the SDLP, conceived the idea of establishing the New Ireland Forum. This forum examined in a radical way the future development of Ireland. All the constitutional parties north and south of the border, with the exception of Sinn Féin who were not invited due to their refusal to condemn violence, were invited but the Forum was weakened by the refusal of the Northern Unionist parties to attend. It's first session was held in Dublin Castle on the 30 May, 1983. In all, 137 written submissions were received, from Ireland and abroad. There were 28 private sessions, 13 public sessions and 56 meetings of the steering group.

As the Forum began drafting its final report, the Irish government felt that close contact with the United States government was necessary, for according to Fitzgerald, 'with the New Ireland Forum and the preparation for a negotiation with the British government, we needed to ensure as much sympathy and support for this policy as we could muster.' Moreover, Fitzgerald wanted to ensure greater American investment in Ireland and in addition Ronald Reagan, the United States President, had indicated an interest in visiting the country later in the year.

It was for these reasons that Fitzgerald visited the United States in 1984. On 15 March he addressed a joint session of Congress in Washington:

Address to the Joint Session of Congress in the US

Mr. Speaker, Mr. Vice-President, distinguished members Congress of the United States, with the Irish hospitality for which America is famous, you have been good enough to invite me to address you in the week of St. Patrick – Féile Phádraig in the language of the Gael. On behalf of the Irish people, close, as always, in feeling to their American cousins, I thank you for this honour.

This is the second time in eight years you have paid tribute in this way, by hearing from this dais the Head of an Irish Government, in celebration of the friendship and cousinship that binds our two peoples. The tradition is a long one, going back over a century to the year 1880, when you offered a platform to one of the first people from outside of the United States ever permitted to address this Congress, the great Irish leader, Charles Stewart Parnell.

I have said that we are cousins: our countries are linked by a special relationship, not built on mutual calculations of interest, but on human links of kinship and friendship: a unique relationship founded primarily and profoundly on people. The family relationship between us extends to 44 million Irish Americans, but in this week of each year, the whole people of this great nation, our friends for 51 weeks in the year, become our cousins in spirit as we honour together Ireland's national saint.

One of the great characteristics of the American people has always been your pride – your justified pride – in the achievements of the new nation that you have forged over several centuries in the land to which your forefathers came from the other continents of the world. That pride has sustained you in many troubles, many trials, many tragedies. It is founded on achievement and is sustained by an abiding faith in your capacity to face any challenge, and by a spirit of generous optimism.

We in Ireland also take pride in our country and in the achievements of our people. We are proud not only of the ancient origins of our race, of the survival of our people through so many struggles and hardships, of the cultural empire we have carved out in literature in the English language complementing our own ancient Gaelic tradition; we are proud also of being a mother country, a people of five million in their own island, but with tens of millions of children scattered throughout the world, keeping fresh the memory of their homeland, most jubilantly on the occasion of this feast of St. Patrick.

An ancient nation, we are a modern state, modern in the sense that the present Irish state took its place in the world community a mere sixty years ago; modern also in the sense that much of our economic development and specifically our industrialisation, is new, created in recent decades, partly by our native effort, but also in significant measure by investment from outside our shores. Pre-eminently, this external investment has come from the United States. Allied to the skills and dynamism of our youthful labour force, it has given us a place in the new technology of our European continent that is quite disproportionate to our size.

Our high technology industries – chemicals, electronics and above all, computers, are the source of a dynamism which, even in the absence of export growth in other sectors, last year increased our total manufactured exports by 14 per cent in the midst of world recession – the highest rate of export increase in Europe. Within twelve years during which two major oil crises have stopped in its tracks world economic growth, we have doubled our share of the world market for manufacturers.

An ancient nation: a modern state, and a youthful people: amongst all the developed countries of the world, Ireland has the youngest population, almost one-third of the electorate being under thirty. Within barely two decades the number of our young people in their twenties has virtually doubled.

There is, of course, another side to all this. Like so many other developed countries we face today a serious employment problem – the more acute because of our young population. The growth of our economy at home, as in so many other countries, has been halted by the recession of recent years – now perhaps coming to an end in response to the American recovery. For many of our people these problems have loomed large, seeming at times indeed to fill the horizon and so dim some of the hopes that the achievements of recent decades had aroused.

And there is another problem, one which constantly overshadows us – and has often touched us directly: the sombre tragedy of Northern Ireland. There is hardly a family on either side of the divided community in the North that has not known insecurity, suffering and all too often, bereavement. This is a fact that must be remembered by all those from outside Northern Ireland who claim to apportion blame or to offer simplistic solutions.

Locked into a corner of our small island, in a piece of territory 100 miles long and sixty miles across, live one-and-a half million people drawn from two different Irish traditions: the ancient Gaelic, Catholic tradition stretching back through several millennia, and the Protestant tradition of those who settled from Britain in much of the north-eastern corner of our island at the same time as compatriots of theirs were settling on the eastern edge of this great continent.

These two traditions in Northern Ireland have maintained their distinct identities through the centuries. Their loyalties face in two different directions – the forty per cent Catholic nationalist minority looking south towards their kinsmen in the Irish state and the sixty per cent majority looking instead towards Britain, whence their ancestors came four centuries ago.

In passing I cannot help reflecting that here in the United States people from these two separate Irish backgrounds have without difficulty given their allegiance to a common flag and a single Constitution, while on their home ground the clash of their identities has remained undiminished by time. This has created in Northern Ireland one of the most complex political problems in the world today: complex in its intensity and in the apparent irreconcilability of the two traditions within this small piece of territory. But a problem which, nevertheless, so often viewed from outside is exceedingly simplistic: seen by all too many as involving no more than the end British rule in Northern Ireland.

Would that this were indeed the only problem! Then the British and ourselves could have solved it in agreement long ago. But the real problem at the human level lies in the North itself – in the inter-relationship between the two traditions in that divided community.

Britain, with the responsibility for governing Northern Ireland, has not hitherto addressed this problem with the combination of determination and even-handedness that it requires. Nor has it given to it the priority which, as a great human tragedy, it demands. Britain has, moreover, hitherto seemed often to be preoccupied with the security symptoms of the problem, at the expense of its fundamentally political character.

But can we, for our part, in our Irish State – although we had neither direct responsibility nor opportunity to solve this problem – truthfully say that we have done all in our power to understand and face the realities of this tragedy? Have we efficiently tried to reach out with sympathy and understanding to both sides in Northern Ireland?

The answer can only be that not one of us, in Britain or in Ireland, is free of some measure of guilt for what has been happening in Northern Ireland. None of us has a right to shift the whole of the blame on to others. Both the London and Dublin Governments have a duty now to break out of ancient moulds and attitudes and to make the imaginative leap of understanding.

This moral obligation, to put Northern Ireland, its people, and their interests first, imposes itself also, I believe, upon those lands, such as this great United States of America, who are concerned, as I know so many of you are concerned with this problem. It can be fulfilled only by the most resolute support for peace and reconciliation amongst the people of Northern Ireland. It can be fulfilled only by a corresponding rejection of – revulsion against – the very idea of aid by way of money, or by way of weapons, or by way of moral support, to any of those who are engaged in the acts of horrific violence that are corrupting and destroying the life of a whole community. And when I call for rejection of such 'moral support', I necessarily include the act of making common cause for any purpose, however speciously well-meaning, with people who advocate, or condone, the use of violence in Ireland for political ends.

Let me tell you, for a few brief moments how the democratically-based political parties of our state have been attempting, in conjunction with the constitutional nationalists of the SDLP Party in the North, led by John Hume, to take our responsibilities in seeking a resolution of this tragic problem. These four parties viz. the two parties in our Government (my own Fine Gael Party and the Labour Party) together with the opposition Fianna Fáil Party, and the SDLP in Northern Ireland, have between them been elected by the votes of ninety per cent of the nationalist people of the island of Ireland and consequently represent seventy per cent of all its inhabitants Nationalist and Unionist. For nine months past, our parties – the parties which aspire to Irish unity achieved by peaceful means – have been working together within the framework of a New Ireland Forum, in search of ways of bringing peace and stability to Northern Ireland and, indeed, to the whole island of Ireland.

Week after week, the Forum has been in session. We four party leaders have already met either in Committee together, or in conjunction with our fellow members in the Forum, no less than sixty-nine times – setting aside our other differences and giving to this work our highest priority.

The Forum has been studying, and hearing personal evidence on submissions made to us by a wide range of people and groups. These have included many that have been representatives of aspects of the Protestant and Unionist tradition of Northern Ireland.

Finally, we have been seeking to find together ways by which political structures could be created in the future that would accommodate not only our own nationalist tradition which aspires to Irish unity achieved peacefully and by agreement, but also that of the Unionist community.

It is our hope that we will find common ground amongst our parties. We hope that this common ground might provide a basis upon which the governments of Britain and Ireland, in conjunction with representatives of both sides of the community in Ireland, could eventually construct a political solution. Such a solution would have to be one that would reconcile the conflicting rights and identities of Unionists and Nationalists: one that would render totally irrelevant those who seek to impose their tyranny of violence on the people of our island.

What we of the constitutional Irish nationalist tradition are attempting together is unique. It is our hope that it will find a response in Britain. There are indications already that responsible opinion in that neighbouring island has taken note of that initiative and is awaiting its outcome with growing interest. When our task is completed it will in turn be Britain's duty to do as we are doing: to review and revise its approach to the problem.

In thus telling you something of what the constitutional parties of nationalist Ireland are currently engaged upon, and of the hopes of an equally generous response from the British government and political parties, I am frankly seeking to engage your interest in, and your commitment to, this process which, we believe, offers a constructive alternative – the only constructive alternative to the violence and terrorism in Northern Ireland.

I believe that you will be glad to hear a message of hope in respect of a problem which many of you must have tempted to write off as insoluble. We know that in this Congress there are very many people whose affection for Ireland and concern for the welfare of our island and its people are deep and strong. I know that in speaking here today, I am speaking to friends of Ireland. We need the help and encouragement of our friends.

America's voice in the world is a strong one. It is listened to. We call it in aid of our efforts, not in support of any narrow sectional interest but in support of a generous attempt to resolve once and for all the conflict of traditional identities in Ireland on a basis that will secure the interests and concerns of both sections of the community in the North – in recognition of the equal validity of the two traditions.

And we ask our friends in the United States that, in the context of any agreement that might emerge from our present efforts, to secure peace and stability in Ireland, they would support in a practical way its implementation.

I have not come to the United States to speak only of this problem, although you will readily understand that it looms foremost in my mind, as it must in the mind of any Irishman who has political responsibilities. We have other common interests to pursue with you, the political leaders of the United States and the European Community, the Presidency of which Ireland will be assuming for the third time on July 1st next.

When, in January 1975, Ireland first undertook that presidential responsibility in the Community, your administration invited me as Minister for Foreign Affairs of Ireland to come to Washington to discuss together the common concerns at that time of the United States and the Community. This was, I think, the first full scale consultation between the European Community and the United States in a new process that had been decided upon during the previous year. I was happy on that occasion to be able to play a part in bringing Europe and the United States closer together.

On this visit I shall be engaged once again upon a similar task – recognising that the common concerns of Europe and the United States are matched also by divergent interests in certain areas of commerce and finance – as also by somewhat different perceptions of the political situation in various parts of the world. It is well that together Europe and America should seek to reconcile these divergent interests and different perceptions, so far as we may be able to do so without doing violence to the legitimate interests, and the principles, of each of the partners in this relationship.

Let me revert for a moment to a festive note appropriate to the joint celebration of St. Patrick's Day by our two peoples. I know that we are two days ahead of time and such earliness is more an American than a European characteristic, exemplified perhaps by your addiction to breakfast television, and as I have found to my cost, working breakfasts. But I feel that no one in the United States would object if I propose that the celebrations of St. Patrick's Day this year be a three-day affair, starting today, and culminating on Saturday – with a very necessary day of rest before we all return to our humdrum daily activities next week!

Peter Robinson
26 November 1985

FOLLOWING the publication of the report of the New Ireland Forum in May 1984, a period of intense dialogue took place between the British and Irish governments. This culminated in the signing of the Anglo-Irish agreement by the British Prime Minister, Margaret Thatcher and An Taoiseach, Garret Fitzgerald at Hillsborough on 15 November, 1984. The agreement, which was registered at the United Nations as an international agreement, provided a framework within which both Dublin and London governments could structure the long-term problems of Northern Ireland.

Whereas the agreement was broadly welcomed by Northern Catholics, it was flatly rejected by an overwhelming majority of Northern Unionists, who felt that the British government was selling out to Dublin. Many Unionists responded with bitterness and violence; there were a succession of marches, rallies and boycotts.

One of the most vigorous opponents of the agreement was the vice-head of the Democratic Unionist Party, Peter Robinson, who spoke against the matter in the House of Commons on 26 November. He began:

Speech at the Debate on the Anglo-Irish Agreement

This debate provides a unique occasion for Ulster Unionist representatives, because it is not often that a man gets the opportunity to deliver the oration at his own funeral. When the Prime Minister signed the agreement in Hillsborough Castle, she was in reality drafting the obituary of Ulster as we know it in the United Kingdom.

It is important for the House to understand why Ulster Unionists came to that conclusion. We did not reach that conclusion simply because of one document that arrived on the 15th November. A long series of events led to that occasion. I am old enough to remember when, in 1969, the Labour Government issued the Downing Street declaration, which said: 'The affairs of Northern Ireland are entirely a matter of domestic jurisdiction.'

I can recall how our Prime Minister, on the 8th December 1980, when in Dublin Castle, signed a communiqué with Charles J. Haughey which altered that stance, because the communiqué said that 'the totality of relations within these islands' was now a fit subject for discussion between the two Governments. From that moment we had the out-working of the unique relations between the Governments of the United Kingdom and the Republic of Ireland. We had joint studies, cross-border cooperation and then the Anglo-Irish Intergovernmental Council, the purpose of which was 'to provide the overall framework for inter-governmental consultation . . . on all matters of common interest and concern' – wait for it – 'with particular reference to the achievement of peace, reconciliation and stability and the improvement of relations.' At that stage, the council had a responsibility to deal with matters of mutual interest and concern. We have moved from that to a new status which, under this situation, is to give the Republic of Ireland – a foreign Government – a direct role in the government of Northern Ireland.

It does not end there, because the agreement announced at Hillsborough Castle is but the tip of the iceberg. I know that the Prime Minister, the Secretary of State and others have been careful to say that there is no other agreement. But then, we were told that there was no agreement right up until it was signed at Hillsborough Castle. Indeed, some weeks in advance of the 15th November, the deputy Prime Minister of the Irish Republic had already had a document printed which he sent to every member of his party. It indicated the full text of the agreement. Incidentally, he said that that agreement was signed by 'the Taoiseach and the Prime Minister of Great Britain.'

It represents quite a change in our status when the deputy Prime Minister of the Irish Republic recognises that Northern Ireland is not to be one of our Prime Minister's responsibilities.

The document says that the task upon which the conference will embark involves trying to achieve an agreement with our Government on matters such as parades and processions, and putting the UDR out of business. It implies – although we have not yet been told – that the meeting of Ministers will take place in Belfast. It is clearly a framework for further agreements. What other reason could there be for a front cover entitled, 'The Republic of Ireland No. 1 Agreement?'

I note that the Honourable Member for Foyle [*Mr Hume*] is in the Chamber. He has at least been honest with the people of Northern Ireland in saying that the agreement is a process. In the Irish News – where else? – he said that it was 'a first step.' The next day he said that there were to be 'progressive stages.' Those who had any doubt about where they were to lead were told by him on RTE: 'We are not waiting for Irish unity. We are working for it.'

I accept that there is no harm in the Honourable Gentleman wanting to work towards that goal, but I wish to ensure that the unionist community in Northern Ireland knows what he and the Republic are working towards. It is clear that this process is intended to take us out of the United Kingdom. Yet the people of Northern Ireland have democratically expressed their wish to stay within it. The agreement is intended to trundle Northern Ireland into an all-Ireland Republic.

The unionist community in Northern Ireland has identified this process. It is not an end in itself, and was never intended to be. It is one step towards a united Ireland. Indeed, the Prime Minister has excused the deal by saying that its laudable aim is to achieve peace, stability, reconciliation and co-operation. That is my aim too. Like some other Honourable Members, I live in Northern Ireland. Our stake and investment are in the Northern Ireland community and, most importantly, our families and constituents live there. It is in our interests to have peace, stability, reconciliation and co-operation. If I felt that they were achievable I would grasp them with a heart and a half, but not outside the union. That would be too high a price to pay.

The document reminds me of another piece of paper waved by a former Prime Minister. In many ways the words are too similar. That Prime Minister's words were 'Peace in our time.' Under this agreement, peace, stability, reconciliation and co-operation are not achievable. How can they be achieved by alienating the majority of people in Northern Ireland? It was never intended that there should be peace, stability, reconciliation and co-operation as a result of this agreement. After all, if that had been the intention, the Government would have wanted, above all, to take the elected representatives of the majority community in Northern Ireland along with them . . .

. . . If the document has been intended to do us good, the prime Minister would have been only too willing to allow the unionist community to be consulted. She would have been only too pleased to take it along with her and to ensure that the representatives of the Unionist people in Northern Ireland could have some input into the discussions.

The Government of the Irish Republic were only too happy to have some input to the discussions to give the Honourable Member for Foyle that facility. The Governnment of the Irish Republic and this Government briefed people all over the world. The Government of the Irish Republic briefed the Secretary of State to the Vatican. The President of the United States was briefed, as were the United Nations and the European Community. But those who were to be affected by the deal were kept in the dark . . .

I ask the Government to scrap this one-sided, anti-unionist deal and to involve Unionists in the process of obtaining peace, stability, reconciliation and co-operation in Northern Ireland. As I have said, we would participate with a heart and a half. More than many, I recognise that it is not my duty simply to say, 'No, we will not have it.' It is my duty and that of other Unionist representatives to say what can be done in a positive way in Northern Ireland. Before the debate ends, I hope that I shall have had the opportunity to do that.

I want to point out what unionists have done, and are prepared to do within the union . . .

I call upon the Government to consult and not to confront the unionist community. Unionists have been positive. The former Secretary of State for Northern Ireland who laid the Assembly legislation before the House knows very well that it was the unionist community in Northern Ireland that went into the Assembly and that co-operated with the Government. It was the Honourable Member for Foyle and his party who stayed outside and withdrew their consent. Is it the reward for those who co-operate with the Government that an agreement that is ultimately to their destruction should be foisted upon them to the benefit of the Honourable Member for Foyle and his party?

The Northern Ireland unionist parties – the Ulster Unionist party with its document, 'The Way Forward' and the Democratic Unionist party with its document, 'Ulster – the Future Assured' put forward positive proposals for peace, stability, reconciliation and co-operation in Northern Ireland.

Even in the Northern Ireland Assembly, with the help of the conciliator, Sir Frederick Catherwood, the parties sat down and reached agreement on a framework that the Government could use in negotiations with the political parties – not only the Unionist parties but the Alliance Party. We have been positive in Northern Ireland.

I say again that we are prepared to remain positive within the United Kingdom. We are prepared to allow the Prime Minister to engage unionists in constructive politics, and if the Prime Minister wishes to call my bluff, I should be only too happy. Do not confront us and put us out of the union with this deal.

The willingness of the unionist community to seek an agreement is undeterred. If the Government want peace and stability in Ulster, I ask them where that can best be achieved? There seems to be a new rule in British politics – if there is a dispute within a house, the way to solve it is to reach an agreement with the two neighbours. It is even more strange the agreement reached between the two neighbours gives aid and succour to one of the parties to the dispute.

If the Government want peace, stability, reconciliation and co-operation in Northern Ireland, they must recognise that that can only be achieved by the politicians – the elected representatives of the people of Northern Ireland – reaching agreement. They cannot impose reconciliation; they cannot impose peace and stability and they certainly cannot impose such an agreement which strikes at the fundamental principle in which the majority in Northern Ireland believe, and that is the union. That is the strangest of British strategies.

Does the agreement measure up to the Government's test for the sort of proposal that would be acceptable? The former secretary of State for Northern Ireland brought the 1982 Act before the House on the basis of 'widespread acceptance throughout the community.'

He argued passionately that there had to be 'cross-community support.' Throughout the years there have been homilies from politicians of one party or another about the necessity for consent in Northern Ireland. They told us that Northern Ireland could not be governed without the consent of the minority.

If that is true, I have to tell the Government that they can never govern Northern Ireland without the consent of the majority. Do they have the consent? Have they tried to access whether there is such consent? Will they test whether there is consent? The people of Northern Ireland have the right and entitlement to be consulted about their constitutionality.

Our citizenship of the United Kingdom does not allow the Government to do whatsoever they may wish with Northern Ireland.

Our citizenship of the United Kingdom must be on the same basis as applies in any other part of the United Kingdom.

If, for whatever reason – be it good or ill – the Government decide that Northern Ireland must be treated differently from the remainder of the United Kingdom, it can be done only if there is consent, and the consent not only of the Government and Parliament, but of the people of Northern Ireland.

It was that principle, enunciated in the House, that resulted in the referendums for Wales and Scotland. Have not the people of Ulster the same right to be consulted as the people of Wales and Scotland? Do they not have the same right to give their approval to any deal that, ultimately, will affect their future and the way that they are governed? I believe that they have that right and that they should be given it. If this House is not prepared to give them that right, it is incumbent upon the elected representatives of Northern Ireland to give them that right.

Right Honourable and Honourable Members criticise me, but I ask them how they would like it if the governance of their people was not directly by this House, but by a structure that allowed a foreign power, at its own behest, to make challenges and to request consultation. The agreement goes even further than that and requires that 'a determined effort is made to resolve the differences' between the two Governments. I doubt whether many Right Honourable and Honourable Members would want that for themselves or their constituents.

The agreement is not merely consultative. The House should not pass this measure believing that it is only a talking shop, in which the Irish Republic can make comments. It is much more than that. I am sure that the Prime Minister will not mind if I divulge certain comments made during our meeting yesterday, when we put the point about consultation to her on two occasions. On the first occasion, she was about to speak when the question was answered by the Secretary of State for Northern Ireland. I asked whether only a consultative role was involved or whether it was more than that. He said, 'It is not executive.' On the second occasion, the Prime Minister said, 'It is what it is in this agreement.' What do those who have been more candid say about the agreement?

The Prime Minister of Irish Republic says: 'it is more than consultation.' The Prime Minister of the Irish Republic says 'the agreement goes beyond the right to consult.' John F. O'Conner, the Dean of Faculty of Law at UCC, said: 'Whatever the eventual political results, the legal result of the new agreement is that Northern Ireland has now become subject to a status in international law which has no real parallels elsewhere. It never was, nor has it become, a separate entity in international law. It is not a condominium. It is a province of the United Kingdom which for first time has become subject to the legal right of two foreign governments to determine how all matters which go to the heart of sovereignty in that area shall in future be determined.'

It is not only the Unionists – Honourable Members may not like what the Dean of the Faculty of law said, but if they want to dispute it, they had better do so with him.

It is not only the unionists who believe that the deal is unfair to the unionist community in Northern Ireland. Senator Mary Robinson of the Irish Republic – no relation of mine, I assure the House – rejected the agreement because it went too far. She said: 'This is the most serious moment in the political development of this island since we gained independence.' That lady is no unionist – she was one of the signatories to the Forum report. Yet even she says that the agreement goes too far. *The Belfast Telegraph*, never a close friend of the unionist said: 'Even those who, like this newspaper, can see benefit flowing from closer consultation with Dublin, must draw the lines at such institutionalised links between the two countries.'

I say again that it is not only the Ulster Unionists and the Democratic Unionists who believe that the deal goes too far. The ordinary citizens of Northern Ireland, never previously involved in politics, were present at the mass demonstration at the city hall in Belfast.

I was born a free citizen of the United Kingdom. I was brought up to respect the Union flag. At my father's knee I was taught the love that I should have for the monarchy, and throughout my life I have put that into practice. I was nurtured on the principle of the greatness of our British heritage. I have taught all that to my children. I now have to tell this House that over the last seventeen cruel years, when Ulster has been confronted by a vicious campaign of terrorism, not one of the unionist community was prepared to allow that campaign to shatter his loyalty to the United Kingdom.

It is not a one-way street. It never has been for Ulster. We cheered with this country during the Falklands campaign. Ulster suffered its losses just as many did on this side of the Irish sea. During the Second World War, we made sacrifices, just as many people in this part of the United Kingdom, and we did it without conscription. During the First World War, Ulster gave of its best for Britain. After watching the

Ulster Volunteers on the Somme when 5,000 Ulstermen lost their lives at the enemy's hand, a great British general – General Spender – said, 'I am not an Ulsterman but there is no one in the world whom I would rather be after seeing the Ulster Volunteers in action.' In peace and in war Ulster stood by the kingdom. That has been the way of loyal Ulster.

I never believed that I would see a British Government who were prepared to damage Ulster's position in the United Kingdom. Our resolve has been hardened by the bitter times in past years when a terrorist campaign was aimed at undermining our position in the United Kingdom. There would never have been a Hillsborough Castle agreement if the IRA had not been bombing and shooting. That is a fact of life. Can one blame the people of Northern Ireland for thinking that violence works? It makes the task harder for those of us who chose the way of constitutional politics to tell people not to involve themselves in violence.

I wish that the House had a sense of the deep feeling of anger and betrayal in Northern Ireland. Yesterday, while I was waiting in an anteroom in No. 10 Downing Street before meeting the Prime Minister I saw on the wall a portrait of Rudyard Kipling, who was a great patriot. I recall the words of his poem 'Ulster 1912,' which begins:

> The dark eleventh hour
> Draws on and sees us sold
> To every evil power
> We fought against of old.

Later it states:

> The blood our fathers spilt,
> Our love, our toils, our pains,
> Are counted us for guilt,
> And only bind our chains.
> Before an Empire's eyes
> The traitor claims his price.
> What need of further lies?
> We are the sacrifice.

John Hume
26 November 1985

O N 15 NOVEMBER, 1984, the Anglo-Irish Agreement was signed by the British Prime Minister, Margaret Thatcher, and the Irish Taoiseach, Garret Fitzgerald. The agreement, while falling short of many Nationalist aspirations, did nevertheless give the Irish Republic a say in Northern Ireland's affairs by establishing an Intergovernmental Conference which would be 'concerned with Northern Ireland and with the relations between the two parts of Ireland, to deal on a regular basis with political matters, security and related matters, legal matters, including the administration of justice, and the promotion of cross-border co-operation.' One of the Nationalist parties, the Social Democratic Labour Party, under the leadership of John Hume, was supportive of the agreement.

On 26 November, 1984, a lively and sometimes aggressive debate on the Anglo-Irish Agreement took place in the House of Commons.

John Hume began:

Speech at the Debate on the Anglo-Irish Agreement

Listening to some of the Honourable Members who have spoken in the debate one could have been forgiven for thinking that we were not discussing a serious problem, but, after listening to the Honourable Member for Belfast East [*Mr. Robinson*], one should not be in doubt that we are discussing a serious problem.

I was glad to see a full House at the beginning of the debate. That is the first achievement of the Anglo-Irish conference. It shows that the serious human problem facing the peoples of these islands has at last been given the priority that it deserves. It has been put at the centre of the stage.

I was glad also that a meeting took place at the highest level between the British and the Irish Governments at which a framework for ongoing discussion was set up. In an excellent Unionist speech, the Honourable Member for Eastbourne [*Mr Gow*] told us what we already knew – that he was a committed unionist and that he did not particularly like to associate with the loud-mouthed persons with whom I have to live. We did not learn from him of the problem in Northern Ireland – that we have a deeply divided society. The Honourable Gentleman did not bother to analyse why we have a deeply divided society and the political instability and violence which the agreement seeks to address.

This is the first time that we have had a real framework within which to address the problem. The problem is not just about relationships with Northern Ireland. One need only listen to the speeches of Northern Ireland Members to know that it is about relationships in Ireland and between Ireland and Britain. Those interlocking relationships should be addressed within the framework of the problem. The framework of the problem can only be the framework of the solution, and that is the British-Irish framework. There is no road towards a solution to this problem that does not contain risks. The road that has been chosen by both Governments is the road of maximum consensus and is therefore, the road of minimum risk. We should welcome that.

Our community has just gone through fifteen years of the most serious violence that it has ever seen. Northern Ireland has a population of 1.5 million people. About 2,500 people have lost their lives in political violence – the equivalent of 86,000 people in Britain. Twenty thousand people have been seriously maimed. When I say 'maimed,' I mean maimed. That is the equivalent of 750,000 people on this island. About £11 billion worth of damage has been caused to the economies of Ireland – North and South. In 1969, public expenditure by the British Government in subsidy, subvention or whatever one calls it was £74 million; today it is £1.5 billion. Two new prisons have been built and a third is about to be opened – our only growth industry. There are eighteen-year-olds who have known nothing but violence and armed soldiers on their streets. Young people reach eighteen and then face the highest unemployment we have ever had. Forty-four per cent of the population is under twenty-five.

If that is not a time bomb for the future, what is? If that is not a problem that needs the serious attention of the House and the serious attention that the Prime Ministers of Britain and of the Republic of Ireland have given it in the past eighteen months, what is? Is this not a subject that screams out for political leaders in Northern Ireland to take a good look at themselves, their parties and the leadership that they have given? There is only one clear-cut lesson to be learnt from this tragedy – that our past attitudes have brought us where we are. Unless we agree to take a hard look at our past attitudes, we shall be going nowhere fast and we shall be committing ourselves to the dustbin of history, clutching our respective flagpoles.

We are being given some choices. The agreement gives us no more than an opportunity to begin the process of reconciliation. The choices offered to the people of Northern Ireland are the choices offered by Honourable Members here present. The unionist parties have consistently sought to protect the integrity of their heritage in Ireland – the Protestant heritage – and no one should quarrel with that. A society is richer for its diversity. My quarrel with the unionist parties has been that they have sought to protect their heritage by holding all the power in their own hands and by basing that on sectarian solidarity. That is an exclusive use of power which is inherently violent because it permanently excludes a substantial section of the community from any say in its affairs.

That was spelt out clearly by the Right Honourable, Member for Lagan Valley [*Mr Molyneaux*] when he said that he offered an act of leadership. He was sincere. He said that the majority should assure the minority that they would be made part of society. He tells me that it is an act of leadership to make me and the people I represent part of our society sixty-five years after Northern Ireland was created.

We have been lectured about democracy and the democratic process by Honourable Members from both unionist parties. They are practitioners of the democratic process. I do not want to spend too much time on examples of their practice, but they were the masters of gerrymander. Today their voices are somewhat muted, but they have not changed much.

In Belfast City Council not one position on any board has gone to a minority representative. One council has even apologised to the electorate because it made a mistake of appointing a member of the SDLP to one position out of 105 . . .

Honourable Members from both unionist parties have lectured us about democracy. That brings us to the heart of the Irish problem. The sovereignty of this Parliament is the basis of the British system and of the rule of law. The sovereignty of Parliament has been defined only twice in this century – on both occasions by Ulster Unionists.

In 1912 the Ulster Unionists defied the sovereign wish of Parliament to grant home rule. That was only devolution within the United

Kingdom. They objected and accepted instead home rule for themselves. That taught them a lesson which they have never forgotten –
that if one threatens a British Government or British Parliament and
produces crowds in the streets from the orange lodges, the British will
back down. Others learnt from that that if one wins by the democratic
process the British will back down to their loyalist friends and then
they say, 'Why not use force instead?' Those two forces are still at the
heart of preventing a development in relationships within Ireland.
Those who threaten violence are those who use it. The same two forces
are opposing the agreement today . . .

   The logic of the road down which the unionist leadership is taking
its people is inescapable. Unionists once again are prepared to defy the
sovereign will of this Parliament. When they come back after their
elections and Parliament says that it refuses to back down, what will
they do? Where will that lead us? They are going down the UDI road.
That is their logic. They say that they are loyal to the United Kingdom.
They are the loyalists and they must accept the sovereignty of Her
Majesty's Parliament. But they do not.

   What would happen if London Members resigned, were re-elected
and returned saying that the majority in Greater London wanted to keep
the Greater London Council? That would lead to a complete break-
down of parliamentary sovereignty. That is where the unionists are
leading us and they must know it.

   It is sad in 1985 to meet people who are suspicious of everybody.
They are suspicious of London, suspicious of Dublin and suspicious of
the rest of the world. Worst of all, they are suspicious of the people
with whom they share a little piece of land – their neighbours. It is sad
that they never talk of the future except with fear. They talk always of
the past. Their thoughts are encapsulated in that marvellous couplet:

>   To hell with the future and Long live the past
>   May God in his mercy look down on Belfast.

That is more relevant than the words of Rudyard Kipling.

   There has to be a better way. However grand we think we are, we are
a small community. We cannot for ever live apart. Those sentiments
were expressed in 1938 by Lord Craigavon, one of their own respected
leaders. What are we sentencing our people to if we continue to live
apart? People are entitled to live apart, but they are not entitled to ask
everyone else to pay for it.

The other opposition to the agreement comes from the Provisional IRA and its political surrogates. They murder fellow Irishmen in the name of Irish unity. They murder members of the UDR and RUC – fellow Irishmen. Those members see themselves as protectors of their heritage, but the Provisional IRA brutally murders UDR and RUC members in the name of uniting the Irish people, the heritage with which we must unite if we are ever to unite Ireland.

The IRA's political wing is full of contradictions. I hope that none in the House has any sympathy with it. Its members blow up factories, yet complain about unemployment. Its political spokesmen complain about cuts in public expenditure and in the same evening the military wing blows up £2 million of public expenditure in one street. A motion rightly condemns the execution of a young South African poet, but the IRA then shoot in the back of the head a young unemployed man and puts bullets in the head of a young man and his wife in West Belfast. The IRA complains about Diplock courts, yet runs kangaroo courts. What does that offer Ireland?

The Honourable Member for Belfast East [*Mr Robinson*] asks about Irish unity. In the late 20th century it is nonsense that there should be divisions. If European nations which twice in this century alone have slaughtered one another by the millions can build institutions that allow them to grow together at their own speed, why cannot we do the same? He quoted me in an interview as saying that I was working for Irish Unity, but I went on to say that those who think that Irish unity is round the corner are wired to the moon.

The divisions in Ireland go back well beyond partition. Centuries ago the leaders of Irish republicanism said that they wanted to unite Ireland by replacing the name of 'Catholic-Protestant dissenter' with the common name of 'Irishman.' That was in 1795. Thirty years before partition Parnell said that Ireland could never be united or have its freedom until the fears of the Protestant minority in Ireland could be conciliated. This is a deep problem. It will not be solved in a week or in a fortnight. The agreement says that if Ireland is to be united it will be united only if those who want it to be united can persuade those who do not want it to be united. Sovereignty has nothing to do with maps but everything to do with people.

The people of Ireland are divided on sovereignty. They will be united only by a process of reconciliation in which both traditions in Ireland can take part and agree. If that happens, it will lead to the only unity that matters – a unity that accepts that the essence of unity is the acceptance of diversity.

Our third choice is the Agreement. For the first time it sets up a framework that addresses the problem of the interlocking relationships between the people of both Irelands. It is the approach of maximum consensus. It is the way of minimum risk. For the first time – this is a positive element in the agreement – it respects the equal validity of both traditions. That is what the Right Honourable and Honourable Members of the Unionist party are complaining about. It is not a concession to me or to the people whom I represent. It is an absolute right to the legitimate expression of our identity and of the people I represent. Nobody can take that from us. The recognition of the equal validity of both traditions removes for the first time every excuse for the use of violence by anybody in Ireland to achieve his objective. A framework for genuine reconciliation is provided. Both sections of our community can take part in it.

Several Honourable Members have said that the SDLP has a double veto on devolution. I have already said several times to them in public, but let me say it again so that they may hear it, that I believe in the partnership between the different sections of the community in Northern Ireland. That is the best way to reconcile our differences. By working together to build our community we shall diminish the prejudices that divide us. The Agreement means that I am prepared to sit down now and determine how we shall administer the affairs of Northern Ireland in a matter that is acceptable to both traditions . . .

The second question that appears to excite people about my party's attitude relates to the security forces and to policing in Northern Ireland. Our position – this is not a policy but a statement of fact that applies to every democratic society – is that law and order are based upon political consensus. Where political consensus is absent there is an Achilles heel. Violent men in Northern Ireland take advantage of that Achilles heel. For the first time the intergovernmental conference will address that question. It has committed itself to addressing that question. It has also committed itself to addressing the relationship between the community and the security forces. I want to give every encouragement to the conference to do so at the earliest possible opportunity. If it does so, it will have our fullest co-operation. I want the people whom I represent to play the fullest possible part, as do any citizens in a democratic society, in the process of peace and order. While we await the outcome we shall continue to give our full and unqualified support to the police force in impartially seeking out anybody who commits a crime in Northern Ireland.

What is the alternative to the process of reconciliation and the breaking down of barriers? Why should anybody be afraid of the process of reconciliation? Anybody who is afraid has no confidence in himself or herself. It means that they cannot engage in a process of reconciliation. If they cannot retain mutual respect for their own position as well as for that of somebody else, they have no self-confidence. Therefore, they should not be representatives of the people of Northern Ireland. The only alternative is the old one of hopelessness, tit-for-tat, revenge – the old doctrine of an eye for an eye which has left everybody blind in Northern Ireland.

This is well summed up by a better poet than Kipling, the good, honest voice of the North, Louis MacNeice. Describing the old hopelessness, which is what we are being offered by those who will not take this opportunity, he said:

> Why should I want to go back
> To you, Ireland, my Ireland?
> The blots on the page are so black
> That they cannot be covered with shamrock.
> I hate your grandiose airs,
> Your sob stuff your laugh and your swagger.
> Your assumption that everyone cares
> Who is the king of your castle.
> Castles are out of date,
> The tide flows round the children's fancy,
> Put up what flag you like, it is too late
> To save your soul with bunting.

It is far too late for the people of Northern Ireland to save their souls with bunting or with flag-waving. We should note that the followers of those who wave flags as though they were the upholders of the standards of those flags paint their colours on kerbstones for people to walk over. In other words, there is no leadership and no integrity in that approach and no respect. The alternative that we are offered is an opportunity which, like others, may fail. It poses great challenges and risk. The challenges are daunting and difficult, but the choices are not. There is no other choice. There is no other road.

Gordon Wilson
1987

O N SUNDAY, 8 November, 1987, Remembrance Day, the people of Northern Ireland were honouring the dead and injured from the two World Wars by taking part in a series of services, parades and marches. Remembrance Day, even though thousands of Irish Catholics had fought and died for Britain during both World Wars, was regarded by the Irish Nationalists as a 'British' occasion, and, as a result, few Catholics took part in the Remembrance Day ceremonies.

The IRA active service unit who planted the bomb that day in Enniskillen would have known that the vast majority of people gathered that morning were either Protestant, or the alleged targets, the security forces. Ten people lost their lives in the explosion and many more were injured. It plunged the Northern conflict to greater depths of depravity than ever before.

Some days after the bombing, a grieving father, who had narrowly missed death himself, gave an interview to Mike Gaston, a freelance radio journalist. Gaston later said of the interview, 'I've never ever heard anything like it before and I never will again.' Gordon Wilson's words, as they were broadcast on BBC Radio Ulster, gave hope, where before there appeared none. Wilson himself became an international symbol of hope and peace for Northern Ireland. The reporter simply asked him to describe what happened that morning.

Radio Interview concerning the Loss of his Daughter.

As we crossed the bridge just beside where the bomb went off – and ten minutes before it did – I said to Marie 'I hope the police have checked that bridge – that's a very open target.' We walked back and we just positioned ourselves with our backs to the wall that collapsed, the wall of the house or hall or school.

And ten seconds later we were both thrown forward. Rubble and stones and whatever in and round and over us and under us. I remember thinking I'm not hurt. Then I was aware of a pain in my right shoulder. I shouted to Marie was she all right and she said 'Yes' and she found my hand and said, 'Is that your hand, Dad?' Now remember, we were under six foot of rubble. I said, 'Are you all right?' and she said, 'Yes.' but she was shouting in between. Three or four times I asked her and she always said, 'Yes' she was all right.

When I asked her the fifth time, 'Are you all right, Marie?' She said, 'Daddy I love you very much.' Those were the last words she spoke to me. She still held my hand quite firmly and I kept shouting at her, 'Marie, are you all right?' . . . There wasn't a reply.

We were there about five minutes. Someone came and pulled me out. I said, 'I'm all right . . . but for God's sake my daughter is lying right beside me . . . and I don't think she's too well.'

She's dead . . . She didn't die there . . . She died later.

The hospital was magnificent, truly impressive, and our friends have been great, but I have lost my daughter, and we shall miss her. But I bear no ill-will, I bear no grudge. Dirty sort of talk is not going to bring her back to life. She was a great wee lassie. She loved her profession. She was a pet and she's dead. She's in Heaven, and we'll meet again. Don't ask me, please, for a purpose. I don't have a purpose. I don't have an answer. But I know there has to be a plan. If I didn't think that, I would commit suicide. It's part of a greater plan and God is good. And we shall meet again.

The Rights of Man

Jonathan Swift
1725

IN JUNE, 1713, Jonathan Swift was appointed Dean of Saint Patrick's Cathedral in Dublin. He took up his position in August of the following year and quickly busied himself with his church duties. As a result he wrote very little over the next few years.

Following the dispute in 1720, as to whether the Irish Parliament had the right to full legal jurisdiction in Ireland, Swift became involved in writing political pamphlets and addressing his parishioners on a wide range of social, political and economic matters.

Except in questions where religion may have distorted his judgement, Swift was animated by a fierce and deep hatred of injustice and by a deep sense of compassion for material suffering. This is quite apparent in one of his most famous sermons, 'The Causes of the Wretched Condition of Ireland.' He began this sermon in Saint Patrick's Cathedral by reciting Psalm 144, verses 13 and 14. He then continued:

Sermon on the Wretched Condition of Ireland

It is a very melancholy reflection, that such a country as ours, which is capable of producing all things necessary, and most things convenient for life, sufficient for the support of four times the number of its inhabitants, should yet lie under the heaviest load of misery and want, our streets crowded with beggars, so many of our lower sort of tradesmen, labourers and artificers, not able to find clothes and food for their families.

I think it may therefore be of some use, to lay before you the chief causes of this wretched condition we are in, and then it will be easier to assign what remedies are in our power towards removing, at least, some part of these evils.

For it is ever to be lamented, that we lie under many disadvantages, not by our own faults, which are peculiar to ourselves, and which no other nation under heaven hath any reason to complain of.

I shall, therefore first mention some causes of our miseries, which I doubt are not to be remedied, until God shall put it in the hearts of those who are the stronger, to allow us the common rights and privileges of brethren, fellow-subjects, and even of mankind.

The first cause of our misery is the intolerable hardships we lie under in every branch of our trade, by which we are become as hewers of wood, and drawers of water, to our rigorous neighbours.

The second cause of our miserable state is the folly, the vanity, and ingratitude of those vast numbers, who think themselves too good to live in the country which gave them birth, and still gives them bread; and rather choose to pass their days, and consume their wealth, and draw out the very vitals of their mother kingdom, among those who heartily despise them.

These I have but lightly touched on, because I fear they are not to be redressed and, besides I am very sensible how ready some people are to take offence at the honest truth; and, for that reason, I shall omit several other grievances, under which we are long likely to groan.

I shall therefore go on to relate some other causes of this nation's poverty, by which, if they continue much longer, it must infallibly sink to utter ruin.

The first is, that monstrous pride and vanity in both sexes, especially the weaker sex, who, in the midst of poverty, are suffered to run into all kind of expense and extravagance in dress, and particularly priding themselves to wear nothing but what cometh from abroad, disdaining the growth or manufacture of their own country, in those articles where they can be better served at home with half the expense; and this is grown to such a height, that they will carry the whole yearly rent of a good estate at once on their body. And, as there is in that sex a spirit of envy, by which they cannot endure to see others in a better habit than themselves; so those, whose fortunes can hardly support their families in the necessaries of life, will needs vye with the richest and greatest amongst us, to the ruin of themselves and their posterity.

Neither are the men less guilty of this pernicious folly, who, in imitation of a gaudiness and foppery of dress, introduced of late years into our neighbouring kingdom, – as fools are apt to imitate only the defects of their betters – cannot find materials in their own country worthy to adorn their bodies of clay, while their minds are naked of every valuable quality.

Thus our tradesmen and shopkeepers, who deal in home goods, are left in a starving condition, and only those encouraged who ruin the kingdom by importing among us foreign vanities.

Another cause of our low condition is our great luxury, the chief support of which is the materials of it brought to the nation in exchange for the few valuable things left us, whereby so many thousand families want the very necessaries of life.

Thirdly, in most parts of this kingdom the natives are from their infancy so given up to idleness and sloth, that they often choose to beg or steal, rather than support themselves with their own labour; they marry without the least view or thought of being able to make any provision for their families; and whereas, in all industrious nations, children are looked on as a help to their parents, with us, for want of being early trained to work, they are an intolerable burthen at home, and a grievous charge upon the public, as appeareth from the vast number of ragged and naked children in town and country, led about by stroling women, trained up in ignorance and all manner of vice.

Lastly, a great cause of this nation's misery, is that Egyptian bondage of cruel, oppressing, covetous landlords, expecting that all who live under them should make bricks without straw who grieve and envy when they see a tenant of their own in a whole coat, or able to afford one comfortable meal in a month, by which the spirits of the people are broken, and made for slavery; the farmers and cottagers, almost through the whole kingdom, being to all intents and purposes as real beggars, as any of those to whom we give our charity in the streets. And these cruel landlords are every day unpeopling their kingdom, by forbidding their miserable tenants to till the earth, against common reason and justice, and contrary to the practice and prudence of all other nations, by which numberless families have been forced either to leave the kingdom, or stroll about, and increase the number of our thieves and beggars.

Such, and much worse, is our condition at present, if I had leisure or liberty to lay it before you; and, therefore, the next thing which might be considered is, whether there may be any probable remedy found, at the least against some part of these evils; for most of them are wholely desperate.

But this being too large a subject to be now handled, and the intent of my discourse confining me to give some directions concerning the poor of this city, I shall keep myself within those limits. It is indeed in the power of the lawgivers to found a school in every parish of the kingdom. For teaching the meaner and poorer sort of children to speak and read the English tongue, and to provide a reasonable maintenance for the teachers. This would, in time, abolish that part of barbarity and ignorance, for which our natives are so despised by all foreigners; this would bring them to think and act according to the rules of reason, by which a spirit of industry, and thrift, and honesty, would be introduced among them. And indeed, considering how small a tax would suffice for such a work, it is a public scandal that such a thing should never have been endeavoured, or, perhaps, so much as thought on.

To supply the want of such a law, several pious persons, in many parts of this kingdom, have been prevailed on, by the great endeavours and good example set them by the clergy, to erect charity-schools in several parishes, to which very often the richest parishioners contribute the least. In these schools, children are, or ought to be, trained up to read and write, and cast accompts; and these children should, if possible, be of honest parents, gone to decay through age, sickness, or other unavoidable calamity, by the hand of God; not the brood of wicked strolers; for it is by no means reasonable, that the charity of well-inclined people should be applied to encourage the lewdness of those profligate, abandoned women, who crowd our streets with their borrowed or spurious issue.

In those hospitals which have good foundations and rents to support them, whereof, to the scandal of Christianity, there are very few in this kingdom; I say, in such hospitals, the children maintained, ought to be only of decayed citizens, and freemen, and be bred up to good trades. But in these small parish charity schools which have no support, but the casual good will of charitable people, I do altogether disapprove the custom of putting the children apprentice except to the very meanest trades; otherwise the poor honest citizen who is just able to bring up his child, and pay a small sum of money with him to a good master is wholely defeated, and the bastard issue, perhaps, of some beggar, preferred before him. And hence we come to be so over-stocked with apprentices and journeymen, more than our discouraged country can employ; and, I fear, the greatest part of our thieves, pickpockets, and other vagabonds are of this number.

Therefore, in order to make these parish charity schools of great and universal use, I agree with the opinion of many wise persons, that a new turn should be given to this whole matter.

I think there is no complaint more just than what we find in almost every family, of the folly and ignorance, the fraud and knavery, the idleness and viciousness, the wasteful squandering temper of servants, who are, indeed, become one of the many public grievances of the kingdom; whereof, I believe, there are few masters that now hear me, who are not convinced by their own experience. And I am very confident, that more families, of all degrees, have been ruined by the corruptions of servants, than by all other causes put together. Neither is this to be wondered at, when we consider from what nurseries so many of them are received into our houses. The first is the tribe of wicked boys, wherewith most corners of this town are pestered, who haunt public doors. These, having been born of beggars, and bred to pilfer as soon as they can go or speak, as years come on, are employed in the lowest offices to get themselves bread, are practiced in all manner of villainy, and when they are grown up, if they are not entertained in a gang of thieves, are forced to seek for a service. The other nursery is the barbarous and desert part of the country, from whence such lads come up hither to seek their fortunes, who are bred up from the dunghill in idleness, ignorance, lying, and thieving. From these two nurseries, I say, a great number of our servants come to us, sufficient to corrupt all the rest. Thus, the whole race of servants in this kingdom have gotten so ill a reputation, that some persons from England, come over hither into great stations, are said to have absolutely refused admitting any servant born among us into their families. Neither can they be justly blamed; for, although it is not impossible to find an honest native fit for a good service, yet the inquiry is too troublesome, and the hazard too great for a stranger to attempt.

If we consider the many misfortunes that befall private families, it will be found that servants are the causes and instruments of them all: Are our goods embezzled, wasted, and destroyed? Is our house burnt down to the ground? It is by the sloth, the drunkenness or the villainy of servants. Are we robbed and murdered in our beds? It is by confederacy with our servants. Are we engaged in quarrels and misunderstandings with our neighbours? These were all begun and inflamed by the false, malicious tongues of our servants? Are the secrets of our family betrayed, and evil repute spread of us? Our servants were the authors. Do false accusers rise up against us – an evil too frequent in this country – they have been tampering with our servants. Do our children discover folly, malice, pride, cruelty, revenge, undutifulness in their words and actions? Are they seduced to lewdness or scandalous marriages? It is all by our servants. Nay, the very mistakes, follies, blunders, and absurdities of those in our service, are able to ruffle and discompose the mildest nature, and are often of such consequence, as to put whole families into confusion.

Since therefore not only our domestic peace and quiet, and the welfare of our children, but even the very safety of our lives, reputations, and fortunes have so great a dependence upon the choice of our servants, I think it would well become the wisdom of the nation to make some provision in so important an affair: but, in the mean time, and perhaps, to better purpose, it were to be wished, that the children of both sexes, entertained in the parish charity-schools, were bred up in such a manner as would give them a teachable disposition, and qualify them to learn whatever is required in any sort of service. For instance, they should be taught to read and write, to know some somewhat in casting accompts, to understand the principles of religion, to practice cleanliness, to get a spirit of honesty, industry, and thrift, and be severely punished for every neglect in any of these particulars. For, it is the misfortune of mankind, that if they are not used to be taught in their early childhood, whereby to acquire what I call a teachable disposition, they cannot without great difficulty, learn the easiest thing in the course of their lives, but are always awkward and unhandy; their minds, as well as bodies, for want of early practice, growing stiff and unmanageable, as we observe in the sort of gentlemen, who, kept from school by the indulgence of their parents but a few years, are never able to recover the time they have lost, and grow up in ignorance and all manner of vice, whereof we have too many examples all over the nation. But to return to what I was saying: if these charity-children were trained up in the manner I mentioned, and then bound apprentices in the families of gentlemen and citizens, – for which a late law giveth great encouragement – being accustomed from their first entrance to be always learning some useful thing, they would learn in a month more than another without those advantages can do in a year; and, in the mean time, be very useful in a family, as far as their age and strength would allow. And when such children come to years of discretion, they will probably be a useful example to their fellow servants, at least they will prove a strong check upon the rest; for, I suppose, every body will allow, that one good, honest, diligent servant in a house may prevent abundance of mischief in the family.

These are the reasons for which I urge this matter so strongly, and I hope those who listen to me will consider them.

I shall now say something about that great number of poor, who, under the name of common beggars, infest our streets, and fill our ears with their continual cries, and craving importunity. This I shall venture to call an unnecessary evil, brought upon us for the gross neglect, and want of proper management, in those whose duty it is to prevent it: but, before I proceed farther, let me humbly presume to vindicate the justice and mercy of God and his dealings with mankind. Upon this particular he hath not dealt so hardly with. His creatures as some would imagine, when they see so many miserable objects ready to perish for want: for it would infallibly be found, upon strict inquiry, that there is hardly one in twenty of those miserable objects who do not owe their present poverty to their own faults; to their present sloth and negligence; to their indiscreet marriage without the least prospect of supporting a family, to their foolish expensiveness, to their drunkenness, and other vices, by which they have squandered their gettings, and contracted diseases in their old age. And, to speak freely, is it any way reasonable or just, that those who have denied themselves many lawful satisfactions and conveniencies of life, from a principle of conscience, as well as prudence, that they might not be a burthen to the public, should be charged with supporting others, who have brought themselves to less than a morsel of bread by their idleness, extravagance, and vice? Yet such and no other, are for the greatest number not only in those who beg in our streets, but even of what we call poor decayed housekeepers, whom we are apt to pity as real objects of charity, and distinguish them from common beggars, although, in truth, they both owe their undoing to the same causes; only the former is either too nicely bred to endure walking half naked in the streets, or too proud to own their wants. For the artificer or other tradesman, who pleadeth he is grown too old to work or look after business, and therefore expecteth assistance as a decayed house-keeper; may we not ask him, why he did not take care, in his youth and strength of days, to make some provision against old age, when he saw so many examples before him of people undone by their idleness and vicious extravagance? And to go a little higher; whence cometh it that so many citizens and shopkeepers, of the most creditable trade, who once made a good figure, go to decay by their expensive pride and vanity, affecting to educate and dress their children above their abilities or the state of life they ought to expect?

However, since the best of us have too many infirmities to answer for we ought not to be severe upon those of others; and, therefore, if our brother, thro' grief, or sickness, or other incapacity, is not in a condition to preserve his being, we ought to support him to the best of our power, without reflecting over seriously on the causes that brought him to his misery. But in order to do this, and to turn our charity into its proper channel, we ought to consider who and where those objects are, whom it is chiefly incumbent upon us to support.

By the ancient law of this realm, still in force, every parish is obliged to maintain its own poor, which although some may think to be not very equal, because many parishes are very rich, and have few poor among them, and others the contrary; yet, I think, may be justly defended: for, as to remote country parishes in the desert parts of the kingdom, the necessaries of life are there so cheap, that the infirm poor may be provided for with little burden to the inhabitants. But in what I am going to say, I shall confine myself only to this city, where we are over-run, not only with our own poor, but with a far greater number from every part of the nation. Now, I say, this evil of being encumbered with so many foreign beggars, who have not the least title to our charity, and whom it is impossible for us to support, may be easily remedied, if the government of this city, in conjunction with the clergy and parish officers, would think it worth their care; and I am sure few things deserve it better. For, if every parish would take a list of those begging poor which properly belong to it, and compel each of them to wear a badge, marked and numbered, so as to be seen and known by all they meet, and confine them to beg within the limits of their own parish, severely punishing them when they offend, and driving out all inter-lopers from other parishes, we could then make a computation of their numbers; and the strolers from the country being driven away, the remainder would not be too many for the charity of those who pass by, to maintain; neither would any beggar, although confined to his own parish, be hindered from receiving the charity of the whole town; because in this case, those well-disposed persons who walk the streets, will give their charity to such whom they think proper objects, where-ever they meet them, provided they are found in their own parishes, and wearing their badges of distinction. And, as to those parishes which border upon the skirts and suburbs of the town, where country strolers are used to harbour themselves, they must be forced to go back to their homes, when they find no body to relieve them, because they want that mark which only gives them licence to beg. Upon this point, it were to be wished, that inferior parish officers had better encouragement given them, to perform their duty in driving away all beggars who do not belong to the parish, instead of conniving at them, as it is said they do for some small contribution; for the whole city would save much more by ridding themselves of many hundred beggars, than they would lose by giving parish officers a reasonable support.

It should seem a strange, unaccountable thing, that those who have probably been reduced to want by riot, lewdness, and idleness, although they have assurance enough to beg alms publicly from all they meet, should yet be too proud to wear the parish badge, which would turn so much to their own advantage, by ridding them of such great numbers, who now intercept them: yet, it is certain that there are many who publicly declare they will never wear those badges, and many others who either hide or throw them away: but the remedy for this is very short, easy, and just, by tying them like vagabonds and sturdy beggars, and forcibly driving them out of the town.

Therefore, as soon as this expedient of wearing badges shall be put in practice, I do earnestly exhort all those who hear me, never to give their alms to any public beggar who doth not fully comply with this order; by which our number of poor will be so reduced, that it will be much easier to provide for the rest. Our shop-doors will be no longer crowded with so many thieves and pick-pockets, in beggars habits, nor our streets so dangerous to those who are forced to walk in the night.

Thus I have, with great freedom delivered my thoughts upon this subject, which so nearly concerneth us. It is certainly a bad scheme, to any Christian country which god hath blessed with fruitfulness, and where the people enjoy the just rights and privileges of mankind, that there should be any beggars at all. But, alas! among us, where the whole nation itself is almost reduced to beggary by the disadvantages we lye under, and the hardships we are forced to bear; the laziness, ignorance, thought-lessness, squandering temper, slavish nature, and uncleanly manner of living in the poor popish natives, together with the cruel oppressions of their landlords, who delight to see their vassals in the dust; I say, that in such a nation, how can we otherwise expect than to be over-run with objects of misery and want? Therefore, there can be no other method to free this city from so intolerable a grievance, than by endeavouring, as far as in us lies, that the burden may be more equally divided, by contribut-ing to maintain our own poor, and forcing the strolers and vagabonds to return to their several homes in the country, there to smite the conscience of those oppressors, who first stripped them of all their substance.

I might here, if the time would permit, offer many arguments to persuade to works of charity; but you hear them so often from the pulpit, that I am willing to hope you may not now want them. Besides, my present design was only to shew where your alms would be best bestowed, to the honour of God, your own ease and advantage, the service of your country, and the benefit of the poor. I desire you will all weigh and consider what I have spoken, and, according to your several stations and abilities, endeavour to put it in practice; and God give you good success, to whom, with the Son and Holy Ghost, be all honour.

Edmund Burke
22 March 1775

IN SEPTEMBER, 1774 fifty-five delegates from the twelve American colonies met in Philadelphia. They drew up a 'Declaration of Rights' claiming that the privileges of Englishmen were still theirs. On those grounds they demanded the repeal of recent legislation such as the Boston Port Act, which had been designed to punish the Bostonians for their destruction of tea in Boston Harbour on 16 December, 1773. Until their demands were met the Bostonians agreed to stop exporting and importing to and from Britain.

As the situation deteriorated, King George III and the British Government under Prime Minister Frederick North agreed that a policy of concession had been tried and had failed, and that the only option was to coerce the colonies. Some politicians, notably William Pitt and Edmund Burke disagreed.

In January, 1775 Pitt tabled a motion in the House of Lords to withdraw the troops from Boston and to conciliate America by yielding to the demands of the Philadelphia Congress. This proposal and subsequent ones by Pitt were rejected.

Two months later, on 22 March, 1775 Edmund Burke proposed that the Americans should be treated to an 'equal interest in the British Constitution,' and be placed 'on the footing of other Englishmen.'

The following is an extract from that 25,000 word Speech [it took five hours to deliver], which consisted of an argued analylsis into the value and nature of the American colonies to Britain; of the defence of colonists' rights; and of how conciliation could come about.

Conciliation with the Colonies

I hope Sir, that notwithstanding the austerity of the Chair, your good nature will incline you to some degree of indulgence towards human frailty. You will not think it unnatural, that those who have an object depending, which strongly engages their hopes and fears, should be somewhat inclined to superstition. As I came into the House full of anxiety about the event of my motion, I found, to my infinite surprise, that the Grand Penal Bill, by which we had passed sentence on the trade and sustenance of America, is to be returned to us from the other House. I do confess I could not help looking on this event as a fortunate omen. I look upon it as a sort of providential favour; by which we are put once more in possession of our deliberative capacity, upon a business so very questionable in its nature, so very uncertain in its issue. By the return of this Bill which seemed to have taken its flight for ever, we are at this very instant nearly as free to choose a plan for our American Government as we were on the first day of the session. If, Sir, we incline to the side of conciliation, we are not at all embarrassed by any incongruous mixture of coercion and restraint. We are, therefore, called upon, as it were by a superior warning voice, again to attend to America; to attend to the whole of it together; and to review the subject with an unusual degree of care and calmness . . .

America, gentlemen say, is a noble object. It is an object well worth fighting for. Certainly it is, if fighting a people be the best way of gaining them. Gentlemen in this respect will be led to their choice of means by their complexions and their habits. Those who understand the military art will, of course, have some predilection for it. Those who wield the thunder of the State may have more confidence in the efficacy of arms. But I confess, possibly for want of this knowledge, my opinion is much more in favour of prudent management than of force; considering force not as an odious, but a feeble instrument for preserving a people so numerous, so active, so growing, so spirited as this, in a profitable and subordinate connection with us.

First, Sir, permit me to observe, that the use of force alone is but temporary. It may subdue for a moment, but it does not remove the necessity of subduing again; and a nation is not governed which is perpetually to be conquered.

My next objection is its uncertainty. Terror is not always the effect of force; and an armament is not a victory. If you do not succeed, you are without resource; for, conciliation failing, force remains; but, force failing, no further hope of reconciliation is left. Power and authority are sometimes bought by kindness, but they can never be begged as alms by an impoverished and defeated violence.

A further objection to force is that you impair the object by your very endeavours to preserve it. The thing you fought for is not the thing which you recover; but depreciated, sunk, wasted, and consumed in the contest. Nothing less will content me than whole America. I do not choose to consume its strength along with our own, because in all parts it is the British strength that I consume. I do not choose to be caught by a foreign enemy at the end of this exhausting conflict, and still less in the midst of it. I may escape; but I can make no insurance against such an event.

Let me add, that I do not choose wholly to break the American spirit, because it is the spirit that has made the country.

Lastly, we have no sort of experience in favour of force as an instrument in the rule of our colonies. Their growth and their utility indulgence have been owing to methods altogether different. Our ancient indulgence has been said to be pursued to a fault. It may be so; but we know, if feeling is evidence, that our fault was more tolerable than our attempt to mend it; and our sin far more salutary than our penitence.

These, Sir, are my reasons for not entertaining that high opinion of untried force, by which many gentlemen, for whose sentiments in other particulars I have great respect, seem to be so greatly captivated.

But there is still behind a third consideration concerning this object, which serves to determine my opinion on the sort of policy which ought to be pursued in the management of America, even more than its population and its commerce – I mean its temper and character. In this character of the Americans a love of freedom is the predominating feature which marks and distinguishes the whole; and, as an ardent is always a jealous affection, your colonies become suspicious, restive, and, untractable, whenever they see the least attempt to wrest from them by force, or shuffle from them by chicane, what they think the only advantage worth living for. This fierce spirit of liberty is stronger in the English colonies, probably, than in any other people of the earth, and this from a variety of powerful causes, which, to understand the true temper of their minds, and the direction which this spirit takes, it will not be amiss to lay open somewhat more largely.

The people of the colonies are descendants of Englishmen. England sir, is a nation which still, I hope, respects, and formerly adored, her freedom. The colonists emigrated from you when this part of your character was most predominant; and they took this bias and direction the moment they parted from your hands. They are, therefore, not only devoted to liberty, but to liberty according to English ideas and on English principles. Abstract liberty, like other mere abstractions, is to be found. Liberty inheres in some sensible object; and every nation has formed to itself some favourite point which, by way of eminence, becomes the criterion of their happiness. It happened, you know, sir, that the great contests for freedom in this country were, from the earliest times, chiefly upon the question of taxing. Most of the contests in the ancient commonwealths turned primarily on the right of election of magistrates, or on the balance among the several orders of the state. The question of money was not with them so immediate. But in England it was otherwise. On this point of taxes the ablest pens and most eloquent tongues have been exercised; the greatest spirits have acted and suffered. In order to give the fullest satisfaction concerning the importance of this point, it was not only necessary for those who in argument defended the excellence of the English constitution, to insist on this privilege of granting money as a dry point of fact, and to prove that the right had been acknowledged in ancient parchments and blind usages to reside in a certain body called the House of Commons. They went much further: they attempted to prove, and they succeeded, that in theory it ought to be so, from the particular nature of a House of Commons, as an immediate representative of the People, whether the old records had delivered this oracle or not. They took infinite pains to inculcate, as a fundamental principle, that, in all monarchies the people must, in effect, themselves, mediately or immediately, possess the power of granting their own money, or no shadow of liberty could subsist. The colonies draw from you, as with their life-blood, these ideas and principles. Their love of liberty, as with you, fixed and attached on this specific point of taxing. Liberty might be safe or might be endangered in twenty other particulars, without their being much pleased or alarmed. Here they felt its pulse; and, as they found that beat, they thought themselves sick or sound. I do not say whether they were right or wrong in applying your general arguments to their own case. It is not easy, indeed, to make a monopoly of theorems and corollaries. The fact is, that they did thus apply those general arguments; and your mode of governing them, whether through lenity or indolence, through wisdom or mistake, confirmed them in the imagination that they, as well as you, had an interest in these common principles.

They were further confirmed in this releasing error by the form of their provincial legislative assemblies. Their governments are popular in

a high degree; some are merely popular; in all, the popular representative is the most weighty; and this share of the people in their ordinary
government never fails to inspire them with lofty sentiments, and with
a strong aversion from whatever tends to deprive them of their chief
importance.

If anything were wanting to this necessary operation of the form of
government, religion would have given it a complete effect. Religion,
always a principle of energy, in this new people is no way worn out or
impaired; and their mode of professing it is also one main cause of this
free spirit. The people are Protestants; and of that kind which is the most
adverse to all implicit submission of mind and opinion. This is a persuasion not only favourable to liberty, but built upon it. I do not think,
sir, that the reason of this averseness in the dissenting churches from all
that looks like absolute government, is so much to be sought in their
religious tenets as in their history. Every one knows that the Roman
Catholic religion is at least coeval with most of the Governments where
it prevails; that it has generally gone hand in hand with them; and received
great favour and every kind of support from authority. The Church of
England, too, was formed from her cradle under the nursing care of
regular government. But the dissenting interests have sprung up in direct
opposition to all the ordinary powers of the world, and could justify that
opposition only on a strong claim to natural liberty. Their very existence
depended on the powerful and unremitted assertion of that claim. All
Protestantism, even the most cold and passive, is a kind of dissent. But
the religion most prevalent in our colonies is a refinement on the principle
of resistance; it is the dissidence of dissent, and the Protestantism of the
Protestant religion. This religion, under a variety of denominations,
agreeing in nothing but in the communion of the spirit of liberty, is
predominant in most of the northern provinces; where the Church of
England, notwithstanding its legal rights, is in reality no more than a
sort of private sect, not composing most probably the tenth of the
people. The colonists left England when this spirit was high, and in the
emigrants was the highest of all; and even that stream of foreigners,
which has been constantly flowing into these colonies, has, for the
greatest part, been composed of dissenters from the establishments of
their several countries, and have brought with them a temper and
character far from alien to that of the people with whom they mixed.

Sir, I can perceive by their manner, that some gentlemen objected to
the latitude of this description; because in the southern colonies the

Church of England forms a large body, and has a regular establishment. It is certainly true. There is, however, a circumstance attending these colonies, which, in my opinion, fully counterbalances this difference, and makes the Spirit Of liberty still more high and haughty than in those to the northward. It is that in Virginia and the Carolinas they have a vast multitude of slaves. Where this is the case in any part of the world, those who are free are by far the most proud and jealous of their freedom. Freedom is to them not only an enjoyment, but a kind of rank and privilege. Not seeing there that freedom, as in countries where it is a common blessing, and as broad and general as the air, may be much abject toil, with great misery, with all the exterior of servitude, liberty looks, amongst them, like something that is more noble and liberal. I do not mean, sir, to commend the superior morality of this sentiment at least as much pride as virtue in it, but I cannot alter the nature of man. The fact is so; and these people of the southern colonies are much more strongly, and with a higher and more stubborn spirit, attached to liberty, than those to the northward. Such were ancient commonwealths; such were our Gothic ancestors; such, in our days, were the Poles; and such will be all masters of slaves, who are not slaves themselves. In such a people the haughtiness of domination combines with the spirit of freedom, fortifies it, and renders it invincible.

Permit me, Sir, to add another circumstance in our colonies, which contributes no mean part toward the growth and effect of this untractable spirit – I mean their education. In no other country, perhaps, in the world is the law so general a study. The profession itself is numerous and powerful; and in most provinces it takes the lead. The greater number of the deputies sent to Congress were lawyers. But all who read, and most do read, endeavour to obtain some smattering in that science. I have been told by an eminent bookseller, that in no branch of his business, after tracts of popular devotion, were so many books as those on the law exported to the Plantations. The colonists have now fallen into the way of printing them for their own use. I hear that they have sold nearly as many of Blackstone's Commentaries in America as in England. General Gage marks out this disposition very particularly in a letter on your table. He states that all the people in his government are lawyers, or smatterers in law; and that in Boston they have been enabled, by successful chicane, wholly to evade many parts of one of your capital penal constitutions. The smartness of debate will say that this knowledge ought to teach them more clearly the rights of legislature, their obligations to obedience, and the penalties of rebellion. All this is mighty well. But my honourable and learned friend [*Mr, afterward Lord. Thurlo*] on the floor, who condescends to mark what I say for animadversion, will disdain that ground. He has heard, as well as I, that when great honours and great emoluments do not win over this knowledge to the service of the state, it is a formidable adversary to Government. If spirit be not tamed and broken by these happy methods, it is stubborn and litigious. Abeunt studia in mores [*studies pass into habits*]. This study renders men acute, inquisitive, dexterous, prompt in attack, ready in defence, full of resources. In other countries, the people, more simple, and of a less mercurial cast, judge of an ill principle in government only by an actual grievance; here they anticipate the evil, and judge of the pressure of the grievance by the badness of the principle. They augur misgovernment at a distance; and snuff the approach of tyranny in every tainted breeze.

The last cause of this disobedient spirit in the colonies is hardly less powerful than the rest, as it is not merely moral, but laid deep in the natural constitution of things. Three thousand miles of ocean lie between you and them. No contrivance can prevent the effect of this distance in weakening government. Seas roll, and months pass, between the order and the execution; and the want of a speedy explanation of a single point is enough to defeat the whole system. You have, indeed, 'winged ministers' of vengeance, who carry your bolts in their pounces to the remotest verge of the sea. But there a power steps in, that limits the arrogance of raging passions and furious elements, and says, 'So far shalt thou go, and no further.' Who are you, that should fret and rage, and bite the chains of nature? Nothing worse happens to you than does to all nations who have extensive empire; and it happens in all the forms into which empire can be thrown. In large bodies, the circulation of power must be less vigorous at the extremities. Nature has said it. The Turk cannot govern Egypt, and Arabia, and Curdistan, as he governs Thrace: nor has he the same dominion in Crimea and Algiers which he has at Brusa and Smyrna. Despotism itself is obliged to truck and huckster. The sultan gets such obedience as he can. He governs with a loose rein, that he may govern at all; and the whole of the force and vigour of his authority in his centre, is derived from a prudent relaxation in all his borders. Spain, in her provinces, is, perhaps, not so well obeyed as you are in yours. She complies too; she submits; she watches times. This is the immutable condition, the eternal law, of extensive and detached empire.

Then, sir, from these six capital sources of descent, of form of government, of religion in the northern provinces, of manners in the southern, of education, of the remoteness of situation from the first mover of government; from all these causes a fierce spirit of liberty has grown up. It has grown with the growth of the people in your colonies, and increased with the increase of their wealth; a spirit that, unhappily meeting with an exercise of power in England, which, however lawful, is not reconcilable to any ideas of liberty, much less with theirs, has kindled this flame that is ready to consume us.

I do not mean to commend either the spirit in this excess, or the moral causes which produce it. Perhaps a more smooth and accommodating spirit of freedom in them would be more acceptable to us. Perhaps ideas of liberty might be desired, more reconcilable with an arbitrary and boundless authority. Perhaps we might wish the colonists to be persuaded that their liberty is more secure when held in trust for them by us, as guardians during a perpetual minority, than with any part of it in their own hands. But the question is not whether their spirit deserves praise or blame. What, in the name of God, shall we do with it? You have before you the object, such as it is, with all its glories, with all its imperfections on its head. You see the magnitude, the importance, the temper, the habits, the disorders. By all these considerations we are strongly urged to determine something concerning it. We are called upon to fix some rule and line for our future conduct which may give a little stability to our politics, and prevent the return of such unhappy deliberations as the present. Every such return will bring the matter before us in a still more untractable form. For, what astonishing and incredible things have we not seen already? What monsters have not been generated from this unnatural contention? . . .

We are indeed, in all disputes with the colonies, by the necessity of things, the judge. It is true, Sir; but I confess that the character of judge in my own cause is a thing that frightens me. Instead of filling me with pride, I am exceedingly humbled by it. I cannot proceed with a stern, assured, judicial confidence, until I find myself in something more like a judicial character. I must have these hesitations as long as I am compelled to recollect that, in my little reading upon such contests as these, the sense of mankind had at least as often decided against the superior as the subordinate power. Sir, let me add too, that the opinion of my having some abstract right in my favour, would not put much at my ease in passing sentence, unless I could be sure that there were no rights which, in their exercise under certain circumstances that I see the same party at once a civil litigant against me in the point of right and a culprit before me; while I sit as criminal judge on acts of his whose moral quality is to be decided on upon the merits of the very litigation. Men are every now and then put, by the complexity of human affairs, into strange situations; but justice is the same, let the judge be in what the situation he will.

Sir, these considerations have great weight with me, when I find things so circumstanced that I see the same party at once a civil litigant against me in point of right and a culprit before me; while I sit as criminal judge on acts of his whose moral quality is to be decided on upon the merits of that very litigation. Men are every now and then put, by the complexity of human affairs, into strange situations; but justice is the same, let the judge be in what situation he will.

In this situation, let us seriously and coolly ponder, what is it we have got by all our menaces, which have been many and ferocious. What advantage have we derived from the penal laws we have passed, and which, for the time, have been severe and numerous? What advances have we made toward our object, by the sending of a force which, by land and sea, is no contemptible strength? Has the disorder abated? Nothing less. When I see things in this situation, after such confident hopes, bold promises, and active exertions, I cannot, for my life, avoid a suspicion that the plan itself is not correctly right.

If, then, the removal of the causes of this spirit of American liberty be, for the greater part, or rather entirely, impracticable; if the ideas of criminal process be inapplicable, or, if applicable, are in the highest degree inexpedient, what way yet remains? No way is open but the third and last – to comply with the American spirit as necessary, or, if you please, to submit to it as a necessary evil.

If we adopt this mode, if we mean to conciliate and concede, let us see of what nature the concessions ought to be. To ascertain the nature of our concessions, we must look at their complaint. The colonies complain that they have not the characteristic mark and seal of British freedom. They complain that they are taxed in Parliament in which they are not represented. If you mean to satisfy them at all, you must satisfy them with regard to this complaint. If you mean to please any people, you must give them the boon which they ask; not what you may think better for them, but of a kind totally different ...

Such is steadfastly my opinion of the absolute necessity of keeping up the concord of this empire by a unity of spirit, though in a diversity of operations, that, if I were sure the colonists had, at their leaving this country, sealed a regular compact of servitude; that they had solemnly abjured all the rights of citizens; that they had made a vow to renounce all ideas of liberty for them and their posterity to all generations, yet I should hold myself obliged to conform to the temper I found universally prevalent in my own day, and to govern two millions of men, impatient of servitude, on the principles of freedom. I am not determining a point of law. I am restoring tranquillity, and the general character and situation of a people must determine what sort of government is fitted for them. That point nothing else can or ought to determine.

My idea, therefore, without considering whether we yield as matter of right, or grant as matter of favour, is to admit the people of our colonies into an interest in the Constitution, and, by recording that admission in the journals of parliament, to give them as strong an assurance as the nature of the thing will admit, that we mean forever to adhere to that solemn declaration of systematic indulgence . . .

The Americans will have no interest contrary to the grandeur and glory of England, when they are not oppressed by the weight of it; and they will rather be inclined to respect the acts of a superintending legislature, when they see them the acts of that power which is itself the security, not the rival, of their secondary importance. In this assurance my mind most perfectly acquiesces, and I confess I feel not the least alarm from the discontents which are to arise from putting people at their ease; nor do I apprehend the destruction of this empire from giving, by an act of free grace and indulgence, to two millions of my fellow citizens, some share of those rights upon which I have always been taught to value myself . . .

But to clear up my ideas on the subject; a revenue from America transmitted hither – do not delude yourselves – you never can receive it – no, not a shilling. We have experienced that from remote countries it is not to be expected. If, when you attempted to extract revenue from Bengal, you were obliged to return in loan what you had taken in imposition, what can you expect trom North America? For certainly, if ever there was a country qualified to produce wealth, it is India; or an institution fit for the transmission, it is the East India Company. America has none of these aptitudes. If America gives you taxable objects on which you lay your duties here, and gives you, at the same time, a surplus by a foreign sale of her commodities to pay the duties on these objects which you tax at home, she has performed her part to the

British revenue. But with regard to her own internal establishments, she may, I doubt not she will, contribute in moderation; I say in moderation, for she ought not to be permitted to exhaust herself. She ought to be reserved to a war, the weight of which, with the enemies that we are most likely to have, must be considerable in her quarter of the globe. There she may serve you, and serve you essentially.

For that service, for all service, whether of revenue, trade, or empire, my trust is in her interest in the British Constitution. My hold of the colonies is in the close affection which grows from common names, from kindred blood, from similar privileges, and equal protection. These are ties which, though light as air, are as strong as links of iron. Let the colonies always keep the idea of their civil rights associated with your government; they will cling and grapple to you, and no force under heaven will be of power to tear them from their allegiance. But let it be once understood that your government may be one thing, and their privileges another; that these two things may exist without any mutual relation; the cement is gone; the cohesion is loosened; and everything hastens to decay and dissolution. As long as you have the wisdom to keep the sovereign authority of this country as the sanctuary of liberty, the sacred temple consecrated to our common faith, wherever the chosen race and sons of England worship freedom, they will turn their faces toward you. The more they multiply, the more friends you will have. The more ardently they love liberty, the more perfect will be their obedience. Slavery they can have anywhere. It is a weed that grows in every soil. They may have it from Spain; they may have it from Prussia; but, until you become lost to all feeling of your true interest and your natural dignity, freedom they can have from none but you. This is the commodity of price, of which you have the monopoly. This is the true Act of Navigation, which binds to you the commerce of the colonies, and through them secures to you the wealth of the world. Deny them this participation of freedom, and you break that sole bond which originally made, and must still preserve, the unity of the empire. Do not entertain so weak an imagination as that your registers and your bonds, your affidavits and your sufferances, your cockets and your clearances, are what form the great securities of your commerce. Do not dream that your letters of office, and your instructions, and your suspending clauses, are the things that hold together the great contexture of this mysterious whole. These things do not make your government. Dead instruments, passive tools as they are, it is the spirit of the English communion that gives all their life and efficacy to them. It is the spirit of the English Constitution which, infused through the mighty mass, pervades, feeds, unites, invigorates, vivifies every part of the empire, even down to the minutest member.

Is it not the same virtue which does everything for us here in England? Do you imagine, then, that it is the land tax which raises your revenue, that it is the annual vote in the committee of supply which gives you your army? or that it is the mutiny bill which inspires it with bravery and discipline? No! surely no! It is the love of the people; it is their attachment to their government, from the sense of the deep stake they have in such a glorious institution, which gives you your army and your navy and infuses into both that liberal obedience, without which your army would be a base rabble, and your navy nothing but rotten timber.

All this, I know well enough, will sound wild and chimerical to the profane herd of those vulgar and mechanical politicians, who have no place among us; a sort of people who think that nothing exists but what is gross and material, and who, therefore, far from being qualified to be directors of the great movement of empire, are not fit to turn a wheel in the machine. But to men truly initiated and rightly taught, these ruling and master principles, which, in the opinion of such men as I have mentioned, have no substantial existence, are in truth everything and all in all. Magnanimity in politics is not seldom the truest wisdom; and a great empire and little minds go ill together. If we are conscious of our situation, and glow with zeal to fill our place as becomes our station and ourselves, we ought to auspicate all our public proceeding on America with the old warning of the church, sursum corda [*lift up your hearts*]! We ought to elevate our minds to the greatness of that trust to which the order of Providence has called us. By advertising to the dignity of this high calling, our ancestors have turned a savage wilderness into a glorious empire, and have made the most extensive and the only honourable conquests, not by destroying, but by promoting, the wealth, the number, the happiness of the human race. Let us get an American revenue as we have got an American empire. English privileges have made it all that it is; English privileges alone will make it all it can be.

In full confidence of this unalterable truth, I now, quod felix faustumque sit [*and it maybe lucky and fortunate*], lay the first stone in the temple of peace; and I move you, 'That the colonies and plantations of Great Britain in North America, consisting of fourteen separate governments, and containing two millions and upwards of free inhabitants, have not had the liberty and privilege of electing and sending any knights and burgesses, or others, to represent them in the high court of parliament.'

Burke's proposals were rejected by the house of Commons and with this rejection began the eight-year struggle which culminaled in the severance of the Americam Colonies from Britain.

Richard Lalor Sheil
24 October 1828

A FTER DANIEL O' Connell's overwhelming victory in the Clare by-election of July, 1828, it became apparent that the British government, under Sir Robert Peel and the Duke of Wellington was considering the introduction of Catholic Relief legislation. The fears of Protestants were consequently aroused, and many meetings were held to protest against any concessions.

When Mr. Richard Sheil, one of the leaders of the Catholic Association, heard of an impending meeting, on Penenden Heath, in Kent he proceeded to London, purchased a freehold which entitled him to speak, and went to Kent. When he eventually spoke, 20,000 people gave voice against him. The philosopher, Jeremy Bentham, later commented, 'So masterly a union of logic and rhetoric as Mr. Sheil's speech, scarcely have I ever beheld.'

An extract from that speech follows:

Catholic Emancipation Speech

Let no man believe that I have come here in order that I might enter the lists of religious controversy and engage with any of you in a scholastic disputation. In the year 1828, the Real Presence does not afford an appropriate subject for debate, and it is not by the shades of a mystery that the rights of a British citizen are to be determined. I do not know whether there are many here by whom I am regarded as an idolater, because I conscientiously adhere to the faith of your forefathers, and profess the doctrine in which I was born and bred; but if I am so accounted by you, you ought not to inflict a civil deprivation upon the accident of the cradle. You ought not to punish me for that for which I am not in reality to blame. If you do you will make the misfortune of the Catholic the fault of the Protestant, and by inflicting a wrong upon my religion, cast a discredit upon your own. I am not the worse subject of my King, and the worse citizen of my country, because I concur in the belief of the great majority of the Christian world; and I will venture to add, with the frankness and something of the bluntness by which Englishmen are considered to be characterised, that if I am an idolater, I have a right to be one if I choose; my idolatry is a branch of my perogative, and is no business of yours. But you have been told by Lord Winchelsea that the Catholic religion is the adverse of freedom. It may occur to you, perhaps, that his lordship affords a proof in his own person that a passion for Protestantism and a love of liberty are not inseparably associated; but without instituting too minute or embarrassing an inquiry into the services to freedom which in the course of his political life have been conferred by my Lord Winchelsea, and putting aside all personal considerations connected with the accuser, let me proceed to the accusation.

Calumniators of Catholicism, have you read the history of your country? Of the charges against the religion of Ireland the annals of England afford the confutation. The body of your common laws was given by the Catholic Alfred. He gave you your judges, your magistrates, your high sheriffs (you, Sir, hold your office, and have called this great assembly, by virtue of his institutions) your courts of justice, your elective system, and the great bulwark of your liberties, the trial by jury. When Englishmen peruse the chronicles of their glory, their hearts beat high with exultation, their emotions are profoundly stirred, and their souls are ardently expanded. Where is the English boy who reads the story of his great island, whose pulse does not beat at the name of Runnymede, and whose nature is not deeply thrilled at the contemplation of that great incident when the mitred Langton, with his uplifted crozier, confronted the tyrant, whose sceptre shook in his trembling hand, and extorted what you have so justly called the Great, and what, I trust in God, you will have cause to designate as your everlasting Charter? It was by a Catholic pontiff that the foundation-stone in the temple of liberty was laid; and it was at the altars of that religion which you are accustomed to consider as the handmaid of oppression, that the architects of the Constitution knelt down. Who conferred upon the people the right of self-taxation, and fixed if he did not create, the representation of the people? The Catholic, Edward the First; while in the reign of Edward the Third, perfection was given to the representative system, parliaments were annually called, and the statute against

constructive treason was enacted. It is false, foully, infamously false, that
the Catholic religion, the religion of your forefathers, the religion of
Seven millions of your fellow-subjects, has been the auxiliary of debasement, and that to its influences the suppression of British freedom can,
in a single instance, be referred. I am loath to say that which can give
you cause to take offence; but when the faith of my country is made the
object of imputation I cannot help, I cannot refrain from breaking into
a retaliatory interrogation, and from asking whether the overthrow of
the old religion of England was not effected by a tyrant, with a hand of
iron and a heart of stone? Whether Henry did not trample upon freedom, while upon Catholicism he set his foot; and whether Elizabeth
herself, the virgin of the Reformation, did not inherit her despotism
with her creed; whether in her reign the most barbarous atrocities were
not committed; whether torture, in violation of the Catholic common
law of England, was not politically inflicted, and with the shrieks of
agony the Towers of Julius, in the dead of night, did not re-echo? And
to pass to a more recent period, was it not on the very day on which
Russell perished on the scaffold that the Protestant University of
Oxford published the declaration in favour of passive obedience, to
which your Catholic ancestors would have laid down their lives rather
than have submitted?

These are facts taken from your own annals, with which every one of
you should be made familiar; but it is not to your own annals that the
recriminatory evidence, on which I am driven to rely, shall be confined.
If your religion is the inseparable attendant upon liberty, how does it
come to pass that Prussia, and Sweden, and Denmark, and half the
German states should be Protestants, and should be also slaves? You
may suggest to me that in the larger portion of Catholic Europe freedom does not exist; but you should bear in mind that at a period when
the Catholic religion was in its most palmy state freedom flourished in
the countries in which it is now extinct. Look at Italy, not indeed as she
now is, but as she was before Martin Luther was born, when literature
and liberty were associated, and the arts imparted their embellishments
to her free political institutions. I call up the memory of the Italian
Catholic republics in the great cause which I am sufficiently adven-
turous to plead before you. Florence, accomplished, manufacturing, and
democratic, the model of your own municipal corporations, gives a
noble evidence in favour of Catholicism; and Venice, Catholic Venice,
rises in the splendour of her opulence and the light of her liberty, to

corroborate the testimony of her celebrated sister with a still more lofty and majestic attestation. If from Italy I shall ascend the Alps, shall I not find, in the mountains of Switzerland, the sublime memorials of liberty, and the reminiscences of those old achievements which preceded the theology of Geneva, and which were performed by men by whom the ritual of Rome was uttered on the glaciers, and the great mystery of Catholicism was celebrated on the altars which nature had provided for that high and holy worship? But Spain, I may be told, Spain affords the proof that to the purposes of despotism her religion has always lent its impious and disastrous aid. That mistake is a signal one, for when Spain was most devotedly Catholic, Spain was comparatively free – her Cortes assumed an attitude nobler even than your own Parliament, and told the King, at the opening of every session in which they were convened, that they were greater and invested with a higher authority than himself. In the struggles made by Spaniards within our own memory we have seen the revival of that lofty sentiment; while amongst the descendants of Spaniards, in the provinces of South America, called into existence in some sort by yourselves, we behold no religion but the Catholic, and, no government of which the principle is not founded in the supremacy of the people. Republic after republic has arisen at your bidding through that immeasurable expanse, and it is scarce an exaggeration to say – if I may allude to a noble passage in one of the greatest writers of our time – that liberty, with her 'meteor standard' unfurled upon the Andes, 'Looks from her throne of clouds o'er half the world.'

False, I repeat it, with all the vehemence of indignant asseveration, utterly false is the charge habitually preferred against the religion which Englishmen have laden with penalties, and have marked with degradation. I can bear with any other charge but this; to any other charge I can listen with endurance. Tell me that I prostrate myself before a sculptured marble; tell me that to a canvas glowing with the image of heaven I bend my knee; tell me that my faith is my perdition and as you traverse the churchyards in which your forefathers are buried, pronounce upon those who have lain there for many hundred years a fearful and appalling sentence. Yes, call what I regard as the truth not only an error, but a sin to which mercy shall not be extended – call this I will bear – to all this I will submit – nay, at all this I will but smile, but do not tell me that I am in heart and creed a slave, that my countrymen cannot brook; in their own bosoms they carry the high consciousness that never was imputation more foully false or more detestably calumnious.

I do not believe that with the passion for true liberty a nation was ever more enthusiastically inspired – never were men more resolved – never were men more deserving to be free than the nation in whose oppression, fatally to Ireland and to themselves, the statesmen of England have so madly persevered.

What have been the results of that system which you have been this day called together to sustain? You behold in Ireland a beautiful country, with wonderful advantages agricultural and commercial, a resting-place for trade on its way to either hemisphere; indented with havens, watered by numerous rivers, with a fortunate climate in which fertility is raised upon a rich soil, and inhabited by a bold, intrepid, and, with all their faults, a generous and enthusiastic people. Such is Ireland as God made her. What is Ireland as you have made her? This fine country, swarming with a population the most miserable in Europe, of whose wretched-ness, if you are the authors you are beginning to be the victims – the poisoned chalice is returned in its just circulation to your lips. Harvests the most abundant are reaped by men with starvation in their faces; all the great commercial facilities of the country are lost; the rivers that should circulate opulence, and turn the machinery of a thousand manu-factures, flow to the ocean without wafting a boat or turning a wheel; the wave breaks in solitude in the silent magnificence of deserted and shipless harbours. In place of being a source of wealth and revenue to the empire, Ireland cannot defray its own expenses; her discontent costs millions of money; she debilitates and endangers England. The great mass of her population are alienated and dissociated from the state – the influence of the constituted and legitimate authorities is gone; a strange, anomalous, and unexampled kind of government has sprung up, and exercises a despotic sway; while the lower class, inferior in numbers, but accustomed to authority, and infuriated at its loss, are thrown into formidable reaction – the most ferocious passions rage from one extremity of the country to the other. Hundreds and thousands of men, arrayed with badges, gather in the south, and the smaller faction, with discipline and with arms, are marshalled in the north; the country is like one vast, magazine of powder, which a spark might ignite into an explosion, and of which England would not only feel, but, perhaps, never recover from the shock. And is this state of things to be permitted to continue? It is only requisite to present the question in order that all men should answer something must be done. What is to be done? Are you to re-enact the Penal Code? Are you to deprive Catholics of their properties, to shut up their schools, to drive them from the Bar, to strip them of the elective franchise, and reduce them to Egyptian bondage?

It is easy for some visionary in oppression, to imagine these things. In the drunkenness of sacerdotal debauchery, men have been found to give vent to such sanguinary aspirations, and the teachers of the Gospel, the ministers of a mild and merciful Redeemer, have uttered in the midst of their ferocious wassails, the bloody orison, that their country should be turned into one vast field of massacre, and that upon the pile of carnage the genius of Orange ascendancy should be enthroned. But these men are maniacs in ferocity, whose appetites for blood you will scarcely undertake to satiate. You shrink from the extirpation of a whole people. Even suppose that, with an impunity as ignominious as it would be sanguinary, that horrible crime could be effected, then you must needs ask, what is to be done? In answering that question you will not dismiss from your recollection that the greatest statesmen who have for the last fifty years directed your councils and conducted the business of this mighty empire, concurred in the opinion, that, without a concession of the Catholic claims, nothing could be done for Ireland ...

But supposing that authority, that the coincidence of the wisest and of the best in favour of Ireland was to be held in no account, consider how the religious disqualifications must necessarily operate. Can that be a wise course of government which creates not an aristocracy of opulence, and rank, and talent, but an aristocracy in religion, and places seven millions of people at the feet of a few hundred thousand? Try this fashion of government by a very obvious test, and make the case your own. If a few hundred thousand Presbyterians stood towards you in the relation in which the Irish Protestants stand towards the Catholics, would you endure it? Would you brook a system under which Episcopalians should be rendered incapable of holding seats in the House of Commons, should be excluded from sheriffships, and corporate offices, and from the bench of justice, and from all the higher offices in the adminis-tration of the law; and should be tried by none but Presbyterian juries, flushed with the insolence of power and infuriated with all the ferocity of passion? How would you brook the degradation which would arise from such a system, and the scorn and contumelies which would flow from it? Would you listen with patience to men who told you that there was no grievance in all this – that your complaints were groundless, and that the very right of murmuring ought to be taken away? Are Irishmen and Roman Catholics so differently constituted from yourselves, that they are to behold nothing but blessings in a system which you would look upon as an unendurable wrong?

Protestants and Englishmen, however debased you may deem our country, believe me that we have enough of human nature left within us – we have enough of the spirit of manhood, all Irishmen as we are, to resent a usage of this kind. Its results are obvious. The nation is divided into two castes. The powerful and the privileged few are patricians in religion, and trample upon and despise the plebeian Christianity of the millions who are laid prostrate at their feet. Every Protestant thinks himself a Catholic's better; and every Protestant feels himself the member of a privileged corporation. Judges, sheriffs, crown counsel, crown attorneys, juries, are Protestants to a man. What confidence can a Catholic have in the administration of public justice? We have the authority of an eminent Irish judge, the late Mr. Fletcher, who declared that, in the north, the Protestants were uniformly acquitted, and the Catholics were as undeviatingly condemned. A body of armed Orangemen fall upon and put to death a defenceless Catholic; they are put upon their trial, and when they raise their eyes and look upon the jury, as they are commanded to do, they see twelve of their brethren in massacre empanelled for their trial; and, after this, I shall be told that all the evils disqualification lie in the disappointed longing of some dozen gentlemen after the House of Commons. No, it is the ban, the opprobrium, the brand, the note and mark of dishonour, the scandalous, the flagitious bias, the sacrilegious and perjured leaning, and the monstrous and hydra headed injustice, that constitute the grand and essential evils of the country. And you think it wonderful that we should be indignant at all this . . .

I have heard since I came here that it is a familiar saying, that 'the men of Kent have never been conquered.' That you will never be vanquished in any encounter where men shall be arrayed in arms against you is my belief and my desire; but while in this regard you will always prove unconquered and unconquerable, there is one particular in which I hope that proof will be afforded that you can be subdued. Be no longer invincible, but let the victory be achieved by yourselves. The worst foes with which you have to contend are lodged in your own breasts – your prejudices are the most formidable of your antagonists, and to discomfit them will confer upon you a higher honour than if in the shouts of battle you put your enemies to flight. It is over your antipathies, national and religious, that a masterdom should be obtained by you, and you may rest assured that if you shall vanquish your animosities, and bring your passions into subjection, you will, in conquering yourselves, extend your dominion over that country by which you have been so long resisted, your empire over our feelings will be securely established, you will make a permanent acquisition of the affections of Irishmen, and make our hearts your own.

Daniel O'Connell
1831

DANIEL O'CONNELL'S impact stretched far beyond Dublin.
The great French realist novelist Honoré de Balzac, wrote 'I
would like to have met three men only this century: Napoleon, Curvier
and O'Connell.' These few words testify to the extraordinary impact
left by O'Connell on both England and mainland Europe. Undoubtedly,
this was partly due to O'Connell's concern for civil liverties, regardless
of race or religion.

In the following, speech delivered in the House of Commons in
1831 O'Connell shows his utter detestation for colonial slavery:

Speech against Colonial Slavery

No man can more sincerely abhor, detest, and abjure slavery than I do. I
hold it in utter detestation, however men may attempt to palliate or
excuse it by differences of colour, creed, or clime. In all its gradations,
and in every form, I am its mortal foe. The speech of an opponent on
this question has filled me with indignation. 'What!' said this party,
'would you come in between a man and his freehold!'

I started as if something unholy had trampled on my father's grave
and I exclaimed with horror, 'A freehold in a human being!' I know
nothing of this individual; I give him credit for being a gentleman of
humanity; but, if he be so, it only makes the case the stronger; for the
circumstance of such a man upholding such a system shows the horrors
of that system in itself and its effect in deceiving the minds of those
who are connected with it, wherever it exists. We are told that the slave
is not fit to receive his freedom – that he could not endure freedom
without revolting. Why, does he not endure slavery without revolting?
With all that he has to bear, he does not revolt now; and will he be
more ready to revolt when you take away the lash? Foolish argument!

But I will take them upon their own ground – the ground of gradual amelioration and preparation. Well; are not eight years of education sufficient to prepare a man for anything? Seven years are accounted quite sufficient for an apprenticeship to any profession, or to any art or science; and are not eight years enough for the negro? If eight years have passed away without preparation, so would eighty, if we were to allow them so many. There is a time for everything – but it would seem there is no time for the emancipation of the slave. Mr. Buxton most ably and unanswerably stated to the House of Commons the awful decrease in population; that, in fourteen colonies in the course of ten years, there had been a decrease in the population of 145,801 – that is, in other words, 145,801 human beings had been murdered by this system, their bodies gone to the grave, – their spirits before their God. In the eight years that they have had to educate their slaves for liberty, but which have been useless to them – in those eight years one twelfth have gone into the grave murdered! Every day, ten victims are thus dispatched! While we are speaking, they are sinking, while we are debating, they are dying! As human, as accountable beings, why should we suffer this any longer? Let every man take his own share in this business. I am resolved, if sent back to parliament that I will bear my part. I purpose fully to divide the House on the motion; That every negro child born after the first of January, 1832, shall be free. They say; Oh! do not emancipate the slaves suddenly, they are not prepared, they will revolt! Are they afraid of the insurrection of the infants? Or, do you think that the mother will rise up in rebellion, as she hugs her little freeman to her breast, and thinks that one day, that he will one day become her protector? Oh! no, there can be no such pretence . . .

I will carry with me to my own country, the recollection of this splendid scene. Where is the man that can resist the argument of this day? I go to my native land under its influence; and let me remind you that land has its glory, that no slave ship was ever launched from any of its numerous ports. I will gladly join any party to do good to the poor Negro slaves. Let each extend to him the arm of his compassion; let each aim to deliver his fellow man from distress. I shall go and tell my country men that they must be first in this race of humanity.

Daniel O'Connell
1833

IN 1833, the Church of Ireland was the church of about one tenth of the Irish population, yet it received income from the entire population in the form, called a tithe. This caused great resentment within the Catholic and Presbyterian.

The hostility towards paying the tithe was exacerbated by the extreme poverty of the Irish masses. Sir Walter Scott, who visited Ireland in 1825 noted in his diary: 'Their poverty has not been exaggerated: It is on the extreme verge of human misery.'

As the agitation against tithes increasingly took the form of intimidation and violence, the British Government decided to introduce coercive legislation to help eliminate the disorder.

Daniel O'Connell, the leader of the Catholic Association, made this forcefull speech in the House of Commons against the impending legislation:

Speech against Coercive Legislation

I do not rise to fawn or cringe to this house; I do not rise to supplicate you to be merciful towards the nation to which I belong – towards the nation which, though subject to England yet is distinct from it. It is a distinct nation; it has been treated as such by this country, as may be proved by history, and by seven hundred years of tyranny. I call upon this House, as you value the liberty of England, not to allow the present nefarious Bill to pass. In it are involved the liberties of England, the liberty of the press, and of every other institution dear to Englishmen.

Against the Bill I protest in the name of the Irish people, and in the face of heaven. I treat with scorn the puny and pitiful assertions that grievances are not to be complained of, that our redress is not to be agitated, for, in such cases, remonstrances cannot be too strong, agitation cannot be too violent, to show to the world with what injustice our fair claims are met, and under what tyranny the people suffer.

There are two frightful clauses in this Bill. The one which does away with trial by jury, and which I have called upon you to baptise; you call it a court martial – a mere nickname; I stigmatise it as a revolutionary tribunal. What, in the name of heaven, is it, if it is not a revolutionary tribunal? It annihilates the trial by jury: it drives the judge off his bench, the man who, from experience, could weigh the nice and delicate points of a case – who could discriminate between the straightforward testimony and the suborned evidence, who should see, plainly and readily, the justice or injustice of the accusation. It turns out this man who is free, unshackled, unprejudiced – who has no previous opinions to control the clear exercise of his duty. You do away with that which is more sacred than the throne itself, that for which your King reigns, your Lords deliberate, your Commons assemble.

If ever I doubted before of the success of our agitation for repeal, this Bill, this infamous Bill, the way in which it has been received by the House, the manner in which its opponents have been treated, the personalities to which they have been subjected, the yells with which one of them has this night been greeted, all these things dissipate my doubts, and tell me of its complete and early triumph. Do you think those yells will be forgotten? Do you suppose their echo will not reach the plains of my injured and insulted country; that they will not be whispered in her green valleys, and heard from her lofty hills? Oh! They will be heard there; yes, and they will not be forgotten. The youth of Ireland will bound with indignation; they will say, 'we are eight millions and you treat us thus, as though we were no more to your country than the Isle of Guernsey or Jersey!'

I have done my duty, I stand acquitted to my conscience and my country: I have opposed the measure throughout; and I now protest against it as harsh, oppressive, uncalled for, unjust, as establishing an infamous precedent by retaliating crime against crime, as tyrannous, cruelly and vindictively tyrannous.

Charles Stewart Parnell
2 February 1880

HAVING been appointed president of the Home Rule Confederation of Great Britain in 1879, Charles Stewart Parnell also accepted the Presidency of the newly formed Irish National Land League before the year was out. The Land League advocated peaceful and lawful means to obtain justice for the Irish tenant farmers. Its main objectives were 'Ireland for the Irish' and 'Land for the People.'

With the aim of soliciting funds for the newly founded Land League and for the relief of the starving people, particularly in the West of Ireland, Charles Stewart Parnell, accompanied by John Dillon, undertook a tour of the United States of America on 2 January, 1880. Over the following two months he travelled 16,000 miles throughout the United States and Canada, speaking in over 60 cities. His speeches aimed to evoke the sympathy of the American people for the starving, evicted tenants in Ireland and to impart the ultimate objectives of the Land League. So successful was Parnell's fund-raising tour that by the time he returned to Ireland on the 11 March, 1880, he had raised about £60,000 for famine relief and an additional £12,000 for the general purposes of the Land League.

Perhaps the most significant of all his speeches was that given before the House of Representatives on 2 February, 1880. Speaking before an audience that was somewhat unsympathetic to the Irish situation, Parnell, in a well-prepared speech, described the Irish Land Question as he viewed it:

Speech to the Joint Houses of Congress in the US

Mr. Speaker and gentlemen of the House of Representatives, I have to thank you for the distinguished honour that you have conferred upon me in permitting me to address this august assembly upon the state of the affairs of my unhappy country.

Until I landed in America nothing was known of the imminence or threatened extent of the famine which has now assumed such horrible proportions as to attract the attention and compassion of all civilized nations. To every thinking man it must be a matter of perplexity how such a famine could burst upon a people without giving any warning of its approach. But in fact this catastrophe was clearly foreseen and predicted six months ago in Ireland, and government was repeatedly warned to make timely preparations to deal with it. But the British government not only refused to do anything, but with extraordinary perversity persisted in denying that there was any danger of famine. And now that thousands are starving the singular spectacle is presented of a government which refuses to come to the aid of its own subjects sanctioning appeals to the charity of America or any other nation which may be ready to feed them.

The present famine, as all other famines in Ireland, has been the direct result of the system of land tenure which is maintained there. And while we have been compelled by the frightful condition of our people to appear before the American people in the guise of beggars, and to use every exertion to collect money to save life, I feel it to be equally my duty to point out to you the cause which keeps Ireland in a condition of chronic poverty and brings on from time to time such horrible famines as that which is at present raging there. When the task is thrown upon America of feeding a people who have been driven into starvation by ruinous and unjust laws, surely you acquire a right to express your opinion very freely on the character of those laws and on the policy of maintaining them. And I have every confidence that the public sentiment of America will be a great assistance to our people in their present effort to obtain a just and suitable settlement of the Irish land question.

Since I have been in this country I have seen so many tokens of the good wishes of the American people toward Ireland that I feel entirely at a loss to express my sense of all the enormous advantage and service which is being daily done in this way to our cause. We do not seek to embroil your Government with the government of England; but we claim that the public opinion and sentiment of a free country like America is entitled to find expression wherever it is seen that the laws of freedom are not observed.

Mr. Speaker and gentlemen, the most pressing question in Ireland at the present moment is the tenure of land. That question is a very old one; it dates from the first settlement of Ireland from England. The struggle between those who own the land on the one side and those who till it on the other has been a constant one. But up to the present moment scarcely any ray of light has ever been let in upon the hard fate of the tillers of the soil in that country. But many of us who are now observing the course of events believe that the time is fast approaching when the artificial and cruel system of land tenure prevailing in Ireland is bound to fall and be replaced by a more natural and a more just one.

I could quote many authorities to show you what this system is. The feudal tenure has been tried in many countries, and it has been found wanting everywhere. But in no country has it wrought so much destruction and proved so pernicious as in Ireland. As the result of that feudal tenure we have constant and chronic poverty; we have our people discontented and hopeless. Even in the best of years theirs is one of continual misery. And when, as on the present occasion, the crops fail and a bad year comes around, we see terrific famines sweeping across the face of our land, claiming their victims in hundreds of thousands, driving multitudes into a forced and pauperized immigration and leaving a settled gloom and terror behind as the inheritance, for years, of the survivors.

Mr. Froude, the distinguished English historian, who cannot be accused of being a prejudiced witness in our favour, gives his testimony with regard to this land system in the following words:

'But of all the feudal gifts which we bestowed upon our unhappy possession was the English system of owning lands. Land, properly speaking, cannot be owned by any man. It belongs to all the human race. Laws have to be made to secure the profits of their industry to those who cultivate it. But the private property of this or that person which he is entitled to deal with as he pleases never ought to be and never strictly is. In Ireland, as in all primitive civilizations, the soil was divided amongst the tribes. Each tribe collectively owned its own district. Under the feudal system the proprietor was the crown as representing the nation; while the subordinate tenures were held with duties attached to them, and were liable on non-fulfilment to forfeiture.'

Now, I look upon this testimony of Mr. Froude's as a most important and valuable one coming as it does from an English source, and a source which cannot be called prejudiced in favour of Ireland. As Mr. Froude says, property has its duties under the feudal system of tenure as well as its rights. But in Ireland those enjoying the monopoly of the land have only considered that they had rights, and have always been forgetful of their duties; so that bad as the feudal tenure must be it has there been worked in a way to intensify its evils tenfold. I find that a little further on Mr. Froude again writes to the following effect: 'And if we had been more faithful in our stewardship, Ireland would have been as wealthy and prosperous as the sister island, and not at the mercy of a potato blight. We did what we could; we subscribed money; we laid a poor-law on the land. But it was to no purpose. The emigrants went away with rage in their hearts, and a longing hope of revenge hereafter with America's help.' [*Cheers and applause*]

But I could multiply testimony from distinguished sources, and of well-known men, to the same effect. I shall content myself with quoting from one more source, Professor Blackie, the Professor of Greek in Edinburgh University, who in the *Contemporary Review* for this month writes as follows: 'Among the many acts of baseness branding the English character in their blundering pretense of governing Ireland, not the least was the practice of confiscating the land, which, by Brehon Law, belonged to the people, and giving it not to honest resident culti-vators – which might have been a politic sort of theft – but to cliques of literature, and whose opinion is entitled to very great weight and greedy and grasping oligarchs, who did nothing for the country which they had appropriated but suck its blood in the name of rent, and squander its resources under the name of pleasure, and fashion, and courtliness in London.'

Now, we have been told by the landlord party as their defense of this system that the true cause of Irish poverty and discontent is the crowded state of that country, and the only remedy emigration; and I admit to the fullest extent that there are portions of Ireland which are too crowded. The barren hills of the west of Ireland, whither the people were driven from the fertile lands after the famine, are too crowded; but the fertile portions of Ireland maintain scarcely any population at all, and remain as vast hunting-grounds for the pleasure of the landlord class.

Before, then, we talk of emigration as the cure of all the ills of Ireland, I should like to see a more natural distribution of the soil of that country. I should like to see the rich plains of Meath, Kildare, Limerick and Tipperary, instead of being the desert wastes that they are to-day, supporting the teeming and prosperous population that they are so capable of maintaining. At the present moment you may drive for ten or twenty miles through those great rich counties without meeting a human being or seeing a single house. And it is a remarkable testimony to the horrible way in which the land system has been administered in

Ireland that the fertility of the country has proved the destruction of the population, instead of being their support. Only on the poor lands have our people been allowed to settle, and there they are crowded in numbers far too great for the soil to support. Let the next emigration be from the West to the East, instead of from the East to the West – from the hills of Connemara back to the fertile lands of Meath. When the resources of my country have been fully taken advantage of and developed, when the agricultural prosperity of Ireland has been secured, then if we have any surplus population we shall cheerfully give it to this great country. Then our emigrants will go willingly and as free men – not shovelled out by a forced emigration, a disgrace to the Government whence they come and to humanity in general, [*Applause.*] Then our emigrants would come to you as come the Germans, with money in their pockets, and education to enable them to obtain a good start in this great and free country, with sufficient means to enable them to push out to your western lands, instead of remaining about the eastern cites, doomed to hard manual labor, and many of them falling a prey to the worst evils of modern city civilization.

I have noticed within the last few days a very remarkable refutation to this argument of overcrowding, in one of the newspapers of this country – *The Nation* – a journal, I believe, distinguished in the walks of literature, and whose opinion is entitled to very great weight and consideration. *The Nation* says: 'That the best remedy for Irish poverty is to be found in the multiplication of peasant properties and not by emigration, as many suppose, there is little question. Emigration is good for those who emigrate: but it leaves gaps in the home population which are soon filled by a fresh poverty-stricken mass.' A writer in the *London Times*, giving an account of the island of Guernsey, shows that it supports in marvelous comfort a population of thirty thousand by the cultivation of ten thousand acres, while Ireland has a cultivable area of 15,500,000 acres and would, if as densely peopled as Guernsey, support a population of forty-five million instead of five million.' [*Applause*]

The climate of Guernsey, too, is as moist as that of Ireland, and the island is hardly any nearer the great markets. But nearly every man in it owns his farm, and the law facilitates his getting a farm in fee on easy terms.

Now, Mr. Speaker and gentlemen of the House of Representatives, the remedy that we propose for the state of affairs in Ireland is an alteration of the land tenure prevailing there. We propose to imitate the example of Prussia and other continental countries, where the feudal tenure has been tried, found wanting, and abandoned; and we desire to give an opportunity to every occupying tenant-farmer in Ireland to become the owner of his own farm.

This may, perhaps, seem at first sight a startling proposition; and I shall be told about the 'rights of property' and 'vested interests' and 'individual ownership'. But we have the high authority of Mr. Froude, the English historian, whom I have just quoted, to the effect that 'Land, properly speaking, cannot be owned by any man. It belongs to all the human race. Laws have to be made to secure the profits of their industry to those who cultivate it; but the private property of this or that person which he is entitled to deal with as he pleases, land never ought to be and never strictly is.'

And we say if it can be proved, as it has been abundantly proved, that terrible sufferings, constant poverty, are inflicted on the millions of the population of Ireland, we may then reasonably require from the legislature that, paying due regard to vested interests and giving them fair compensation, the system of ownership of the soil by the few in Ireland should be terminated and replaced by one giving that ownership to the many.

As I have pointed out, we have historical precedents for such a course. The King of Prussia in 1811, seeing the evils of the feudal tenure, by a royal edict transferred all the land of his country from the landlords to the tenants. He compensated the landlords by giving them government bonds bearing 4 per cent interest; and he ordained that the tenants should repay to the state the principal and interest of these bonds by annual instalments of 5 per cent, extending over forty-one years, and that then all payments should cease. The preamble to this edict is so very remarkable that I venture to trespass on your time for a few moments by reading it:

> 'We, Frederick William, by the grace of God, King of Prussia, having convinced ourselves both by personal experience in our own domains and by that of many lords of manors of the great advantages which have accrued both to the lord and to the peasant by the transformation of peasant holdings into property and the commutation of the rents on the basis of a fair indemnity, and having consulted in regard to this weighty matter experienced farmers, ordain and decree as follows:

That all tenants of hereditary holdings, whatever the size of
the holding, shall by the present edict become proprietors of
their holdings, after paying to the landlord the indemnity
fixed by this edict.'

But we have also precedents for the course we propose afforded by the
legislation of Great Britain. The Parliament of England has already,
under the Bright clauses of the Land Act, expressed its approval of the
principal that a class of tenant or peasant owners should be created in
Ireland. That act permitted the state to advance to tenants desirous of
purchasing their holdings two-thirds of the purchase money, to be
repaid by instalments of 5 per cent, extending over thirty-five years.
Those clauses, for a variety of reasons which I dare not trespass on your
time long enough to explain, have remained a dead letter. But I see that
Mr. John Bright, the eminent reformer, one of the originators of the
movement for the repeal of the corn laws, and a fellow-labourer with
Cobden in that movement, now comes forward and proposes to amend
those clauses very considerably so as to make them more workable. By a
cable dispatch from London I find that, speaking at Birmingham the
other day, Mr. Bright proposed:

'To appoint a government commission to go to Dublin with
power to sell farms of landlords to tenants willing to buy, and to
advance three-fourths of the purchase-money, principal and
interest to be repaid in thirty-five years. Such a measure, Bright
believed, would meet the desire of the Irish people. The commission should assist the tenant to purchase whenever the landlord
was willing to sell. He recommended compulsory sale only where
the land is owned by London companies, as is the case with large
tracts near Londonderry. He expressed the conviction that, if his
plan was ever adopted, self-interest or public opinion would soon
compel individual landlords to sell to the tenants.'

Now, this proposal is undoubtedly a very great reform and an immense
advance upon the present state of affairs. While we could not accept it
as a final settlement of the land question, yet we should gladly welcome
it as an advance in our direction; and we are willing to give it a fair trial.
The radical difference between our proposition and that of Mr. Bright
is that we think the state should adopt the principle of compulsory

expropriation of land, whereas Mr. Bright thinks it may be left to self-interest and the force of public opinion to compel the landlords to sell. For that is the word which he uses, 'compel.'

While I concur with Mr. Bright in thinking that, in all probability, if his proposals were adopted the present land agitation in Ireland, if maintained at its present vigor, would compel the landlords to sell to tenants at fair prices, yet I ask the House of Representatives of America what would they think of a statesman who, while acknowledging the justness of a principle, as Mr. Bright acknowledges the justness of our principle that the tenants of Ireland ought to own the lands, shrinks at the same time from asking the legislature of his country to sanction that principle and leaves to an agitation such as is now going on in Ireland the duty of enforcing that which the Parliament of Great Britain should enforce. [*Loud applause*] I think you will concur with me that this attempt on the part of the British Parliament to transfer its obligations and duties to the helpless, starving peasantry of Connemara is neither a dignified nor a worthy one, and that the sooner our Parliament comes to recognize its duties in this respect the better it will be for all parties and the government of Great Britain.

Mr. Speaker and gentlemen, I have to apologize for having trespassed on your attention at such great length, and to give you my renewed and heartiest thanks for the very great attention and kindness with which you have listened to my feeble and imperfect utterances. I regret that this great cause has not been pleaded by an abler man, but at least the cause is good, and, although put before you imperfectly, it is so strong and so just that it cannot fail in obtaining recognition at your hands and from the people of this country. It will be a proud boast for America if, after having obtained, secured, and ratified her own freedom by sacrifices unexampled in the history of any nation, she were now, by the force of her public opinion alone, by the respect with which all countries look upon any sentiment prevailing here, if she were now to obtain for Ireland, without the shedding of one drop of blood, without drawing the sword, without one threatening message, the solution of this great question. For my part, I, as one who boasts of American blood, [*loud and long-continued applause*] feel proud of the importance which has been universally attached on all sides to American opinion with regard to this matter, and I am happy in seeing and believing that the time is very near at hand when you will be able to say you have in the way I have mentioned, and in no other way, been a most important factor in bringing about a settlement of the Irish land question. [*Applause*] And then, Mr. Speaker and gentlemen, these Irish famines now so periodical, which compel us to appear as beggars and mendicants before the world, a humiliating position for any man but a still more humiliating position for a proud nation like ours. Mr. Speaker, these Irish famines will have ceased when their cause has been removed. We shall no longer be compelled to tax your magnificent generosity, and we shall be able to promise you that with your help this shall be the last Irish famine. [*Great applause*]

Charles Stewart Parnell
29 September 1880

IN APRIL 1880, Gladstone began his second term as Liberal Prime Minister of Britain. He immediately appointed W.E. Forster as the Chief Secretary of Ireland, with implicit instructions to quell the disturbances in Ireland and to restore law and order. One of Forster's first moves was to introduce the Compensation for Disturbances Bill, on 18 June, in the House of Commons. It stated that an evicted tenant should be entitled to compensation if he could prove to the courts that he could not pay his rent for some good reason [*e.g.* failure of harvest]. The Bill proceeded through the House of Commons with ease but was thrown out by the House of Lords on 3 August. This immediately heightened agrarian tension in Ireland.

Charles Stewart Parnell, the President of the Irish National Land League and the leader of the Home Rule Party, hoped that Gladstone would do something to retrieve the worsening situation but as the days passed it became apparent that it was not going to happen. Parnell finally broke his silence on 19 September, 1880, with a rousing address to a crowd of over 12,000 in Ennis, Co. Clare.

After the local Home Rule MP, Lysaght Finegan, had spoken in favour of the Bill, Parnell rose upon the platform to address the waiting audience:

Boycott Speech in Ennis

You must take hand and band yourselves together in Land Leagues. Every town and village must have its own branch. You must know the circumstances of the holdings and of the tenures of the district over which the League has jurisdiction – you must see that the principles of the Land League are inculcated, and when you have done this in Clare, then Clare will take her rank with the other active counties, and you will be included in the next Land Bill brought forward by the government [*cheers*]. Now, what are you to do with a tenant who bids for a farm from which another tenant has been evicted?

I think I heard somebody say shoot him [*cheers*]. I wish to point out to you a very much better way – a more Christian and charitable way, which will give the lost man an opportunity of repenting [*laughter and hear, hear*]. When a man takes a farm from which another has been evicted, you must shun him on the roadside when you meet him – you must shun him in the streets of the town – you must shun him in the shop – you must shun him in the fairgreen and in the marketplace, and even in the place of worship, by leaving him alone, by putting him into a moral Coventry, by isolating him from the rest of his country as if he were the leper of old – you must show him your detestation of the crime he has committed. If you do this, you may depend on it there will be no man so full of avarice, so lost to shame, as to dare the public opinion of all the right-thinking men in the country and transgress your unwritten code of laws [*cheers*].

People are very much engaged at present in discussing the way in which the land question is to be settled, just the same as when a few years ago, Irishmen were at each other's throats as to the sort of parliament we would have if we got one. I am always thinking it is better first to catch your hare before you decide how you are going to cook him [*laughter*]. I would strongly recommend public men not to waste their breath too much in discussing how the land question is to be settled, but rather to help and encourage the people in making it, as I said just now, ripe for settlement [*applause*].

When it is ripe for settlement, you will probably have your choice as to how it shall be settled, and as I said a year ago that the land question would never be settled until the Irish landlords were just as anxious to have it settled as the Irish tenant [*cheers*].

There are indeed so many ways in which it may be settled that it is almost superfluous to discuss them; but I stand here today to express my opinion that no settlement can be satisfactory or permanent which does not ensure the uprooting of that system in landlordism which has brought the country three times in a century to famine. The feudal system of land tenure has been tried in almost every European country and it has been found wanting everywhere, but nowhere has it brought more exile, produced more suffering crime and destitution than in Ireland [*cheers*].

Within a week of Parnell's Ennis speech, Captain Charles Boycott of Lough Mask House, County Mayo, became the first victim of the proposed policy of putting offending landlords into 'moral Coventry.' The much publicised event also added a new word to the English language: boycotting.

William Butler Yeats
4 February 1907

O N THE OPENING night of John Millington Synge's play, '*The Playboy of the Western World*,' in the Abbey Theatre in Dublin, members of the audience began to demonstrate: their decency outraged by the use of the word 'shift', their anger aroused by the bad reflection the play threw on the people of the west of Ireland, who were depicted welcoming a young man who purported to have killed his father with the blow of a shovel.

The disruptions continued throughout the first week of performances continued with the play being made entirely inaudible due to shouting, hissing and the blowing of trumpets. There were disturbances outside the theatre as well as inside and rioting took place in some of the neighbouring streets. Every day of that first week, newspaper articles appeared ridiculing the play and calling for its withdrawal. Things got so bad that on the last night five hundred policemen kept order in and around the theatre.

A public meeting, advertised as a 'Discussion on the Freedom of the Theatre and Mr. Synge's Play' was held the following Monday in the Abbey. William Butler Yeats, the President of the Abbey, fought the play's case against a hostile audience.

Speech Supporting the staging of Synge's 'Playboy'

During the performances every now and then some one got up in his place and tried to make a speech. On Saturday night an old gentleman stood up in the front row of the pit after the opening of the third act, and is probably very indignant that the police did not allow him to speak. I hope he is here tonight, and all those other speakers. We have never desired anything but the most free discussion that we may get at last some kind of sound criticism in this country. But before the discussion commences I will do my best to answer a few of the more obvious arguments, for there is no use wasting our time on stupidities or on misunderstandings of each other's point of view. I see it said again and again that we have tried to prevent the audience from the reasonable expression of dislike. I certainly would never like to set plays before a theatrical audience that was not free to approve or disapprove, even very loudly, for there is no dramatist that does not desire a live audience. We have to face something quite different from reasonable expression of dislike. On Tuesday and on Monday night it was not possible to hear six consecutive lines of the play, and this deafening outcry was not raised by the whole theatre, but almost entirely by a section of the pit, who acted together and even sat together. It was an attempt to prevent the play from being heard and judged. We are under contract with our audiences, receive money on the understanding that the play shall be heard and seen; we consider it is our duty to carry out our contract.

It has been said in to-day's *Freeman* [*a newspaper*] that the forty dissentients in the pit were doing their duty because there is no government censor in Ireland. The public, it is said, is the censor where there is no other appointed to the task. But were these forty – we had them counted upon Monday night and they were not more alone, the public and the censor? What right had they to prevent the far greater number who wished to hear from hearing and judging? They themselves were keeping the plays from the eyes and ears, of its natural censor. We called to our aid the means which every community possesses to limit the activities of small minorities who set their interests against those of the community – we called in the police. There is no stalwart member of the Sinn Fein party who would not do the same if he were to find a representative of that active minority – the burglars – fumbling with the lid of his strong box. We think it folly to say, that we cannot use the laws common to all civilised communities to protect ourselves and our audience against the tyranny of cliques. At no time would we have ever hesitated to do what we have done. When *The Countess Cathleen* was denounced with an equal violence we called in the police, That was in 1899, when I was still President of the '98 Association of Great Britain.

I would indeed despise myself if for the sake of popularity of a vague sentiment I were to mar the task I have set my hands to, and to cast the precious things of the soul into the trodden mire. A deputation of young Catholic students came to see me the other day, and the one who spoke their thoughts the most thanked us especially for this, for he said

that the little domineering cliques presume upon the fur of lost popularity that keeps a Nationalist from calling to his aid those powers
which hold together every community of the world, and silence the
rattling bells on the cap of the fool. The struggle of the last week has
been long a necessity; various paragraphs in newspapers describing Irish
attacks on theatres had made many worthy young men come to think
that the silencing of a stage at their own pleasure, even if hundreds
desired that it should not be silenced, might win them a little fame, and
perhaps, serve their country. Some of these attacks have been on plays
which are themselves indefensible, vulgar and old-fashioned farces, or
demoded comedies. But the attack being an annihilation of civil rights
was never anything but an increase of Irish disorder. The last I heard of
was in Liverpool, and there a stage was rushed, and a priest, who had
set a play upon it, withdrew his play and apologised to the audience.
We have not such pliant bones, and did not learn in the houses that
bred so suppliant a knee. But behind the excitement of example there is
a more fundamental movement of opinion. Some seven or eight years
ago the National Movement was democratised and passed from the
hands of a few leaders into those of large numbers of young men
organised in clubs and societies. These young men made the mistake of
the newly enfranchised everywhere; they fought for causes worthy in
themselves with the unworthy instruments of tyranny and violence.
Comic songs of a certain kind were to be driven from the stage, everyone was to wear Irish cloth, everyone was to learn Irish, everyone was
to hold certain opinions of political policy, and these ends were sought
by personal attack, by virulent caricature and violent derision. It needs
eloquence to persuade and knowledge to expound; but the coarser
means come to every man's hand, as ready as a stone or a stick, and
where these coarse means are all, there is nothing but mob, and the
commonest idea most prospers and is most sought for. Means come
ready to every man's hand, as ready as a stone or a stick, and where
these coarse means are all, there is nothing but mob, and the commonest idea most prospers and is most sought for.

Gentlemen of the little clubs and societies, do not mistake the
meaning of our victory; it means something for us, but more for you.
When the curtain on *The Playboy* fell on Saturday night in the midst of
what the *Sunday Independent* – no friendly witness – described as
'thunders of applause,' I am confident that I saw the rise in this country
of a new thought, a new opinion, that we had long needed. It was not

all approval of Mr. Synge's play that sent the receipts of the Abbey Theatre this last week to twice the height they had ever touched before. The generation of young men and girls who are now leaving schools or colleges are wary of the tyranny of clubs and leagues. They wish again for individual sincerity, the eternal quest of truth, all that has been given up for so long that all might crouch upon the one roost and quack or cry in the one flock. We are beginning once again to ask what a man is, and to be content to wait a little before we go on to that further question: What is a good Irishman? There are some who have not yet their degrees that will say to friend or neighbour, 'You have voted with the English, and that is bad;' or 'you have sent away your Irish servants, or thrown away your Irish clothes, or blocked your face and sung a coon song. I despise what you have done, I keep you still my friend; but if you are terrorized out of doing any of these things, evil things though I know them to be, I will not have you for my friend any more.' Manhood is all, and the root of manhood is courage and courtesy.

The inconclusive end to the meeting meant that the first run of 'The Playboy' lasted for only one week. Yeats and the Abbey Company took the play on tour to Britain the following June, where it encountered serious objections and even more violent protests greeted the company when it performed the play in America. But the determination of the Abbey to continue presenting the play never faltered and today it is widely regarded as a classic.

Jim Larkin
October 4th 1913

IN 1909, Jim Larkin formed his own trade union organisation, the Irish Transport and General Workers Union. Between 1911 and 1913 the ITGWU organised a series of successful strikes involving carters, dockers and railwaymen. In response to this growing threat to Dublin employers, the Dublin Employers Association was set up, with the great entrepreneur William Martin Murphy as its chairman.

By 1913, the membership of the ITGWU had grown to over 10,000; it published its own newspaper, 'The Irish Worker' with a circulation of over 90,000 a week, and had a substantial headquarters in Liberty Hall near Dublin's city centre.

1913, proved to be a testing year for the employers and employees of Dublin. Between January and August there were over thirty strikes in Dublin. The response of the employers was to refuse to employ anyone who was a member of the ITGWU. Larkin and the ITGWU reacted by calling a general strike on the 26 August, 1913. The employers immediately reacted by closing their businesses and locking their employees out. That evening Larkin told members, 'We are fighting for bread and butter. By the living God, if they want war, they can have it.'

As the strike worsened, a tribunal of inquiry was set up to find a solution. Larkin acted as the spokesman for the workers. His address to the tribunal, which is printed below, clearly demonstrates his ability as an orator.

Speech at 1913 Lockout Tribunal

I hope you will bear with me in putting before you as plainly as possible a reply somewhat of a personal character, but which I think will cover the matters dealt with during the last few days. The first point I want to make is that the employers in this city, and throughout Ireland generally, have put forward a claim that they have a right to deal with their own; that they have a right to use and exploit individuals as they please; that they have duties which they limit, and they have responsibilities which they also limit, in their operation. They take to themselves that they have all the rights that are given to men and to societies of men, but they deny the right of the men to claim that they also have a substantial claim on the share of the produce they produce, and they further say that they want no third party interference. They want to deal with their workingmen individually. They say that they are men of such paramount intelligence and so able in their organising ability as captains of industry, who can always carry on their business in their own way, and they deny the right of the men and women who work for them to combine and try to assist one another in trying to improve their conditions of life . . .

There must be fair play between man and man. There are rights on both sides, but these men opposite assume to themselves certain privileges, and they deny to the workingmen, who make their wealth and keep them in affluence, their rights.

Shakespeare it was, who said that, 'He who holds the means whereby I live, holds my life and controls me.' That is not the exact quotation, but I can give it

> 'You take my house when you do take the prop,
> That doth sustain my house, you take my life,
> When you doth take the means whereby I live.'

It means that the men who hold the means of life control our lives, and, because we workingmen have tried to get some measure of justice, some measure of betterment, they deny the right of the human being to associate with his fellow. Why, the very law of nature was mutual co-operation. Man must be associated with his fellows. The employers were not able to make their own case. Let him help them. They had had all the technique and the craftsmanship, but they have not been able to put their case in proper focus. What was the position of affairs in connection with life in industrial Ireland? Let them take the statement made by their own apologist. Take Dr. Cameron's statement that there are 21,000 families – four and a half persons to a family – living in single rooms. Who are responsible? The gentlemen opposite would have to accept the responsibility. Of course they must. They said they control the means of life; then the responsibility rests upon them. Twenty-one thousand people multiplied by five, over 100,000 people huddled together in the putrid slums of Dublin, five in a room in cubic space less than 1,000 feet, though the law lays it down that every human being should have 300 cubic feet.

We are determined that this shall no longer go on; we are determined the system shall stop; we are determined that Christ will not be crucified in Dublin by these men. Mr. Waldron was good enough to say yesterday that Larkin had done what was right and just in getting facilities for the workers on the Canal to be enabled to get to Mass on Sundays. Let them go further with the argument and add a little more to the picture. There were phases of the subject that he was not going to enter into in a mixed audience. The argument was used that Larkin came from Liverpool. Well, if that was so, it was time that someone came from some place in order to teach those whom he addressed their responsibilities. What about the gentlemen on the other side? Were they to be asked to produce their birth certificates? Could they all speak as men who represented the Irish race? These men had no feeling of respect for the Dublin workman or for its development. The only purpose and desire they had was to grind out wealth from the poor men, their wives and children.

Let people who desire to know the truth go to the factories and see the maimed girls, the weak and sickly, whose eyes are being put out and their bodies scarred and their souls seared and when they were no longer able to be useful enough to gain their £1 a week, or whatever wage they earned, were thrown into the human scrap heap. These things were to be found in their midst, and yet the people who caused these conditions of wretchedness described workingmen as loafers.

True it was that Mr. Murphy said that the Dublin workman was a decent man; but he would deny the right of the Dublin workmen to work in their city on terms of decency, on the streets or on the quays. He would deny their right to develop their activities and to receive proper and living wages. He was an instrument to bring down the wages. The souls of these men were steeped in the grime of profit-making. This dispute would do one thing and had already done something in that direction – it would arouse the social conscience. It had done what every man would thank God for. Let him go closer to the subject. He was out in this struggle to elevate the class he belonged to and he believed it to be his duty, and in doing it he believed he did much even to elevate those who were opposed to them.

They should all work together in a co-operative way, and they wanted to address them in a way that he hoped would not fall on barren ground. I hope that Mr. Murphy would not take anything I said in a personal light. Mr. Murphy had very strong views on the subject of the rights of property, and he is one of the strongest amongst the capitalists in this country, in Western Europe, or in America . . .

Mr. Murphy admitted he did not know the details of his own business, and stated that had no right to interfere with him to induce the men to fight him. Mr. Murphy was absolutely unable to state his own case. He admitted he had no knowledge of the details of his own business. He admitted he had no strikes at any moment during his connection with industry concerns, but had proved that his life had been one continuous struggle against the working classes. I give him credit, too, that in a great many cases he came out on top, because he had never been faced by a man who was able to deal with him; he had never been faced by a social conscience such as now existed, and according to which the working classes could combine to alter the present conditions of labour. There was such a thing as human thought, and no one had killed it yet, not even the theologians or the politicians, and Mr. Murphy might try to realise during the later hours of his life, before 'he passed hence' that those who gave him affluence and wealth deserved something to encourage them from the lower plane on which they existed to a higher plane on which they might live. He had been an able man, backed up by able men; he was backed up at that inquiry by one of the ablest counsel at the Bar, who used his power relentlessly. That could be seen up to a certain point, but there must be a break. There was a point where all that abuse would meet with its own result, and that result would be that the power wielded by such men would be smashed, and deservedly smashed . . .

I am concerned in something greater, something better, and something holier – a mutual relation between those carrying on industry in Ireland . . . These men with their limited intelligence cannot see that. I cannot help that. I cannot compel them to look at the thing from my point of view. Surely they have a right to realise the work in which I am engaged. It is not to our interest to have men locked-out or on strike. We don't get double wages. They say 'Larkin is making £8 a week,' and has made more than £18 a week, but he never got it unfortunately. I have lived among the working classes all my life. I have starved because men denied me food. I worked very hard at a very early age. I had no opportunities like the men opposite, but whatever opportunities I got I have availed of them. I am called an anti-Christ and an atheist. If I were an atheist I would not deny it. I am a Socialist and have always claimed to be a Socialist.

I believe in a co-operative commonwealth. That is a long way ahead in Ireland. Why cannot I help as you can help in working the present system in a proper, reasonable way, conducive to both sides, and I have suggested the machinery that may be put into operation . . .

Can anyone say one word against me as a man? Can they make any disparagement of my character? Have I lessened the standard of life? Have I demoralised anyone? Is there anything in my private life or my public life of which I should feel ashamed? These men denounced me from the pulpit, and say I am making £18 a week and that I have a mansion in Dublin. The men who are described as Larkin's dupes are asked to go back. All this is done two thousand years after Christ appeared in Galilee. Why, these men are making people atheists – they are making them godless. But we are going to stop that.

When the position of the workers in Dublin was taken into consideration, was it any wonder that there was necessity for a Larkin to arise, and if there was one thing more than another in my life of which I will always be proud it was the part I have taken in rescuing the workers of Dublin from the brutalising and degrading conditions under which they laboured.

We are out to break down racial and sectarian barriers. My suggestion to the employers is that if they want peace we are prepared to meet them, but if they want war, then war they will have.

The tribunal came down on the side of the workers, but the 'war' as Larkin called it continued into 1914. By the end of January most of the workers had returned to work; their aims had not been accomplished as they had been starved into submission.

Biographies

Biographies

George Berkeley (1685–1753)

GEORGE BERKELEY was born in Kilkenny on 12 March, 1685. He attended Kilkenny College, and later studied at Trinity College, Dublin, where he became deeply influenced by the views of the English philosopher John Locke. In 1709, he completed *Essay Towards a New Theory of Vision*, in which he extended Locke's ideas on the character of matter. This he followed with *The Principles of Human Knowledge* and when it failed to convince people of his theory, he published a more popular version, *The Three Dialogues Between Hylas and Philonous*, in 1713. Meanwhile he had been ordained a deacon in the Anglican Church of Ireland but his writings were considered controversial and foolish by his contemporaries and so in 1716 he moved to Italy. After many travels abroad Berkeley was appointed Dean of Derry, in 1724. In 1728, he resigned his deanery and went to America to attempt to found a missionary college in Bermuda; due to lack of finance, however, he spent the next three years in the colony of Rhode Island. One of Berkeley's lasting legacies has been his influence on higher education in America, assisting in the development of Yale and Columbia universities and a number of other schools. In 1732, Berkeley was made Bishop of Cloyne, in Ireland. He remained in this position until his retirement, a year before his death on 14 January, 1753.

Edmund Burke (1729–97)

EDMUND BURKE was born in Dublin on 1 January, 1729. He was educated at Baltimore Boarding School in County Kildare and then at Trinity College, Dublin, where he studied logic, metaphysics and history. In 1750, two years after graduation, Burke went to London where he briefly studied law before embarking on a literary career. His first important work, *Vindication of Natural Society*, a satire ridiculing the reasoning of the British statesman Henry Bolingbroke, was published anonymously in 1756. Later in the same year he published an essay, *The Philosophical Inquiry into the Origin of Our Ideas on the Sublime and Beautiful*. In 1761, he became private secretary to the British Chief Secretary for Ireland, William Hamilton, and demonstrated an aptitude for political service. Four years later he became private secretary to the Marquis of Rockingham, and in 1766, Burke was elected as a Whig Member of Parliament. Almost immediately he sought repeal of the Stamp Act. In a pamphlet, *Thoughts on the Cause of the Present Discontents* (1770), and in two parliamentary speeches, *On American Taxation* (1774) and *Conciliation with America* (1775), he urged justice and conciliation toward the American colonies. Burke took a deep interest in India and advocated a reversal of the British policy that allowed the East India Company to exploit the population of that country. On 15 February, 1788, Burke began a four-day-long opening speech in Westminster Hall in the unsuccessful impeachment proceedings against the statesman and colonial administrator Warren Hastings for high crimes and misdemeanours committed in India. Burke's celebrated, *Reflections on the Revolution in France*, which criticised the French Revolution, was published in 1790. The text, which was read through-out Europe, encouraged European rulers in their hostility to the French Revolution. Burke retired from Parliament in 1794. He died three years later on the 9 July, 1797.

Isaac Butt (1813–79)

ISAAC BUTT, the son of a Church of Ireland clergyman, was born, in Glenfin, County Donegal on the 6 September, 1813. He was educated at the Royal School, Raphoe, in Donegal and at Trinity College, Dublin, where he had an outstanding academic career. In 1836 he was appointed Professor of Political Economy in Trinity and was called to the Irish Bar in 1838. Following the Great Famine in the late 1840s he came to believe that the Parliamentary Union with Britain needed to be broken. He founded the Home Government Association in 1870. In 1873 this became the Home Rule League, and in the General Election of 1874 the party won 59 out of the 103 Irish seats. From the beginning there was a lack of consensus among the Home Rulers. At a meeting held in Dublin at which they committed themselves to forming a 'separate and distinct party' which would demand unity on only one single issue, Irish Home Rule; on all other issues, even those concerned with important Irish matters, Home Rule MPs were permitted to do as they pleased. As divisions within the party grew Butt resigned as its head in February, 1879. He died in May of that year.

Edward Carson (1854–1935)

EDWARD HENRY CARSON, the son of an architect, was born, on 9 February, 1854 in Harcourt Street, Dublin. He studied classics at Trinity College, Dublin, qualified and practiced as a barrister, married at the age of twenty-five, fathered four children, and became Crown Prosecutor in Ireland. After his election as Member of Parliament for Trinity College in 1892, he moved to London where he quickly established a sizeable reputation at the English Bar and in the House of Commons. In 1910, he was elected leader of the Irish Unionist Party and took a leading role in opposing the Liberal government's Home Rule Bill of 1912. During World War I he acted as a minister in the Lloyd George led coalition government. But ultimately, he failed to prevent Home Rule becoming law. He did, however, succeed in securing the exclusion of the six counties of today's Northern Ireland from the all Ireland Parliament. After the Government of Ireland Act became law in December, 1920 Carson resigned his position as head of the Irish Unionist's and took up a post as a Lord of Appeal in the House of Lords. He died on 22 October, 1935.

Roger Casement (1864–1916)

ROGER CASEMENT, the son of a British army officer was born in Sandycove, Dublin on 1 September, 1864. After working for a time with a Liverpool Shipping Company, in 1892 he joined the British consular service where he gained such a considerable international reputation for his reports on human right abuses in Africa and South America that in 1911 he was knighted by the British government. After retiring from the colonial service in 1913, he returned to Ireland where he became involved in the nationalist movement. He went to Germany to secure arms for the Irish Volunteers and also made to raise an Irish Brigade from British prisoners of war. The ship carrying the arms, the *Aud*, was intercepted off the Kerry coast on Good Friday 1916 and Casement, who was in a German submarine which was escorting the consignment, barely managed to escape to the Irish shore. He was captured soon afterwards and tried in London for treason. Casement was found guilty of high treason and sentenced to death. An international campaign attempted to have his sentence commuted but it lost momentum when the British government circulated a number of diaries, supposedly containing details of Casement's homosexuality. He was hanged in Pentonville prison on 3 August, 1916.

Michael Collins (1890–1922)

MICHAEL COLLINS was born in Clonakilty, County Cork on the 16 October, 1890. After being educated in Lisavaird National School in County Cork, Collins went to work as a clerk in the British Post Office at the age of fifteen. Whilst living in London Collins became involved in the GAA and the Gaelic League and he also joined the Irish Republican Brotherhood, a revolutionary group working for the independence of Ireland from British rule. In January 1916, he returned to Ireland to avoid conscription into the British army and then took part in the ill-fated Easter Rising in Dublin. He was released from internment in December of that year, and became Secretary of the Irish Volunteers' Dependants Fund and Adjutant General of the Provisional Executive. He was elected MP for the South Cork constituency and, as did all other Sinn Féin candidates, choose to take his seat in an Irish Parliament which was to be named, Dáil Éireann. He was appointed Minister of Home Affairs in 1918, and Minister for Finance, from 1919 to 1922. Between the years 1919 to 1921 he organised the guerrilla warfare that succeeded in forcing Britain to negotiate for peace. Collins reluctantly represented Ireland in London and signed the peace treaty that brought the Irish Free State into existence. Later he was appointed head of the Provisional Government and Commander-in-Chief of the Irish Free State forces. In the Civil War that followed the Treaty, Collins lost his life on 22 August, 1922 in an ambush in Béal na mBláth, County Cork.

John A. Costello (1891–1976)

JOHN ALOYSIUS COSTELLO was born in Dublin in 1891. He was educated in the O'Connell School in Dublin, at University

College, Dublin, and at the Kings Inns. Costello participated in the 1916 Rising and then from 1926 to 1932 he acted as Attorney-General for the Irish Free State and was its delegate to the League of Nations. In 1933 he became TD for Dublin County for Cummann na nGaedhael. After the 1948 general election, the Dáil elected him prime minister to replace Éamon de Valera, who had served since 1932. Costello and de Valera dominated Irish politics for the next ten years, with Costello serving as Taoiseach from 1948 until 1951 and from 1954 until 1957 and as leader of the opposition from 1951 to 1954 and from 1957 to 1959. He held his parliamentary seat until 1969 and maintained his legal practice almost until his death in 1976.

James Craig (1871–1940)

JAMES CRAIG, the son of a wealthy distiller, was born on the 8 January, 1871 in north County Down. He was educated at the local Presbyterian school and at Merchiston Castle in Edinburgh. After serving as Captain with the Royal Irish Rifles in the Boer War he returned to Ireland in 1901. With the financial help of his father he was elected to House of Commons as the Unionist MP for East Down in 1906. Craig took the lead in the fight against Home Rule and became the vice-leader of the Ulster Unionists. As deputy to Edward Carson he proved a superb military and political organiser, and was the main co-ordinator of the Ulster Covenant which was signed by over half a million people. When Carson resigned as leader of the Ulster Unionists in February, 1921, Craig took his place and went on to become the first Prime Minister of Northern Ireland in June of that year. In 1927, he was bestowed with the honour of Viscount. He died suddenly, whilst still in office, on 24 November, November 1940.

John Philpot Curran (1750–1817)

JOHN PHILPOT CURRAN was born of humble origins near Cork, in 1750. Educated at Trinity College, Dublin he subsequently went to London where he qualified as a barrister. After initial difficulties, he was called to the Irish Bar in 1775 and became one of Ireland's leading advocates. He became a member of the Irish Parliament for the constituency of Kilbeggan in 1783. In 1806 the Whig government appointed him Master of the Irish Rolls and Privy Council, an office he was to hold until his retirement in 1814. He died in London in 1817.

Richard de Ledrede (1227–1360)

The English born Franciscan monk, RICHARD DE LEDREDE, was consecrated Bishop of Ossory in 1317 by Pope John XXII. He arrived to Kilkeny fresh from the papal court at Avignon in 1317 and held that position until his death in 1360.

Éamon de Valera (1882–1975)

ÉAMON DE VALERA, the son of an Irish mother and Spanish father, was born in New York on 14 October, 1882. After his parents seperated, de Valera's mother sent him back to Ireland to be raised by his grandmother in Bruree, Co. Clare. He was educated in the local national school and the Christian Brothers' School in Charleville, and finished his schooling in Blackrock College in Dublin. He went on to study for an arts degree at Williamstown Castle, which was at the time affiliated to the Catholic University. After a variety of teaching posts he became Professor of Mathematics at Carysfort teacher training college in Dublin. De Valera became immersed in Irish affairs first with the Gaelic League and then with the Irish Volunteers. In 1916 he led a group of 140 Volunteers during the Easter Rising, for which he was sentenced to death but his sentence was commuted to life imprisonment and he was released in the general amnesty of 1917. After the signing of the Treaty with Britain and the ending of the Civil War, de Valera formed the Fianna Fáil party which came to power in 1932, with de Valera as Taoiseach. During the same year, de Valera became president of the League of Nations Council and in 1938 became President of its Assembly. During World War II de Valera successfully advocated a policy of neutrality for Ireland. He lost the Taoiseachship in 1948, but occupied the post twice again before his election as President of Ireland. In 1973 de Valera retired from public life. He died near Dublin on 29 August, 1975.

John Dillon (1851–1927)

JOHN DILLON, the son of the Young Irelander, John Blake Dillon, was born, in Blackrock, County Dublin on 4 September, 1851. After qualifying as a doctor he switched his attentions to politics becoming the MP for County Tipperary in 1880, and proceeded to take a major role in the struggle to improve the plight of the Irish tenant farmer. He was the leader of the anti-Parnell camp following the split in the Irish Parliamentary Party in 1891. In 1900, differences within the party were resolved and the party re-united under John Redmond's leadership. The re-united party then led Ireland's fight for independence from Britain. After Redmond's death in 1918, Dillon became head of the party, only to loose his seat to de Valera in the 1918 general election. He died in London on 4 August, 1927.

James Dillon (1902–86)

JAMES DILLON, the son of the Irish parliamentarian John Dillon, was born, on 26 September, 1902. He was educated at Mount Saint Benedicts in Gorey, County Wexford, UCD and the King's Inns, Dublin. He also studied business management in London and Chicago He was elected to Dáil Éireann in 1932 as an independent candidate for Donegal. He then joined the National Centre Party and one year later coalesced with other small political groups to form what later became Fine Gael. During World War II he was expelled from the Fine Gael party for breaking the all-party consensus in the Dáil on neutrality and for arguing that Ireland should join the War on the Allies side. After a period as an Independent TD, he rejoined Fine Gael in 1951 and became its leader in 1959. In 1965 he resigned the leadership and continued to hold his seat until 1969. He died in 1986.

Robert Emmet (1778–1803)

ROBERT EMMET, the youngest of seventeen children was born, in Dublin, in 1778. His father, a noted doctor, had him educated at Whyte's Academy on Grafton Street in Dublin. He subsequently entered Trinity College, Dublin, in 1793, but resigned in 1798 before obtaining a degree rather than submit to questioning by the strongly anti-nationalist Lord Chancellor of Ireland, John Fitzgibbon, Earl of Clare, who was trying to appraise student support for the United Irishmen. The young Emmet became the guiding light for the United Irishmen in Dublin and after an attempt to capture him failed, Emmet escaped to the Continent where he sought the help of Napoleon Bonaparte in aiding Ireland 'take her place among the nations of the world.' His attempts failed and he secretly returned to Ireland in October, 1802, and immediately set about laying plans for a rebellion in Dublin on the night of Saturday, 23 July, 1803. A trail of disasters led up to the event and when the supposed rebellion started, what Emmet had was not a well-disciplined rebellious force, but a mob of thugs and drunkards. As he later conceded, what had happened did not even have the respectability of an insurrection. In all, thirty people, including Lord Chief Justice Kilwarden, lost their lives that night in an evening of desultory rioting. Emmet himself escaped but was caught a month later. He was tried at Green Street court-house where he was found guilty of high-treason and sentenced to death by hanging.

Brian Faulkner (1921–77)

BRIAN FAULKNER was born in Helen's Bay, County Down, on the 18 February, 1921. He was educated in St. Columba's College, Dublin, after which he entered the family textile business. In 1949, aged 28, he was elected to the Northern Ireland assembly as representative for East Down. After serving in various government ministerial positions he was appointed Prime Minister in March, 1971, in succession to James Chichester-Clark. He exacerbated the political rift between Nationalists and Unionists by introducing internment in August, 1971. The Northern situation deteriorated rapidly over the winter of 1971–2 and in response to this, the British government suspended the Northern Ireland Parliament and began ruling the North directly from London. In December, 1973 Faulkner, as leader of the Ulster Unionists, signed the Sunningdale Agreement which provided for power-sharing within Northern Ireland. The reaction in some Unionist quarters was one of utter shock and dismay. Protests followed and, with the Unionist Party split over the issue, Faulkner resigned to found, the Unionist Party of Northern Ireland. The party received little support in the 1975 general election and Faulkner resigned from politics. In 1977 he was made a life peer but died later that year in a riding accident.

Garret Fitzgerald (1926–)

GARRET FITZGERALD was born in Dublin on the 9 February, 1926. He was educated at Belvedere College and UCD. Between the years 1948–58 he worked in Aer Lingus where he became an expert on the economics of transport. In 1959 he started lecturing in Political Economics in UCD and in 1969 obtained a doctorate in economics. In 1965 he was appointed a Senator for the Fine Gael party and in 1969 was elected TD for the Dublin South-East constituency. When the coalition of Fine Gael and Labour took office in March, 1973, Fitzgerald was appointed Minister for Foreign Affairs. The government fell in 1977, and he was appointed leader of Fine Gael. He immediately set about implementing a policy of change within the party. Following the election of June, 1981 Fitzgerald formed a coalition government of Fine Gael and Labour. After various terms in and out of office he resigned the leadership of Fine Gael in 1987. He took little part in active politics thereafter and completely retired from politics in 1992. He now spends his life writing and lecturing, and is a regular columnist in the *Irish Times*.

Henry Grattan (1746–1820)

HENRY GRATTAN was born in Dublin in 1746. He was educated at Trinity College, Dublin and in London where he studied law. In 1772, he was called to the Irish Bar, and three years later became a member of the Irish Parliament. His brilliance as a speaker quickly marked him apart from his contemporaries and he became a leader of the reform faction known as the 'Patriots.' His demand for free trade for Ireland was granted by the British in 1779, and his campaign to abolish the authority of the British Parliament to legislate for Ireland bore fruit when on 16 April,1782, the Irish Parliament triumphantly passed his resolutions demanding legislative independence. Despite these concessions the Irish Parliament had no power over the executive authorities, who were still appointed from England; moreover, the majority of the Irish people could not vote because they were Roman Catholics. Although a Protestant, Grattan campaigned tirelessly for the political rights of the Roman Catholics. British resistance to change increased in the 1790s, and in 1797 Grattan seceded from Parliament with other constitutional nationalists. He took no part in the Irish Rebellion of 1798, but in 1800 he returned to Parliament to lead an unsuccessful fight against the Act of Union, under which the parliaments of Ireland and Britain were merged. In later life Grattan became a member of this new parliament in London and continued his activities on behalf of Roman Catholic emancipation. He died in London in 1820.

Henry Flood (1732–92)

HENRY FLOOD, the son of the Chief-Justice, was born on the family estate near Kilkenny in 1732. After studying classics at Trinity College, Dublin and at Oxford, he entered the Temple in London, where he studied law. In 1759 he was elected as a member of the Irish Parliament for Kilkenny. His eloquent, forthright speeches led to him becoming head of the 'patriots,' who had as their aim the abridgement of the corrupt influence of the English government and the establishment of parliamentary independence. He died, from pleurisy on 2 December, 1792.

Arthur Griffith (1871–1922)

ARTHUR GRIFFITH was born in Dublin on 31 March, 1871 and was educated in the Christian Brother's School in Strand Street. A printer by trade, he co-founded the Celtic Literary Society in 1893, became a member of the Gaelic League and of the secret organisation, the Irish Republican Brotherhood. After three years working in South African gold mines, Griffith returned to Ireland to edit the weekly newspaper, *United Irishman*. It adopted a policy of separation and took as its motto a quotation from Wolfe Tone: 'We must have Ireland not for certain peers, or nominees of peers in College Green, but Ireland for the Irish.' In 1900, Griffith proposed an amalgamation of all the patriotic clubs and societies which had recently grown up in Ireland. The organisation that emerged became known as Cumann na nGaedheal. When it later joined with other such organisations it became known as Sinn Féin. Griffith went on to become a British Member of Parliament but he, like the other Sinn Fein members elected, refused to take his seat. Instead they set up a parliament of their own in the Mansion House, Dublin. The War of Independence followed in the aftermath of which

Griffith led the Peace Treaty negotiations with Britain. In the Treaty Debates that followed de Valera resigned as President of Dáil Éireann and walked out of the Dáil with the other anti-treaty members. Griffith took his place but during the subsequent civil war, died of a brain haemorrhage on 12 August, 1922.

Cahir Healy (1877–1970)

CAHIR HEALY was born in Mountcharles, County Donegal in 1877. At the age of eighteen he moved to Enniskillen where he worked as a journalist for various local newspapers. After being interned in 1922, he was elected Sinn Féin MP for Fermanagh-Tyrone. He was elected to the Stormont Parliament in 1925 and held a seat until 1965. He was Nationalist leader in the Stormont Parliament for many years. He died in 1970.

John Hume (1937–)

JOHN HUME was born in Derry on 18 January, 1937. He was educated in St. Columb's College, Derry and at Maynooth College. While a school teacher in Derry in the 1960s he became active in the Northern Ireland Civil Rights Association. In October, 1968, following police attacks on NICRA members, he was elected vice-chairperson of the Derry Citizens' Action Committee and in 1969 he was elected to the Northern Ireland assembly. In 1970, he co-founded the Social Democratic and Labour Party. After the collapse of the power sharing Executive in 1974, he failed to get elected to the British Parliament but did succeed, in 1979, in winning a seat in the European Parliament, and within a few months he replaced Gerry Fitt as the leader of the SDLP. Hume's diligent involvement in the Peace process helped lead to the setting up of the New Ireland Forum in 1984, the signing of the Anglo-Irish Agreement in 1985, the Downing Street Declaration in 1993, the ceasefire by the IRA in 1994, the beginning of all-party talks in Northern Ireland in 1996 and the signing of the Good Friday Agreement.

Douglas Hyde (1860–1949)

DOUGLAS HYDE, the son of a Church of Ireland rector, was born in Castlerea, County Roscommon on 17 January, 1860. He was educated at home and at Trinity College, Dublin, where he had a brilliant academic career. After graduation he returned to Roscommon where he began to collect and translate Irish folklore and poetry. In 1889, he published his first book, *Beside the Fireside* and then in 1891, he co-founded the Irish Literary Society in London, and became President of the National Literary Society, Dublin in 1892. After breaking away from the National Literary Society in 1893, he co-founded, together with Eoin MacNeill, the Gaelic League, which aimed to promote Irish language, music, dance and sports. In 1908, he became the first Professor of Modern Irish in University College Dublin, a post he held until his retirement in 1932. In 1937 Hyde became the first Irish President under the new constitution. He died in Dublin on the 12 July, 1949.

Jim Larkin (1876–1947)

JIM LARKIN was born near Newry, County Down in 1876, but spent the earlier part of his life in Liverpool. While working for a shipping company in Liverpool he became involved in the National Union of Dock Labourers. In 1907 he transferred to the National Union of Dock Labourers in Belfast and immediately began organising worker agitation throughout Ireland. As a result of a strike in Cork in 1908, the Irish Transport and General Workers Union was formed. In 1911 Larkin was made President of the Irish Trade Union Congress and, in 1912 he was elected to the Dublin Corporation and during the following year he was the workers leader in the Dublin strikes of 1913. The famous Dublin lock-out followed, during which employers refused to open their doors to employees. In the end the strike was broken but Larkin became a national figure. In 1914 after his newspaper, the *Irish Worker* was suppressed Larkin left for the US where he stayed until 1923. On his return to Ireland he founded the Worker's Union of Ireland, of which he was general secretary until his death. In 1927 he was elected TD for Dublin North and held a seat in Dáil Éireann on and off until 1944. He died in 1947.

Jack Lynch (1917–)

JACK LYNCH was born in Cork City on 15 August, 1917. He was educated at CBS, North Monastery, Cork and studied law at the King's Inns whilst working as a civil servant in Dublin. After an outstanding career in Gaelic football and hurling for Cork he was elected to the Dáil in 1948 as a Fianna Fáil TD for Cork City. He became Minister for Education in de Valera's 1948 government and held various cabinet posts in later Lemass governments. After Sean Lemass retired as leader of Fianna Fáil, Lynch was elected head of the party, a position he held, together with that of Taoiseach until 1979. On retirement from politics Lynch took up a number of company directorships. He lives in Rathgar, Dublin.

The Manchester Martyrs

WILLIAM PHILIP ALLEN was born near the town of Tipperary, in April, 1848. After failing to complete his apprenticeship as a carpenter, Allen worked in Cork, Dublin and Chester. An enthusiastic Fenian he incited some of his fellow countrymen in Manchester to attempt the rescue of the Fenian, Colonel Kelly. However in the melee that surrounded the attack, a police officer died. Allen together, with Michael Larkin, and Michael O'Brien, both from Cork, was tried and sentenced to death. The three were executed at the old prison in Manchester on 23 November, 1867.

Constance Markievicz (1868–1927)

CONSTANCE MARKIEVICZ was born Constance Gore-Booth in London on 4 February, 1868. She was educated at her family home in Lissadell, County Sligo. She studied art in London and Paris, where she met the Ukranian-Polish Count Casimir Markievicz, whom she married in 1900. They settled in Dublin where she became increasingly involved in the Nationalist cause. She joined the Gaelic League, the Abbey Theatre, Inghinidhe na hÉireann and the Irish Citizen Army. She took part in the 1916 Rising and was imprisoned for her role. After release from jail in 1917, she became the first woman elected to the

British Parliament. She did not take her seat, however, and instead involved herself in the establishment of the first Dáil, in which she was appointed Minister for Labour. She opposed the Treaty in 1921 and helped found Fianna Fáil in 1926. She died in Dublin on the 15 July, 1927.

Thomas Francis Meagher (1823–67)

THOMAS FRANCIS MEAGHER was born into a wealthy family in Waterford, on the 3 August, 1823. He was educated at Clongowes Wood College, and Stonyhurst, in England. He joined the Catholic Association and became a supporter of the Repeal of the Act of Union. Together with O'Brien, Mitchel, Davis, and others, they soon carried the name of Young Irelanders. In 1846, the Association split following Meagher's famous 'sword' speech. In January, 1847, he helped found the Irish Confederation and in the following year took part in the failed Smith O'Brien rising. Meagher was captured, tried and found guilty of high-treason. He was sentenced to death but the sentence was commuted to penal servitude for life, in Tasmania. Here he was allowed considerable freedom and in 1852 he escaped to New York where he became a lawyer, journalist and a distinguished popular lecturer. After leading a battalion in the Civil War he became Secretary of the State of Montana, a post he held until his death on the 1 July, 1867.

Terence MacSwiney (1879–1920)

TERENCE MACSWINEY was born in Cork in 1879. He was educated locally and at the Royal University of Ireland. He helped set up the Cork Celtic Literary Society in 1901 and was co-founder with Daniel Corkery of the Cork Dramatic Society in 1908. He was one of the main figures in the setting up of the Cork branch of the Irish Volunteers in 1913. Two years later he became a full time organiser in that organisation. He was elected to the First Dáil in 1918 as a member for Cork. In March, 1920 he was elected Lord Mayor of Cork, following the murder of Tómas MacCurtain. In August of that year he was arrested and sentenced to two years imprisonment in Brixton Gaol. He immediately went on hunger strike and died 74 days later on the 24 October.

Daniel O'Connell (1775–1847)

DANIEL O'CONNELL was born to a wealthy Kerry family on 6 August, 1775. Like most of the wealthy Irish Catholics of the day, O'Connell was educated on the continent. After studying law in London he was called to the Irish bar in 1798. On 13 January, 1800, O'Connell, at a meeting of leading Catholics at the Royal Exchange, Dublin made his first public speech, in which he attacked the Act of Union. From that day onwards O'Connell became immersed in Irish politics and, in particular, became identified with the causes and grievances of the Irish Catholics. Under his leadership, the Irish Catholics received increased rights from the Protestant establishment, culminating in Catholic Emancipation in 1829, which resulted in O'Connell becoming the first Irish Catholic Member of the British Parliament. Throughout his life O'Connell led the Irish public in peaceful agitation – at one meeting in Tara it is reported that one million people heard him speak for the Repeal of the Act of Union and the restoration of an Irish Parliament. Although the Repeal of the Act of Union was not achieved during his lifetime, O'Connell demonstrated the power of democracy to countless generations. He died a broken man, on the 15 May, 1847, the worst year of the Irish Famine, at Genoa whilst on a pilgrimage to Rome.

Terence O'Neill (1914–90)

TERENCE O'NEILL, the son of the Unionist MP for Mid-Antrim, Arthur O'Neill, was born on the 19 September, 1914. He was educated at Eton before joining the army. In 1946, he was elected member of the Northern Ireland Parliament for Bannside. In 1963, after serving for seven years as Minister for Finance, he succeeded Basil Brooke as Prime Minister. O'Neill was never fully trusted by some of the extreme Unionists and their limited trust was further reduced when O'Neill met the Irish Taoiseach, Seán Lemass, in Stormont in 1965. Following the civil rights demonstrations in 1968, O'Neill introduced a series of reforms to combat religious discrimination in Northern Ireland. After receiving heavy criticism from some Unionists for his actions, he found his position untenable, and resigned as Prime Minister in April 1969. He was subsequently knighted Lord O'Neill of the Maine and moved to England in 1975. He died in his Hampshire home on the 13 June, 1990.

Charles Stewart Parnell (1846–91)

CHARLES STEWART PARNELL was born on 27 June, 1846, in Avondale, County Wicklow. He was educated at home, at a boarding school in Derbyshire, England and at the University of Cambridge. After Parnell was first elected to the British Parliament as Home Rule MP for Meath in 1875 he created a name for himself by pursuing a policy of obstructionism, resorting to all-night filibusters to draw attention to the severity of the Irish problem. Having become an active opponent of the land laws he was elected president of the newly founded National Land League in 1879. In the elections of 1880, Parnell supported the Liberal party leader, William Gladstone, but when Gladstone sponsored the Land Act, which fell far short of nationalists' demands, he joined the opposition. In 1881 Parnell encouraged boycott as a means of influencing landlords and land agents. The promulgation of these policies led to the jailing of Parnell and several of his principal followers at Kilmainham prison and to the suppression of the Land League. One of Parnell's first acts after entering prison was to issue a manifesto calling upon the Irish peasants not to pay their rents. Soon afterwards, Parnell and Gladstone reached an agreement, known as the Kilmainham Treaty, whereby Parnell abandoned the 'no-rent' policy and urged his followers to avoid physical violence. In return for these compromises he was released. In 1885, when the Gladstone government moved to extend new coercive legislation, Parnell, whose party held the balance of power in Parliament, voted against Gladstone, and brought down the Gladstone led ministry. In 1889, Parnell was cited as co-respondent in the O'Shea divorce petition. The ensuing scandal brought about a split in the Irish Nationalist League (which had replaced the dissolved National Land League), with the majority of the members turning against Parnell. From this time until his death in Brighton, on 6 October, 1891, Parnell waged a vain struggle to reunite the nationalists.

Patrick Henry Pearse (1879–1916)

PATRICK HENRY PEARSE was born in Dublin on the 10 November, 1879. He was educated at CBS Westland Row, UCD and the King's Inns. His love for Irish drew him into the Gaelic League and in 1903, he became the editor of its journal, *An Claidheamh Soluis*. He went to Belgium where he studied the education system and on his return to Ireland founded a school, St. Enda's, in 1908. In 1913 he helped found the Irish Volunteers and shortly afterwards joined the secret militant organisation, the Irish Republican Brotherhood. He led the rising in Easter 1916 and after establishing his headquarters at the GPO on O'Connell Street read out the infamous proclamation of an Irish Republic. The rebellion was soon quashed and after surrendering on 29 April, he was executed on 3 May, in Kilmainham gaol.

Oliver Plunkett (1625–81)

OLIVER PLUNKETT was born on the 1 November, 1625, near Oldcastle, County Meath. On the advice of his first teacher and cousin, Patrick Plunkett, who was also the local priest, Oliver journeyed to Rome to study philosophy and theology in the Irish College there. After his ordination in 1654 he was made Professor of Theology at Propaganda College in Rome. He held this post until 1669 when Pope Clement IX chose Plunkett as the Archbishop of Armagh. He immediately set about enforcing, with great vigour, the new ideals of the counter-reformation movement. Following the falsely concocted popish plot to assassinate the King of England and to rid England of all Protestants, anti-Catholic frenzy spread throughout the country. The Irish administration's overzealous reaction was to arrest many of the leading Irish clergy, including the Primate of Ireland, Oliver Plunkett. In a widely publicised trial he was sentenced to death for the crime of organising a French invasion of Ireland – a crime of which he was innocent – and was executed in Tilburn, London on the 1 July, 1681. He was beatified in 1920 and canonized in 1975.

William Conyngham Plunket (1764–1854)

WILLIAM CONYNGHAM PLUNKET, the son of a Presbyterian minister in Enniskillen, was born in the north of Ireland in 1764. He studied at Trinity College, Dublin and, after qualifying as a barrister, became a member of the Irish Parliament. After the abolition of the Irish Parliament, following the passing of the Act of Union in 1800, he practised at the Bar and later became the Solicitor-General and

Attorney General for Ireland. In 1812, he became a Member of the British Parliament for Trinity College, Dublin, and then in 1827 he was made a peer and the Chief Justice of the Common Pleas in Ireland. In 1830, he was appointed Lord Chancellor of Ireland, a position he was to hold for eleven years. He died in 1854.

John E. Redmond (1856–1918)

JOHN EDWARD REDMOND, the son of an MP, in Ballytrent, County Wexford, was born on the 1 September, 1856. He was educated at Clongowes Wood College, Trinity College, Dublin and Gray's Inn, London where he qualified as a barrister. At the age of twenty-five he was elected an MP in New Ross for the Irish Parliamentary Party. After the Irish Parliamentary Party split in 1890, Redmond remained loyal to Parnell. In 1900, the party reunited under Redmond's leadership and set about agitating within the British Parliament for reforms in Ireland and most importantly of all, Home Rule. In 1912, under pressure from Redmond and his party, Asquith's Liberal party introduced the third Home Rule Bill. However when Redmond accepted the British government's decision to suspend Home Rule's implementation until the end of the war and then offered the services of the Irish Volunteers to the war effort, he provoked an outraged response from the more militant members of the Volunteers. These more militant Volunteers went on to stage the Easter Rising in 1916. In the aftermath of the rising his popularity and support dwindled and he lost his position as leader of the Irish Nationalists. He died in 1918.

Mary Robinson (1944–)

MARY ROBINSON was born in Ballina, Co. Mayo, in May 1944. Her parents, who were both medical doctors sent her to be educated in Hollymount, Mayo and Mount Anville in Dublin. She studied law in Trinity College, Dublin and Harvard University, before becoming a barrister of some note. At the age of twenty-five she was appointed Reid Professor of Law in Trinity College, Dublin and later in the same year, was chosen to represent Trinity College in the Irish Senate. After joining the Labour party in 1976 she unsuccessfully contested the 1977 and 1981 Dáil elections. Her resignation from the party in 1985 and her decision not to run for Senate election in 1989 appeared to show that her political career was at an end. But in 1989, the Labour party nominated her as its candidate for the Presidency. She defeated Brian Lenihan, the Fianna Fáil candidate, by a small majority, and became Ireland's first woman President. Her energy and vigour redefined the role of the President in both Irish and world affairs. In 1997, she was appointed High Commissioner for Human Rights in the United Nations.

Peter Robinson (1948–)

PETER ROBINSON was born in Belfast in 1948. He was educated in Annadale Grammar School, Belfast and Castlereagh College. In 1975, he became the general secretary of the Democratic Unionist Party. Following several unsuccessful electoral attempts he was elected to the Castlereagh District Council in 1977 and then to the British Parliament in 1979. In recent years his profile has increased considerably, and today he is vice-leader of the Democratic Unionist Party.

George Bernard Shaw (1856–1950)

GEORGE BERNARD SHAW was born in Dublin on the 26 July, 1856. After attending the Marlborough Street Central Model School and Wesley College, Shaw, took a clerical job in a land agents office; at the age of sixteen; thereafter he was self-educated. When his parents' marriage failed, his mother and sisters went to London, and Shaw joined them there in 1876. The next decade was one of frustration and near poverty. Between 1879 and 1883, Shaw wrote five unsuccessful novels, of which *Cashel Nyron's Profession* was the best. By the mid-1880s Shaw discovered the writings of Karl Marx and became the force behind the newly founded Fabian Society (1884), a middle-class socialist group that aimed at the transformation of English government and society. He also became a firm (and life-long) believer in vegetarianism, a spellbinding orator, and tentatively, a playwright. It was through the Fabian Society's founders, Sidney and Beatrice Webb, that Shaw met his future wife, the Irish heiress Charlotte Payne-Townshend, whom he married in 1898. Shaw's first real fame was as a music critic, a position from which he championed the controversial work of the German composer Richard Wagner. He then embarked on writing plays which entertained and flouted romantic conventions. Success followed success, the pinnacle being reached in 1925 when Shaw was awarded the Nobel Prize for his play about Joan of Arc, *Saint Joan*. Until his death on 2 November, 1950, Shaw continued to publish brilliantly argued prefaces to his plays and, to flood publishers with books, articles, and cantankerous letters to the editor.

John Sheares (1776–98)

JOHN SHEARES, the son of a banker, was born in Cork in 1776. After an education in Trinity College he was called to the Bar in 1788. John and his brother, Henry, became sympathetic to the French Revolutionaries. Both became members of the Society of United Irishmen, John often taking the chair at meetings. After 1795 they became actively involved in the organisation of the proposed 1798 rising. After the imprisonment of some of the leaders of the rebellion in March, 1798, John took his place as chief organiser of the forthcoming rebellion. But on the 21 May, both brothers were arrested and tried for treason. They were later executed outside Newgate Prison on the morning of 14 July, 1798.

Richard Brinsley Sheridan (1751–1816)

RICHARD BRINSLEY SHERIDAN was born in Dublin's Dorset Street in September, 1751. He was educated at Whytes Academy on Grafton Street, Dublin and at Harrow in England. In 1772 the youthful Sheridan eloped with Miss Linley, a most accomplished young singer, and was secretly married to her in France. Efforts to become a writer proved successful when his first comedy, *The Rivals*, was staged to acclaim in London in 1775. This was quickly followed by his best known comedy, *School for Scandal* and his popularity was acknowledged by his election as Member of Parliament for Stafford. Over the next thirty years he proved to be an extraordinarily able and eloquent politician. Unfortunately, Sheridan's financial situation declined, and he died a pauper in London, on Sunday, 7 July, 1816.

Richard Lalor Sheil (1791–1851)

RICHARD L. SHEIL was born on 16 August, 1791, at his parents residence in County Kilkenny. He was initially educated at home, then at the Jesuit schools in Kensington House, London and Stonyhurst College, Lancashire. He then entered Trinity College, Dublin, where he studied classics. On completion of his degree he went to London where he studied law at the Lincolns Inn. He was called to the Irish Bar in 1814, and wrote successfully for Dublin and London theatres. From the establishment of the Catholic Association in 1822, Sheil began to take a serious interest in the Catholic cause. He distanced himself from Daniel O'Connell after Catholic Emancipation was achieved in 1829, and was elected to the British Parliament for the borough of Milborne Port, in England in 1831. He attached himself to the Whig camp, became Queen's Council and Privy Councillor, and afterwards, in succession, a commissioner of Greenwich Hospital, Vice-President of the Trade Board, Judge Advocate-General, and Master of the Mint. He died suddenly in Florence on 25 May, 1851, whilst acting as a British Government representative in Tuscany.

Jonathan Swift (1667–1745)

JONATHAN SWIFT was born in Dublin in 1667. He attended school at Kilkenny College before studying, with little distinction, Greek and Latin at Trinity College, Dublin. After graduation he went to England where he acted as the secretary to the diplomat and writer, Sir William Temple. On completing a master's degree at Oxford he returned to Ireland and was ordained a clergyman in the Church of Ireland in 1894. Swift spent much of the next twenty years in London where he built himself a considerable reputation as writer, one of his works, Gulliver's Travels became a timeless classic. He returned to Ireland in 1699, becoming a prebend of St. Patrick's Cathedral, Dublin. In 1713, Swift was made Dean of St. Patrick's, and spent the remainder of his life in this post, his career advancement blocked by his irreligious satirical writing. Before he died in 1745, Swift bequeathed the greater part of his fortune to the founding of St. Patricks Hospital for Imbeciles Dublin.

Theobald Wolfe Tone (1763–98)

THEOBALD WOLFE TONE was born in Dublin on 20 June, 1763, the eldest son of Peter and Margaret Tone. His father, a farmer and a coach-builder, insisted in him entering Trinity College where he studied logic. Whilst at Trinity, he fell in love with a fifteen year old girl named Matilda Witherington and married her in 1785. After graduating in 1786, Tone spent two years in London where he studied to be a barrister. On returning to Ireland he became interested in politics: the two fashionable political issues of the day, parliamentary reform and Catholic Emancipation had obvious appeal. In his first important publication, *Spanish War: An Enquiry how far Ireland is bound, of right, to Embark on the Impending Contest on the Side of Great Britain*, Wolfe Tone outraged the authorities by arguing that Ireland was not, as a separate kingdom with its own independent parliament, bound to support a war declared by Great Britain. In September, 1791, Wolfe Tone published a pamphlet entitled, *An Argument on Behalf of the Catholics of Ireland*, in which he attempted to persuade the Ulster Presbyterians, 'to forget all former feuds, to consolidate the entire strength of the whole nation and to form for the future but one people.' The following month the first open meeting of the United Irishmen took place in Belfast: it was agreed that a union between all religious persuasions was needed to counteract the British influence in Ireland and to secure a reform of the Irish parliament. As it became apparent that a rebellion was needed Wolfe Tone went to France in 1795 in an effort to persuade the revolutionary French government to invade Ireland to achieve Irish independence from British rule. Two French invasions were attempted, but both failed. Wolfe Tone was captured aboard a French ship off the Donegal coast in October, 1798. He was tried for high treason, found guilty and sentenced to death by hanging, but committed suicide or was murdered, as has been alleged, before his sentence could be carried out.

Gordon Wilson (1927–95)

GORDON WILSON, the son of a Methodist draper, was born on the 25 September, 1927 in Manorhamilton, a small town in the Irish Republic, near the border with Northern Ireland. He was educated in the local national school and Wesley College, in Dublin. In 1945, Wilson went to work for his father's new drapery business in Enniskillen. Ten years later he married, and with his wife, Joan had three children, two girls and one boy. On 8 November, 1987 he was with his daughter, Marie, when she was killed in an IRA bombing at the Remembrance Day ceremony in Enniskillen. The simple and beautiful way in which Gordon Wilson described her final words and his Christian explanation of the events were so moving that he became the embodiment of the desire for peace in Northern Ireland. In 1993, the Irish Government nominated him to be a member of the Irish Seanad, a position he accepted in the hope that he could make a contribution towards peace. The following year he was appointed a delegate at the Forum for Peace and Reconciliation. Gordon Wilson died peacefully on 27 June, 1995.

William Butler Yeats (1865–1939)

WILLIAM BUTLER YEATS, the eldest child of the artist John Butler Yeats, was born in Sandymount, Dublin, on the 13 June, 1865. He spent most of the first sixteen years of his life in London, bar the long summers which he spent with his mother and family in Sligo. In 1881, the Yeats family returned to Ireland where William Butler attended High School. Having failed to gain entrance to Trinity College, he studied at the Metropolitan School of Art. There he became friendly with George Russell, and together they founded the Dublin Hermetic Society a year later. His first work, *The Isle of Statues* was published in 1885, and the following year the play, *Mosada* was published. When the Yeats family returned to London in 1887, W.B. began collecting and publishing Irish folk tales and the following year he was one of the founder members of the Pan-Celtic society, a group set up to revive and publish poems and ballads of Irish interest. After returning to Ireland in 1899, he founded the Irish Literary Theatre, which led in 1904 to the formation of the Abbey, of which Yeats was president for many years. In 1922 Yeats was appointed a senator by the Irish government and the following year he received the Nobel Prize for Literature. He died while on holiday in the south of France on 28 January, 1939.

Bibliography

All in a Life, Garret Fitzgerald, Gill and Macmillan, 1991.

Burke's Speech on Conciliation With America, F.G. Selby (ed.), Macmillan, London, 1955.

De Valera, Tim Pat Coogan, Huchinson, London, 1993.

Edmund Burke, Stanley Ayling, John Murray, 1988.

Enduring the Most: the Life and Times of Terence MacSwiney, F.J. Costello, Brandon, 1995.

Famous Dubliners, Michael Stanley, Wolfhound Press, 1996.

Gordon Wilson, An Ordinary Hero, Alf McCreary, Marshall Pickering, 1996.

Great Irish Speeches of the Twentieth Century, Michael McLoughlin (ed.), Poolbeg, 1996.

Great Northerners, Art Byrne and Sean McMahon, Poolbeg, 1991.

High Upon the Gallows Tree, Anthony Glynn, Anvil, 1967.

In Their Own Voices, Margaret Ward, Attic Press, 1995.

In Time of War, by Robert Frisk, Gill and Macmillan, 1985.

Ireland 1912–1985, Joseph Lee, Cambridge University Press, 1989.

Irish Orators and Oratory, T.M. Kettle, The Talbot Press, 1924.

Irish Historical Documents 1172–1922, R.B. McDowell and E. Curtis (eds), Methuen, London, 1968.

Irish Historical Documents Since 1800, Alan O'Day and John Stevenson (eds), Gill and Macmillan, Dublin, 1992.

Irish Political Documents 1869–1916, Arthur Mitchell and Padraig O'Snodaigh (eds), Irish Academic Press, 1985.

Irish Political Documents 1916–1949, Arthur Mitchell and Padraig O'Snodaigh (eds), Irish Academic Press, 1989.

Lend Me Your Ears, William Safire (ed.) Norton, 1992.

Lord Plunket's Speeches, J.C. Hoey (ed.), James Duffy, 1862.

Mary Robinson: A President in Progress, Deirdre McQuillan, Gill and Macmillan, 1994.

Michael Collins, Tim Pat Coogan, Huchinson, London, 1990.

Modern Ireland, R.F. Foster, Penguin, 1989.

Modern Irish Lives, Louis McRedmond (ed.), Gill and Macmillan, 1996.

Nineteenth Century Ireland: The Search for Stability, D.G. Boyce, Gill and Macmillan, 1990.

Northern Ireland: The Orange State, Michael Farrell, Pluto, 1976.

P. Pearse, Political Writings and Speeches, Dublin, 1952.

Phrases Make History Here, Conor O'Clery, O'Brien Press, Dublin, 1986.

Playboy Riots, J.F. Kilroy, Dolmen Press, 1971.

Rowan, W.H. Drummond (ed.), Irish University Press, 1972.

Sheil's Speeches, T. MacNevin (ed.), James Duffy.

Sheridan, Lewis Gibbs, Kennikat Press, 1970.

Speeches and Statements by Éamon de Valera, Maurice Moynighan (ed.), Gill and Macmillan, Dublin, 1980.

Speeches from the Dock, T.D., A.M., and D.B., O'Sullivan (eds), Gill and Macmillan, Dublin, 1968.

The Annals of Clonmacnoise, Dennis Murphy (ed.), University Press, Dublin, 1896.

The Green Flag, Robert Kee, Weidenfeld and Nicolson, 1972.

The Irish Republic, Dorothy Macardle, Irish Press, Dublin, 1951.

The Laurel and the Ivy, Robert Kee, Penguin, 1993.

The Making of Modern Ireland, J.C. Beckett, Faber and Faber, 1981.

The Penguin Book of Historical Speeches, Brian MacArthur (ed.), Viking, 1995.

The Senate Speeches of W.B. Yeats, Donald R. Pearce (ed.), Faber and Faber, 1971.

The Sorcery Trial of Alice Kyteler, 1324, L.S. Davidson and J.O. Ward (eds), Medieval and Renaissance Texts and Studies, New York, 1993.

The Treasury of British Eloquence, R. Cochrane (ed.) W.P. Nimmo, Hay and Mitchell, 1882.

The Trial of Oliver Plunkett, Alice Curtayne, Sheed and Ward, 1953.

The Writings and Speeches of Edmund Burke, Boston, Mass., 1901.

The Works of George Berkeley, Oxford, 1901.

Twentieth Century Ireland, Nation and State, Dermot Keogh, Gill and Macmillan, Dublin, 1994.

Ulster at the Crossroads, Terence O'Neill, Faber and Faber, 1969.

Sources

SPEECHES FROM THE DOCK

Oliver Plunket, 1681 *The Trial of Oliver Plunkett*, Alice Curtayne, Sheed and Ward, 1953.

John Sheares, 1798 *Irish Orators and Oratory*, T.M. Kettle, The Talbot Press, 1924.

Wolfe Tone, 1798 *Speeches from the Dock*, T.D., A.M., and D.B., O'Sullivan (eds), Gill and Macmillan, Dublin, 1968.

Robert Emmet, 1803 *Irish Historical Documents Since 1800*, Alan O'Day and John Stevenson (eds), Gill and Macmillan, Dublin, 1992.

The Manchester Martyrs, 1867 *Speeches from the Dock*, T.D., A.M., and D.B., O'Sullivan (eds), Gill and Macmillan, Dublin, 1968.

Roger Casement, 1916 *Speeches from the Dock*, T.D., A.M., and D.B., O'Sullivan (eds), Gill and Macmillan, Dublin, 1968.

THE BIRTH OF A NATION

Countess Markievicz, 1909 *In Their Own Voices*, Margaret Ward, Attic Press, 1995.

John Redmond, 1914 *Hansard*, 3 August, 1914.

Patrick Pearse, 1915 *P. Pearse, Political Writings and Speeches*, Dublin, 1952.

Patrick Pearse, 1916 *Irish Historical Documents Since 1800*, Alan O'Day and John Stevenson (eds), Gill and Macmillan, Dublin, 1992.

John Dillon, 1916 *Hansard*, May 11, 1916.

Terence MacSwiney, 1920 *Speeches from the Dock*, T.D., A.M., and D.B., O'Sullivan (eds), Gill and Macmillan, Dublin, 1968.

Arthur Griffith, 1921 *Dáil Éireann, Official Report*, December 1921–January 1922.

Michael Collins, 1921 *Dáil Éireann, Official Report*, December 1921–January 1922.

Éamon de Valera, 1921 *Dáil Éireann, Official Report*, December 1921–January 1922.
John A Costello, 1948 *Dáil Debates*, 24 November, 1948.

IRELAND DURING THE EMERGENCY

James Craig (Lord Craigavon), 1939 *Northern Ireland Parliament Debates*, 2 September, 1939.
Éamon de Valera, 1940 *Speeches and Statements by Éamon de Valera*, Maurice Moynighan (ed.), Gill and Macmillan, Dublin, 1980.
James Dillon, 1941 *Dáil Debates*, 17 July, 1941.
Éamon de Valera, 1945 *Speeches and Statements by Éamon de Valera*, Maurice Moynighan (ed.), Gill and Macmillan, Dublin, 1980.

EULOGIES

Edmund Burke, 1783 *The Writings and Speeches of Edmund Burke*, Boston, Mass., 1901.
George B. Shaw, 1930 *Lend Me Your Ears*, William Safire (ed.) Norton, 1992.

SPEECHES OF VISION

George Berkeley, 1712 *The Works of George Berkeley*, Oxford, 1901.
Edmund Burke, 1774 *The Treasury of British Eloquence*, R. Cochrane (ed.) W.P. Nimmo, Hay and Mitchell, 1882.
Edmund Burke, 1780 *The Treasury of British Eloquence*, R. Cochrane (ed.) W.P. Nimmo, Hay and Mitchell, 1882.
Douglas Hyde, 1892 *Irish Historical Documents 1172–1922*, R.B. McDowell and E. Curtis (eds), Methuen, London, 1968.
Éamon de Valera, 1943 *Speeches and Statements by Éamon de Valera*, Maurice Moynighan (ed.), Gill and Macmillan, Dublin, 1980.
Mary Robinson, 1990 *Mary Robinson: A President in Progress*, Deirdre McQuillan, Gill and Macmillan, 1994.
Mary Robinson, 1995 *Irish Emigrant Weekly*, February, 1995.

UNION AND THE FIGHT FOR HOME RULE

Henry Grattan, 1780 *The Treasury of British Eloquence*, R. Cochrane (ed.) W.P. Nimmo, Hay and Mitchell, 1882.

Henry Grattan, 1782 *Irish Orators and Oratory*, T.M. Kettle, The Talbot Press, 1924.

Henry Flood, 1783 *Irish Orators and Oratory*, T.M. Kettle, The Talbot Press, 1924.

Lord Plunket, 1799 *Lord Plunket's Speeches*, J.C. Hoey (ed.), James Duffy, 1862.

Henry Grattan, 1800 *Irish Orators and Oratory*, T.M. Kettle, The Talbot Press, 1924.

Daniel O'Connell, 1843 *Irish Orators and Oratory*, T.M. Kettle, The Talbot Press, 1924.

T.F. Meagher, 1846 *Irish Orators and Oratory*, T.M. Kettle, The Talbot Press, 1924.

I. Butt, 1874 *Hansard*, 20 march, 1874.

Charles Stewart Parnell, 1885 *Irish Historical Documents Since 1800*, Alan O'Day and John Stevenson (eds), Gill and Macmillan, Dublin, 1992.

THE GREAT ADVOCATES

Bishop of Ossory, 1324 *The Sorcery Trial of Alice Kyteler*, 1324, L.S. Davidson and J.O. Ward (eds), Medieval and Renaissance Texts and Studies, New York, 1993.

Edmund Burke, 1788 *The Treasury of British Eloquence*, R. Cochrane (ed.) W.P. Nimmo, Hay and Mitchell, 1882.

R.B. Sheridan, 1788 *The Treasury of British Eloquence*, R. Cochrane (ed.) W.P. Nimmo, Hay and Mitchell, 1882.

John P. Curran, 1794 *Irish Orators and Oratory*, T.M. Kettle, The Talbot Press, 1924.

THE ULSTER QUESTION

Edward Carson, 1914 *Hansard*, 11 February, 1914.

William Butler Yeats, 1924 *The Senate Speeches of William Butler Yeats*, Donald R. Pearce (ed.), Faber and Faber, 1971.

Cahir Healy, 1934 *Northern Ireland Parliament Debates*, 24 April, 1934.

James Craig (Lord Craigavon), 1934 Northern Ireland Parliament Debates, 24 April, 1934.

Terence O'Neill, 1968 *Ulster at the Crossroads*, Terence O'Neill, Faber and Faber, 1969.

Jack Lynch, 1970 *Dáil Debates*, 6 May, 1970.

Brian Faulkner, 1972 *Northern Ireland Parliament Debates*, 28 March, 1972.

Garret Fitzgerald, 1984 *The Irish Times*, 16 March, 1984.

Peter Robinson, 1985 *Hansard*, 26 November, 1985.

John Hume, 1985 *Hansard*, 26 November, 1985.

Gordon Wilson, 1987 *Gordon Wilson, An Ordinary Hero*, Alf McCreary, Marshall Pickering, 1996.

THE RIGHTS OF A MAN

Jonathan Swift, 1725 *The Works of Jonathan Swift*.

Edmund Burke, 1775 *Burke's Speech on Conciliation With America*, F.G. Selby (ed.), Macmillan, London, 1955.

Richard L. Sheil, 1828 *Sheil's Speeches*, T. MacNevin (ed.), James Duffy.

Daniel O'Connell, 1831 *The Treasury of British Eloquence*, R. Cochrane (ed.) W.P. Nimmo, Hay and Mitchell, 1882.

Daniel O'Connell, 1833 *The Treasury of British Eloquence*, R. Cochrane (ed.) W.P. Nimmo, Hay and Mitchell, 1882.

Charles Stewart Parnell, 1880 *Irish Historical Documents Since 1800*, Alan O'Day and John Stevenson (eds), Gill and Macmillan, Dublin, 1992.

Charles Stewart Parnell, 1880 *Irish Historical Documents 1172–1922*, R.B. McDowell and E. Curtis (eds), Methuen, London, 1968.

William Butler Yeats, 1907 *The Arrow*, 23, February, 1907, Dublin.

Jim Larkin, 1913 *The Freeman's Journal*, 6 October, 1913, Dublin.

Index